Bevan Ashford

Unparalleled legal advice

Our aim is to add value to your business and help you tackle the challenges you face.

We concentrate on exceptionally well-focused advice for our private and public sector clients, many of which are household names.

As nationally recognised specialists we offer a full range of legal services at the complex and increasingly common interface between the public and private sectors.

The result is truly in-depth commercial legal advice to specific markets:

- Built Environment
- Insurance and Finance
- Public Sector
- Technology and Manufacturing

Our focus is your business. If you are looking for specialist expertise from lawyers who have a genuine understanding of your view of the markets and talk your language please call 0117 923 011

Bristol   Birmingham   London   **www.bevanashford.co.uk**

the
SUSTAINABLE
ENTERPRISE

AccountAbility
institute of social and ethical accountability

Promoting accountability for sustainable development

Established in 1995, AccountAbility is the leading international non-profit institute that brings together members and partners from business, civil society and the public sector from across the world. AccountAbility provides effective assurance and accountability management tools and standards through its AA1000 Series, offers professional development and certification, and undertakes leading-edge research and related public policy advocacy.

Core to the AccountAbility Community are our members, who govern us, support us and participate in our programmes as well as play a vital role in shaping our direction and work.

AccountAbility has always valued and relied upon input from members, and now more than ever is looking towards working with, servicing and developing strong relationships with our members.

Membership

Our membership scheme is based on what our members, partners and collaborators tell us is needed, directly, and indirectly, through our international, representative Council. The comprehensive packages provide you with a range of benefits that can be tailored to meet your specific needs, however developed your corporate responsibility approach is.

Membership of AccountAbility is an invaluable asset for those committed to advancing and promoting greater accountability in business, civil society or public institutions across the world. Joining the AccountAbility Community delivers members access to; our unrivalled international networks, our unique blend of strategic research, professional development, and our prominent position in standards and public policy development.

AccountAbility has developed a series of membership levels that have been designed to meet the requirements of different types of members. Packages are accessible to both large and small businesses, service providers, academic institutions, NGO's and individuals.

To find out more about AccountAbility membership packages, and how you can benefit by joining, please visit **www.accountability.org.uk/membership** or email **membership@accountability.org.uk**

the
SUSTAINABLE ENTERPRISE
Profiting from Best Practice

consultant editor:
christopher stephen brown

The Chartered Institution
of Wastes Management

London and Sterling, VA

This book has been endorsed by the Institute of Directors.

The endorsement is given to selected Kogan Page books which the IoD recognizes as being of specific interest to its members and providing them with up-to-date, informative and practical resources for creating business success. Kogan Page books endorsed by the IoD represent the most authoritative guidance available on a wide range of subjects including management, finance, marketing, training and HR.

The views expressed in this book are those of the authors and are not necessarily the same as those of the Institute of Directors.

Publisher's note

First published in Great Britain and the United States in 2005 by Kogan Page Limited

120 Pentonville Road
London N1 9JN
United Kingdom
www.kogan-page.co.uk

22883 Quicksilver Drive
Sterling VA 20166-2012
USA

© Kogan Page and individual contributors, 2005

The right of Christopher Stephen Brown to be identified as the author of this work has been asserted by him in accordance with the Copyright, Designs and Patents Act 1988.

ISBN 0 7494 4220 4

British Library Cataloguing-in-Publication Data

A CIP record for this book is available from the British Library.

Library of Congress Cataloging-in-Publishing Data

Brown, Chris.
  The sustainable enterprise: profiting from best practice / Chris Brown
    p. cm.
  Includes indexes.
  ISBN 0-7494-4220-4
  1. Social responsibility of business. 2. Business enterprises–Environmental aspects. 3. Small business–Environmental aspects. 4. Industrial management. 5. Factory and trade waste–Environmental aspects. 6. Pollution prevention. 7. Business ethics. I. Title.
  HD60.B758 2005
  658.4'08–dc22

2004026546

Typeset by Datamatics Technologies Ltd, Mumbai, India
Printed and bound in Great Britain by Cambrian Printers Ltd, Aberystwyth, Wales

the cat's pyjamas

The Corporate Social Responsibility approach is not enough! We believe that profit and sustainability go hand in hand and that all too soon this will become a competitive imperative.

Directors must increasingly understand the social and environmental impact of their companies activities on stakeholders. Do you have an understanding of your impacts? Can you measure, report and improve upon them? Do you have the systems in place to deal with these demands?

The Cat's Pyjamas organises bespoke events to showcase how successful business have tackled these issues and won national awards for their work. Our events offer a warts and all approach and you'll go away from our events with plenty to think about and a host of ideas to implement back at work

The Cat's Pyjamas is part of the award winning FRC Group, winners of ACCA's Best Social Report in the Accountability 2002 awards.

If you would like to find out more about how we can help your business tackle these challenges please call Jeremy Nicholls on 0151 734 5869 or Alison Ball on 0151 702 0550 or. Or have a look at our website www.the-cats-pyjamas.com

RENEWABLE ENERGY
– OPTIMISE YOUR STRATEGY

To get the most out of your green initiative - talk to London Energy.

London Energy combines renewable energy supply with great products to help manage your green targets effectively:

Our Energy Reporting Service combines a series of monitoring tools that identify underlying energy consumption and the practical advice to realise the 'on-paper' benefits that are relevant to your organisation.

Performance Partnerships is an exciting new option that focuses on reducing your organisation's total energy cost over a three year period by combining your energy supply and utilities management requirements into one single contract.

FIND OUT MORE:
0845 744 8910

OR VISIT OUR WEB SITE:
www.london-energy.com/business

TSE.04/04

Contents

The CIWM Waste Awareness Certificate

✓ SAVE MONEY! ✓ STAY OUT OF JAIL? ✓ SAVE THE ENVIRONMENT!

TOO GOOD TO BE TRUE?!

The Chartered Institution of Wastes Management (CIWM) has launched a new training initiative designed to make employees "aware of waste".

By attending this short five-hour training course employees will be able to:

✓ **Understand what is waste**

✓ **Reduce, re-use, and recycle waste**

✓ **Know about disposal routes for remaining waste**

✓ **Deal with waste safely**

✓ **Know the legal responsibilities for waste**

✓ **Identify sources of help for those difficult waste questions**

The course is supported by DEFRA, DTI, the Environment Agencies in England, Scotland, Wales and Northern Ireland and WRAP.

Candidates receive a certificate from the CIWM and a Reference Book to ensure they keep "thinking about waste" thus saving money and helping to save the environment by managing waste better.

Contact us now to book!

T: 01604 620426 E: training@ciwm.co.uk

Training Services Department, CIWM 9 Saxon Court, St Peters Gardens, Northampton, NN1 1SX

TRAINING BY THE EXPERTS IN WASTE MANAGEMENT

The Chartered Institution of Wastes Management

vision...

...can take you places you've never dreamed of, helping you stay at the forefront of the latest procurement thinking.

strength...

...in numbers will ensure you'll always find the right people for your company, and the resources to help them grow.

support...

...at the moment you need it most, will give you the confidence to keep moving forward, taking your career to new heights.

Unlocking The Value Of Sustainability: Are Your People Prepared?

EABIS
European Academy
of Business in Society

The European Academy of Business in Society (EABIS) was founded to help business answer this question.

Bringing together more than 30 of Europe's leading companies and business schools, EABIS finds collaborative solutions to the challenge of developing more and better knowledge and skills on business sustainability issues.

Enabling integration into core business

Although often overlooked, the next step in mainstreaming sustainability is developing the right knowledge and skills amongst your people. This step is not overlooked at EABIS: membership gives you the opportunity to draw on the strengths of Europe's leading business educators and develop the mainstream management education you need to help your people tackle 'real life' business sustainability issues.

Connecting Europe's leading businesses and educators

By joining EABIS, you will work in partnership with the leading organisations in Europe:
- More than half of Europe's top 20 Business Schools (Financial Times)
- Five of the top 20 Global companies (Business Week)
- Business network members with over 1,000 European companies

Unilever's view of membership

" *EABIS offers us the unique opportunity to work in partnership with a network of leading European business schools and universities to help improve awareness and understanding of the broad debate on corporate responsibility. In addition to contributing to the body of academic research, this collaboration is also enabling us to learn how we can better integrate wider societal concerns within our business decisions.* "

Andre Van Heemstra, Personnel Director of the Executive Committee, Unilever

**Find out more about joining EABIS at www.eabis.org or contact
Peter Lacy, Executive Director: peter.lacy@eabis.org, Tel. + 32 2 541 1615**

Who Are We?

We are a community development finance institution - a new breed of financial intermediary. We trade for social and ethical purposes, rather than private profit. We issue ethical shares to our members, and operate a one-member one-vote constitution. We channel finance from public and private sectors into under invested communities encouraging sustainable regeneration and development

What Do We Do?

- Provide finance to social and ethical enterprises that cannot access mainstream finance. Three funds generally lend between £5,000 - £50,000:

  - *Social Enterprise Fund — loans to organisations in social ownership that trade for community benefit rather than private profit.*

  - *Assistance and Business Loans for Ethical Enterprises - aimed at businesses which may be privately owned, but which have a strong social and / or environmental aim.*

  - *Mutual Aid Fund — this small loan fund is for emerging community-based enterprises, with no or few assets and needing to develop their business skills. Groups invest in the fund by buying shares in London Rebuilding Society, they can borrow as they save — like a credit union, and can pool their skills and trade ideas.*

- Run a Financial Support Programme for new and growing social enterprises to get them "investment ready" so that they will be more sustainable.
- Develop a Home Improvement Fund in East London to provide advice and finance to older people, and in particular black and minority ethnic communities. The fund will improve their health and well being, whilst renewing existing housing stock.

How Do We Work?

- Across London through our local development managers based in, and trusted by the community.
- Through strong strategic, London wide and local partnerships with public and voluntary bodies.
- By jointly financing enterprises with Charity Bank, Triodos Bank, Industrial Common Ownership, Local Investment Fund, as well as mainstream banks.
- With support from the private sector — banks such as Barclays, the RBS Group, Unity Trust Bank, and professional firms

How Are We Financed?

- By the public sector and through charitable funds
- Corporate sponsors
- Individual as well as corporate investors (shareholders)

london rebuilding society

227c City Road   London   EC1V 1JT
Tel: 020 7682 1666
Fax: 020 7682 1417
info@londonrebuilding.com
www.londonrebuilding.com

Funded and supported by

Foreword

The concepts of what have been broadly defined as sustainable development and corporate social responsibility are commanding increasing public attention in the United Kingdom and all the other advanced industrialized countries. The huge impact that business can have in today's world, with the continuous growth of economic activity, the spread of globalization and the advance of technology, is increasingly being recognized. It shapes our lives and it shapes our environment. Accordingly, the issues are becoming ever more important on the board agenda.

Of course, the primary goal of any business – to generate profit – remains unchanged. Any business that loses sight of that isn't going to be around long enough to influence the environment or society one way or another. But contrary to popular opinion, few boardrooms nowadays single-mindedly pursue profit to the exclusion of all other considerations. The average board has a far higher sense of social responsibility than most people realize. Directors live and raise families in the same world as everyone else.

What has also become clear is that socially responsible policies need not be in conflict with the pursuit of commercial goals – quite the opposite. As public awareness changes, so too do the attitudes of customers, shareholders and employees. This means that businesses not only have to pursue policies that command confidence and support, but also have to ensure that those policies are well communicated and fully understood.

This book aims to assist those running or advising organizations of all types and sizes in understanding the business case for sustainable development and corporate social responsibility. It tackles the subject from many different perspectives. It also offers advice and guidance in preparing and implementing programmes and policies appropriate for the different contexts in which businesses operate.

The book sheds light on an area that has become a critical consideration for business in the 21st century.

George Cox
immediate past Director General of the Institute of Directors
recently appointed Chair of the Design Council

The South East England Development Agency (SEEDA) is focused on driving sustainable economic and social development across its vibrant region. The need for sustainability permeates through every aspect of SEEDA's operations. Sustainability is visibly factored into the decision making process before major programmes can be approved and delivered.

For the last four years, SEEDA has been energetically challenging businesses to embrace the requirements of sustainability through its Sustainable Business Awards for the South East. The aim is to accelerate business competitiveness and to show how to leverage an advantage in the marketplace, while at the same time providing benefits for the environment and the community. The Awards recognise and celebrate businesses that are harnessing the benefits of sustainability in both their daily operations and strategic planning.

SEEDA works collaboratively with seven sub regional Sustainable Business Partnerships (SBPs) on the Awards to foster a local engagement with business. This relationship also champions the positive commercial and reputational returns for businesses seizing the sustainability agenda. A compelling series of case studies from the finalists has also inspired other organisations to emulate successful implementation of sustainable business practices.

SEEDA also supported the development of 'egeneration' – a unique interactive web-based centre of excellence, demonstrating leadership to small and medium enterprises to help them become more sustainable. The site promotes replicable best practice programmes. Last year, SBPs helped 17,000 companies to enhance their bottom line by improving their sustainability performance.

For further details, please visit **www.seeda.co.uk** and **www.egeneration.co.uk**

Foreword

The growth of globalization continues at an unprecedented rate, bringing benefits across the world and at the same time increasing public awareness and concern about the role of business. As Minister for Corporate Social Responsibility (CSR), I believe that responsible business practice is good not only for wider society and the environment, but also for business. CSR offers a view of businesses and their activities that can help stimulate better policies, decision-making and business practices based on a broader understanding of business impacts beyond the purely financial.

Our ambition at the Department of Trade and Industry is 'prosperity for all'. We can only achieve this ambition if we build the productivity and competitiveness of the UK economy. We see the drivers of productivity as investment, innovation, skills, enterprise and competition. Corporate responsibility and sustainable business practices can make a contribution to each of these – for example, through the potential to build motivation, skills, commitment, innovation and new business ideas.

Our role in government is to help set the right policy framework to boost socially and environmentally responsible performance. Where regulation is the right solution, it should be well designed and focused, recognizing the need for a flexible rather than a 'one size fits all' approach. And that is reflected in our proposals for a statutory Operating and Financial Review for quoted companies, which we expect to secure greater accountability by encouraging companies to report on broader matters such as employees, the environment and social and community issues where these are necessary for an understanding of the business.

We want profitable, successful and competitive businesses whose entrepreneurial and innovative strengths are contributing fully to ensuring a fairer society and a cleaner environment. To achieve this goal, responsible behaviour needs to become just part and parcel of the way we do business, which means that the understanding and skills for CSR practice need to be widespread across business and integrated into decision-making. One of my priorities is therefore to establish a CSR Academy, which will support the development of CSR skills across business practice.

This valuable handbook will also support this goal by showing how businesses can strengthen the delivery of their sustainability objectives in a way that is consistent with commercial success. Our aim must be to marry competitiveness with responsibility, and I welcome this.

Stephen Timms MP
immediate past Minister for Energy, e-Commerce and Postal Services

Foreword

This is a fast-changing world, where business and society continue to adjust to new realities and the myriad impacts of globalization. As World Bank President James Wolfensohn emphasizes, this is also 'a world out of balance', where 1 billion of the world's 6 billion people own 80 per cent of global GDP and another billion-plus struggle to survive on less than a dollar a day. Within this context, the sustainable approach outlined in this volume is crucial for delivering positive, lasting change.

The private sector has increased opportunities and influence, but also faces new risks and responsibilities. Around the world, public attitudes are shifting, with concerns ranging from climate change to business – community relations to corruption. 'Business as usual' is no longer an option, but sustainable business practice and competitive success can go hand in hand. Business, together with entrepreneurialism, is now a vital partner in creating economic and social development. Within the World Bank, the World Bank Institute takes a lead on capacity-building and knowledge sharing for development. Its private-sector development work is greatly enhanced by partnerships with companies and business associations, highlighting approaches that work for business and communities. Not by chance is the WBI programme titled 'Corporate Social Responsibility and Sustainable Competitiveness'.

Handbooks such as this are important tools to enable businesses to adopt practical steps to strengthen the sustainability of their operations for the benefit of the company and all its stakeholders. The importance of disseminating best practices, encapsulated here, lies at the heart of the World Bank Institute's approach. Representative organizations such as the Institute of Directors are uniquely positioned to assist in capturing such best practices and partnering to give businesses the tools to build a 'sustainable enterprise' in the United Kingdom and the global marketplace. Sustainable enterprises can reinforce not just their own long-term success, but also that of the local, national and global community.

Michael Jarvis
Corporate Social Responsibility and Sustainable Competitiveness Program,
World Bank Institute

Oldmoor Wetlands Centre, RSPB Dearne Valley, transforming coalfield land into a tourist attraction and business centre.

Turning energy efficiency into economic growth.
1 forward thinking agency

Over the past year Yorkshire Forward has helped to lower CO_2 emissions in Yorkshire and Humber by 1.1m tonnes. That's equivalent to one in six people in Yorkshire and Humber leaving their cars at home for a year or a forest around the size of Huddersfield being preserved from deforestation.

Yorkshire Forward is committed to working with the environment, not against it.

Over the past five years we have changed the way that we work as an organisation in terms of our own impact on the environment, and have built sustainability requirements into the support that we offer, to ensure a better quality of project with increased environmental benefit.

Projects like Old Moor Wetlands Centre and Gibson Mill in West Yorkshire, which will generate it's power onsite, are making a positive difference to both enterprise and the environment.

If you would like more information on sustainable development at Yorkshire Forward, get in touch with Yorkshire Forward on marketing@yorkshire-forward.com or visit www.yorkshire-forward.com

Yorkshire Alive with Opportunity!

YORKSHIRE FORWARD

Are you interested in IMPROVING YOUR CAREER PROSPECT? or CONTINUING PROFESSIONAL DEVELOPMENT?

We offer postgraduate level courses in:

- ❑ Climate Change Management
- ❑ Environmental Impact Assessment and Management
- ❑ Environmental Policy and Management
- ❑ Environmental Resource Planning
- ❑ Environmental and Sustainability Management for Business
- ❑ Integrated Waste Management
- ❑ Landscape Design and Architecture
- ❑ Tourism and Sustainable Development
- ❑ Water and Environmental Management

Contact Details:
School of Environment Office
Tel: + 44 (0) 1242 532922/532948
Email:pgelcourses@glos.ac.uk

Are you looking for ENVIRONMENTAL RESEARCH or CONSULTANCY EXPERTISE?

We offer services in :

- ❑ Corporate social responsibility/business sustainability
- ❑ Ecological surveys
- ❑ Environmental impact assessment
- ❑ Environmental management systems/ISO14001
- ❑ Graduate industry placements (KTPs)
- ❑ Green transport planning
- ❑ Monitoring, sampling and laboratory services
- ❑ Strategic waste management/life cycle analysis
- ❑ Surveying, mapping and GIS
- ❑ Water resource assessment

Contact Details:
School of Environment Office
Tel: + 44 (0) 1242 532922/544002
Email:soe@glos.ac.uk

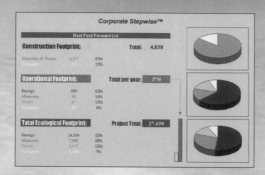
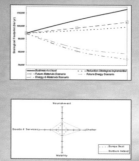

Sustainable value

Sustainable value: introduction

Jonathon Porritt

It's been a long haul, but it's clear that the so-called 'business case for sustainable develop-ment' (or corporate social responsibility (CSR), depending on which particular dialect you speak!) has at last come of age. The idea that good companies (big or small) will become even better companies if they go about their business in more environmentally and socially responsible ways was once heresy: sustainable development was seen as 'someone else's concern', a source of increased regulatory hassle, increased costs and runaway expectations. Not any more.

The business world is nothing if not pragmatic. It's practice that counts, not theory; 'what works' works. And the truth of it is that enough companies have started to make a fist of CSR to give the lie to all those misery-guts who continue to assert that business should 'stick to the knitting' – generating profits, dividends, jobs and tax revenues – and do nothing that isn't required by law or demanded by the consumer. You'll find dozens and dozens of these countervailing success stories dotted throughout this timely and informative publication.

Some of those stories are risk based: keeping out of trouble in an ever more environ-mentally conscious world makes a lot of sense. Some of them are value driven: there really are new markets and new opportunities for highly profitable business off the back of the sustainable development agenda. Some are externally driven (by new regulation or eco-nomic incentives), some internally driven, by employees or company leaders who just feel better about themselves and their company by reducing impacts and doing right by their stakeholders even as they build a successful company.

You will also discover that this is not just about the big multinationals: the same old band of do-gooding suspects. It's true that it's often harder for small and medium-sized enterprises (SMEs), for which survival remains the overarching imperative. But gearing up for a world that will demand ever-higher environmental and ethical standards already makes a great deal of commercial sense.

All this doesn't let governments off the hook. They still bear the principal responsibility for shaping markets in such a way as to reward responsible wealth creation and ensure that companies can't go on externalizing their costs on to other people, the environment and future generations. But one's got to be either congenitally gloomy or professionally cynical not to be encouraged by the multitude of ways in which the private sector is now reaching out beyond that regulated minimum to achieve far higher standards and improved performance.

And that's the principal message for all those SMEs that have yet to see the light!

Sustainable value: legal overview

Kathryn Mylrea, Simmons & Simmons

There is no legal standard against which sustainable value can be measured, but as a concept it is underpinned by many issues subject to legislation and regulation. This can be at an international and national level, for example climate change and biodiversity. Although a consensus has been slow to emerge about the connections between corporate objectives and social and environmental ones, recognition that businesses have responsibilities to a wide group of stakeholders is gradually gaining acceptance. It is this relationship that underpins the concept of corporate social responsibility (CSR).

CSR has developed as a way of encouraging organizations to take broader social and environmental issues into account in their day-to-day operating activities. CSR has advanced rapidly since the mid-1990s, when it first began to gain widespread attention. Initially it was focused more on revenue and cost benefits, but growing awareness of the importance of reputational issues and how a poor record on environmental matters can adversely affect a company's standing and business prospects has broadened the definition.

The British Standards Institution established a new committee to develop standards on CSR and sustainable development in October 2003, and the International Organization for Standardization is currently looking to develop an International Standard for social responsibility. The objective is to produce 'a guidance document, written in plain language which is understandable and usable by non-specialists' and not intended for use in certification.

In July 2002 the European Commission issued a Communication on Corporate Social Responsibility that emphasized the voluntary nature of CSR but supported the creation of a Multi-Stakeholder Forum on CSR to discuss the issues and provide advice. The report of the Multi-Stakeholder Forum was published in June 2004 and concludes that there is no need for EC rules on CSR and that the approach to reporting on environmental and community activities should remain voluntary.

The United Kingdom's proposed new Operating and Financial Review (OFR) will involve some consideration of sustainable value in that it requires a more forward-looking view of the business prospects. Climate change is specifically mentioned as an example of something that should be considered.

Risk management

Greg Pritchard, CPAAudit

The balance between risk and reward is the very essence of business; it is necessary to take risks in order to generate returns. There is, however, a difference between risks taken as a result of careful judgement and those taken unwittingly or unknowingly. In today's world of increasing complexity and uncertainty, businesses must manage risk more rigorously than ever before.

Thus, risk management should be a key feature of any successful business, and carrying out a thorough risk assessment is the starting point. Completion of such an assessment typically follows the following process:

■ Step 1. Identify the risk drivers for each category of risk, including business strategy, market, political and economic environment, customers, products and services, operations and distribution, suppliers, credit and financial soundness, management and staff. This activity is usually carried out in a workshop, brainstorming or focus group setting.

■ Step 2. Allocate a probability of the risks identified arising. This is a subjective assessment and can be in the form of a simple high, medium, low categorization. Alternatively, a more sophisticated approach could be adopted by allocating time-frames such as:

  – rare occurrence: less than once every 10 years;
  – unlikely occurrence: once every 5–10 years; and so on.

■ Step 3. Assess the business exposure, such as loss of a customer, damage to reputation or a financial penalty, in the event of each risk arising.
■ Step 4. Assess the degree of impact resulting from the business exposure. Again, this can be a subjective assessment in the simple form of high, medium, low, or a more sophisticated approach can be taken based on likely monetary losses, such as:

– insignificant: loss less than £10 million;
– minor: loss between £10 million and £25 million; and so on.

With the risk assessment complete, the business will know with some degree of certainty what risks it faces, how likely they are to arise and the likely impact on the business in the event they do arise. Naturally, the risk assessment should be monitored and reviewed on a regular basis in case the risk profile of the business changes.

Not surprisingly, the next step is to identify the control mechanisms in place to prevent the risks arising or to mitigate their effects. Here the focus should be on those risks that are more likely to arise and have a significant detrimental impact on the business when they do arise; these are the areas where the most robust internal controls are required.

The nature and extent of the systems and controls that a business will need to maintain will depend upon a variety of factors including:

■ the nature, scale and complexity of its business;
■ the diversity of its operations;
■ the volume and size of its transactions;
■ the degree of risk associated with each area of its operations.

Typical control mechanisms include supervision, monitoring and review, reconciliations, segregation of duties, exception reporting, disaster recovery and business continuity planning, physical security, documentation, insurance and, of course, internal audit. Other constituents of the risk management toolkit include risk committees and stress and scenario testing. To be truly effective, a company's internal control system should:

■ be embedded within its operations and not treated as a separate exercise;
■ be able to respond to changing risks within and outside the company;
■ enable each company to apply it in an appropriate manner related to its risks.

Here, factors to consider include:

■ the nature and extent of the risks facing the company;
■ the extent and categories of risk that it regards as acceptable for the company to bear;
■ the likelihood of the risks concerned materializing;
■ the company's ability to reduce the incidence and impact on the business of risks that do materialize;
■ the costs of operating controls relative to the benefit obtained from managing the risks.

A convenient tabular format for recording and displaying the results of the risk assessment process, based on a company operating in the financial sector, is shown in Table 1.3.1.

Table 1.3.1 Format for recording and displaying the results of a risk assessment

Category of Risk	Risk Driver	Probability	Exposure	Impact	Control Mechanism	Audit Test
Staff	Loss of key individuals	Medium	Loss of knowledge, expertise and commercial contacts	Low to high depending on business area	Cross-training and spreading client relationships Procedures manuals, work schedules and other documentation, particularly relating to IT systems Provision of attractive career opportunities and competitive compensation packages	Review results of employee skills audit and client relationship management arrangements Review procedures manuals, work schedules, IT system documentation etc for completeness Compare remuneration packages against comparable industry benchmark data
	Insufficient segregation of duties	Low	Potential for fraud or hiding mistakes resulting in loss to the company	Medium	Exception reporting from IT systems Management review Independent confirmation and/or reconciliation with third parties	
	Critical systems not supported when staff are absent	Low to high depending on business area	Interruption of normal business cycle	High	Cross-training Use of subcontractors where no suitable internal resource exists	Review results of employee skills audit Review procedure for selecting, and assessing the competence of, subcontractors

(Continued)

Table 1.3.1 *(Continued)*

Category of Risk	Risk Driver	Probability	Exposure	Impact	Control Mechanism	Audit Test
	Normal procedures not carried out and normal controls not applied when staff are absent	Low	Potential for error or fraud increases Breach of client investment guidelines	Medium	System controls and warnings and other manual procedures Cross-training and absence cover	
	Poor quality or inexperienced staff deliver inadequate client service and/or provide inadequate advice	Low	Client dissatisfaction Damage to reputation Regulatory concern	High	Tight recruitment procedures to ensure only suitably qualified individuals are employed Staff training and professional development	
Systems	Loss or corruption of data	Low	Interruption of normal business cycle	High	Daily back-up procedure Anti-virus software	
	System failure	Low	Inability to conduct business	High	Presence of emergency site Emergency power supply	
	Confidential data strays into the public domain	Low	Client dissatisfaction Damage to reputation Regulatory concern	Low	Use of firewall to protect internet connection Systems protected by passwords	Attempt to penetrate the firewall

Category	Risk		Consequence		Controls
Compliance and regulation	Failure to comply with regulations	Low	Fines, loss of licences	High	Regular review of activities by Compliance Officer
	Loss of Compliance Officer	Low	Increased risk of non-compliance and breach of regulations due to inadequate supervision	Medium	Use of other members of staff (with appropriate experience) or external consultants
Health and safety	Accidents to personnel	Low	Temporary loss of personnel Claims for compensation	Low	See staff section above Periodic checks conducted by Health and Safety Officer Insurance
Security	Unauthorized intrusion	Low	Physical attacks on personnel Loss of equipment Confidential information stolen	Low	Insurance Door entry security system Nightwatchman Data back-ups
Operational and delivery	Incorrect order execution	Low	Company assumes an unintentional proprietary position Company required to compensate client(s) for profits that would have arisen on the correct trade or losses incurred on the incorrect trade	Medium	Order read back to client Fill confirmed to client Transaction note sent to client

(Continued)

Table 1.3.1 (*Continued*)

Category of Risk	Risk Driver	Probability	Exposure	Impact	Control Mechanism	Audit Test
	Incorrect recording of trades	Low	Company assumes an unintentional proprietary position Unknown open positions give rise to losses for which the company will eventually have to provide compensation	Medium	Back-office reconciliations to order confirmations Transaction note sent to client	
	Late settlement of futures contracts which go to delivery	Low	Fines imposed by the London Clearing House Clients dissatisfied	Medium	Exception report of trades approaching delivery sent to dealing desk and followed up by back office	
	Late or incorrect payment instructions when funds are remitted to clients or counterparties	Low	Possible financial loss to the company	Medium	Standard settlement payments are checked against a list daily; US$ payments require sign-off by one authorized signatory, GB£ payments require sign-off by two authorized signatories All other payments are confirmed by telephone	

	Risk		Description		Controls	Audit review
Counter-party and credit	Failure of counterparty	Low	The cost of settling open foreign exchange contracts and open futures contracts would accrue to the company Loss of cash deposits lodged with counterparty as margin to collateralize trading lines	Low	Trade only with approved counterparties Periodic review of financial standing of counterparties	
	Volatile market conditions result in exceptional losses that clients are unable or unwilling to cover	Medium	Client losses accrue to company	Medium	Periodic review of client creditworthiness Management of the size of positions in relation to individual limits and in relation to the size of the overall market Awareness of events likely to cause market volatility and associated contingency planning Margin call management	Review documentation relating to recent client creditworthiness checks for high-value positions in volatile commodities Review the size of positions in relation to individual limits and the size of the overall market Review contingency plans for events currently likely to cause market volatility

(*Continued*)

Table 1.3.1 (*Continued*)

Category of Risk	Risk Driver	Probability	Exposure	Impact	Control Mechanism	Audit Test
						Review recent margin call activity, noting the speed with which clients respond
Market and performance	Poor advice given to advisory and discretionary clients	Low	Damage to reputation affecting client retention and new business development	Medium	Selection procedures for recruiting dealers who are required to pass FSA exams. Client agreements absolve responsibility for bad advice	

If the business has an internal audit department, it should use the risk assessment to direct the business's resources in order to evaluate whether an adequate level of internal control exists to reduce business risks to an acceptable level. Thus, internal audit resource should be focused on reviewing and testing the effectiveness of those internal controls in place to prevent, mitigate, minimize or transfer risk caused by events that have a high to medium probability of occurrence and give rise to a correspondingly high to medium detrimental impact. Naturally, internal control mechanisms should be refined or created where these are found to be ineffective or missing. Used in this way, internal audit will become a valuable tool for corporate boards in their endeavours to achieve business objectives efficiently and objectively by maintaining and improving internal controls commensurate with business risk. Such an approach also constitutes best practice with regard to corporate governance.

CPAAudit provides professional advice to the financial services sector in the areas of:

■ regulatory compliance;
■ risk management;
■ internal audit;
■ corporate governance.

It also provides a range of consultancy and support services, including executive search, company secretarial services, fund administration and the preparation of FSA financial returns. For more details, please go to http://www.cpaaudit.co.uk.

The long-term sustainability of your business depends on you meeting your responsibilities to all your stakeholders – not just customers and investors, but also employees, suppliers, neighbours, regulators and society as a whole.

Take the long view

As one of the UK's leading corporate social responsibility consultancies, csrnetwork can help you fulfil your social and environmental responsibilities.

We'll benchmark your CSR management against best practice and then help you develop your CSR strategy, engage with your stakeholders and manage and report your performance.

Contact us or visit our website to find out why so many companies in the UK and beyond turn to csrnetwork when they want to make CSR a reality.

Corporate social responsibility

Elizabeth Ness, csrnetwork

Put simply, corporate social responsibility (CSR) is the necessity and the duty of a company to behave responsibly, ethically and sustainably, and to be transparently accountable to its stakeholders. The concept is not new, but it has now joined the often-despised ranks of ill-understood three-letter abbreviations.

To those who firmly believe that 'the business of business is business', CSR can be seen as a distraction from the bottom line. To those who have proactively assessed their impacts on local and global economies, the environment, and society, there is a growing under-standing that the long-term sustainability and profitability of an enterprise mean managing these impacts in an accountable manner.

To those who believe that 'like environmental issues, CSR is a passing fashion', I would pose the question: since when did honesty go out of fashion? Since when did oper-ating with basic decency and integrity move into the purview of the fashionista? And how can today's money markets, which are increasingly remote from the wealth-generating activities (eg commodities and derivatives trading), retain stability if there is no basic underlying integrity?

In April 2004 Alan Greenspan[1] spoke on 'capitalizing reputation'. His emphasis was that to maintain stable economies, 'the importance of reputation cannot be overstated' – but also that 'rules cannot substitute for character'. 'Rules guide only a few of the day-to-day decisions of… executives'; the rest is 'governed by personal codes of values'.

The concept underpinning the forerunner of modern-day CSR was the social philanthropy of the 18th and 19th centuries, which recognized that, in order to have an efficient workforce, the workers' housing, healthcare and nourishment had to be adequate. Thus appeared the worker villages of the industrial revolution, company medical facilities and the subsidized works canteen. Societal concern was seen in the context of enlightened self-interest, and was carried out in the context of the prevailing moral codes of the day – a typical example in the United Kingdom being the 1802 Health and Morals of Apprentices Act.

During the 1960s, 70s and 80s, environmental concern grew with books such as Rachel Carson's *Silent Spring*, causes célèbres such as the fate of the Brent Spar oil rig, and disasters such as Chernobyl. Corporations and governments were seen as increasingly unresponsive and remote, leading to the growth in number, type and effectiveness of pressure groups – or NGOs. It should also be recognized that, even when companies put in considerable effort to assess the environmentally least damaging option (as in the case of the Brent Spar), the NGO view can prevail. Scientific arguments still debate whether disposal of the oil rig at sea should have been the preferred environmental option.

As corporations continued to grow, the public became conscious of their supply-chain effects – but this time, environmental concern was coupled with social issues. A breed of 'ethical consumer' began to emerge, concerned not just about the loss of virgin rain forest to make mass-produced furniture, but also about the human misery dimension: the 'sweatshops' producing the consumer products for the affluent nations. Nike in particular faced a major threat to profitability from a boycott by US universities on this issue – the result being the creation of the Fair Labor Association, active policies towards and monitoring of manufacturing practices in less developed nations, and much wider public reporting among global suppliers of sports, clothing and other consumer goods.

The role of the state and regulatory bodies has gradually increased: the Sarbanes–Oxley requirements for corporate reporting in the United States were drafted as a direct result of the scandals associated with Enron, Tyco and the like. In the United Kingdom the 1992 Cadbury Report can be seen as a forerunner of many approaches to reforming corporate governance: the 1995 Greenbury Report, the 1998 Hampel Report, the 1999 Turnbull Report and the 2003 Higgs Report. The UK Government is at present consulting on revision of the Operating and Financial Review (OFR).[2]

On the world stage the governments of the 30 OECD countries have approved a revised version of the OECD's Principles of Corporate Governance, adding new recommendations for good practice in corporate behaviour with a view to rebuilding and maintaining public trust in companies and stock markets.[3] This growth in regulation mirrors public loss in trust in what is seen as increasingly remote and detached management of multinational corporations.

The sustainable enterprise

The title of this book – *The Sustainable Enterprise* – encompasses two strands: 1) business sustainability; 2) sustainability of the earth and its resources. The two are inseparable and interactive – but timescales can differ. For quoted companies, the financial time-frame can be as little as three months – the cycle of reporting on the New York Stock Exchange. These are often the companies with the greatest global impact; the 100 largest quoted companies (as listed by Fortune) have turnovers greater than the GDP of many nations. It should follow that these companies should display, and report, leadership in corporate social responsibility. There has recently been a step change in reporting by this largest 100 since 2003 – up from 48 to 72. In the latest survey of CSR[4] reporting and accountability, 66 companies produced stand-alone sustainability reports, 4 reported on sustainability on the web (sometimes accompanied by a hard-copy summary) and 2 provided sustainability performance information as an integrated part of their annual report.

As John Kay recently wrote, 'No one will ever be buried with the epitaph "He maximized shareholder value."'[5] Companies that changed their objectives and values from aspiring to greatness in their fields to an emphasis on shareholder value achieved neither shareholder value nor sustainable company growth (eg ICI and Boeing). In other words, argues Kay, focus on maximizing short-term earnings per share results ultimately in an unsustainable enterprise. In essence, a sustainable business sees itself as a value maximizer rather than a profit maximizer.[6]

CSR in practice

CSR in practice for the small and medium-sized enterprise (SME) is the same as for global multinational companies:

- Behave ethically according to societal norms, and treat others as you would wish to be treated.
- Discover, assess, manage and improve economic, environmental and societal risks and opportunities as an integral part of your business strategy.
- Relate your reward structure to behaviours that promote and integrate CSR into business practice.
- Make your actions transparently available to (all of) your stakeholders.
- Tell it like it is.

The envelope of CSR and sustainability issues surrounding the organization is dynamic. To reap the value on the bottom line, CSR must be an accepted norm within daily business

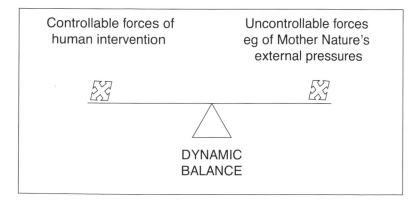

Figure 1.4.1 Dynamic nature of issues related to corporate social responsibility and sustainability

operations. In addition, it is essential to understand not only the organization's greatest impacts, but also where its scope of control is effective.[7]

Within this publication are many case studies illustrating approaches and bottom-line benefits. What they will all have in common is that success will have come from a clearly stated leadership vision of what CSR and sustainability mean to the growth and profitability of the organization, and how individuals are required to respond to this vision in practice.

Companies that successfully practise CSR and reap the rewards do so because they have integrated CSR into business reality. Once they have implemented the legal minimum, policy development is best conducted inclusively around real examples, such as the following:

- Equal opportunities policy can be developed to support a retention and recruitment drive.
- Supplier engagement can be developed around a review of debtors/creditors and security of supply.
- Environmental improvement programmes can be developed around the need to:
  - reduce waste/energy/travel costs;
  - change haulage supplier;
  - create new product and service opportunities.
- Supply chain ethics can be developed with a key supplier or key vulnerable product – and maybe learnt in partnership with a key corporate customer – potentially yielding considerable business benefit.

CSR guidelines

The UN Global Compact[8]

The United Nations is a leading focus for the engagement of business in the CSR agenda. Businesses of all sizes can engage with the UN programmes according to their vision and scope of influence.

The vision of the UN Global Compact is 'a more sustainable and inclusive global economy by fostering a more beneficial relationship between business and societies'. Business is seen as part of the solution to problems related to globalization. The Global Compact asks companies to 'embrace, support and enact, within their sphere of influence, a set of core values in the areas of human rights, labour standards and the environment'.

The nine Global Compact principles are:

- to support and respect the protection of internationally proclaimed human rights;
- to avoid complicity in human rights abuses;
- to uphold freedom of association and the effective recognition of the right to collective bargaining;
- to eliminate all forms of forced and compulsory labour;
- to effectively abolish child labour;
- to eliminate discrimination with respect to employment and occupation;
- to support a precautionary approach to environmental challenges;

- to promote greater environmental responsibility;
- to promote development and diffusion of environmentally friendly technologies.

These nine principles enjoy universal consensus and are derived from:

- the Universal Declaration of Human Rights (www.un.org/overview/rights.html);
- the International Labour Organization's Declaration on Fundamental Principles and Rights at Work (www.ilo.org/public/english/standards/decl/declaration/text);
- the Rio Declaration on Environment and Development (www.un.org/esa/sustdev/ agenda21.htm).

The Global Compact provides guidance for businesses on how to approach the nine principles in practice.

Many, if not all, of the principles of the Global Compact seem self-evident in today's Western society. We no longer indulge in child labour or forced labour, or abuse human rights in the workplace... or do we? What answer do we get when we look at our purchasing decisions and our supply chain? This is one of the most difficult issues to tackle, not least because a small business is likely to be uncertain about its influence on the supply chain, and will not have the time to research all the issues. There is, however, a major learning opportunity for the SME should a major corporate involve it in a supply chain management exercise.

The Global Reporting Initiative (GRI)[9]

Started in 1997, the GRI was a project of CERES[10] and the United Nations Environment Programme (UNEP)[11]. The GRI became independent in 2002, is an official collaborating centre of UNEP, and works in cooperation with UN Secretary-General Kofi Annan's Global Compact. The GRI is a 'practical expression' of the Global Compact, and those businesses that wish to report on their CSR performance can use the GRI Guidelines as a template. The reporting framework covers Vision and Strategy, Profile, and Governance Structure and Management Systems, plus the 'three pillars' of sustainability: Economic, Environmental and Social (see Figure 1.4.2). The GRI recognizes that not all its indicators are relevant to all businesses – and also that businesses embracing CSR have begun a journey. Incremental reporting against the Guidelines is the expected progression.

In many ways, reporting is the easy bit: an organization that properly consults its stakeholders, and that has a strategy of integrating CSR into business practices, can just tell the story.

Other resources

There are many other programmes and resources to assist businesses aspiring to apply CSR – many of which are described in this publication. Trade associations can be a rich source of information and assistance, as can local government, chambers of commerce and other business groups. Particular examples in the United Kingdom are Business in the Community[12] and the Prince of Wales's Business Leaders Forum – the CSR Forum.[13] Globally, the World Business Council for Sustainable Development is a leading focus for business.[14]

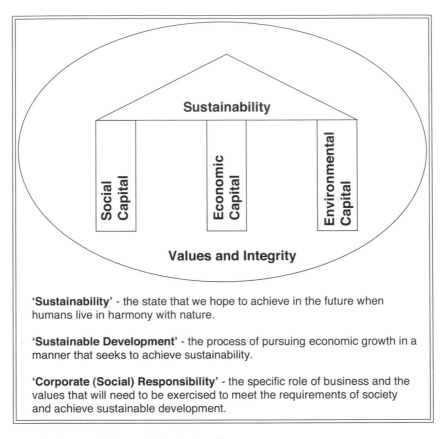

Sustainability - the state that we hope to achieve in the future when humans live in harmony with nature.

'Sustainable Development' - the process of pursuing economic growth in a manner that seeks to achieve sustainability.

'Corporate (Social) Responsibility' - the specific role of business and the values that will need to be exercised to meet the requirements of society and achieve sustainable development.

Figure 1.4.2 Sustainability and the three pillars

The business benefits of CSR

Many companies consider CSR, sustainability, environmental issues and the like as a part of their risk management process. This is an honest approach, and can contribute much to the integrity and health of a company if treated sufficiently broadly – ie by considering timescales beyond the next financial year. The effects of global warming are uncertain, but if you are giving 25-year financial undertakings they are highly relevant – as is found today when one tries to buy insurance.

In addition, the truly entrepreneurial company has the opportunity to break the mould by integrating CSR into its business activities and creating opportunities for differentiation and product development. Small start-ups are particularly well placed as they are unencumbered by the baggage of history and stock market expectations – an obvious example being Café Direct.[15]

The benefits of integrating CSR into a business range across:

- the straight fiscal: increased profit, better access to capital, reduced operating costs;
- an increased ability to attract and retain the best employees;
- market benefits in terms of image and reputation, and customer retention.

Nice people to do business with!

At its simplest, CSR is the practice of enlightened self-interest by a company. Staying in business, licence to operate, access to capital, sustainable growth – all require that a company can demonstrate response to its stakeholders' concerns.

To bring to an end these thoughts, here is a piece of news reported by the BBC[16] that I feel illustrates the battle we really face if sustainable development is to become reality: 'At the beginning of 2004 bicycles will be banned from certain portions of Shanghai's main thoroughfares… to make way for the more than the 11,000 new cars pouring into China's roads every week.'

Good news, bad news: prosperity is growing in China – but not sustainably.

Notes

1   Greenspan, A (2004) Capitalizing reputation, speech to 2004 Financial Markets Conference of the Federal Reserve Bank of Atlanta, Sea Island, Georgia, April 2004, www.federalreserve.gov/boarddocs/speeches/2004/20040416/default.htm.

2   Department of Trade and Industry (2004) Operating and Financial Review (OFR) consultation document, May, www.dti.gov.uk/cld/financialreview.htm.

3   The OECD Principles of Corporate Governance, Organisation for Economic Co-operation and Development, www.oecd.org.

4   Encoding accountability: the accountability rating® 2004, **csr**network and AccountAbility, www.csrnetwork.com and www.accountability.org.uk.

5   Kay, John (2004), Forget how the crow flies, *The Financial Times*, 16 January 2004, www.ft.com.

6   O'Malley, Charley (2004) European Business Forum, February, www.ebfonline.com.

7   Figure by Lucy Candlin on behalf of **csr**network.

8   The UN Global Compact, www.unglobalcompact.org. 0

9   For additional information on the Global Reporting Initiative, www.globalreporting.org.

10 CERES Coalition for Environmental Responsible Economics, www.ceres.org.

11 The United Nations Environment Programme, www.unep.org.

12 Business in the Community, www.bitc.uk.org and International Business Leaders Forum, www.iblf.org.

13 The Prince of Wales International Business Leaders Forum, CSR Forum, www.pwblf.org.

14 World Business Council for Sustainable Development, www.wbcsd.ch.

15 Café Direct, www.cafedirect.co.uk.

16 BBC News, www.news.bbc.co.uk/2/hi/asia-pacific/3513119.stm. It is also reported that the city has now 'back-pedalled' and that 'cycle paths would be integrated into urban renewal projects in the run-up to the 2010 World Expo in Shanghai'.

Elizabeth Ness, csrnetwork Ltd
E-mail: elizabeth.ness@csrnetwork.com

Confronting the challenges related to reducing greenhouse gas emissions

Pedro Moura Costa, EcoSecurities Group

Introduction

Among all environmental challenges currently facing industry, the reduction of greenhouse gas (GHG) emissions is among the most topical. Given its direct link to global climate change, how countries and industries will reduce emissions of GHGs has become an issue of significant international relevance and public interest. It is widely acknowledged that the potential impact of climate change on the global economy could be enormous: re-insurance companies estimate that it could be of the order of hundreds of billions of dollars per year in the form of natural disasters and disruptions to agricultural cycles. The extent of these impacts provides ample justification for the introduction of drastic measures for prevention and mitigation of climate change. The targets set out by the Kyoto Protocol of the Climate Convention are only a first step in this direction, but undoubtedly any measure to limit emissions will come with a cost.

Limitations in the emissions of GHGs could lead to reductions in the levels of industrial output and economic activity. In the absence of innovation, it has been estimated that the cost of compliance to meet the targets outlined by the Kyoto Protocol could reach tens of billions of euros per year in Europe alone. Moreover, traditional policy measures such as command-and-control systems or taxation mechanisms can be difficult and expensive to administer, can result in prohibitive costs for industry, and do not provide any guarantee that targets will actually be met. Regulatory systems that cap overall emissions and allow for the trading of these (known as cap-and-trade systems) provide flexibility for individual companies to explore the full extent of their comparative advantages and are proven to be cheaper and more effective than other approaches. It is expected that an international trading system for GHGs could significantly reduce costs of reaching global targets while at the same time rewarding innovation and entrepreneurship.

This chapter describes the initiatives related to GHG mitigation currently being implemented at global and European levels, and how they could impact British industry and economy. The chapter and the accompanying case study (page 33) outline how companies can take advantage of the opportunities afforded by the various mechanisms established for reducing GHG emissions.

The Climate Convention and its flexibility mechanisms

The underlying policy initiative steering international efforts to reduce GHG emissions is the United Nations Framework Convention on Climate Change. Launched in 1992 during the United Nations Conference on Environment and Development in Rio de Janeiro, the Climate Convention created the basis for current efforts related to controlling GHG emissions. Specifically, the Convention establishes the stabilization of GHG concentrations in the atmosphere as its main objective.

In December 1997 the Kyoto Protocol was created to further define the rules and regulations for the implementation of the targets established in the Climate Convention. The most important aspect of the Kyoto Protocol is the adoption of binding commitments by 37 developed countries and economies in transition (collectively called 'the Annex 1 countries') to reduce their GHG emissions by an average of 5.2 per cent below their 1990 levels for the years 2008–12. The commitments are different for different countries, with some required to reduce up to 8 per cent below their 1990 levels (eg the European Union as a whole), while others only have to limit the growth of their emissions to 1990 levels. The United Kingdom's target is to reduce emissions by 12.5 per cent below 1990 levels. At the same time, the Protocol establishes the use of three 'flexibility mechanisms' for facilitating the achievement of these GHG emission reduction targets. These are:

■ *emissions trading*, allowing the international transfer of national allotments of emission rights between Annex 1 countries;

■ *joint implementation* (JI), the creation of emissions reduction credits undertaken through transnational investment between industrial countries and/or companies of the Annex 1 countries;

■ the *Clean Development Mechanism* (CDM), which allows for the creation of Certified Emission Reduction (CER) credits from projects in developing countries and also promotes sustainable development in these countries.

The Kyoto Protocol was a truly international step in the GHG emissions mitigation arena, providing a compromise between substantial emissions reduction targets with a market

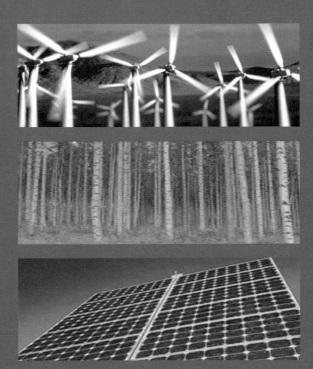

mechanism under which to achieve those emissions reduction requirements. The Protocol opened for signature on March 1998 and will become legally binding after the ratification by a minimum of 55 Annex 1 countries, accounting for at least 55 per cent of the emissions of the developed countries in 1990. The entry into force of the Protocol is now expected to be February 2005, 90 days after Russia's ratification in November 2004.

The UK and EU emissions trading schemes

The objectives established by the Climate Convention have, in turn, to be translated into national rules, regulations and legislation. The United Kingdom was the first European country to develop and implement an emissions trading scheme to assist the country to meet its emission reduction targets. The UK Emissions Trading Scheme (UK ETS) started operating in early 2002, one year after the establishment of a Climate Change Levy on the use of electricity by all companies in the country (the rationale being that electricity generation is one of the main causes of CO_2 emissions in the United Kingdom). The UK ETS was particularly focused on energy-intensive industries such as the steel, aluminium, chemicals, paper, food and drinks, glass, and foundry sectors. These energy-intensive companies were entitled to negotiated emission reduction plans with the government in exchange for a reduction in their Climate Change Levy burden. In order to meet their emission-reduction targets, companies in these sectors were allowed to trade emission permits between themselves, forming the basis for the UK ETS. It is estimated that by 2006 the UK ETS will have led to the reduction of some 4 million tonnes of CO_2 emissions in relation to 1998–2000 levels. In parallel, the UK ETS had the objective of fostering innovation and triggering the beginning of an environmental trading system that would place the City of London at the centre of this new market.

Although the United Kingdom was the first to develop an emissions trading scheme for GHGs, the UK ETS will now be gradually superseded by a European Union-wide trading system, designed to prepare the EU for its Kyoto agreements. Arrangements for the European Union Emissions Trading Scheme (EU ETS) came into force in October 2003, and it is planned that it will begin operating in January 2005. The EU ETS is a cap-and-trade system based on the allocation of limited amounts of emission rights – European Allowance Units (EAUs) – and the associated flexibility to buy or sell surplus allowances from other parties. While the EU ETS is an important tool for meeting the objectives of Kyoto, it is important to point out that it is not dependent on Kyoto ratification: the EU ETS would have been implemented even if Russia had not ratified the Kyoto Protocol. The main elements of the system are as follows.

The system will start operating in January 2005 with the participation of the 15 established EU member states, and will gradually incorporate the accession countries. The first phase of the EU ETS runs from 2005 to 2007, while the second phase coincides with the first commitment period under Kyoto, 2008–12.

The system covers five main sectors of the economies of the EU, namely power and heat generation, iron and steel, mineral oil refineries, mineral industry (cement, glass, ceramics) and the pulp and paper sectors. In total, a total of 12,000–15,000 plants or installations will be covered by the EU ETS. These sectors account for approximately 46 per cent of EU emissions, or over 2 billion tonnes of CO_2 emissions per year. Reduction of emissions from other sources (eg transport) will be promoted directly by individual governments

RISK MANAGEMENT

In a previous article, I quoted one of the suggested board performance criteria post Higgs and the Combined Code. It was: "What has been the board's contribution to ensuring robust and effective risk management?"

Yet again, there are two ways of viewing this issue. In one part of the public sector recently, a 'model' risk management plan was produced by a central body and this was then copied, with few changes, by the institutions within the sector. This enabled each of the institutions concerned to claim 'compliance' with the requirements but gave no ownership of risk management issues to either the Boards or the Management Teams concerned.

The effective way for Risk Management to be embedded into organisations is for the Board to give a lead and to ensure that a proper debate, that focuses on the particular risks faced by the organisation takes place. This is not to make boards or management 'risk averse', but simply to ensure that the evaluation of risk is carried out by all managers who should be required to show how they will beneficially manage the risks faced in their part of the organisation. This is simply a similar approach to the one heard by many of us as children which said "look after the pence and the pounds will look after themselves". In other words, if risk management is truly embedded into an organisation in the same way as equal opportunities, diversity and so on, then the board only has to monitor what management is doing and provide performance criteria for themselves. In developing training in this issue, it is important to take the generalities and work out for yourself what the detail ought to be.

through a combination of internal measures, policy instruments and, as already initiated by some governments (eg the Netherlands, Italy), programmes for the purchase of emission reduction credits from projects outside the European Union (see the next section).

Each country will decide on the total amount of EAUs that will be allocated to its industry and, effectively, the emission reductions burden that it will impose on the sectors of its economy that are covered by the EU ETS. This allocation, however, has to be in line with the country's Kyoto and European emission reduction targets. The process of allocating allowances between sectors and companies in a given country is determined through the establishment of the National Allocation Plans (NAPs), which will be published by each individual member state. The first drafts of these NAPs are currently being issued and negotiated. The process for internal allocation of allowances within a country varies. Some approaches are based on 'grandfathering' (the taking of an inherited right or method), historical and projected emission levels, auctions, etc.

After receiving their EAUs, companies will have to implement measures to ensure that they stay within their CO_2 emission quotas. The allocation of EAUs, however, will be done in such a way that installations will need to effectively reduce their CO_2 emissions.

In order to allow companies to explore fully their comparative advantages, the EU ETS allows companies to trade surplus EAUs between themselves. In this way, companies that are successful in reducing their GHG emissions beyond their target generate surplus allowances and can sell them to companies that do not meet their targets. In addition, companies will be able to purchase a certain number of emission credits from emission reduction projects taking place outside the European Union (see the next section).

Companies that do not meet their targets will be subjected to penalties for non-compliance. These will start at 40 euros per tonne of CO_2 during 2005–07, reaching 100 euros from 2008 onwards. Penalties will not be treated as an 'opt-out', and companies that are fined will still need to meet their emission targets either by reducing their emissions somehow or buying emission credits or EAUs.

Though the United Kingdom's Kyoto target is to reduce GHG emissions by 12.5 per cent below 1990 levels by 2008–12, the country has adopted a more ambitious voluntary national climate change target of reducing CO_2 emissions by 20 per cent as compared with their 1990 levels by 2010. In Phase 1 of the EU ETS (2005–07), the UK plans are based on the reduction of 16.3 per cent of the emission levels in relation to 1990, possibly leading to a higher level of reductions in Phase 2. A total of 1,500 installations will be included, and some 714 million tonnes of CO_2 allowances will be distributed between them during 2005–07. Allocation of EAUs will be based on an average of historical levels of emissions during the 1998–2002 period, taking into account some of the commitments that were made as part of the UK ETS.

Linking the European Union with Kyoto: the use of project-based credits

In parallel to the establishment of the EU ETS, the European Union is finalizing a directive to link it to the flexibility mechanisms of the Kyoto Protocol, in particular the CDM and JI project mechanisms. The main advantage of this link is that the use of the Kyoto flexibility mechanisms would greatly increase liquidity of the EU ETS market and reduce overall costs of compliance. The 'linking directive' is due to be approved in early 2004 and is expected to enter into force in January 2005. The main elements of the linking directive are as follows.

CARBON MANAGEMENT CLUBS

Yorkshire is the base for the UK's first carbon management clubs, which aim to help businesses to minimise the environmental impact of their working practices whilst maximising the benefits that this can bring.

Two pilot programmes, funded by Yorkshire Forward with support from the Carbon Trust, and involving 22 companies from the region began in 2003. The companies, which have an average £500k annual energy bill, have been assisted in establishing a 'carbon footprint' to understand where the carbon emissions are. From this baseline, an analysis of the business risks in terms of cost increases and any emissions trading scheme that may come into force in the future, have helped to establish the priorities for implementation of changes. This should save the companies an average of 10% on their energy costs.

David Kinder, Quality and Environmental Manager from Coca Cola Enterprises in Wakefield explains why they joined the programme.

"Coca-Cola Enterprises Ltd has a strong environmental policy to ensure we are responsible stewards of natural resources. We were keen to participate in the carbon management club which has provided us with an excellent opportunity to share best practices, to focus our efforts and people on initiatives that will reduce our local environmental impact.

"As part of the carbon club, we have attended workshops on energy reduction and travel planning.

"Our goal working with this group is to enhance our environmental performance and support our environmental objectives, which will dovetail with a strong business performance."

Mike Smith, Head of Sustainable Development for Yorkshire Forward comments "We are delighted with the response to this initiative from business. Should the pilot prove successful, lessons learned will be integrated into a wider programme across the region."

In order to provide companies with a larger degree of flexibility, the linking directive enables companies affected by the EU ETS to buy credits from emission reduction projects that are implemented outside the European Union (through the JI and CDM mechanisms).

Companies will be able to purchase an additional 8 per cent of their original EAU allocation in the form of credits from either JI or CDM projects. This could mean an additional volume of 125 million tonnes of CO_2 per year in Europe, or some 19 million tonnes of CO_2 per year in the United Kingdom alone.

The original directive stated that credits from JI and CDM projects would be allowed in the ETS only from 2008. However, a recent amendment put forward by many member states proposes that the use of credits from projects in developing countries should be allowed in the EU ETS from the beginning of 2005. This has already been accepted by the EU Parliament and the EU Commission and is now waiting for final approval.

It is expected that the introduction of project-based credits in the EU ETS will reduce the overall cost of credits and allowances traded from 26 to 13 euros per tonne of CO_2, leading to a reduction in the cost of compliance in the European Union of approximately half a billion euros per year.

Barrier or opportunity?

Given the scale and complexity of the challenge to reduce GHG emissions worldwide, the EU ETS appears to be a sensible way forward. As I have shown, the integration of the EU system with other Kyoto initiatives through international trading has the potential to significantly reduce the overall costs of meeting these targets. In addition, limiting GHG emissions will most likely promote innovation and the development of new technologies both in Europe and internationally. In a recent survey of European electricity companies, more than 50 per cent of those interviewed indicated that they see the EU ETS as an opportunity with the potential to enhance the shareholder value and profitability of their companies in the long term.

Apart from those directly involved in the EU ETS, international emissions trading systems are also fostering the development of a wide range of associated services. These include technical consultancies, project finance, and auditing, verification, financial, insurance and legal services. The United Kingdom can play a significant role in this new service industry, capitalizing on its reputation and tradition as a global financial services centre.

On a wider scale, emissions trading systems can also lead to substantial transfers of resources to developing countries, in the form both of payment for project-based emission reduction credits and of foreign direct investment associated with the development of environmentally sound projects abroad (an example is shown in the case study on page 33). At the same time, the faster uptake of clean technologies promoted by carbon trading could also lead to an increasing demand for new low-emissions European technology.

The combination of these factors suggests that while companies could face increased costs due to limitations set on previously unregulated pollution, they have at their disposal several options for reducing their cost of compliance. As with all regulations, there will be winners and there will be losers, but the ability to craft effective corporate strategies for addressing the challenges of a carbon-constrained economy will allow the more nimble players to limit their burden or even to capitalize on opportunities.

Opportunities for emissions reductions in the iron and steel sector in developing countries

Large quantities of carbon feedstocks (thermo-reduction agents) are used as part of the production process for manufacturing steel. Internationally, the main source of carbon feedstock is coke obtained from the dry distillation of coal, one the most carbon-intensive fossil fuels. The Brazilian steel sector, however, is the only one in the world that uses charcoal as a reducing agent. Given that charcoal is a renewable fuel source, the charcoal-based steel produced by the Brazilian industry can therefore be considered 'carbon neutral'.

During the past 10 years, however, economic trends related to both the industrial operations and the forestry sector in Brazil have led to increased utilization of imported coal, as opposed to locally produced charcoal. This, in turn, has resulted in increases in greenhouse gas (GHG) emissions. Recently a few companies have been trying to reverse this trend by selling carbon credits through the Clean Development Mechanism (CDM) of the Kyoto Protocol.

The charcoal-based steel and iron industry in Brazil has developed in parallel with the plantation forestry sector, its main source of raw fuel material. In order to support the development of these sectors, the Brazilian Government ran a fiscal incentive programme from 1967 to 1989 to encourage investment in afforestation for use in the pulp, paper and charcoal-based pig iron and steel industries. By 1990 over 6 million hectares of forest plantations had been established in Brazil under this programme. At the same time, production levels grew until Brazil became the world's eighth largest producer of steel.

Following the end of the fiscal incentives, a significant reduction in the Brazilian plantation forest base was observed over a period of a few years. In addition, it became more cost-effective to utilize imported coal than to use locally produced charcoal for the iron and steel industries, as a consequence of Brazilian macroeconomic trends. The combination of these factors has led a series of steel manufacturers to move away from charcoal back to coal, leading to a substantial increase in GHG emissions. The current trend of substitution with coal will persist unless incentives are put in place to support the production of charcoal for industrial uses.

The fuel-switch project of Vallourec and Mannesmann Tubes

V&M do Brasil is the Brazilian subsidiary of V&M Tubes, a joint venture between the French group Vallourec and the German company Mannesmannrohren-Werke. V&M do Brasil is the only steel pipe manufacturer in the world to use 100 per cent renewable energy for the production of pig iron and steel. Its forestry division, V&M Florestal, is responsible for the production of all charcoal required by its mills, from its 120,000 hectares of plantation forests (certified as sustainably managed according to the standards of the Forest Stewardship Council). Economic forces were increasingly pressing V&M Tubes to switch to the use of coal for the production of steel.

In 2000 the company decided to develop an emissions reduction project that consists of investments to ensure the use of sustainably produced charcoal for steel manufacture in Brazil, avoiding the use of coal. An additional component of the project relates to the introduction of improved carbonization technologies to avoid the release of methane during the process of charcoal manufacturing. It is estimated that this will result in the reduction of 21 million tonnes of CO_2 emissions during the next 21 years. This project has been validated according to the CDM rules of the Kyoto Protocol by the Norwegian company DNV, and the initial verification of carbon flows was conducted by the Swiss company SGS. The project design is currently under analysis by the CDM Methodologies Panel, and when it has been approved, the company will be able to sell its emission reduction credits in the international market to ensure continuation of project activities. This type of project has great potential in a number of developing countries, given the availability of land and a good climate for tree growth.

Responsible managers need training in business and science to promote sustainable management

As Environmental Management and Corporate Social Responsibility continue to be hotly debated, clearly individuals and organisations need to adopt scientifically and socially responsible management to avoid further damage to our planet.

Professor Ewan Ferlie, Head of the School of Management, Royal Holloway, University of London, explains: "The world needs a new generation of managers, who can understand and respond to serious current environmental issues. Issues such as the hole in the ozone layer, climate change, forest burning, over-fishing, poor quality of air and the escalating number of asthma sufferers are of growing concern. In the past, this knowledge has been confined to those with a purely scientific background. Managers will increasingly need to access this knowledge so as to promote sustainable styles of management in such sectors as energy and tourism."

Royal Holloway intends to become a leading provider of education in the new field of sustainable management. The already popular MBA in International Management has been redesigned to include CSR as a mainstream module, and from September a new MSc in Sustainability and Management will be available, bringing science and business together in one programme.

David Faulkner, the MSc Course Director says "This new degree is unique in providing both scientific and management knowledge in relation to issues that concern us all, and if not tackled on a global scale will make life on the planet unlivable in less than 100 years, according to authorities in the field. At last the universities are taking this seriously. More graduates who are literate and knowledgeable in the area can do nothing but good."

MBA International Management and MSc Sustainability and Management are available from September 2004. Details of the courses are on the School of Management's website: **www.rhul.ac.uk/Management/**

World Bank Institute Program on
**Corporate Social Responsibility
and Sustainable Competitiveness**

WORLD BANK INSTITUTE
Promoting knowledge and learning for a better world

The World Bank Institute is the knowledge and learning arm of the World Bank Group. As outlined by Frannie A. Léautier, Vice President, the World Bank Institute, "Our vision is to spur the knowledge revolution in developing countries to be a global catalyst for creating, sharing, and applying the cutting-edge knowledge necessary for poverty reduction and economic development."

Within this context, the Corporate Social Responsibility and Sustainable Competitiveness program (**www.csrwbi.org**) builds capacity for sustainable and equitable private sector development worldwide. Established by World Bank President James Wolfensohn in January 2000, this rapidly expanding program seeks to address the need for a better understanding of the role of business in society, focusing on issues of competitiveness, social responsibilities, and reputational risk management. It highlights their importance in relation to poverty reduction, good governance, and a sound investment climate. The program also seeks to address the clear need for broader acceptance of corporate social responsibility as a vital component of corporate strategy, thus facilitating efforts for more equitable development.

Together with its partners, the CSR and Sustainable Competitiveness program has developed a strong set of initiatives with the goal of strengthening CSR practices worldwide. These include courses and global e-dialogues for a variety of stakeholder groups and a program component specifically designed to reach young people, addressing the importance of social responsibility and sustainable development for the next generation. Partnership is vital in enabling WBI to reach a diverse body of client country stakeholders who recognize that knowledge is one of the most important and valuable keys to reducing poverty and promoting sustainable development. This program works closely with local and multinational actors from the private sector, including individual companies and business associations, as well as relevant government, academic and civil society stakeholders.

Environment Agency

creating a better place

We are the Environment Agency – the largest environmental regulator in England and Wales. We work with you to ensure that the environment is improved now and protected for future generations.

We want businesses to innovate and grow so when we regulate we look at the risk of each site and focus our effort where it is most needed. We will continue to take tough action on those who do not meet acceptable environmental standards.

The business section of our website: **www.environment-agency.gov.uk /business** gives you comprehensive advice, sector specific technical guidance and information on how and why we regulate your business.

The NetRegs website: **www.netregs.co.uk** has essential information for small and medium businesses in the UK. It will help you to improve your environmental performance, has sector specific information and shows you where to go for further advice.

At the start of 2005 we will launch our business e-bulletin. If you would like to receive this free newsletter please send an email to: **vicky.quill-bishop@ environment-agency.gov.uk**

A new framework for business

A new framework for business: introduction

Jean Lambert, Green Party Member of the European Parliament for London

The Johannesburg Earth Summit of 2002, 10 years after the Earth Summit in Rio, transferred significant responsibility to business, expecting it to play a leading role in the movement towards global sustainable development. Partnerships between the governments of developing countries and business concerning the delivery of basic services such as clean water, energy and education were envisaged. Also at Johannesburg, considerable attention was paid to the core issues of consumption and production, which have significant implications for the amount of raw materials consumed and the management of waste products.

There is now a growing concern within the European Commission to decouple economic growth from environmental degradation: reducing transport emissions, for example, and improving the efficient use of fossil fuels. Past research for the Commission has shown a strong link between economic growth and the production of greenhouse gases, air pollution and toxic waste.

How to provide for people's needs and their supplementary desires in a way that does not destroy our planet is becoming ever more crucial. The Pentagon's recent statement that climate change is a greater threat to the world than international terrorism should also be providing food for thought in the United States, which produces higher greenhouse-gas emissions per capita than anywhere else. There is also growing concern that the economic development of countries such as India and China should not follow a Western path in terms of energy use and non-sustainable resource consumption.

Many businesses understand that they need to change their production patterns and resource use. What is not clear is how to do this in a global economy in which different standards – such as those concerning labour and environmental standards – and pricing mechanisms apply. As legislators, we are frequently told that we cannot keep putting the costs of environmental protection on to business, yet how else can one change behaviour and protect the planet? We need a level playing field so that the best are not undermined by the worst. This implies a strong legislative framework and a fiscal system that support the same goals of sustainability. The European Union is gradually moving in this direction.

A new framework for business: legal overview

Kathryn Mylrea, Simmons & Simmons

There is a widely held view that the expanding number and complexity of legal requirements, particularly in the areas of environmental and health and safety law, are putting an intolerable burden on industry – in particular, on small and medium-sized enterprises (SMEs). Although, with a few exceptions, much of the new legislation has been preceded by extensive discussion and consultation, so should not take industry entirely by surprise, there has needed to be an increase in the amount of environment, health and safety legislation in order to comply with European obligations and deliver UK policy objectives. The importance of having an 'early warning system' to detect changes in law and policy that will have a significant effect on a business is essential, and can be a feature of environmental management systems.

There is also a concern that industry is being exposed to some heavy-handed enforcement by environmental and health and safety regulators. While it is fair to say that one measure of a regulator's success can be by its enforcement statistics, the suggestion that prosecutions are commenced or enforcement notices issued inappropriately is difficult to substantiate. There is no doubt, however, that the days when it was cheaper to 'pay the fine' than comply with a legislative requirement are at an end. Public expectations and government policy fully support higher fines for prosecutions for environmental and health and safety offences.

Personal liability of directors and officers has been a feature of environment, health and safety law for many years. However, there has been an increasing focus on this issue and a sense that the directors of companies must ensure that they are better aware of the situation within their own organization with regard to environment and health and safety performance. Even though, to date, there have been relatively few custodial sentences imposed on company directors, the issue is a real one. The Health and Safety Executive still hopes to see legislation on corporate killing put in place, which would involve increased exposure for individual directors.

Economic instruments, including those establishing and implementing 'green taxes' designed to deliver environmental improvements by making it more costly not to comply can impose additional costs on business as well as being quite complicated to comply with. For example, the steps to be taken to obtain an exemption from the payment of landfill tax for remediation of contaminated land contain many pitfalls.

Changes in company law, to be discussed in more detail in Part 3, will lead to a much more systematic and documented consideration of the impacts of environmental as well as employee and community and social issues on the prospects of the business. The changes are intended to require directors to be both backward and forward looking on these topics.

Green taxes

Jean Lambert, Green Party Member of the European Parliament for London

In my view, climate change is the most severe problem that we are facing today, more serious even than the threat of terrorism.

(Sir David King, the British Government's Chief Scientific Adviser, 2004)

Green taxation is as much about changing behaviour as it is about raising revenue. Its purpose is to promote and reward sustainable conduct, while penalizing the wasteful and the polluters. To achieve sustainable conduct means changing the behaviour of both consumer and producer so that the footprint left on our environment is diminished. Green taxation can only be successful, though, when integrated with a great many other policy measures, including regulation where necessary. When addressing greener forms of taxation we must look further than national fiscal policy. To be successful, the European perspective is just as important as the national perspective.

National green taxation

Nationally, green taxes could be used much more effectively to tax resources put into production processes, as well as being levied on the outputs of those processes, depending on their ecological impact. They could include taxes levied on manufactured products if they require the use of pollutants (eg pesticides or plastic packaging products) or pollute through their waste and emissions (eg toxic gases).

A good example of a national green tax is tax on fuel. Despite government action, fuel prices do not at the moment internalize or reflect the hidden costs of the damage caused by road transport, such as its contribution to climate change, pollution-related respiratory diseases as well as traffic accidents and the need for road maintenance. In the United Kingdom these costs are estimated at over £40 billion each year, and current fuel tax does not begin to cover this debt. Many people remain unaware of the link between road transport and climate change, although their lack of concern about road transport might change if they were better informed.

Varying the level of tax on different fuels, with the higher taxes being put upon the carbon offenders, would promote the use of (and eventually the quality of) alternative fuels such as bio-fuel. Following the Iraq war, rising fuel costs hit the headlines. Increasing the supply and freezing the duty might stabilize fuel prices in the short term, but we are made incredibly vulnerable through our dependence on oil, not to mention the significant contribution the burning of oil makes to climate change. A shift to green taxation on fuel duty is the only way both to tackle global warming and to kick-start the production of greener, and more locally available, alternatives.

If we address an environmental problem through taxation (such as transport), spending on other areas should go down. As an environmental problem is gradually resolved, less expenditure is required on its associated problems. For example, in the event of air pollution being reduced, NHS expenditure on related health problems also falls.

A green tax on fuel would bring about dramatic changes. It would offer an incentive to manufacturers to make vehicles more efficient, and the revenue raised could be invested in alternative methods of public transport, such as the rail network. This policy has already been put into practice in London, where congestion charge revenue goes towards London buses and improved public transport.

Another aspect of green taxation is that it shifts emphasis away from being a levy on labour (ie income) to being a levy on consumption and the use of resources such as water, oil and land. In a world where the wealthy are largely free to buy and consume as much as they wish, at the expense of the poor, this represents an improvement.

An example of this in practice is the Climate Change Levy (CCL), which took effect in April 2002. The levy was imposed on UK businesses but was offset against national insurance reductions. Businesses became liable for a new energy tax that adds about 15 per cent to typical energy bills. With a few exceptions such as low-energy producers and charities, all businesses are now subject to the levy.

The principle of the CCL is to move the burden of taxation from 'efficient operations' to 'inefficient energy users' in order to improve business use of energy. It is hoped that this improved use will, in turn, accelerate the take-up of low-carbon technologies, such as renewables, and stimulate new, more efficient sources of power generation. The revenue raised (around £1 billion per year) was recirculated via a 0.3 per cent cut in employers' National Insurance contributions, and also provided financial support (£50 million) for energy-saving schemes and renewable energy schemes. The levy package was intended to reduce at least 2.5 million tonnes of carbon dioxide emissions per year by 2010. From a Green perspective, the CCL – while well intended – did not go far enough, and business has not yet been empowered or informed about the direct impact its decision-making has on the environment. Green taxation is only constructive if it is accompanied by broad awareness-raising about choices and consequences, and specific assistance to create change.

European Union-level taxation of energy products

A revision of the European regulations on excise duties on mineral oils has recently come into force. This relates to the structure and the rates of these excise duties, putting forward the possibility of a structure for the taxation of all energy products. Here, minimum rates could be agreed, for the first time, on energy products other than mineral oils (coal, coke, natural gas, electricity as substitutable for heating purposes), and with minimum rates for mineral oils being slightly increased. However, there are still many shortfalls within the proposals regarding commitments to the Kyoto Protocol. Moreover, the text is weaker than the European Union's own sustainability strategy. Structures that would give support to member states intending to make their tax system more environmentally friendly and employment-friendly by shifting the tax burden from labour to consumption and environmental degradation are still absent.

Climate taxes: an international perspective

'Climate taxes', such as carbon and energy taxes, are increasingly used to counteract climate change. For various reasons, countries may introduce related border adjustment measures in the form of border tax adjustments on imports and exports. It has been argued that this is one of the most urgent issues to be addressed in the Kyoto Protocol and WTO interface. Under the international trade agreement on trade and tariffs (GATT), climate taxes on consumption, such as carbon and energy taxes on fossil fuels, may be extended to imports through border tax adjustments, provided that such adjustments are not discriminatory in application or in levels of climate taxes and the related adjustments. Charges on imports, equivalent to internal taxes, and charges on inputs or on end products, are also permitted, provided that members do not discriminate against imported products. However, it should be the design of climate taxes and accompanying border tax adjustments that determines whether they are allowed under the GATT or not.

Ideally, climate taxes should be harmonized internationally rather than adjusted at borders. This would ensure a level playing field as well as alleviate pressure on the World Trade Organization (WTO). If this is not realistic in the short term, climate taxes should be introduced gradually (over time and taking into account tax rates). They should also be introduced in a transparent manner. Gradual and transparent introduction would act as a counterbalance to the possible negative effects of competition.

Airport industry: tax breaks

Aviation is the most highly polluting transport mode on earth and the fastest-growing source of greenhouse gas emissions. A comprehensive package of measures to reduce the impact of aviation is desperately required.

Despite this, the aviation industry enjoys tax breaks of an estimated £7 billion per year. The air transport sector pays no external costs, nor does it pay certain taxes. There is no tax on fuel, no VAT, and duty-free sales continue except in the case of trips entirely within the European Union. It is estimated that if aircraft fuel were taxed at the same rate as unleaded petrol, if VAT were levied at the standard rate and if duty-free were abolished, the tax raised would be an astonishing £9.2 billion a year (and rising).

The 'polluter pays' principle would shift the environmental, social and health costs back to the industry. Emissions charging would finally oblige the aviation industry to pay fuel tax, like all other modes of transport.

By abolishing aviation industry tax breaks throughout the European Union and by abolishing the associated hidden subsidies, £13 billion a year would be saved, money that could go towards improving public transport in all member states.

Emissions trading

Governments have largely shown an antithesis to green taxation, preferring instead to develop 'market signals' to trigger behavioural change. An example of this is the European Union-wide emissions trading scheme. Under this system, companies purchase permits to emit greenhouse gases. These are bought from companies that are able to reduce their emissions. It is clear, though, that market signals are not direct enough on their own to promote the degree of change that is necessary. Businesses – in particular, small and medium-sized businesses – can often be more prepared to take the 'hit' rather than undertake a holistic review of performance.

Conclusions: what next after the Johannesburg summit?

Since the 2002 UN sustainability summit in Johannesburg, the European Union has been committed to decoupling economic growth from environmental degradation caused by such policies as transport expansion. The Union has also committed itself to examining issues and patterns around production and consumption, an examination that should be challenging – not least in the movement towards requiring industry to internalize end-of-life responsibility. The EU member states need to fully endorse the movement towards radical thinking if we are to solve the major environmental problems facing us today.

It is often said that environmental taxation puts additional burdens on business, and this is true in the short term. It also impacts on the consumer, as costs are generally handed on through pricing rather than reducing shareholder return. Individual governments are increasingly reluctant to make policy unilaterally in case doing so impacts on their competitiveness globally. The need for concerted and collective action is clear. Inaction may serve business but will not reduce the overall burden on our environment and society as a whole.

Public-sector procurement and corporate social responsibility

Darren Ford, Senior Procurement Specialist, Chartered Institute of Purchasing and Supply

I want Britain to be a leading player in this coming green industrial revolution.
(Rt Hon Tony Blair MP, Prime Minister, www.dti.gov.uk/sustainability)

The public sector accounts for 40 per cent of the United Kingdom's GDP, and central civil government alone spends around £13 billion per year on goods and services. This expenditure can cover almost anything from buying food to buying aeroplanes, to cleaning equipment or cleaning uniforms. With this level of responsibility, the public sector must ensure that it is equipped to operate in an ethical, sustainable and corporately responsible manner in just the same way as any organization in the private sector.

With buying activity levels so high, the impact that the public sector has on economic, social and environmental issues is potentially massive. More commonly, it is 'big business' that comes under the spotlight for its standards of behaviour in matters of the environment, ethics and operating in a sustainable manner. However, the public sector must also take the same level of responsibility when examining the effects it has on the outside world.

Relationships with employees, customers and suppliers all need to reflect and demonstrate that they are protecting the environment, considering human rights and taking care of the local communities within which they operate and also represent.

Like the private sector, the public sector has a huge responsibility in delivering sustainable development, creating practical solutions and having a more innovative approach, including:

- operating in open and dynamic markets – where the environmental costs are signalled effectively;
- examining and using greener technologies and business models in competitive goods and services;
- meeting consumer demand for greater value, performance and choice in more resource-efficient ways and with reduced environmental impact.

The job of government can be seen as twofold. On one level, government has to ensure that the regulatory and fiscal framework encourages and does not stifle corporate social responsibility (CSR) initiatives. Alongside this, government also has to work in partnership with business and others to develop and promote best practice at home and abroad. Within this remit, government has to examine its own actions and ensure that it addresses, where possible, operations and principles that demonstrate an ongoing commitment to sustainability.

Stephen Timms MP, CSR Minister, unveiled a global framework in March 2004 setting out the Government's approach to corporate social responsibility at an international level during a Corporate Responsibility in Practice conference. He said:

> The UK is seen internationally as a pioneer of corporate social responsibility and I am committed to ensuring that we keep up our active contribution to the policy debate…The main priorities are to spread best practice, encourage innovation and ensure approaches that deliver practical outcomes and solutions. This includes encouraging all relevant international and inter-governmental institutions to be engaged and playing to their strengths and competencies. (www.wired-gov.net)

This statement not only clearly positions the United Kingdom at the heart of a global CSR debate but also underlines the importance for governments to get behind legislation and engage in behaving in a sustainable manner.

The Office of Government Commerce

In 1999, Peter Gershon, the then Chief Operating Officer of BAE Systems, conducted a review of civil service procurement in central government, which recommended the creation of the Office of Government Commerce (OGC). The OGC is an independent Office of the Treasury reporting to the Chief Secretary. It is responsible for a wide-ranging programme that focuses on improving the efficiency and effectiveness of central civil government procurement. Its current purpose is assisting departments to set up project and programme management centres of excellence.

An Executive Agency of the OGC is OGCbuying.solutions. Its role is to offer a complete advisory and procurement arrangement service to purchasing professionals working for central government as well as the wider public sector, including the following areas:

■ quality assurance;
■ procurement advice;
■ energy conservation advice;
■ environmental awareness.

The use of agencies such as OGCbuying.solutions is a clear demonstration that the public sector is having to adapt the same skills and approaches to business as private-sector commercial organisations use, thus ensuring that while improvements can still be made from an economic point of view, awareness of issues such as the environment and behaving in a socially responsible manner are of key importance.

The need to conserve energy and protect the environment underscores the policies and practices of the OGC, and these fundamental principles have to be satisfied when evaluating competitive tenders for products and services. Customers and suppliers are strongly encouraged to develop awareness of these issues in their activities at all times.

The Government's Energy White Paper, published in March 2004, examines the role of sustainable procurement by government and highlights the need to make it easy for public-sector customers to locate and buy energy-efficient products. This paper put forward the concept of 'quick wins', which highlighted the need for particular standards to be met and put in place immediately. The 'quick wins' approach includes a variety of products such as energy-saving computers and recycled paper through to low-emission cars, energy-efficient boilers and energy-saving light bulbs.

Supplier relations within the public sector play an integral part in the Government's CSR objectives. There is an increasing emphasis within government on selecting and working with suppliers who can meet delivery commitments to cost, time and quality. The OGC has identified three key elements that must be addressed in improving departments' ability to manage their supplier relationships: 1) realism – the need to check that the supplier can provide and maintain quality services for the quoted price; 2) recognition that long-term partnering relationships must consistently deliver services that meet or exceed the contracted requirement; 3) risk – seeking an optimal transfer of risk based on risks allocated to the parties best able to control them.

EU legislation requires that all contracts from the public sector that are valued above a certain threshold must be published in the *Official Journal of the European Union* (OJEU). The legislation covers organizations and projects that receive public money. Local authorities, NHS trusts, central government departments are all included and must advertise in the OJEU if their contract is covered. The criteria used to evaluate tenders include:

■ financial criteria (accounts, prices, etc);
■ quality systems (ISO 9000, etc);
■ environmental policy (which is becoming a major prerequisite);
■ references.

Although some government departments have set up contracts for other departments to use, there is no one single organization that buys on behalf of the public sector. S-CAT and

Gcat are frameworks run by OGCbuying.solutions that provide the Government with pre-tendered products and services, primarily in the area of IT and professional services (OGCbuying.solutions does offer frameworks for other types of goods as well). Across the public sector, many other departments, local authorities and central purchasing agencies run similar frameworks.

For the IT sector specifically, OGCbuying.solutions has compiled a list of contract holders that have tendered successfully and offer equipment that conforms to the OGC environmental policy. Along the same lines has been the policy introduced on timber products, namely that of ensuring that they are sourced from legal and sustainable sources. Again there is a list of contract holders that have tendered successfully and abide by the guidelines on the sourcing of timber.

The Government has also put in motion a requirement for a significant increase in the uptake of environmental management systems (EMS). These will help support the delivery of improvements in performance, particularly in areas such as energy, water and waste, bringing about greater efficiency, reducing costs and ensuring compliance with environmental regulations. Standards such as ISO 14001, an environmental standard that is part of a series of international standards on environmental management (ISO 1400), specify a framework of control for an environmental management system against which an organization can be certified by a third party.

Impacts on different services

Obviously, the development of bodies such as the OGC has made a significant contribution to streamlining processes and procedures in government procurement and trying to ensure that CSR policies are adopted as widely as possible. However, the size and breadth of the public-sector services operated in the United Kingdom are massive, ranging from education and health to defence, local government and transport, and the task of considering the variety of CSR issues across all those boundaries is a huge feat. Many different sectors are up against their own barriers that they need to work around to ensure that they continue to operate within a sustainable and corporately responsible framework.

In 2003 it was the turn of the public-sector food buyers to come under scrutiny. At a conference of 300 delegates from major public institutions such as hospitals, prison and schools, the Government outlined its Public Sector Sustainable Food Procurement Initiative. This was aimed at fighting what the Government believed to be an epidemic of obesity-related ill health, and suggested that food-sector buyers consider buying more sustainable foods such as organic meat, fruit and vegetables. There was also a desire that buyers should give smaller, local and organic producers the chance to compete more easily for contracts.

The food and farming Minister at the time, Lord Whitty of Camberwell, said, 'The food service sector needs to be encouraged to be part of the solution to unsustainable practices. This Government expects public sector procurement to use purchasing power to help deliver its Sustainable Farming Food strategy and remove barriers to small local suppliers.'

Within the NHS, the Purchasing and Supply Agency (PASA), an executive agency of the NHS, has taken its own steps forward in ensuring a more environmentally friendly outlook. In 2002 it cut use of electricity by 21 per cent and gas by 17 per cent, and in 2003 it was said to have saved 'million of pounds' by sourcing fair-trade tea.

In 2003, Ken Livingstone, the Mayor of London, called on purchasers from the 33 London boroughs to buy food and drink stamped with the fair-trade seal of approval. In the same year, government was also held to account by the pressure group Greenpeace for using rain-forest timber in its new Home Office headquarters. The result was a Government inquiry into its contractors' supply chains.

Changing patterns

In September 2003 the Department for Environment, Food and Rural Affairs (Defra) published *Changing Patterns: The UK Government Framework for Sustainable Consumption and Production*. This report brought together for the first time the economic and environmental case for action to tackle sustainable consumption and production. The report stated:

> The scope for using Government purchasing actively to help deliver sustainable development objectives, and particularly environmental objectives, is greatly underutilised at present. A number of specific 'green' procurement commitments have been made by the Government in recent years – on paper, timber, renewable electricity and alternatively fuelled vehicles – but a much more ambitious and coordinated approach is needed.

A cross-government Sustainable Procurement Group recommended some positive changes to support sustainable procurement. These include:

- an explicit policy commitment to pursue sustainable procurement;
- new central guidance to government departments, making clear, among other things, the approach to value for money with sustainable procurement;
- an initial set of minimum environmental standards (quick wins) for selected product types;
- use of environmental risk assessment for departments' larger procurement projects;
- development of an online information service to enable greener purchasing and contract specification by practitioners.

Many companies have achieved commercial benefits from incorporating CSR into their day-to-day activities and in particular from the active management of their environmental and social impacts. For example, they may have made operational changes resulting in waste reduction, or may have become more energy efficient. For others, the benefits have come about through the protection of intangible assets such as brand and reputation.

As the CSR debate continues to create headlines around the world, consumer and indeed investor awareness are growing on a daily basis, helping consumers and investors to make more informed choices. But all that has gone before is just the tip of the iceberg, and action is needed not only by private business but from governments and society too. The *Changing Patterns* report sums up this need quite concisely; it states, 'The action needed is not only for Government. It also needs the engagement of business, civil society, organisations, international institutions and all of us as consumers, employees and citizens.'

Environmental regulation in the 21st century

Jim Gray, Environment Agency

As business becomes increasingly mobile and global, it is important that British business competitiveness is not hampered by excessive costs of regulation. Business needs efficient regulation that does not stand in the way of flexibility and innovation, but still delivers the safety and reassurance that society wants.

New approaches to meeting a new century's environmental challenges are needed in ways that make sense for the business world as well as the environment. The Environment Agency, the leading environmental regulator in England and Wales, has responded to this challenge of balancing society's demand for high environmental standards with the need to avoid putting unnecessary constraints on business. New EU legislation already on the books means a steady increase in our regulatory duties, so achieving more with less has never been so vital. We have developed an approach to 21st-century regulation that we believe will deliver a better environment more effectively.

Background

Traditionally, environmental regulation has been about prohibition, prescription and control. Beginning with the first Alkali Act in 1863, this approach has delivered substantial benefits for people and the environment. In the last century the Clean Air Acts saved city dwellers from deadly smog, and other pollution laws have delivered cleaner rivers, land and air.

Direct regulation of this kind has traditionally controlled abstractions from and emissions to the environment. Such controls will continue to play an important role but will become smarter through the use of risk-based approaches, greater standardization and intelligent charging mechanisms. Use of these will allow us to target our efforts more effectively, taking action that is more proportionate to the risks.

These new approaches represent a new stage on the regulatory journey, moving on from a traditional command-and-control approach to a framework that provides incentives for good performance and offers dialogue instead of adversarial relationships. It is explained in detail in a discussion document published in October 2003, *Delivering for the Environment: A 21st century approach to regulation.*

Modern regulation

The Environment Agency is working with the Department for Environment, Food and Rural Affairs (Defra) on a joint strategy for this new approach. The priorities are:

- reviewing existing legislation;
- influencing the development of new EU legislation;
- addressing inefficiencies;
- focusing on results.

There is wide acceptance that good regulation is good for business. The aim of modern regulation is to provide more effective ways of achieving a sustainable and improving environment – benefiting both the Environment Agency as regulator and the businesses that we regulate. This requires a regime that encourages businesses to improve, rewarding good performers while remaining tough on those that do not meet acceptable standards. We will use dialogue to solve problems jointly with industry, and will focus on the desired environmental improvement rather than the regulatory process.

Modern regulation focuses on the potential environmental risk of an activity. Risk is determined by several factors, not just the intrinsic hazard of an activity or plant. Risk can be reduced by good environmental management: thus, the effectiveness of companies' environmental management systems will be part of our assessment process for judging what does and does not constitute 'real' risk.

Business benefits

By focusing our resources on the biggest risks (without neglecting less significant risks) we will maximize the impact of our effort to achieve a healthier, safer environment. Focusing on the biggest risks also makes sense for businesses that manage their risks well, because they will be subject to less intrusive and less expensive regulation. On the other hand, those that do not take their environmental responsibilities seriously will see more of our inspectors – but only until they improve their environmental performance.

Importantly for businesses, charges will reflect risk, including the operator's performance in managing the site. This is where environmental management systems come in. By identifying, managing and reducing key risk areas, businesses can reduce their risk profile, which will then be reflected in lower charges and reduced compliance assessment.

Clear evidence is emerging that good environmental management goes hand in hand with good business performance. In other words, going green can actually enhance a company's commercial standing. This relationship was confirmed in a European Commission paper in November 2001. *The Impact of Best Available Technology on the Competitiveness of European Industry* looked at the economic and environmental performance of the cement, non-ferrous metals and pulp and paper industries. The report showed conclusively, across a range of different measures, that companies operating with the highest environmental standards were also the ones with the best economic performance.

We believe that a well-planned and well-implemented environmental management system (EMS) will help to improve the management of environmental risks from a site or activity. In addition, businesses can usually benefit from savings in raw materials and waste disposal costs. We would like to see large companies demonstrate to their supply chains the benefits that can be gained from having an EMS.

Modern regulation in practice

Direct regulation through authorizations, consents and licences will remain a fundamental part of our work. Direct regulation may also be required to underpin instruments such as trading and voluntary agreements to ensure that participants meet a minimum level of performance. But modern regulation means using the best tools for the job rather than a blanket approach regardless of the nature and scale of the environmental risk.

We have developed a wider and smarter range of tools for assessing regulatory compliance, including Operator and Pollution Risk Appraisal (OPRA) schemes, compliance assessment schemes and a sector planning approach.

The OPRA schemes are a good example of modern regulation in practice. This risk assessment tool helps us to formalize judgements about environmental risks, using a standardized scoring system that takes into account the key elements of risk: operator performance and environmental hazard. It allows us to allocate resources and set charges based on the risk involved. Originally developed for large industrial sites, OPRA has been adapted for waste management sites, and now Environmental Protection (EP) OPRA applies to sites under the Integrated Pollution Prevention and Control regime.

A better toolbox

The way in which we tackle sulphur dioxide (SO_2) emissions from power stations shows how modern regulation can bring together different approaches to produce a better solution than command and control on its own. Power stations contribute about 65 per cent of the United Kingdom's SO_2 emissions, which leads to poor air quality and damage to environmentally sensitive areas. Setting industry-wide reduction targets and allowing operators to decide how to achieve them means that the cost of compliance can be significantly reduced. By 2005 this approach will lead to a 60 per cent reduction in emissions of SO_2 from 1999 levels. Conventional regulation through permits will continue to control all the other pollution from power stations.

Our approach to permitting has also been modernized by moving towards a standardized format for all discharge permits rather than starting from scratch with a bespoke approach at each site. We adapt the standard approach with site-specific prescriptions where necessary, but greater standardization means we can ensure common standards throughout England and Wales, while saving our own resources and those of the businesses seeking permits.

We have also developed a compliance classification tool, which will mean that permit breaches are dealt with more consistently.

Sector by sector

We are developing sector-based templates that address the specific issues associated with particular sectors. This approach will allow us to prioritize the regulatory workload between and within sectors.

Examples

■   In the past, the waste industry has been treated uniformly, with all waste sites in the same category treated as being equal. With modern regulation, the Environment Agency will commit most effort to sites that carry the biggest environmental risks, and where the biggest improvement to the environment can be achieved.

■   For water quality, sites that have a potential to discharge dangerous substances are categorized in a range from A to D. Category A applies to locations where there are significant discharges of dangerous substances and where there are agreed numeric limits on discharges to protect water quality. Categories B to D apply where discharges may contain pollutants, but at progressively lower levels, none of which threatens environmental quality standards. Compliance requirements and the resources we need to commit will be proportionate to the discharge, and consequently the cost of regulation for operators in Band D will be least.

These examples illustrate our proportionate, risk-based approach. We do not want to stifle business innovation and growth, but 21st-century citizens expect products and services to be delivered responsibly and safely. Modern regulation aims to find the right balance between these two objectives. It will drive environmental improvements and reward good performance, but still provide the ultimate reassurance that tough action will be taken on those who fail to meet acceptable standards.

The modern approach consists of the following elements.

Direct regulation:

■ permits: bespoke for complex activities; standard where many activities are similar;
■ registrations: where an annual renewal and charging system is required;
■ direct application of legislation: where activities are simple and risks are low.

Economic instruments:

■ environmental taxes such as the Climate Change Levy and Landfill Tax;
■ trading schemes such as the Emissions Trading Scheme.

Voluntary or negotiated agreements:

■ Agreements work best in mature, well-managed sectors with a history of regulatory compliance or a 'good reputation' to uphold. They can be useful where a large number of very similar activities or sites need to be controlled.

Education and advice:

■ Business needs to be more aware of how its actions impact on the environment and human health. Education and advice will raise awareness and offer solutions.

Environmental management systems:

■ EMS will allow business to deliver consistent compliance and reduce the environmental risk from a site or activity.

Delivering for the Environment: A 21st century approach to regulation can be found on the Environment Agency website at www.environment-agency.gov.uk/business.

Written by Jim Gray, the Environment Agency's policy lead on modernizing regulation of the industrial, waste and water sectors. Prior to joining the Environment Agency in 1999, he had 20 years' experience working in industry on regulatory policy and compliance with complex and simple regulation.

Risk and directors

Jeremy Nicholls, The Cat's Pyjamas

Sustainability is not just about reducing environmental impact on the world, nor is it just about the way you treat your customers and your employees, as if it were an ethical code. Sustainability is about understanding the social, environmental and economic impact that the business has, and dealing with issues raised. For some people, corporate social responsibility is the same thing.

Chris Marsden, Chair of Amnesty International Business Group, defines it as follows:

> Corporate Social Responsibility (CSR) is about the core behaviour of companies and the responsibility for their total impact on the societies in which they operate. CSR is not an optional add-on nor is it an act of philanthropy. A socially responsible corporation is one that runs a profitable business that takes account of all the positive and negative environmental, social and economic effects it has on society.

If this seems a huge agenda – and a quick look at the contents of this book might do nothing to calm your fears – then you need a way in. AccountAbility, an organization that develops standards for sustainability reporting, argues that one of the core principles is materiality. You deal with the issues that are material to your business, and these will depend on the nature of your business and your stakeholders. Knowing your material issues needs a system for assessing risk.

Systems for assessing risk are part and parcel of good governance and are part of the responsibilities of company directors. They will also be a way in which directors can know that they are meeting legal requirements, for example in relation to health and safety, emissions or product labelling. An assessment of the material sustainability issues for your business may require better systems and information than are covered by existing legal requirements.

The 2002 Government White Paper *Modernising Company Law* supported the Operating and Financial Review (OFR) as a way of improving disclosure by companies. Draft regulations were published for consultation on 5 May 2004. Practical guidance has also been issued to help directors in producing an OFR. The draft regulations cover an analysis of the development and performance of the business, its objectives, risks and uncertainties, as well as other issues such as environmental matters and social and community issues. It will be up to the directors to decide what should be included in an OFR in order to comply with the regulations and they will need to have the right balance of skills and competencies available from themselves and from their advisors.

Items should be included if their omission, misstatement or inadequate description would change or influence an understanding of other matters reported upon – and so understanding stakeholder issues will be a prerequisite for knowing what is important and what should be included. The guidance specifically mentions that consideration of the inclusion and environment issues that may be relevant to the OFR may require access to additional skills and competencies and that this could be addressed by appointing non-executive directors with relevant backgrounds.

The issue of directors' competence in this sphere crops up in existing standards. For example, the Association of British Insurers guidelines on social responsibility state that:

- The Board takes regular account of the significance of social, environmental and ethical (SEE) matters to the business of the company.
- The Board has identified and assessed the significant risks to the company's short and long term value arising from SEE matters, as well as the opportunities to enhance value that may arise from an appropriate response.
- The Board has received adequate information to make this assessment and that account is taken of SEE matters in the training of directors.
- The Board has ensured that the company has in place effective systems for managing significant risks, which, where relevant, incorporate performance management systems and appropriate remuneration incentives.

Meanwhile, across town the Higgs Report on the role and effectiveness of non-executive directors included the statement that 'Proposals are made to broaden the pool of candidates for non-executive director appointments, including more executive directors and senior executives from other companies and directors of private companies, as well as advisors and those from other backgrounds.' Its recommendation was that 'A small group of business leaders and others will be set up to identify how to bring to greater prominence candidates for non-executive director appointments from the non-commercial sector.'

The Cat's Pyjamas has established a board bank of people with these skills who can be drawn on by businesses. This service responds to both of the issues raised in this chapter: getting better governance from non-executive directors, and ensuring that boards have access to directors with the skills and knowledge necessary to assess material items in relation to social and environmental matters.

Jeremy Nicholls, The Cat's Pyjamas, c/o Furniture Resource Centre, Brunswick Business Park, Atlantic Way, Liverpool L3 4BE.

Tel: 0151 702 0564
Fax: 0151 702 0551
Email: events@the-cats-pyjamas.com

Risk management, corporate social responsibility and compensation

Association of British Insurers

This chapter explores the relationship between risk management, corporate social responsibility and compensation.

The compensation culture: myth or reality?

We are constantly reading stories and watching reports about the 'compensation culture'. Many commentators take the view that in the United States things have got out of hand and we are going in the same direction in the United Kingdom. But what is the truth about the compensation culture?

This is the question that the Better Regulation Task Force (BRTF) addressed in its recently published report *Better Routes to Redress*. The Task Force report is well balanced and it makes some very sensible recommendations aimed at improving systems by which people with genuine grievances are able to get redress – and how we can prevent the need for redress in the first place. The report also comments that 'the perception of the compensation culture is largely, though not entirely, perpetuated by the media'.

The Task Force report points out that the number of accidents at work has been falling for several years. Independent research commissioned by ABI tends to supports this view. However, our research also indicates that the cost of liability claims has been increasing rapidly: between 1996 and 2002 the average cost of a liability claim increased threefold. The reason for this increase cannot be put down to any one single factor; rather, it is the result of a number of factors coinciding. These include:

∎ personal injury inflation due to higher compensation awards, improved medical care and longer life expectancy;
∎ a changing claims mix, from low-value claims such as deafness to higher-value claims such as bodily injury;
∎ the introduction of success fees and 'after the event' insurance;
∎ lower discount rates.

The debate about whether or not there is a compensation culture will no doubt continue, but there is clear evidence that the cost of liability insurance claims has increased substantially in recent years and that these cost increases have had to be passed on by insurers to their customers.

Prevention is better than cure

The BRTF makes several recommendations, primarily aimed at government, intended to improve how the compensation system operates. Two key recommendations are:

∎ promoting better management of occupational health and safety;
∎ managing risk and lower insurance premiums.

Few people would argue against the idea that prevention is better than cure, but the link between insurance prices and risk management is a more complex one. Over the past couple of years we have seen the average cost of employers' liability insurance increase by 30–50 per cent. Businesses that have not made any claims have felt particularly aggrieved by these increases. Thus, it is important to understand how the insurance market operates.

Like all businesses, insurers must take into account their costs when deciding what they are going to charge their customers. The increasing cost of awards as described above will obviously have an influence on insurers' pricing, but there are other reasons for the increasing cost of liability insurance, as will now be discussed.

The insurance cycle

The insurance market in the United Kingdom is both competitive and cyclical. It goes through 'hard' and 'soft' phases of the cycle. In a hard market, premiums will rise, and capacity, or the 'supply' of insurance, is limited. In a soft market, competition is fiercer and rates will level off or even fall. The period 2001–04 has seen a hard market for most commercial classes of insurance and particularly for liability insurances. Prior to 2001 there was a relatively soft market for these insurances, and premium income had stagnated since the early 1990s. The dynamics of this competitive market must be taken into account when considering how insurers set their premiums.

Investment income

Liability insurance is a 'long tail' class of business; that is, there can be a long time lag between the paying of the premium and all the claims being notified to the insurer. In the case of asbestos-related diseases this can be a matter of decades. The problem with long tail business is that it is very difficult to predict the number and the cost of future claims, and employers' liability insurance in particular is therefore a very unattractive class of business to many insurers. The positive aspect of long tail business is that insurers can invest the premium income they receive and can therefore make returns on these investments. In the 1990s, investment returns made a significant contribution to insurers' income, but recent economic conditions have been more difficult. In recent years, insurers have been putting far greater emphasis on trying to make an underwriting profit rather than relying on investment income.

Technical pricing

Most insurance companies are now emphasizing the need for accurate underwriting, with the emphasis on correct 'technical' pricing. Much greater effort has been made to accurately assess likely claims development over a long period. Actuaries are much more actively involved in setting rates than in previous years. Where insurers are competing, there is greater reluctance to offer cover at rates below what the insurer considers to be the technical price. This strategy will, however, be tested as the market softens over the coming months.

Setting premiums

The factors described have an impact on market conditions for liability insurance. However, they do not describe the process whereby an insurer actually underwrites a particular risk. This will depend on a number of factors, including:

- size of the business, turnover, etc;
- trade or sector;
- claims experience;
- risk management features.

Larger businesses will be rated in a different way from smaller businesses. Because larger businesses will have a 'claims experience', insurers are much more able to underwrite these businesses individually. They can more accurately predict the future number, type and cost of claims based on past experience. The larger the firm, the more emphasis will be placed on individual underwriting. It will also be economically viable to send an insurance risk assessor to visit these firms, get to know the management, understand their approach to risk management and make recommendations for risk improvement. With a small business, whose premium may be measured in hundreds of pounds, it is often not viable or cost-effective for the insurer to send a surveyor to the premises. Some companies insure hundreds of thousands of business customers and, like the Health and Safety Executive, they do not have the resources to visit them all.

However, insurers will still need to decide what rate to charge. In order to do this, individual insurers have collated claims experience for groups of firms, usually by sector or trade. This allows the insurer to predict the number of claims that a sector is likely to generate. It should be remembered that many small businesses may not make a claim for many years, but if they are in a trade that generates a lot of claims, they will still have to make their contribution.

The Department of Work and Pensions (DWP), in its review of employers' liability insurance, has emphasized that more effort should be made by insurers to link premiums to health and safety performance. Individual insurers have recently developed questionnaires and software to try to understand better the efforts being made by small and medium-sized enterprises (SMEs) to manage their risks. The competitive insurance market is also a driver for insurers to assess and price risk as accurately as possible. The ABI and member companies are also successfully operating the Making the Market Work initiative (more details from makingthemarketwork@abi.org.uk), which assesses the health and safety performance of trade associations. These assessments are then circulated to all insurers that have agreed to take them into account when underwriting.

Now more than ever, it is essential for all businesses to 'sell' themselves to their insurer. Good brokers will be able to present the case effectively, but businesses need to emphasize the steps that they are taking to manage their risks. Demonstrating good risk management will improve access to the insurance market and improve the terms that can be secured from insurers.

Corporate social responsibility and insurance

Insurance companies have an interest in corporate social responsibility (CSR) both as underwriters of risk and as institutional investors. UK insurers own some 20 per cent of all UK equity. Investors will want to see that the companies they invest in are both aware of the risks that their businesses face and taking steps to manage those risks.

In 2001, reflecting pensions legislation, ABI published guidelines to help companies understand the nature of disclosure on social, ethical and environmental (SEE) risk, which would be helpful to investors. Insurers, on behalf of their pension fund clients and others, are particularly interested in how companies report on SEE and welcome information in the report and accounts (with further details elsewhere when appropriate):

■ defining board responsibilities;
■ identifying risks, their business impact, policies and procedures in place to deal with them;
■ disclosing performance targets;
■ internal or external verification or audit.

It is clear from ABI's recent publication *Risk Returns and Responsibility* by Roger Cowe that CSR issues are gaining momentum. The report comments:

> [S]o far as underlying corporate performance is concerned, risk aspects of corporate responsibility are as important as bottom line impacts. Companies need to incorporate these matters into strategic risk management, because they can have important implications for drivers such as brand value, market acceptability, human capital and new fields such as biotechnology.

The message is clear: risk management makes good business sense. It is worth businesses taking a holistic view of risk and how to manage it. Insurance is one important component of risk management but it is not the whole. Businesses that manage their risks more effectively are more likely to benefit as regards their own performance, the way they are perceived by investors, and the terms they are offered from the insurance market.

The Association of British Insurers (ABI) represents the collective interests of the United Kingdom's insurance industry. The Association speaks out on issues of common interest; helps to inform and participate in debates on public policy issues; and also acts as an advocate for high standards of customer service in the insurance industry. For more information, please go to http://www.abi.org.uk.

Compensation culture: a legal perspective

Paul Taverner, Bevan Brittan

Where there's blame...

Is Britain turning into a nation of opportunistic compensation seekers? Prince Charles certainly thinks so. One of his much-publicized recent letters to the Lord Chancellor spoke of the 'dread' which he and 'countless others' felt about the growth of a US-style personal injury culture in the United Kingdom. He highlighted as an example the felling of horse chestnut trees in Norwich the previous year, apparently motivated by the fear of claims from passers-by injured by falling conkers.

This viewpoint is certainly not unique, and is one that is actively encouraged by certain sections of the media. The fear of a growing compensation culture has been fuelled by media suspicion of conditional agreements (CFAs), and the vilification of claims management companies such as Claims Direct.

It is true that CFAs have opened up the prospect of litigation to huge numbers of people who might not previously have considered bringing a personal injury claim. However, the spectacular demise of Claims Direct has shown that claims management companies that regularly back weak or uneconomic cases will quickly come unstuck when faced with a robust response from the insurance industry. Claims Direct is currently in administration, and is being sued by a large number of disgruntled investors and franchisees – most of whom, ironically, are funded by CFAs.

One benefit of CFAs that is often overlooked is that insurers know they will recover their costs if they successfully defend an unmeritorious claim. The days when a legally aided claimant could continue litigation safe in the knowledge that he or she would never have to pay any costs if unsuccessful are gone.

A further factor to bear in mind is that, however he or she is funded, the claimant will still have to prove his or her case if the claim is going to succeed. On this front, there is still a huge difference between the British and US legal systems.

The contrast is probably best highlighted by the conflicting fortunes of McDonald's on the two sides of the Atlantic. In the United States in 1994, a woman who received scalds after spilling a cup of McDonald's coffee on her lap received damages of nearly $3 million. A similar group action by 36 McDonald's customers in the United Kingdom failed in its entirety in 2003. The judge, Mr Justice Field, took a common-sense approach and ruled that if McDonald's served its coffee cool, then people would simply not want to buy it. Although he accepted that McDonald's owed a duty of care to its customers to guard against injury, the duty was not so great that McDonald's should have refrained from serving hot drinks at all.

A central plank of the claimants' case was that because the hot drinks were served in insulated cups, the customers had no idea of the temperature of the drink. Again adopting a common-sense approach, Mr Justice Field found that McDonald's was entitled to assume that the customers would know their drink was hot. He also found that there were 'numerous ways' by which the customers could cool the drink down, for instance by stirring it or blowing. All 36 claims were rejected.

It is a similar story in the field of tobacco litigation. A jury in California recently ordered cigarette manufacturer Philip Morris to pay $28 billion in damages to a smoker who is now suffering from cancer. In the United Kingdom, meanwhile, the only meaningful group action against tobacco manufacturers was struck out by the court at an interlocutory stage. The staggering size of the Californian award highlights another huge difference between the United Kingdom and the United States: the award was made up entirely of punitive damages, a concept that does not exist in UK personal injury law.

Statistics generated by the Court Service also suggest that Britain is not in fact suffering from a tidal wave of speculative personal injury litigation. The caseload of the Queen's Bench Division of the high court has just dropped significantly for the third year in succession. Twenty per cent fewer claims were issued in the Queen's Bench Division in 2002 than in 2001 – and the division now handles less than a fifth of the volume of claims it had in 1998. By contrast, the caseload of the Chancery Division of the high court – which deals with insolvency, industry and intellectual property disputes – has fallen by only 2 per cent over the same period.

The drop-off in litigation generally has had a serious knock-on effect on court revenues. The Lord Chancellor issued a consultation document predicting a £30 million shortfall in court income, which is blamed on falling litigation levels following the Woolf reforms. The Lord Chancellor has proposed steep increases in court fees to counter the lost revenue – with hikes of up to 30 per cent in the county court and 60 per cent in the high court being suggested.

Insurers will always be faced with spurious or unmeritorious claims. However, the numbers of these claims do not appear to be rising dramatically, and there has been no discernible shift in the attitude of the courts that would allow the weaker claims to succeed.

The real issue for insurers at present is the rising cost of settling successful claims. CFAs have played a large role in this, with success fees and insurance premiums bumping up legal costs significantly. Damages payments are also increasing at well above the rate of inflation, with one of the key factors being the ever-increasing cost of care packages in cases involving long-term injuries. There are external factors to consider as well, such as the Government's proposal to extend the recovery of NHS charges from defendants to the employers' liability sector.

There is nevertheless evidence that a proactive approach by insurers can help to limit the rate of claims inflation. Well-argued cases on costs have led to advantageous results such as *Halloran* v *Delaney*, which limited claimants' success fees to 5 per cent on straightforward personal injury claims settled at the protocol stage. In addition, by focusing on rehabilitation, and making short-term investments in improving claimants' medical conditions, insurers have been able to make significant strides in capping quantum in cases involving substantial care packages or lost earnings. It is in these types of areas, rather than media hype about a tidal wave of phoney claims, that prudent insurers are focusing their efforts.

Paul Taverner
Partner
0870 194 8900
paul.taverner@bevanbrittan.co.uk

LONDON REMADE

The business of recycling

London Remade: Remaking the Capital

London produces over 3 million tonnes of waste per year yet only recycles 14.5%. London Remade is an innovative recycling programme that aims to increase the demand for recycled products and, in turn, increase levels of recycling. A unique partnership between the business, community, public and not-for-profit sectors, London Remade uses recycling as a vehicle to drive economic and social regeneration and is principally funded by the London Development Agency to deliver green procurement and business support programmes.

Focusing on each aspect of the recycling supply chain London Remade can offer advice and support on collection schemes and aims to help develop markets for recycled content products.

The first challenge in the recycling supply chain is ensuring an efficient and consistent supply of quality material, collected from households and commercial waste streams, for reprocessing. The Support Service provides support to London waste authorities and is dedicated to providing quality advice and support on implementing best practice in waste minimisation and waste management across the Capital.

London Remade has also helped develop reprocessing facilities within London to create saleable products from London's waste, including four Eco-sites for paper, glass, construction and demolition waste and organic material. Since the programme began the eco sites have helped divert over 540,000 tonnes of waste material from landfill.

The Mayor's Green Procurement Code, launched in 2001, focuses on stimulating the demand for the purchase of recycled content products and closing the recycling loop. With over 360 signatories the Mayor's Code offers a free, comprehensive brokerage service to find markets for waste materials. This year's annual purchase report demonstrated that signatories to the code have spent over £22 million on recycled content products ranging from stationery to glass aggregate. The Mayor's Code has now extended to include the materials service aiming to facilitate matches of recyclable materials, which currently have no end market, between producers and collectors in London.

For more information on London Remade please see our website **www.londonremade.com** or contact us at **info@londonremade.com** Tel: **020 7061 6360**

BUSINESS SERVICES

The Green Business Support Organisation (GBSO) supports small and medium sized enterprises wanting to improve their environmental performance, providing a single port of call for businesses seeking environmental support and advice.

GBSO is funded by Yorkshire Forward, and is delivered by Business in the Community, providing businesses with a direct link to a support network. GBSO channels its support through four environmental co-ordinators who work out of Business Link's offices in North, South and West Yorkshire, and the Humber. They act as a gateway, signposting local businesses to appropriate business support.

John-Mark Zwyko, environment project manager, BITC said: "Where appropriate, we provide onsite quality assured environmental consultancy specific to individual business processes. The idea is to implement a set of actions at low cost, to reduce waste or energy use and increase profits."

The initial consultancy, including an environmental audit of their practices, is free to businesses. A six-month action plan is devised enabling companies to work towards achieving reductions in waste and energy use.

David White is the owner of A & E Bakers, who produce food for eight shops in Barnsley in addition to supplying retail chains. He joined the GBSO after contacting Business Link South Yorkshire, and was introduced to environmental practitioners Meltzer Consultants.

He explains what happened next:

"Meltzer identified two areas where we could save money: waste disposal and energy use. We concentrated on the waste aspect first of all, because we found we could make savings straight away, without any cost to ourselves."

Almost five tonnes of packaging was literally thrown away each year. By setting up a contract with a local recycling company, the company made an immediate saving of 20% on their waste disposal costs. They are now concentrating on reducing energy costs.

Business standards

Business standards: introduction

Business in the Community

Companies understand that when they manufacture their product, or develop and train their people, principles of good management apply, and will affect the quality of the result. To reassure customers and regulators that they take those principles seriously, they have embraced a range of management standards that deliver reliability around a recognized quality framework.

Companies are beginning to understand that the same rules apply to sustainable development or corporate social responsibility (CSR). Benefits for the business and for society are achieved only by managing these aspects within a quality framework.

The quest for reliable quality standards in a field of intangibles has led to a huge amount of activity and innovation, the result of which can be bewildering for the corporate executive seeking a way through the morass. A range of indices have been built up to apply quality of management measures, both as investment vehicles (Dow Jones Group Sustainability Index, FTSE4good) and as business-led benchmarks (Business in the Community's Corporate Responsibility Index).

Management frameworks have been created to help the company reliably control its operations in relation to key CSR issues, from the well-established ISO 14001 (environment) to SA 8000 (workplace and human rights). In other areas, management frameworks or principles have focused on even more specific areas of activity, such as Business in the Community's Principles of Corporate Community Investment and its Cause-Related

Marketing Principles. The move globally for greater disclosure and reporting has led to the creation of the Global Reporting Initiative, along with other national or sector-based initiatives.

What all these tools and frameworks have in common is that they are part of the quest to identify and deliver quality of management in corporate responsibility. It is not enough that companies seek to do the right thing. They must do it well. And that means managing for corporate responsibility as seriously as they manage every other aspect of their business.

Business standards: legal overview

Kathryn Mylrea, Simmons & Simmons

There are many different voluntary initiatives in the corporate governance and corporate social responsibility area that can be adopted by an organization. These include the Equator Principles (guidelines for banks funding development projects), the CERES principles (10 principles relating specifically to environmental awareness and accountability), the Global Reporting Initiative (GRI) Sustainability Reporting Guidelines and the Association of British Insurers (ABI) Disclosure Guidelines on Socially Responsible Investment. A draft ISO on corporate social responsibility is being developed and is designed to be consistent with ISO 9000 or ISO 14001.

The UK Department of Trade and Industry (DTI) published, on 5 May 2004, draft regulations on a new Operating and Financial Review (OFR) and the Director's Report. The new regulations will make it mandatory for directors of a listed company to prepare an annual OFR. The draft regulations include some mandatory items for inclusion in the OFR, and employee, environmental and social and community issues are 'additional items' for inclusion in the OFR to the extent necessary to enable the directors to comply with the 'review objective' and other general requirements. The review objective is a balanced and comprehensive analysis of development and performance of the business during the financial year, the position of the company at the end of the year, the main trends and factors underlying that development, performance and position, and the main trends and factors that are likely to affect future development, performance and position. Environmental reporting is not therefore mandatory, but there is likely to be a very high hurdle to clear if no environmental information is included in an OFR. The OFR is not intended to replace free-standing environment or sustainability reports, which it is expected will contain more detail than the OFR.

Corporate governance

Greg Pritchard, CPAAudit

Corporate governance is generally regarded as the system by which companies are directed and controlled. It is the way in which the affairs of corporations are handled by their corporate boards and officers.

Since the latter part of 2001, the already lively debate on corporate governance has become a turbulent one, with attention being increasingly focused on the following issues:

- *Spectacular corporate failures* – including Enron, Parmalat and many others.
- *Auditor independence and conflicts of interest.* Non-audit work, such as computer consultancy and internal audit, can often be far more lucrative than pure audit work.
- *Excessive executive remuneration.* Examples include executives of the New York Stock Exchange and SmithKline Beecham.
- *Ineffective non-executive directors.* A survey conducted by KPMG in 2002, for example, found that some 40 per cent of non-executive directors surveyed felt they did not have sufficient knowledge of non-financial factors such as environmental, political and employment issues that could have a material impact on a company.
- *Increasingly active investors* – witness the ousting of Sir Philip Watts and Ian Prosser at Shell and Sainsbury respectively.
- *Legislation* – including, in the United States, the Sarbanes–Oxley Act of 2002.

As details of accounting frauds continued to hit both sides of the Atlantic, the pace of the corporate governance debate increased. Codes of best practice continue to flourish from a wide variety of interest groups. The Organization for Economic Co-operation and

Development (OECD), for example, published a revised draft of its corporate governance principles, originally adopted in 1999, for public comment in January 2003. The governments of the 30 OECD countries subsequently approved the revised version, which incorporates new recommendations for good practice in corporate behaviour with a view to rebuilding and maintaining public trust in companies and stock markets, in April 2004.

There are many cynics, of course. In a letter sent in April 2003 to Patricia Hewitt, Secretary of State at the UK Department of Trade and Industry (DTI), David Blundell, Chairman of the UK Shareholders Association, commented:

> It is time to control the levels of overpayment to underperforming and failing directors, and increase the powers of the legal owners of public companies, namely the shareholders. The Cadbury, Greenbury, Hampel et al reports have spawned an awe-inspiring growth in remuneration consultants, non-executive directors and bureaucratic procedures. But can one argue convincingly that much has been achieved? What one can argue convincingly is that the UK has created a new and fast-growing industry of its own – the corporate governance industry!

Corporate governance had its origins in the 19th century, arising in response to the separation of ownership and control following the formation of joint stock companies. The owners or shareholders of these companies, who were not involved in day-to-day operational issues, required assurances that those in control of the company – the directors and managers – were safeguarding their investments and accurately reporting the financial outcome of their business activities. Thus, shareholders were the original focus of corporate governance. However, current thinking recognizes a corporation's obligations to society generally, in the form of stakeholders.

More recently, the Treadway Commission, formed in the United States in 1985 following a number of financial failures, frauds and questionable business practices, reporting in 1987 found that breakdowns in internal control were a contributory factor in nearly 50 per cent of fraudulent financial reporting. In 1987 the Committee of Sponsoring Organizations (COSO) of the Treadway Commission defined three objectives for internal control in their final framework, which was issued in 1992:

- effectiveness and efficiency of operations;
- reliability of financial reporting;
- compliance with laws and regulations.

Safeguarding of assets was added as a further objective in 1994.

As to the history of corporate governance in the United Kingdom, corporate boards will be well aware of the Cadbury (internal financial control) and Greenbury (disclosure of director's remuneration) Committees of the early to mid-1990s. As the debate on corporate governance continued, a further committee, the Hampel Committee, was formed towards the end of 1995. This committee issued its report early in 1998 and highlighted the role of corporate governance as a contributor to business prosperity in addition to its previous focus on financial reporting.

The Hampel Report, which incorporated the recommendations from both the Cadbury and the Greenbury Committees as well as some amendments from the London Stock

Exchange, was published as the Combined Code in June 1998. The Code was appended to, but was not part of, the London Stock Exchange Listing Rules. It originally consisted of 14 Principles of Corporate Governance, each of which was supported by a number of provisions of which there were 45 in total; these were listed separately as the Code of Best Practice.

Implementation of the Code required a two-part disclosure statement in the annual financial statements. The first part required a description of how a company applied the 14 Principles and the second part required confirmation of compliance with the 45 supporting provisions or, alternatively, an explanation of why the company did not comply. Seven of the original supporting provisions were subject to external audit review for compliance.

The Hampel Report requires directors to review the effectiveness of all internal controls, not simply internal financial controls. A further committee known as the Turnbull Committee was subsequently established to provide guidance on this issue. Compliance with the Code became mandatory for all accounting periods ending on or after 23 December 2000.

Complying with the requirements of the Turnbull Report involves operational compliance with best practice, including a review of internal controls and risk management, and drafting the precise wording of the disclosure required in the financial statements. A Boardroom Briefing is available to assist companies with the implementation of the Turnbull requirements.

More recently, 2003 was a busy year in the field of corporate governance in the United Kingdom. January of that year saw the publication of both the Higgs Report on the role of non-executive directors and the Smith Report on audit committees. The Financial Reporting Council subsequently reissued the revised Combined Code on 23 July 2003. This document includes the Code itself and related guidance comprising the Turnbull guidance on internal control, the Smith guidance on audit committees and various items of good practice guidance from the Higgs Report. The new Code applies to listed companies for reporting years beginning on or after 1 November 2003. Finally, the National Association of Pension Funds codified its own corporate governance policies on 8 December 2003. In so doing, it laid down the ground rules that its voting advisory service will use when recommending how member funds should vote.

Clearly, much has been written on the subject of corporate governance, but what about the practice? In many instances, corporate governance procedures appear overly sophisticated when what is needed is just good old-fashioned accounting and a hint of transparency. Or, as Terry Smith, CEO of stockbroker Collins Stewart commented following public criticism of a bundled resolution at a company EGM on 17 February 2003, 'If anyone thinks that the rise and rise of corporate governance claptrap will save any investor from anything, they're living in a dream world.'

Greg Pritchard is the Senior Partner of CPAAudit UK, an independent consultancy based in the City of London that advises on regulatory compliance, internal audit, risk management and corporate governance issues. Information about the firm can be found at www.cpaaudit.co.uk.

CORPORATE GOVERNANCE

In the wake of the Higgs Report and recommendations, it seems that a whole new industry of corporate governance consultancy has arisen. Boards are asking what development activity they need to undertake for non executive directors in order to comply with the recommendations of the combined code. They are also asking how they might govern better. In reality, the compliance side of this equation does not necessarily result in better governance although it might help.

In trying to make better sense of what some see only as a compliance issue, CPA Audit carried out some research and conducted some development work of their own. In Atlanta Georgia, Dr John Carver has for some years now been preaching the virtues of his 'policy governance' model. Much plaudited by Sir Adrian Cadbury and practised by companies as prestigious as BP, the policy governance model is at once both complex and simple. Its simplicity lies in its generic messages to which it is easy to relate. The complications arise when you are considering whether this model applies with equal certainly to the unitary board as it does to the supervisory board. Without getting into those, or indeed other, complications, let me try and explain the attractiveness of this model in purely generic terms.

First and foremost, it calls for the Board to rethink its whole activity. For example, is the Board working to its own agenda or to that of senior management? Given that the Board is accountable to the shareholders for all activity, how much of that activity is delegated to the Chief Executive and how is that delegation recorded? Are there any limitations that the Board may wish to place on the Chief Executive and, if so, what are they and where are they spelt out? How will the Board monitor the performance of the chief executive? What information will it use and is the chief executive fully aware of the process and in agreement with it, because, once agreed, no other process and no other information can be introduced. The greatest value lies in the clarity that this process produces. The Board is clear about its role, individual directors are clear about their role and the senior management team is clear about what it has to do.

Finally, a word about the Board's role in evaluation. So long as clear objectives have been agreed, it is a relatively easy matter for the Board to monitor the activity of the company, both against targets and within clear value systems. It is less easy for them to monitor their own performance unless they have agreed what it is that will represent success for the Board. I leave you with some suggestions, post Higgs, from the combined code:

- How well has the board performed against any performance objectives that have been set?

- What has been the board's contribution to the testing and development of strategy?

- What has been the board's contribution to ensuring robust and effective risk management?

These are just three of a number of suggestions. For the Board to be really effective, it should consider such suggestions and then devise its own relevant performance criteria and decide how and when achievement of such criteria shall be monitored. Next on the agenda may well be the performance appraisal of individual directors. Senior managers are routinely subject to this, so why not to directors?

An introduction to environmental and sustainability reporting

Rachel Jackson, Head of Social and Environmental Issues, ACCA

Organizations are increasingly coming to realize that, in order to meet the growing demands made on them by their competitors, external stakeholders and the Government, they need to change the way they 'do business'. This change includes becoming more open and accountable for the economic, environmental and social consequences of their activities. This new (and often underestimated) dimension of corporate governance includes taking responsibility for the full range of positive and negative consequences arising from corporate decisions and actions, and disclosing these impacts in an appropriate environmental, social and sustainability report.

Over the past decade, companies worldwide have come under increasing pressure to conduct their business in a more open and responsible manner. The following developments have been identified as the key drivers that have encouraged businesses to become more responsible:

- the increasing size and influence of companies;
- the growth of civil society activism, increasing the influence of non-governmental organizations (NGOs);

■   the increased importance a company places on intangibles;
■   advances in communications technology.

These developments are encouraging more businesses to question what they do and how they do it. In the early 1990s only a handful of companies were sufficiently far-thinking to publish voluntary data on their non-financial impacts. Over a decade on, the situation looks very different, with a growing number of companies reporting each year from an increasing number of countries.

These reports have become highly effective tools for communicating to stakeholders the environmental, social and wider economic performance of an organization. Estimates put the total number of environmental reports produced worldwide at around 4,000. Although environmental and sustainability reporting has yet to reach a generally accepted standard of financial reporting, there has nevertheless been a rapid evolutionary process that has contributed to the high standard of environmental and sustainability reports seen today. Mandatory environmental reporting regimes have been introduced in various parts of the world, including the Netherlands, Denmark, Australia, the United States and, most recently, France.

What is environmental reporting?

'Environmental reporting' is the term commonly used to describe the disclosure by an entity of environmentally related data, verified (audited) or not, regarding environmental risks, environmental impacts, policies, strategies, targets, costs, liabilities or environmental performance to those who have an interest in such information, as an aid to enabling or enriching their relationship with the reporting entity. Disclosure can take place via:

■   the annual report;
■   a stand-alone corporate environmental performance report;
■   a site-centred environmental statement;
■   some other medium (eg staff newsletter, video, CD ROM, website).

The Sustainability Working Party of the European Federation of Accountants (FEE) defines the objective of external environmental reporting as being 'the provision of information about the environmental impact and operational performance of an entity that is useful to relevant stakeholders in assessing their relationship with the reporting entity'.

An excellent environmental report clearly acknowledges and explains the environmental impacts of an organization's operations and products, and publicly demonstrates the organization's commitment to reduce them accordingly.

What is sustainability reporting?

As sustainability reporting is an emerging and rapidly developing practice, there have been several attempts to define what a sustainability report is or should be. In general, however, sustainability reporting involves reporting on the economic, environmental and social impact of organizational performance. A sustainability report should be a high-level strategic document that addresses the issues, challenges and opportunities sustainable development brings to the core business and its industry sector. All material and relevant elements of sustainability – economic, environmental and social – should be addressed, on both a separate and an integrated basis.

As a sustainability report is strategic report, key business issues such as public policy positions, risk management procedures and governance commitment should also be disclosed. Economic indicators can include cost of all goods, materials and services purchased; total payroll and benefits expense; total sum of taxes of all types paid; and donations to community, civil-society or other groups. Social issues can include labour practices, human rights, societal and product responsibility issues.

Reporting by small and medium-sized enterprises

It is well known that fewer small and medium-sized organizations (SMEs) disclose social, economic and environmental information than do their larger counterparts: even on a global scale, the total number of reporting organizations remains small. SMEs have fewer resources – finance, time, knowledge – available to them, which restricts the number of SMEs that report on sustainability issues.

ACCA believes in principle, however, that all businesses, in all areas of industry and of whatever size, need to address the issue of sustainable development and integrate it into their business strategies. The level of effort and expense that SMEs can devote to this will vary, however, and the special circumstances of SMEs need to be respected.

Benefits of environmental and sustainability reporting

Since environmental and sustainability reporting in most countries is a purely voluntary activity, it is necessary for companies to perceive some tangible benefits when establishing the business case to report. The following are some of the benefits most commonly cited by reporting organizations:

- Reporting demonstrates coherence of overall management strategies to important external stakeholders.
- By disclosing management strategies, systems and policies relating to the environment and society, an organization can demonstrate to its stakeholders its holistic approach to environmental responsibility.
- Reporting assists in the aligning of corporate vision and principles with internal business practices and activities.

Strengthened stakeholder relations

One of the benefits of increasing corporate transparency via an environmental or sustainability report is that stakeholder relations are strengthened. Confidence and trust between the two parties are improved when organizations include stakeholders in the reporting process by actively engaging with them. Stakeholder dialogue is increasingly used by large companies to help identify the key issues that are of concern to their stakeholders. Appropriate issues should then be addressed in the environmental report.

Increased competitive advantage

An organization that demonstrates full responsibility for its environmental impacts and then reports on them benefits from gaining a competitive edge over those of its peers in the same sector that are not as open and transparent about such issues. Environmental reporting may provide competitive advantage in capital, labour, supplier and customer markets.

Improved access to lists of 'preferred suppliers'

Corporate environmental stewardship now includes consideration of upstream processes. Suppliers that share the same high environmental values as buyers with green procurement policies, and can openly report on all aspects of their performance, thus giving a more complete and transparent view of the organization's managerial strategy and operations, are more likely to achieve 'preferred supplier' status.

Reduced corporate risk

In the reporting cycle it is now common to identify the areas of environmental and social risk, which previously went unnoticed. By actively lowering these corporate risks, compliance will increase while potential liabilities will decrease, thereby reducing financing costs and, possibly, broadening the range of investors.

Assistance with investment analysis

If a company accounts for all its impacts and performance measures (economic, environmental and social), investors will obtain a clearer picture of its true health. Socially responsible investment, where companies are screened prior to investment, using social and environmental criteria, is growing exponentially. Environmental and sustainability reports aid analysis and, for some funds, reporting are requirements.

Stakeholders and their information needs

Whereas published financial data are assumed to be important primarily to shareholders, lenders and potential investors in enabling them to make economic decisions relating to the reporting entity, with environmental and sustainability reporting there is no such certainty, as there is potentially a much wider audience for environmental, social and economic data.

For example, NGOs need to be shown that secured assets are not impaired in any way; local communities may require site-specific data relating to emission, waste policies and wider community issues; and shareholders and financial analysts will need assurance that poor environmental management will not translate into financial risk. Other stakeholders include customers that may have strict environment and social procurement policies and employees who need assurance on health and safety grounds and assurance that they are working for a responsible and accountable employer.

Many reporters make a considerable effort to identify who their primary stakeholders are and establish an ongoing dialogue with them to ensure that the published reports meet their needs. A comprehensive stakeholder survey is an essential prerequisite for publishing a first environmental or sustainability report. Thereafter, companies may set up stakeholder panels or focus groups to maintain the process of dialogue and feedback. Feedback forms are usually included in published reports, and web-based reports normally incorporate a mechanism for delivering feedback through the website itself.

The Global Reporting Initiative

The Global Reporting Initiative (GRI) was originally established as a voluntary co-operative initiative in late 1997 with the objective of developing a set of reporting guidelines dealing with the economic, environmental and social consequences of organizational activity. The international steering committee that led the initiative brought together the world's leading reporting experts and organizations, including ACCA. The first set of formal 'sustainability reporting' guidelines was published in June 2000.

The growth in support for the objectives of the GRI has been wide-ranging. Apart from around 450 organizations across 45 countries which currently use the GRI in whole or in part as a basis for developing their own corporate sustainability reports, the GRI has received widespread support at the governmental and institutional level as a tool that has the potential to provide the transparency and accountability increasingly being demanded of multinational companies by their stakeholders.

The GRI's mode of working is based around a number of principles or qualities that provide the underpinning legitimacy for its recommendations. The GRI is non-aligned and multi-stakeholder in structure and governance. The organizational model is inclusive and aspires to be global in outreach. Governance and working methods are transparent. Its guidelines are voluntary, not mandatory, and are dynamic in that they are constantly being tested, reviewed and upgraded. The first board of directors was selected in 2003, and Roger Adams, Executive Director – Technical, ACCA, was successfully nominated. The board of directors has the ultimate fiduciary, financial and legal responsibility for the GRI, and exercises final decision-making authority on revisions to the guidelines, technical work and organizational strategy.

The GRI 2002 Guidelines

The second, expanded version of the GRI reporting guidelines was issued in 2002. The 2002 Guidelines represent a significant step forward for sustainability reporting, containing as they do an improved set of environmental indicators alongside much-expanded sets of social and economic performance indicators. The 2002 Guidelines are divided into four parts:

1. Part A: Using the Guidelines. An informative overview of the Guidelines, including a description of what they are, who should use them and how to prepare a report using them.
2. Part B: Reporting Principles. A description of each principle and how it is organized.
3. Part C: Report Content. A description of the content of a GRI report. A GRI report consists of 'Vision and strategy', 'Profile', 'Governance structure and management systems', 'GRI content index' and 'Performance (economic, environmental, social) indicators'.
4. Part D: Glossary and Annexes. A number of annexes are included on issues such as credibility and assurance, and incremental application, together with a glossary.

It should be stressed that the GRI Guidelines can be used and implemented on an incremental basis. The GRI acknowledges that some organizations, particularly smaller ones and first-time reporters, may only be able to adopt part of the Guidelines in the first instance. It is hoped, however, that reporters will increase the quantity and quality of their reporting over time.

The GRI in the future

The GRI has now embarked on creating a 'family' of GRI-related documents. The elements of this family comprise:

1. The core guidelines: the foundation document upon which all other GRI documents are based. These are due to be updated in 2006.
2. Sector-specific supplements providing additional guidance for specific sectors, which address issues pertinent to those industries. Current sector reports being developed include mining and metals, financial services, and public-sector guidelines.
3. Measurement/technical protocols, each one addressing a specific set of indicators and providing technical guidance on their measurement.
4. Issues papers, which are issue-specific supplements to provide additional models for organizing the information.

For further information on the GRI and to download the GRI 2002 Guidelines, please visit www.globalreporting.org.

Components of a sustainability report

Many environmental reporting guidelines have evolved over the past decade to provide organizations with a framework of what to include in an environmental report. More recently, the GRI has provided guidance on what to include in a sustainability report. The following list highlights the main components of an ideal sustainability report.

CEO's statement

A statement from the CEO or the chair of the board of directors helps to demonstrate the degree of commitment to, and support for, corporate accountability. Statements should refer to the organization's policies and should also make reference to achievements and low points of the year, issues and challenges that lie ahead for the company, and its future sustainability strategy.

Organizational profile

The organizational profile is an overview of the organization in terms of its size, structure and spread of activities, as represented, for example, by turnover and number of operational sites and employees and the markets and market segments served. The key interactions with the physical environment with regard to the company's products or services and operations should also be included. Any related health and safety information can also be included in this section.

Scope

A number of report 'boundaries' should be stated to better inform users of the report – for example:

- What part of the organization is included – all the sites or just headquarters? Global or national operations? Are subsidiaries and joint ventures included?
- What is the scope of content – social, environmental and/or economic?
- What period of time does the report cover?

Key impacts

All businesses have an impact on society and the environment, but the extent of this impact depends on many factors, including the size, sector and location of the business. The significant impacts should be clearly explained so that readers can understand the burden of the business. Disclosures under this heading will be strongly influenced by the feedback obtained from organizational stakeholders as to what they consider to be main impacts and the areas on which they request performance disclosures.

Governance

The 2002 GRI Sustainability Reporting Guidelines have a 'Governance and Management Systems' section that should help organizations address this important sustainability issue in future reports. Issues that should be addressed include the governance structure (such as committees and their responsibilities) and the organizational structure of individuals responsible for day-to-day implementation of strategy and policy.

Sustainability-related policies

A public commitment to pursue particular goals and objectives in terms of managing, measuring and reporting environmental, social and/or economic performance against specific targets should be made.

Management systems and procedures

The provision of reliable performance information is impossible without adequate information systems having been established in the first instance. This section typically describes the environmental (and related other) management system in place, including staff contact details and members of the board who are responsible for environmental management training programmes and related educational activities for staff, any external accreditation achieved (eg ISO 14000/EMS) and key managerial responsibilities for the various aspects of the system.

Stakeholder engagement

All organizations' reports should state who the report is intended for, and should disclose who the company's stakeholders are in general. Reports should describe their stakeholder consultation/ dialogue processes and explain how any stakeholder feedback has been used and how stakeholders are involved in the reporting process.

Performance and compliance

Detailed performance data form the central feature of the best reports. Such data comprehensively illustrate success (or failure) in making progress towards achieving the stated targets. This section can include information on physical data, prosecutions and complaints, and financial data. Stakeholder feedback is an excellent pointer as to which specific performance indicators will be of most interest to external parties.

Targets and achievements

Target-setting helps to demonstrate an organization's commitment to continually improve its performance. Feedback on achievements for previously set targets can demonstrate the positive strides the company has made towards meeting its overall objectives. A comprehensive set of targets should cover all key environmental, social and economic issues faced.

Independent verification statement

Most organizations have realized that without independent assurance, their report will have little standing with any external audience. Verification statements cover systems compliance issues and provide assurance as to the completeness of the report. The best verification statements also report on the acceptability performance and offer recommendations for systems improvement and reporting practice. Factors the verifier should bear in mind include:

■ remit and scope;
■ indication of site visits and site-specific testing;
■ interpretation of data or performance reported;
■ identification of any data or information omitted that could or should have been included;
■ independent comment on corporate targets set and impacts identified;
■ shortcomings and recommendations.

Responsible Competitiveness in the East Midlands

Working with business to create the future for our children and generations to come

In today's globalised market-place, thriving businesses understand how motivated staff and positive brand images contribute to a diverse client base and healthy profits. Many companies are now looking beyond to new ways of addressing social and environmental responsibilities whilst achieving commercial success.

Over the last few years the concept of Corporate Social Responsibility has achieved real status in business and Government circles. The important thing about the CSR message is that social and environmental responsibility are not costs, but a real opportunity to improve competitiveness and business performance.

That's why, in the East Midlands we are starting to work towards a vision for responsible competitiveness. Like other English regions we face real challenges in reducing our greenhouse emissions and getting more out of our resources. The vision that we have developed for the region is that by 2010 we will be one of the top 20 European regions. But this vision is not one which will be realised by enhanced economic growth alone!

By adopting a couple of the good practices suggested in this guide, you could do much to help the region become a more attractive place to work, live and invest in.

Why not implement your own CSR or Environmental Policy?

emda is developing a regional strategy related to CSR. If you want to know more about this (or generally about the region) visit our website **www.emda.org.uk** and register for our email news alert service.

WORKING WITH BUSINESSES TO CREATE THE FUTURE WE WANT FOR OUR CHILDREN AND GENERATIONS TO COME

By 2010, the East Midlands will be one of Europe's top 20 regions. It will be a place where people want to live, work and invest because of:

Our vibrant economy

Our healthy, safe, diverse and **inclusive** society

Our quality environment

Safety Values

OHSAS 18001 is the widely respected specification for occupational health & safety management systems. Its adoption can carry many benefits ranging from the reduction of accidents and improved safety performance to employee motivation. By selecting BSI Management Systems for OHSAS 18001 assessment and training, organisations benefit from the international reputation and recognition of a world leader in health & safety management system certification. Contact us now to find out how.

shape the future

- ASSESSMENT
- COMPREHENSIVE TRAINING
- HEALTH & SAFETY SEMINAR
- COMMUNICATION DAYS
- GUIDANCE LITERATURE
- ELECTRONIC TOOLS

Standardization and sustainability

Errol Taylor, The Royal Society for the Prevention of Accidents (RoSPA)

The business case

'New standards can be the source of enormous wealth, or the death of corporate empires' – a perspective that is often overlooked by many executives who see standards and standardization as being synonymous with bureaucracy and red tape. In the fight for commercial survival, in which sustainability is about hitting profit and turnover targets, wider issues such as the enhancement of social, human, manufactured and natural capital are often left as a secondary priority.

This is probably a reflection of the origins of the most widely adopted standard, ISO 9001. At the height of the United Kingdom's Thatcher revolution, when Japanese manufacturers were leading the way with consistently cheaper and better products, the UK Ministry of Defence (MoD) and many government departments started to ask suppliers to be certified to BS 5750, the forerunner of ISO 9001. The quality industry was born, with a new breed of consultants and auditors. They gave organizations clear methodologies for documenting activities, and the result was a step-change improvement in quality control.

Most executives embark on the journey towards compliance with and certification to standards as a leap of faith, since it is very difficult to demonstrate any direct linkage between financial performance and the use of standards. However, Corbett *et al* reviewed the performance of over 300 US companies in three industrial sectors (electronics, chemicals

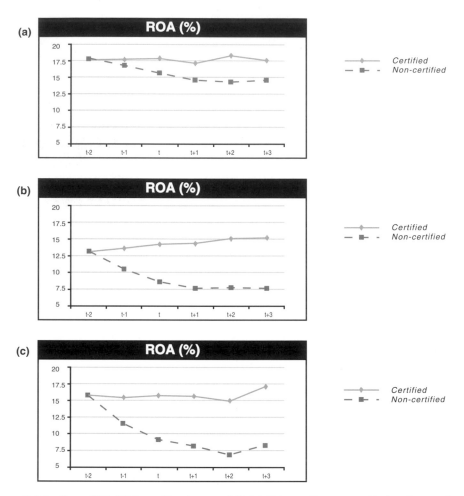

Figure 3.5.1 Does ISO 9000 certification pay? ISO 9000 certification in (a) the chemical industry (SIC 28); (b) the industrial machinery and computer industry (SIC 35); (c) the electronic equipment and components industry (SIC 36) (Source: Corbett *et al*, ISO Management Systems, July–August 2002)

and industrial machinery) and demonstrated that certified organizations improved their return on assets at a higher rate than those that were not certified (Figure 3.5.1).

As yet unpublished research by the British Standards Institution (BSI) shows a similar pattern of performance by the United Kingdom's top listed companies. The findings suggest that better-managed organizations tend to adopt best-practice tools such as ISO certification.

Maybe surprisingly, the positive business case also applies to small to medium-sized enterprises (Figure 3.5.2). Traditionally, entrepreneurs see compliance with regulations as a necessary evil. However, a common pattern for two- to four-year-old businesses is to adopt certification as part of their growth strategy.

AccountAbility
institute of social and ethical accountability

Promoting accountability for sustainable development

Established in 1995, AccountAbility is the leading international non-profit institute that brings together members and partners from business, civil society and the public sector from across the world. AccountAbility provides effective assurance and accountability management tools and standards through its AA1000 Series, offers professional development and certification, and undertakes leading-edge research and related public policy advocacy.

Core to the AccountAbility Community are our members, who govern us, support us and participate in our programmes as well as play a vital role in shaping our direction and work.

AccountAbility has always valued and relied upon input from members, and now more than ever is looking towards working with, servicing and developing strong relationships with our members.

Membership
Our membership scheme is based on what our members, partners and collaborators tell us is needed, directly, and indirectly, through our international, representative Council. The comprehensive packages provide you with a range of benefits that can be tailored to meet your specific needs, however developed your corporate responsibility approach is.

Membership of AccountAbility is an invaluable asset for those committed to advancing and promoting greater accountability in business, civil society or public institutions across the world. Joining the AccountAbility Community delivers members access to; our unrivalled international networks, our unique blend of strategic research, professional development, and our prominent position in standards and public policy development.

AccountAbility has developed a series of membership levels that have been designed to meet the requirements of different types of members. Packages are accessible to both large and small businesses, service providers, academic institutions, NGO's and individuals.

To find out more about AccountAbility membership packages, and how you can benefit by joining, please visit **www.accountability.org.uk/membership** or email **membership@accountability.org.uk**

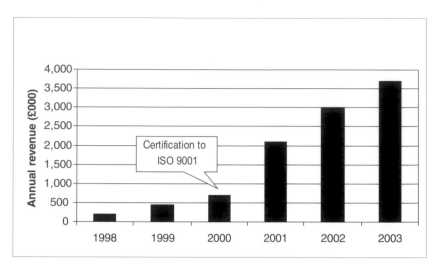

Figure 3.5.2 Growth of a successful small or medium-sized enterprise (SME)

By this stage, they will have saturated their local, start-up market and need to grow either geographically or by appealing to large national and multinational potential clients. For these organizations, certification is useful shorthand proving that the business can manage its fundamental processes effectively and is likely to be a reliable supplier.

Other organizations recognize that the process of standardization can be used to create new markets and exclude some (or all) of their competitors. In fiercely competitive industries such as consumer electronics, manufacturers are constantly fighting to dominate the market with their patented products and services. An industry standard can give significant competitive advantage to certain participants, thereby creating the need for organizations such as BSI to consult widely in the development of standards that are in the public good as well as being beneficial to individual companies.

A strong philosophical argument is that standardization should help build sustainable futures for communities and organizations by finding common ground among interested parties. The quarry or waste treatment plant that ignores the needs of the local villagers is unlikely to remain in business for long: unacceptable levels of noise, dirt, smell and toxic effluent are likely to cause a storm of protest, leading at best to increased security costs and at worst to closure of the operation and redundancies for the workforce.

The roles of standards and standardization

Today's executives face a bewildering array of standards and codes of practice. Their origins can be instructive: ISO 9001 and ISO 14001 were developed as genuine attempts to help organizations improve the quality of their products and reduce their impact on the environment, respectively. In contrast, financial scandals affecting pensions and shareholder value have led to a series of corporate governance reviews starting with the Cadbury Report and culminating in the inclusion of Higgs's recommendations into the London Stock Exchange's Combined Code.

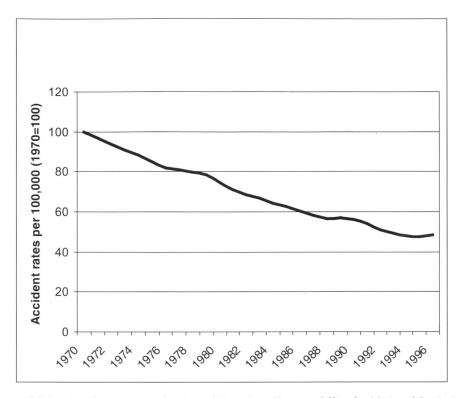

Figure 3.5.3 Accident rates in the United Kingdom (Source: Office for National Statistics)

BSI has pioneered standardization as a means of providing a level playing field for organizations to compete freely in national and international markets while generally improving quality of life for all concerned. Compliance with publicly available specifications (such as Kitemark schemes) provides reassurance to specifiers, buyers and users that the product is safe and its performance will exceed the minimum specified. As a result, injuries due to faulty building materials, toys and electrical goods are far less common than they were in 1974, when the Health and Safety at Work Act was introduced (Figure 3.5.3). Organizations now focus on differentiating their particular combination of products and services to gain market advantage rather than cutting dangerous corners.

In the hi-tech industries such as telecoms and software engineering, the protection of intellectual property has become absolutely paramount: Microsoft's Windows source code can be copied on to a standard CD ROM and would be of immense value to criminals throughout the world trying to gain access to banking details on personal computers. The reputation and ongoing sustainability of all service businesses depends on their clients having total faith in their ability to manage confidential information and keep it secret. At a more fundamental level, market research findings are often controversial, and marketers have to be creative in selectively using the data. Any leaking of the full facts could have a devastating effect on the organization, as can be testified by unfortunate business leaders like Gerald Ratner (who unfavourably compared his best-selling carriage clock with a prawn sandwich).

The SIGMA Project – Sustainability: Integrated Guidelines for Management – was launched in 1999 by BSI, Forum for the Future (a leading sustainability charity and think tank) and AccountAbility (an international professional body for accountability), with the support of the UK Department of Trade and Industry (DTI). The SIGMA project developed the SIGMA Management Framework to provide clear, practical advice to organizations to enable them to make a meaningful contribution to sustainable development. Underpinning the SIGMA Management Framework are the Guiding Principles, which consist of the two core elements of holistic management and accountability.

Holistic management of five different types of capital reflects an organization's overall impact and wealth. The five capitals are:

- *Natural capital* is the natural resources (energy and matter) and processes needed by organizations to produce their products and deliver their services. These include sinks that absorb, neutralize or recycle wastes; resources, some of which are renewable, while others are not; and processes, such as climate regulation and the carbon cycle, that enable life to continue in a balanced and healthy way.
- *Social capital* is any value added to the activities and economic outputs of an organization by human relationships, partnerships and co operation. Social capital includes, for example, networks, communication channels, families, communities, businesses, trade unions, schools and voluntary organizations as well as cultural and social norms, values and trust.
- *Human capital* incorporates the health, knowledge, skills, intellectual outputs, motivation and capacity for relationships of the individual. In an organizational context it includes the elements needed for human beings to engage in productive work and the creation of wealth, thereby achieving a better quality of life.
- *Manufactured capital* is material goods and infrastructure owned, leased or controlled by an organization that contribute to production or service provision, but do not become embodied in its output.
- *Financial capital* reflects the productive power and value of the other four types of capital and covers those assets of an organization that exist in a form of currency that can be owned or traded, including (but not limited to) shares, bonds and banknotes.

All the capitals are heavily interlinked, and there is some overlap between them. This whole system is then encircled by the principle of accountability, representing the relationship that an organization has with the outside world – with its stakeholders and for its stewardship of the five capitals.

The SIGMA Management Framework describes a four-phase cycle to manage and embed sustainability issues within core organizational processes (Figure 3.5.4). Organizations may enter the cycle at different points and work through the phases at different speeds according to their particular circumstances and existing systems.

Selecting the best fit for your organization

'Triple bottom line' reporting, covering social, environmental and economic issues, is becoming the norm for many organizations. Listed in Table 3.5.1 (see pages 104–05) are some of today's main management standards with an indication of their relevance to elements

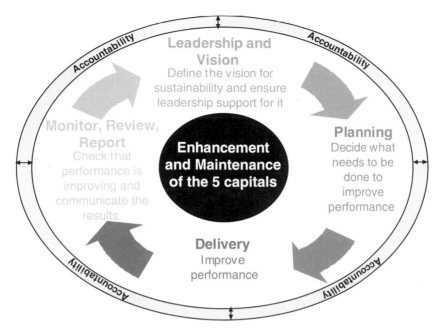

Figure 3.5.4 Embedding sustainability issues within core organizational processes

of the 'triple bottom line'. Generally, these standards are common-sense lists of best current management practice. In some cases they are aspirations, outlining 'next' management practice and therefore giving organizations a clear sense of direction.

By their nature, standards have little to offer that is unusual, unexpected or inappropriate. The challenge for most organizations is how to prioritize their adoption, given the plethora of conflicting pressures they face from stakeholders. To help busy executives make these choices, BSI is pioneering the use of two approaches: the Business Performance Improvement Review (BPIR) and the simpler Systems Prioritization Matrix (SPM). In summary, BPIR is an audit of stakeholder priorities based on the principles of ISO 9004. The needs of stakeholders – ranging from employees and customers to the local community and shareholders – must first be identified and then prioritized. Next, these priorities are used to validate whether communication flows within the organization match the stated priorities. Even in the best-run organizations this deceptively straightforward process turns out to be difficult because it forces unpleasant choices: should the needs of shareholders really be put ahead of those of customers or the local community? More alarming still, resource allocation rarely reflects strategic priorities, and significant work has to be done to reconfigure the organization to focus on its primary objectives.

The SPM (Figure 3.5.5) is far less ambitious in its scope. It was developed specifically to help managers and directors decide whether a management system would add value to their organization using a four-stage process:

- ■ **Stage 1:** List all the systems that you are aware of. The list given here is for illustrative purposes and is not intended to be exhaustive.

Table 3.5.1 Some of today's main management standards

Title of Management System or Framework	Description	Name or Number	Linkage to the Triple Bottom Line			Strategic Context on the Route to Sustainability
			Social	Environmental	Economic	
Sustainability: Integrated Guidelines for Management	Integration of social, environmental and business issues	SIGMA	√	√	√	Management consolidation. Basic needs met
Corporate Governance	Compliance by executives and non-executives with the Combined Code	UK Combined Code (Higgs, Cadbury et al)	√	√	√	Governance and strategy
Managing Risk through Corporate Governance	Guide to help identify business risks and their likelihood together with controls as part of corporate governance requirements	PD 6668	√	√	√	Governance & strategy
EU Eco-Management and Audit Scheme (EMAS)	Allows companies to evaluate, report and improve their environmental performance	EMAS		√	√	Stakeholder engagement and reporting
Environmental Management	Environmental performance evaluation – guidelines	ISO 14031		√	√	Stakeholder engagement and reporting
Accountability	A framework to improve accountability and performance by learning through stakeholder engagement	AA 1000	√			Stakeholder engagement
BPIR	Business Performance Improvement Review – stakeholder review and prioritization using the principles of ISO 9004	BPIR	√		√	Stakeholder engagement

Term	Description	Standard				Category
Business continuity	Review the way your organization provides its products and services and increase its resilience to disruption, interruption or loss	PAS 56	✓			Corporate responsibility and licence to operate
Social Accountability	A tool for retailers, brand companies, suppliers and other organizations to assure just and decent working conditions in the supply chain	SA 8000	✓			Corporate responsibility and licence to operate
European Quality Award	The EFQM Excellence Model was introduced at the beginning of 1992 as the framework for assessing applications for the European Quality Award	EFQM	✓	✓		Growth stage
Quality Management System	The international certifiable standard for quality management systems: the fundamental process-based approach on which other systems can be built	ISO 9001: 2000	✓	✓		Formalization of management systems leading to growth stage
Information Security	Ensures that your organization effectively manages the risks attached to your information data systems	BS 7799			✓	Legal compliance
Occupational Health & Safety	Occupational Health and Safety Management System (OHSMS) helps risk managment strategy to assess changing legislation and to protect the workforce	OHSAS 18001	✓			Legal compliance
Environmental Management System	The international certifiable standard for environmental management systems: a risk-based approach	ISO 14001		✓		Legal compliance
Investors in People	Sets a level of good practice for improving an organization's performance through its people	IIP	✓			Formalization of management systems
Acorn	A five- to six-phase approach to help SMEs implement an EMS in line with ISO 14001 or EMAS	BS 8555			✓	Formalization of management systems

Systems Prioritization Matrix				
Management System	**A** **External** **priority**	**B** **Internal** **priority**	**A × B**	**Rank**
Quality				
Environmental				
Occupational health and safety				
Information security				
Business continuity				
Staff motivation				
Social/ethical				
Corporate governance				

Figure 3.5.5 The Systems Prioritization Matrix (SPM)

■ **Stage 2:** Consider all the external drivers requiring compliance or certification to the system. If the organization is an engineering company supplying the automotive supply chain, it will probably be required to have certified quality and environmental systems. To capture this information, a score of between 1 and 5 has to be allocated. The top score of 5 applies where there are very strong external drivers, such as a customer mandate. The bottom score of 1 is where external drivers are weak or non-existent.

■ **Stage 3:** Repeat stage 2, but this time consider each system from an internal perspective. How valuable is certification to ISO 14001 in helping the organization position itself and generate additional revenues by claiming to be particularly environmentally friendly in an industry that is seen as having a poor pollution record? How could demonstration of excellent procedures for business continuity and protection of intellectual property help a software developer win new contracts from blue-chip clients? Again, the same rationale applies, with a score of 5 where compliance or certification would be highly beneficial to the organization.

■ **Stage 4:** Multiply column A by column B, noting the scores and ranking the systems in order: systems with the highest scores clearly should be receiving higher priority and more resources.

Three worked examples based on the broad primary sectors of the economy (manufacturing, process and services) show how priorities can be very different. The same applies within an organization, where the focus for one plant may be completely different from that of a call centre or the corporate headquarters. Rankings can be checked against intuitive reasoning, as follows.

Manufacturers are tightly controlled by their clients' specifications. Everything has to be geared around consistently delivering product at the right time, place and cost without causing harm or injury to anyone during the production process or during the product's useful life.

Manufacturing organizations

Management System	A External priority	B Internal priority	A × B	Rank
Quality	5	3	15	3
Environmental	4	3	12	2
Occupational health and safety	4	4	16	1
Information security	2	3	6	
Business continuity	2	2	4	
Staff motivation	1	3	3	
Social/ethical	3	2	6	
Corporate governance	3	3	9	

Process industries

Management System	A External priority	B Internal priority	A × B	Rank
Quality	2	4	8	
Environmental	5	4	20	2
Occupational health and safety	5	4	16	1
Information security	2	3	6	
Business continuity	3	4	12	3=
Staff motivation	1	3	3	
Social/ethical	1	2	2	
Corporate governance	4	3	12	3=

Services organizations

Management System	A External priority	B Internal priority	A × B	Rank
Quality	2	3	6	
Environmental	2	2	4	
Occupational health and safety	3	5	15	2=
Information security	4	3	12	
Business continuity	4	5	20	1
Staff motivation	3	5	15	2=
Social/ethical	2	2	4	
Corporate governance	3	4	12	

Figure 3.5.6   The Systems Prioritization Matrix (SPM): three worked examples

For *process* industries (ranging from petrochemicals to electricity generators), relatively long and stable production runs mean that quality is well controlled. Risks associated with damaging people or the environment through spillages and/or explosions must be uppermost in the minds of senior managers.

Within the *services* sector, the ephemeral nature of the product means that the quality and motivation of staff at the point of delivery to the clients are absolutely critical. Clients' needs and well-being have to be top priority.

Conclusion

Standardization can be highly beneficial for whole economic sectors and individual organizations, creating new markets for certified organizations while excluding others. Well-written standards embody best current management practice, and in many cases they show the way forward by describing 'next' practice. Well-managed organizations tend naturally to adopt many of the requirements listed within standards. The perennial challenge for executives and their senior managers is to focus on their strategic priorities and channel finite resources to achieve sustainability.

Errol Taylor is Business Development Director, The Royal Society for the Prevention of Accidents.

www.rospa.com

Corporate social responsibility and assurance

Lucy Candlin, Future Perfect Ltd

All companies want good performance – both financial and, increasingly, in relation to their reputation – and to be trusted. But what do you mean by good performance and how do you ensure that you achieve it? The secret is a combination of good planning – knowing what you want to achieve and how you aim to achieve it – and a quality approach to assurance – monitoring whether you are following the requirements of plans and processes and doing the right things in order to enhance performance and protect reputation. Assurance is a key element of good corporate governance.

What is assurance?

Assurance is the process by which an organization satisfies itself (and others) that it is doing what it intended to do. An essential part of good corporate governance, the assurance process comprises many different tools and approaches, including review, verification and validation, internal audit, external audit, sign-off gateways, and certification. For people with a finance management background, many of these tools will be familiar.

In the context of corporate social responsibility (CSR), assurance is most commonly known in relation to public reporting of CSR performance. (Non-financial reporting can encompass CSR or sustainability, or one or more of their subsets: environmental, health and safety, community, social etc.) However, its application extends to include the certification of management systems, quality control of internal monitoring, and information about plans and performance, systematic checks on performance in relation to business principles/ ethics or activities on the ground, supply chain management, approval mechanisms for developing and implementing projects/products/services, and so on.

External assurance over disclosure of company performance should complement and validate the internal assurance processes undertaken by a company, and which are aimed at getting things right first time and providing appropriate high-quality management of its significant risks and of the management information upon which decisions may be made.

It should be noted that not all significant risks for a company have an immediate (and high) financial impact; risks to reputation and brand, etc, can be acquired over time through lack of action (as well as immediately through poorly judged action) and may be hard to quantify, yet have an enormous impact on a company's ability to do business.

Information and report assurance

For many organizations, a key part of developing their reputation is to enhance the perceptions of people through telling the outside world what the company stands for and how it is performing; so perhaps it is not surprising that CSR and sustainability initiatives have gone hand in hand with communication and reporting on social, environmental and economic impacts and the difference the organization is making. However, the nature and quality of public reports/disclosures vary enormously, so how does an external reader know what to make of them; whether to believe them, and how to respond to the information provided?

The purpose of external non-financial report assurance is to help the report's audience (stakeholders in the organization) make that judgement. The concept is borrowed from financial auditing. Historically, as shareholders became less directly involved in the running of a company, they commissioned someone else (the auditor) to look at the report and accounts and provide an opinion to them directly. Financial auditing has turned into a very complex art, and one that has not been without its own challenges in recent years.

The current practice of assurance for non-financial reports is very confusing and there is much debate about various approaches, elements and the meanings and value of different levels of assurance. There are no generally accepted standards and principles for non-financial report assurance, although AA1000AS (the standard for accountability) is becoming more accepted, and the principles of ISO 19011 (the standard for management systems audits) can be applied to some extent. In addition, companies have very different motives for commissioning external assurance, and their tolerance of qualified opinions (which are the norm for this stage of development of non-financial reporting) is variable.

Some assurance statements are very short, some long and detailed. Some conform to AA1000AS, while some struggle with standards designed for financial reporting. Even those operating to the same standard can produce very different results depending on the approach taken by the assurance provider. And in all this, it is currently unusual to find much input from the stakeholders to whom reports are directed.

So, while it was perhaps useful to borrow from the world of financial auditing, this may not necessarily be the best foundation. Financial auditing is a very technical discipline, and one that relies primarily on the fact that money can be readily quantified. However, social impacts, such as how well a local community has been consulted about a development proposed in its area, or even environmental impacts, such as the level of biodiversity, are not so readily quantified. Bearing this in mind, how can a company achieve the same level of credibility through external analysis of its non-financial reports?

Different companies use different approaches; some self-certify their own reports. One common approach to gaining credibility has been to seek the opinion of credible people, perhaps from NGOs. Some reports therefore include short statements from those whom the audience, hopefully, already respects. The reasoning is that if the 'celebrity' or 'guru' thinks well of the company, so can the audience. But this approach is somewhat limited, as such opinions are not often founded on a systematic review of the company and its report. Also, the 'celebrity' or 'guru' may be valued only amongst a limited audience or may be perceived to represent an organization that is itself not particularly accountable.

Another approach similar to that used in financial reporting is to commission a technical review by an external, impartial organization. While such reviews follow systematic processes, they may not point out omissions (that is, what the report is not covering) – although they should.

So, what would the ideal assurance of a non-financial report look like? Ideally it should answer three key questions in order to provide stakeholders with confidence:

- Are the things in the report right?
- Are the right things in the report?
- Are the underlying performance management and reporting systems sufficiently robust (including the internal assurance mechanisms) to be able to place reliance upon them?

The answer to the first question about correctness requires some technical knowledge of the issues being reported as well as how the organization manages itself to deal with its issues – for example, through certified performance management systems, integration with mainstream business and risk management mechanisms, and quality-controlled information management processes. This may also include review of a company's stakeholder engagement, including the witnessing of dialogue as it is executed by the company – assuming that dialogue is taking place.

However, knowing that the statements within a report are correct may be of little value unless the things being reported are the significant ones. But how do you answer the second question, which relates to the materiality of issues and the scope of disclosures? Without reference to stakeholders this cannot be adequately done. To determine whether the right things are in a report requires an understanding of what is material to stakeholders. This should not, of course, in any way replace the stakeholder engagement that a company will have had; but it raises questions that may need to be confronted in a practical way by both the company and the external assurance provider – for example:

- To what extent should the report (and the assurance) cover issues raised by every stakeholder?

- Does the company understand the difference between material accuracy and material issues coverage?
- Does the company understand the difference between high-level assurance and lower, or reasonable levels, of assurance?

Lastly, the assurance provider needs to be able to identify and evaluate the company's internal performance management, reporting and assurance mechanisms in order to determine whether reliance can be placed upon the systems and controls in place. In other words, will the assurance provider have to do a full depth and breadth, detailed evaluation of information and data – or can they rely on internal assurance mechanisms sufficiently to be able to undertake a risk assessment and focus their efforts in those areas of high business and/or high reporting risk?

In part, the last question is also determined by the level of assurance being sought. Where the degree of certainty over accuracy and material issues coverage required is high, then either more work will be required or very robust internal controls need to be in place. Where the requirement is geared to the level of 'reasonable', a limitation on scope of work may be acceptable, provided that the material (to stakeholders) issues have been disclosed.

Levels of assurance

There is as much debate over levels of assurance as there is ignorance of the meaning of the term. Simplistically, assurance may be provided at a high level, at a 'reasonable' level or at a low level. In the technical sense the difference relates to the breadth and depth of the scope of work and testing undertaken to provide assurance, and the degree of influence that the company has in selecting the areas for interview/testing, etc. This is as true for data accuracy as it is for issues materiality. For the former, the testing is likely to be internal to the company; for the latter, testing is likely to extend to examining the views of stakeholders on the company's performance and reporting, and researching the areas of concern for both the relevant industrial sector and the company.

A key question for companies is what level of assurance is appropriate. For example, for climate change-related data, a high level of assurance may be required where the information will be used to support applications for a tax rebate or for credits in an emissions trading scheme. For other non-financial information, a reasonable or lower level of assurance may be more appropriate.

However, the question still remains – is it as important to get a high level of assurance concerning data accuracy as it is to get a high level of assurance concerning the completeness of the report and the inclusion of all material issues? The answer to this will depend on the function of the disclosure and who the primary audience will be. However, the level of confidence that stakeholders will have in public disclosures is likely to be that much greater where they are involved in the process, particularly in relation to what is of importance to them (ie what is material).

Summary

- Assurance is part of good corporate governance.
- The process of assurance is both an internal and an external process.

■ The process of assurance uses a number of different tools and mechanisms.
■ The process of assurance should look at internal systems and controls; people's actual behaviours in the context of company codes; policies and principles; and performance reporting (internal and external), etc.
■ Internal and external assurance should include the perspectives of stakeholders and take account of their concerns.
■ The level of assurance sought will depend upon the nature and use of the performance being assured.

Lucy Candlin (Future Perfect Ltd)
Tel: 020 7237 9986
E-mail: lucy.candlin@fpsustainability.com

ACCA is the largest and fastest-growing international accountancy body. Over 320,000 students and members in 160 countries are served by more than 70 staffed offices and other centres. ACCA's mission is to work in the public interest to provide quality professional opportunities to people of ability and application, to promote the highest ethical and governance standards and to be a leader in the development of the accountancy profession.

ACCA has promoted greater transparency in the reporting of organisations' social and environmental impacts for over a decade. ACCA is involved in reporting awards in more than 20 countries throughout Europe, Africa, North America and the Asia Pacific region. In addition, we participate in a number of influential organisations including the Global Reporting Initiative (GRI). In recognition of our UK social and environmental issues programme, we have been awarded a Queen's Award for Sustainable Development. ACCA issue a free quarterly web-based newsletter, *Accounting & Sustainability*, providing a comprehensive guide on developments in accounting and sustainable development.

Further information on ACCA is available on ACCA's website, **www.accaglobal.com/sustainability**

London Registrars Ltd

Quick, comprehensive business support from a personable, friendly team

Do you know the Data Protection Act and Health and Safety requirements? Can an Environmental Policy help your business? Are your contracts of employment adequate? Are you starting a new company or too busy to complete your annual return?

We deal with the administrative tasks necessary for you to comply with the law, allowing you to concentrate on your business aims. Our friendly, down to earth team of legal and accountancy consultants are ready to help, with years of company experience behind them.

As an internet based company we can offer our services extremely cost effectively and we are also available for consultation by phone and in person. Our website gives you basic information about your legal requirements and we provide a free email 'surgery' to establish your needs.

For a business to be successful it is important to demonstrate its commitment to staff, customers and society. Health and safety standards and procedures can help avoid accidents and work related ill-health. A sound environmental policy can save money, satisfy increasingly demanding customers and promote good public relations. Comprehensive contracts of employment can help avoid misunderstandings, disputes and potentially disastrous litigation.

In most cases you need do little more than fill out a straightforward questionnaire for us to draw up your required policy statements or contracts. We can also advise on how you could improve and add value to your business.

Our services include company incorporation, registered office, company secretary, annual return completion, debt recovery, health and safety policy, VAT registration, environmental policy, contracts of employment, data protection act registration and solvent company dissolution. All fees are listed on our website, **www.london-registrars.co.uk** For more information please contact Peter Driver: peter@london-registrars.co.uk
Tel: 0870 766 8407 Fax: 020 7404 1373.

4

Marketing and consumption

Marketing and consumption: introduction

Mark Fairbrass, Beacon Press

Some say that the only business of business is business. King Canute would have been proud of them. In the real world, it's a point of view that's being constantly challenged by consumers (and those other ubiquitous stakeholders) who increasingly believe that industry and commerce should do more to face up to their social responsibilities. Our legislators in London and Brussels, not to mention special-interest pressure groups, are also tightening the screws.

Not surprisingly, most of the wealth of advice, encouragement and cajoling on offer from a growing army of environmental communications consultants is directed at business. That's all to the good, because when it comes to changing public attitudes – to the environment, for instance – the commercial endorsement is usually a far more attractive persuader than any amount of 'education and persuasion' from government, pressure groups or a distrusted media. In my view, business – with its direct daily links to the consumer, many of these links being in the home and high street – is the major influence on changing public perceptions, attitudes and behaviour.

Much of the increased public awareness of health messages was sparked in the 1970s when food manufacturers and health educationists overcame many of their mutual suspicions and joined together in mutually beneficial promotions directed at the consumer. The same process can work for the environment through a powerful chain reaction. Suppose that a company has a green message and realizes the promotional benefits of communicating it. By so doing, it informs and educates the consumer, encourages relevant stakeholders, gains goodwill from environmentalists and even, perhaps, holds unwanted legislation at bay.

Whatever the reason, pragmatic or otherwise, the cause of green consumerism is promoted and the environment wins. After all, you can't have too much awareness. Even the humble claim that the cereal packet is made from recycled cardboard goes to the heart of sustainability itself by indicating the need to husband our resources.

Of course, companies must be able to substantiate their claims. There is an expert and valuable environmental lobby at work which, rightly, is on the lookout for 'greenwash'. This is why third-party external endorsement of these claims (through accreditation to ISO 14001 or formal links with special-interest groups like the Forest Stewardship Council, for instance) is so important to provide objective evaluation and favourable consumer perception of a company's commitment.

In my view, this is no time for any company to be hiding its green light, no matter how dim, under a bushel. Comprehensively committing yourself to the strategic importance and commercial value of promoting the environmental dimension of your business has become good commercial sense.

Incidentally, this applies as much to small and medium-sized enterprises (SMEs) as international corporations. As Jonathon Porritt has pointed out, many smaller companies shy away from the idea that they have any meaningful environmental impact, or a duty to tackle it, and in so doing they miss out on some juicy business opportunities.

Mark Fairbrass is Chairman of Beacon Press.

Marketing and consumption: legal overview

Kathryn Mylrea, Simmons & Simmons

Sustainable consumption is one of the fastest-developing themes in the sustainability framework. The UK Government has committed itself to 'encourage and promote the development of a ten year framework of programmes… to accelerate the shift towards sustainable consumption and production'. In September 2003 the UK Department for Environment, Food and Rural Affairs (DEFRA) issued *Changing Patterns*, setting out a broad framework of programmes designed to break the link between economic growth and environmental pollution. It also issued a consultation paper on 'decoupling indicators' of sustainable consumption and production to assess the progress in breaking the link.

At European level, integrated product policy (IPP) was first debated in 1998, and September 2003 saw the Commission releasing a Communication to the Council and the European Parliament on IPP: 'Building on Environmental Life-Cycle Thinking'. The Communication outlines the strategy for reducing the environmental impact caused by products, and implementation actions include 'IPP Regular Meetings' with member states, countries from the European Economic Area and stakeholders. A pilot product exercise is also planned.

® FAIRTRADE

Guarantees a **better deal** for Third World Producers

THE FAIRTRADE MARK MEANS PRODUCTS ARE CERTIFIED TO INTERNATIONAL FAIRTRADE STANDARDS.

ASK YOUR SUPPLIER FOR PRODUCTS THAT CARRY THE FAIRTRADE MARK, OR VISIT OUR WEBSITE FOR MORE DETAILS.

www.fairtrade.org.uk

Brand integrity in the sustainable enterprise

Ian Bretman, Fairtrade Foundation

The increasing attention given to sustainability issues, whether by investors, consumers or wider society through government and the media, creates a new set of challenges for brand management.

There are almost as many approaches to branding as there are brand names in the market, and it is not the intention of this chapter to try to summarize them; but the trend for brands to be more than just a marketing tool is undeniable. The contemporary brand is increasingly the framework, usually defined through a set of explicit or implicit values through which relationships within and outside the organization are managed in order for the organization to pursue its mission. It therefore defines the way that people think and feel about your company and its products or services. Indeed, Richard Branson says that 'It is feelings – and feelings alone – that account for the success of the Virgin brand in all its myriad forms.'

In an increasingly busy and complex world in which we all have more choice than ever, but less time in which to exercise it, we usually rely on our feelings to summarize what we feel about a particular product from among the hundreds available to us. Those feelings might be suggested through advertising (think Volvo and safety, or Volkswagen and reliability), but advertising is effective only if it reflects people's experience of the brand. In other words, your brand is what a customer thinks about you at least as much as the image you try to convey, and so branding is, more than anything, about establishing and retaining the trust of consumers in your company. It's that trust that enables Virgin to sell us everything from flights to mobile phones and from cars to drinks; and it's trust that has enabled Tesco to be more than just a grocer and to take over 12 per cent of all retail spending in Britain. Rita Clifton, Chair of Interbrand, has said that 'Public relations for brands will succeed only if they are based on the brand promise and the internal reality of the company. People have become increasingly sceptical, and in a 24-hour news culture, organizations have nowhere to hide, either inside or outside.'

If people trust you and your brand, then they clearly have expectations of you – and these are in a different realm from the expectations they have of your core business, which you can identify, evaluate and measure your performance against. If you're taking the trouble to read this book, then you probably aim to meet or, more likely, exceed those expectations. But how do you know what people expect of you in terms of sustainability? And how can you ensure that – at the very least – your company is not associated with practices that if exposed, now or in the future, could result in damage to your brand?

This is the question that has tended to be the starting point for most corporate social responsibility (CSR) initiatives. As a first step, scrutiny of internal policies and operations is essential, but in today's business environment, in which companies outsource many of their non-core activities, consideration of supply chains is also important, as companies can also be held accountable for the activities of their suppliers. This is far more complex, especially when production is outsourced to developing countries. Even in Britain, where there is a regulatory framework for employment conditions, we have seen incidents like the deaths in February 2004 of 18 Chinese workers while picking cockles in Morecambe Bay.

Companies have responded to the need for closer control of supply chain management by developing codes of conduct for their own operations and those of their suppliers. In Britain the Ethical Trading Initiative (ETI) was set up in 1998 as an alliance of companies, NGOs and trade unions to share learning on the implementation of codes relating to working conditions across corporate supply chains. The ETI Base Code provides a template of minimum provisions based on the established conventions of the International Labour Organization covering areas such as the avoidance of forced, bonded or child labour, freedom of association, safe working conditions, limits on working hours, the payment of living wages and the avoidance of discrimination and harsh treatment. Thirty-seven companies are currently members of ETI, including the market leaders in food, clothing and houseware retailing, many of their largest suppliers and a number of leading international brands such as Levi Strauss, Gap and Chiquita.

Although work in this area is at an early stage and there is still a great deal to do, the Base Code has enabled companies to identify areas of good practice and those that need to be improved. It has also taken place quietly and with little communication to consumers as companies recognize that they are working towards the expectations of the market. Companies that aim for excellence in their business relationships are therefore looking at how they manage the impact of their business on issues such as human rights and the environment in a way that will exceed society's expectations of them. To quote Rita Clifton of Interbrand again, 'Corporate social responsibility should be about genuinely solving problems, not just about brand reputation management.'

So, in addition to implementing ethical sourcing across their supply chain, many companies are also offering their customers the chance to buy products certified by the FAIR-TRADE Mark, an independent certification label awarded by the Fairtrade Foundation, one of 18 such initiatives operating across Europe, North America, Japan and Mexico – and currently being formed in Australia and New Zealand. Fairtrade standards aim to improve the position of marginalized and disadvantaged farmers and workers in the developing world, and to help them compete more effectively in international markets. Crucially, Fairtrade products mean that the producers have been paid a sustainable price for their products, a price that includes a premium for investment in social or economic improvements. The Mark was launched in the UK in 1994 and is currently available on over 500 retail products made with or from tea, coffee, cocoa, sugar, honey, and a wide range of fruits. Companies that do not trade in these products directly are also getting involved by sourcing their catering supplies as Fairtrade certified as part of their wider CSR policies.

Sales of Fairtrade products have been rising by 40 per cent a year over the past four years and hit an annual rate of £100 million at the end of 2003 as more and more consumers become aware of the Mark – 39 per cent of the UK population, according to a MORI survey in May 2004. The same survey also found that 86 per cent of people who buy Fairtrade products rate the independent guarantee offered by the FAIRTRADE Mark as either 'very' or 'quite' important. Yet some companies are wary of using an external label, preferring to rely on consumer trust in their own brand, although the success of companies such as Cafédirect, Clipper, Green & Black's and Percol, which have built strong brand reputations in their own right through a long association with the FAIRTRADE Mark, demonstrates that these concerns are misplaced.

The Fairtrade Foundation's experience over the past 10 years suggests that an increasing number of companies would like to do more to promote sustainable development because they see it as a better way of doing business for its own sake, and not just to respond to consumer interest. There is therefore a further challenge in securing the sustainability of this process itself and to ensure that, in an increasingly sceptical world, we do not promise more than we can deliver in the pursuit of marketing advantage. In this respect, independent, standards-based certification labels such as the FAIRTRADE Mark can be a valuable tool for brand integrity.

The virtuous circle

It is in the enlightened self-interest of the business community to, in partnership with government, governmental agencies and non-governmental organisations, lead and promote the delivery of sustainable development values. For sustainable development read quality of life. For quality of life read doing things better now and into the future than we have in the past and thereby securing quality of life for today's and tomorrow's society.

To understand better where we want to get to is a good starting point. There is a choice. Society can adopt an ostrich like attitude to the challenges that confront us and bury its head in the sand. That is the unsustainable route to social meltdown. Or we can demonstrate our intelligence and select an alternative route – the sustainable route. Fundamentally, this has to be much more than a top down and seemingly remote governmental political aspiration. It needs to be something people want. However, public "buy in" will only be achieved if the alternative route is understood. It isn't at the moment.

In a "vision" of the alternative route we will utilise resources better, moving away from our current culture of production, consumption and disposal. We will properly account and pay for the costs of our actions and the choices we make. We will use energy differently. What we do use will come from renewable sources. We will live in environments that create thriving communities in which benefits are widely inclusive. Where we live will have quality in design, quality of build, and will encourage and stimulate biodiversity. We will travel differently – with our needs to travel changed by technological advances that impact on both the home and workplace. When we do travel, the choice will be between efficient and effective public transport and our own, non-fossil fuel powered vehicle, if we care to have one.

To get from where we are to where this vision is will need new and innovative products. New markets are already emerging and as they grow and others follow, they will need to be fed by new supply chains. An already visible example is the rush to wind power, a huge investment programme that needs engineering, manufacturing and support services input. Equally, the multi-billion pound rebuild of our towns and cities is another example and, slowly, the emergence of non-fossil fuelled vehicles is another. Together, these and other examples add up to probably the biggest and fastest growing opportunity that has ever been encountered by the business community. If widespread public buy-in to the sustainable development vision, supported by appropriate political frameworks, policies and procurement activity, impacted on market demands as it could, the supply needs from the business community would be enormous.

It is, therefore, in the business interest to promote the sustainable development agenda. There is an immediate snag though. Currently, the trust the public has in the business community in general is low, just one degree above the trust it has in politicians! That is why the Corporate Responsibility (CR) agenda, within the context of sustainable development aspirations, is so important. CR gives business a 'licence to operate' and will be increasingly important in delivering against ever increasing stakeholder expectations. It is, therefore, imperative that the business community wins public trust. It also needs to demonstrate it can itself perform to high standards of sustainable development. Only when it does these things in its own enlightened self-interest can it take a leading role in promoting change.

David Middleton
CEO
Business Council for Sustainable Development-UK

BUSINESS COUNCIL FOR SUSTAINABLE DEVELOPMENT UNITED KINGDOM

The affiliated branch in the UK of the World Business Council for Sustainable Development (WBCSD).

A multi-sectored business group exploring the business opportunities in sustainable development.

 Translating sustainable development from aspirational concepts into projects delivered by the business community with demonstrable sustainability outcomes.

 Providing cross-sectoral networking and exchange of experience and knowledge, a signposting connection service and links to major organisations such as the WBCSD.

 Developing and delivering world leading projects such as, in the field of resource utilisation, the National Industrial Symbiosis Programme.

 Working with national and regional government, regulators, and others to improve the delivery of sustainable development.

 Helping business understand the practical implications of sustainable development and linking it to – risk management, competitiveness, efficiency and corporate responsibility, etc.

 Taking, where possible, the practical experience of BCSD-UK projects into the learning and skills development arena.

 Providing a programme of activity throughout the year including General Meetings, Political Round Table, Annual Dinner, Project related events.

 Regular, globally distributed newsletters providing a platform for news from the BCSD-UK and its members. An active web site – www.bcsd-uk.co.uk

Ethical sourcing in your supply chain

Robert Brown

Ignore your ethical or social responsibilities at your peril. This chapter is designed to give a rough overview and some initial pointers to how companies can begin to manage these issues.

Ethical sourcing, social accountability, ethical trading, triple bottom line...

Think of the terms 'ethical sourcing', 'social accountability' and 'triple bottom line' and their relevance to your organization, and you could be forgiven for being confused already. These and similar phrases within the arena of corporate social responsibility (CSR) are increasing in number almost on a weekly basis, it seems!

However, this perceived confusion does not mean they can be ignored. A company wishing to manage its social responsibilities must work through the fog to develop its own approach.

In this chapter I hope I can highlight some of the reasons why ethical sourcing is an important aspect of any organization's operations, and the benefits and pitfalls involved. I also want to share some experiences on ways to prevent reinvention of the 'ethical sourcing' wheel.

OK, so what definition from those listed is the right one and which one should your organization work to? In essence, what you call it is up to you; it does not really matter that much as long as your organization fully understands your definition, its implications and the way in which it is managed. For the purpose and duration of this chapter, I will refer to ethical sourcing, which, to adopt a broad definition, is 'the inclusion of explicit social, ethical and/or environmental criteria into supply chain management policies, procedures and programmes'.

There are a number of misconceptions associated with ethical sourcing. Let's have a look at some of these first.

Ethical sourcing has no effect on my operations?

Wrong. We, as consumers, are demanding more and more; we desire increased levels of innovation and we want more choice and better performance, all at the cheapest possible price. To meet these requirements, organizations are having to utilize materials, ingredients and manufacturing operations from outside their conventional areas of trading. As a consequence, pressure is increasing not only on the traditional features of a supplier relationship such as quality, but also on other aspects of the relationship such as treatment of workers in an organization's supply chain.

Basic human right contraventions can arise anywhere in the world. Examples can be found daily in newspapers and on the internet and elsewhere. Contraventions include the use of child labour, unsafe working conditions, poor rates of pay and lack of worker representation.

Pressure for action on this issue is only from minority groups?

Wrong. Ethical sourcing is no longer just the domain of selected non-governmental organizations (NGOs). Consumers, shareholders, the media, investment managers and pension funds, among others, all want to be sure that the products, ingredients and their investments are being managed in an ethical manner. Nowadays, an individual with a home computer and knowledge of website development can have an influence on an organization if he or she presents a strong message that may impact upon the marketplace.

There is no benefit to ethical sourcing...

Wrong. There is an ever-growing body of evidence highlighting a strong link between responsible ethical sourcing, sustainable business and financial performance. As always, bad news such as that associated with sweatshop labour and collapses of organizations owing to poor corporate governance dominates the headlines. These examples highlight the potential for brand erosion if the risks are not managed. There are, however, examples that argue for the benefits of ensuring that workers in the supply chain are treated in an ethical manner.

The benefits for organizations can include the following, among others:

- ■ a more stable share price, supporting the opportunities for sustainable investment;
- ■ stronger relationships with suppliers;
- ■ increased awareness and proactive understanding of risks and opportunities;
- ■ increased productivity – more motivated staff;
- ■ process improvements and cost reductions;
- ■ a positive corporate image.

A well-known high street bank is a recent example. It adopted a strong ethical stance by setting defined policies regardless of any potential financial gain. In 2002 the bank reported that this stance meant that it turned down business that would have been worth £4.4 million over five years. However, in doing so, its ethical stance more than offset the lost deals, helping to gain about £30 million in new business. These actions highlight the fact there is an appetite among ordinary consumers to engage with ethically minded organizations.

Another example of the increased benefits for all from adopting ethical sourcing principles is the growth in the market for fair-trade products. A generic definition of fair trade is 'an alternative approach to conventional international trade. It is a trading partnership that aims at sustainable development for excluded and disadvantaged producers. It seeks to do this by providing better trading conditions, by awareness-raising and by campaigning.'

It has a slightly different approach from that in the above examples in that it applies to products rather than companies. Its aims are to give disadvantaged small producers more control over their own lives. It addresses the injustice of low prices by guaranteeing that producers receive fair terms of trade and fair prices – however unfair the conventional market is.

In the United Kingdom the fair-trade market topped £100 million in 2003, which resulted from the 250 or so products on offer, ranging from coffee to flowers. It has been estimated that consumers in the United Kingdom spend £3.17 every second on fair-trade products.

I hope that you can now see the benefits of ethical sourcing, or, at the very least, can see that businesses cannot afford to ignore ethical sourcing issues. So, how does a business wishing to source ethically begin?

Supply chains are often complex and ever-changing. As an example, take one UK leading health and beauty retailer:

- ■ It has 30,000 product lines.
- ■ It has 8,000 cosmetics and toiletry lines.
- ■ Every day 6 products change (on average).
- ■ It has 5,000 suppliers.
- ■ It uses 5,500 raw materials.
- ■ It uses 15,000 packaging components per year.

It is impossible to cover every aspect in one attempt. Every company needs to adopt a strategy that suits it. However, it must reflect meaningful elements of the supply chain, while being robust enough to withstand scrutiny. There is a wide variety of help and guidance available from bodies such as consultancies, auditing companies, trade unions and NGOs.

The list in the next section provides an initial checklist as to how a business can begin to tackle ethical sourcing. By answering each of the questions and completing the actions listed in the next section, a company will go a long way towards managing its responsibilities.

What does ethical sourcing mean to your organization and what are the risks and opportunities?

■ Develop and agree a strategy and processes to identify the scope and delivery of the commitments, bearing in mind the potential risks and benefits to your organization.
■ Gain support from the highest possible level.
■ Identify a senior champion with accountability and responsibility for ethical sourcing.
■ Embed processes into current business and key decision-making practices.
■ Act upon issues arising within defined timescales.
■ Identify and develop partnerships to support your business (and your supply chain) and avoid reinvention of the ethical sourcing wheel.
■ Share learning and experience (positive and negative).
■ Develop and implement an ethical sourcing policy or code of conduct for your organization. Live its principles throughout your business operations.

There are also some relevant organizations that have been in existence for several years. I highlight here just two of these, which lead the way in tackling and influencing the ethical sourcing debates. Information is taken from their respective websites: www.ethicaltrade. org and www.cepaa.org.

The Ethical Trading Initiative

The Ethical Trading Initiative (ETI) is an alliance of companies, NGOs and trade unions. It exists to promote and improve the implementation of corporate codes of practice that cover supply chain working conditions. Its ultimate goal is to ensure that the working conditions of workers producing for the UK market meet or exceed international labour standards.

Underpinning all this work is the ETI Base Code and the accompanying Principles of Implementation. The Base Code contains nine clauses, which reflect the most relevant international standards with respect to labour practices. The Principles of Implementation set out general principles governing the implementation of the Base Code.

The Base Code and Principles of Implementation have two related functions: they provide a basic philosophy or platform from which ETI identifies and develops good practice; and they provide a generic standard for company performance. The labour standards incorporated in the Base Code constitute a minimum requirement for any organization.

The ETI Base Code is as follows:

1. Employment is freely chosen.
2. Freedom of association and the right to collective bargaining are respected.
3. Working conditions are safe and hygienic.
4. Child labour shall not be used.
5. Living wages are paid.
6. Working hours are not excessive.
7. No discrimination is practised.

8.   Regular employment is provided.
9.   No harsh or inhumane treatment is allowed.

The ETI works on a continuous improvement basis. It will not certify or accredit suppliers, factories, companies or products.

Social Accountability International

Social Accountability International (SAI) works to improve workplaces and combat sweatshops through the expansion and further development of the currently operative international workplace standard, SA 8000, and its associated verification system.

SAI is a United States-based non-profit organization dedicated to the development, implementation and oversight of voluntary verifiable social accountability standards. SAI is committed to ensuring that standards and the systems for verifying compliance with such standards are highly reputable and publicly accessible. To accomplish this, SAI:

■   convenes key stakeholders to develop consensus-based voluntary standards;
■   accredits qualified organizations to verify compliance;
■   promotes understanding and encourages implementation of such standards worldwide.

SAI's social accountability system approach is based on transparency, credibility and verification.

Companies that operate production facilities can seek to have individual facilities certified to SA 8000 through audits by one of the accredited certification bodies. The SA 8000 system became fully operational in 1998, and there are now certified facilities in 30 countries on 5 continents and across 22 industries.

In summary, engaging in ethical sourcing for any organization is not easy, nor is there one answer that fits all cases. However, there is help available. Ethical sourcing need not be a necessary evil for an organization, but can in fact become an intrinsic part of the business decision process, one that helps to realize real benefits for organizations and the millions of workers operating in the global supply chain.

Robert Brown works as a Sustainable Development Manager for Boots the Chemist. His key area of expertise is the management of environmental and ethical impacts within the supply chain. He can be contacted directly at the following e-mail address: Robert.Brown@boots.co.uk.

Green labelling

Nick Cliffe, Forest Stewardship Council

More and more products now carry information about their environmental profile, whether it's regarding their potential for recycling, the lack of toxic substances used in their manufacture or how the impact of their production on the environment is less than that of other, competitor products. Though it is useful to consumers, there is not yet much legal requirement to provide this information, so why are so many companies seeking to offer this kind of information to consumers? There are several reasons why you may wish to make a green claim about your company's products:

- To inform consumers of the environmental benefits of your product. Consumer interest in environmental issues is increasing, and the percentage of consumers who weigh the environmental cost of what they buy is growing steadily.
- Environmental labels are a useful tool for demonstrating your corporate social responsibility to customers, partners and other regulators.
- They help raise awareness of issues that are important to your sector.
- They help to improve product standards, and keeping a careful eye on the environmental profile of your product range may help you to avoid problems as new environmental legislation or labelling requirements are introduced.

There are two ways to make an environmental claim: it can be self-declared or done via an existing environmental labelling or declaration scheme.

Self-declared environmental claims

A self-declared environmental claim is considered to be any statement, symbol or graphic that refers to any environmental aspect of a product, component of a product or packaging. Such a claim can appear on the product or packaging itself, or on any associated marketing materials.

Before considering making such a claim, you should establish whether your product is the subject of legal labelling requirements. These are not common, but there are some – such as the European Energy Label (see page 139). Mandatory requirements also exist for the food and drink and the pharmaceutical sectors, and where necessary you should seek detailed advice from the appropriate trade association or your local Trading Standards Officer. For more information, see www.tradingstandards.gov.uk.

There are two references that should guide the process of making self-declared environmental claims in the United Kingdom: *ISO 14021* (developed by the International Organization for Standardization) and the *Green Claims Code* (published by the Department of Environment, Food and Rural Affairs (DEFRA) and the Department of Trade and Industry (DTI)). The Green Claims Code is a user-friendly introduction to ISO 14021 and provides guidance on best practice. Copies can be obtained from DEFRA. DEFRA also publishes specific guidance for several sectors, such as growing media, greetings cards, decorative coatings, cleaning products and aerosols. For more information, see www.defra.gov.uk/environment/consumerprod.

Generally speaking, there are three things you need to take account of when making a self-declared environmental claim:

- content;
- presentation;
- assurance of accuracy.

Content

Any claim should be accurate and truthful. Avoid making claims that, while true, are not particularly relevant. Don't make multiple claims about one environmental benefit of the product using different wordings. You should also ensure that any claim is relevant to that particular product. Do not, for example, make a claim about the packaging of a product that might be interpreted as being a claim about the product itself. A misinterpretation of this kind is often possible when the Möbius loop (see page 137) is used to indicate recycled content or recyclability. It is also important to ensure that you regularly review any claim you are making to ensure it is still accurate.

Your claim should also be specific and unambiguous. Descriptions such as 'environmentally friendly' are essentially meaningless, and claims such as this have, in the past, discredited green claims. You should state a specific benefit (such as the absence of a previously used toxic substance in the product) or make a clear positive comparison with alternatives to the product. Note that when making comparisons it is important to have hard data to back up your claims.

Presentation

Once you have developed a claim that is accurate, relevant and unambiguous, it is important to present it clearly. Avoid using small print or language that may exaggerate the nature of the claim. Remember too that many consumers may lack in-depth knowledge of technical terms, so use plain English wherever possible.

A common way to communicate information is graphically through the use of symbols or icons. If you decide to do this, make sure the meaning is clear, and add supporting statements if required.

Accuracy

When you are making a self-declared environmental claim, there is no need to seek third-party verification, but you must be able to substantiate the claim and provide this supporting information to anyone who requests it. Bear in mind that a false claim could result in prosecution by trading standards authorities. Ensure that any claim you make has been tested and verified. Also, be wary of making a claim that may require you to reveal sensitive commercial information if you are asked to verify its accuracy.

Always keep appropriate records of testing, as this is particularly important if you are making a comparative claim, especially against a competitor product. In this instance you may wish to consider getting an independent organization to carry out the work. You should keep all information relevant to a claim for the entire lifetime of the product.

The alternative to making a self-declared environmental claim is another method of demonstrating the environmental benefits of your products – using existing labelling schemes that offer independent, third-party verification. The next section looks at these.

Existing labelling schemes

There are many benefits to using existing labelling schemes. Most obviously, they provide a ready-made system, thus saving you time in quantifying the environmental costs inherent to your particular business. By researching and selecting a suitable and respected labelling system that already exists for your sector, you in effect receive a ready-made checklist to ensure that your product meets a suitable environmental standard. The certification process will most likely take care of all requirements related to accuracy and verification, and regular audits will ensure that your claim is always up to date.

Many of these schemes also offer you pre-existing consumer awareness. Some carry out a great deal of direct marketing to customers, both business and consumer, informing them directly of the environmental benefits of products that meet their criteria. The scheme may also offer you free entry in catalogues or websites that list products certified under the scheme. Some schemes may even host trade and consumer shows where you can promote your products directly to target markets, and have a system for developing market linkages, thereby helping you find new markets for your products.

These schemes provide independent assurance for your customers. Most are operated on a not-for-profit basis and so are viewed as more trustworthy than a commercial concern. Some are even endorsed by major environmental charities, such as Greenpeace, Friends of the Earth and WWF.

A reverse benefit of such schemes is that they can assist in your own purchasing: many of these schemes operate a chain-of-custody system to track goods from source to consumer. By seeking suppliers already certified under a particular scheme, you can become another link in the chain, providing you with a ready-made buyer's specification.

But bear in mind that most of these schemes will carry a cost, both in terms of adjusting your operations to meet the criteria and for any auditing that gaining certification entails. You should explore the costs of becoming certified under any scheme carefully, and where there are several relevant schemes (or auditors that offer the same form of certification), compare costs.

There are many existing labelling schemes. Some are sector or issue-specific, whereas others are more general. In all cases you should select the scheme that offers the best fit with your company activity. When you have selected a scheme, the first step is to contact those running it and ascertain what the procedure is for gaining the use of the mark. In many cases this will require an independent audit and also changes to your systems and supply chains, so careful planning and budgeting are strongly advised. Note also that many schemes may require you to use accredited certifiers for auditing, in which case it's important to shop around to get the best deal.

In addition to gaining use of an appropriate mark, you may also need to consider communicating to your customers what the mark is and what it represents.

Möbius loop

The Möbius loop is used throughout the world to denote goods that are either recyclable or contain recycled content. It is both the most widely used and most widely recognized of green labels. There are many versions of the logo in use, but they all share the same basic structure of three arrows (representing the three stages of recycling: collection, reprocessing and resale). Where a percentage appears within the loop, it indicates the percentage of recycled content. If no percentage appears, this indicates that the product itself is recyclable. Full guidelines on the use of the loop are given in ISO 14020.

EU Ecolabel

The European Ecolabel is an official EU mark awarded to products with the highest environmental performance in the marketplace. The system was developed by the European Commission and is managed in the United Kingdom by DEFRA. The environmental impact of the product throughout its entire life cycle must be assessed and independently certified in order to use the mark. There are currently 21 product groups covered by the system, as shown in Figure 4.5.1. For more information, see www.defra.gov.uk/environment/consumerprod/ecolabel/index and www.europa.eu.int/comm/environment/ecolabel.

Green Dot (der Grüne Punkt)

The Green Dot is a system for packaging that indicates that the company has paid a financial contribution to a packaging recovery company within the country of origin. It is not currently in operation within the United Kingdom, which instead has packaging regulations based on a system of Packaging Waste Recovery Notes (PRNs). The system is used within many EU states, including Austria, Belgium, France, Germany, the Republic of Ireland,

Textiles	Paper (copying and graphic)	Paper (tissue)
All-purpose cleaners	Soil improvers	Footwear
Personal computers	Portable computers	Televisions
Refrigerators	Tourist accommodation	Mattresses
Detergents (dishwashers)	Detergents (laundry)	Detergents (hand washing)
Indoor paint and varnish	Hard floor coverings	Washing machines
Light bulbs	Dishwashers	Vacuum cleaners

Figure 4.5.1 Product groups covered by the European Ecolabel

Luxembourg, Portugal, Spain and Sweden. If your company operates in these countries, your operation may be eligible for participation in the scheme. For more information, see www.green-dot.com.

Fairtrade

The FAIRTRADE mark on a product demonstrates that the product has met the international Fairtrade standards, which guarantee that producers in developing countries receive a fair price that covers costs and provides a premium for producers to invest in their communities: clean water, healthcare, education and the environment.

The FAIRTRADE mark is widely recognized, and consumer demand for Fairtrade products is growing. In addition, the mark is being heavily promoted by participating companies as well as the Fairtrade organization itself. Currently, the majority of Fairtrade products are food or beverages, but this is beginning to change, and any company sourcing materials from developing countries can apply to use the mark. For more information, see www.fairtrade.org.uk.

Marine Stewardship Council

The Marine Stewardship Council certifies products of fishing, based on an internationally recognized environmental standard for well-managed fisheries. For more information, see www.msc.org.

Forest Stewardship Council

The Forest Stewardship Council operates a system for the certification of well-managed woodlands according to strict environmental, social and economic standards. There is also a chain-of-custody system for tracking timber from these forests to final products. Certification is carried out by independent, third-party auditors, and if the appropriate standard is met, the FSC logo may be shown on-product. Certification is available for all timber and timber fibre products, including paper and recycled timber. For more information, see www.fsc-uk.org.

Leaf Marque

The Leaf Marque system operates on the basis of linking the environment and farming. Products carrying the Leaf Marque are produced by farmers who have demonstrated their commitment to improving the environment for the benefit of both wildlife and the countryside. For more information, see www.leafmarque.com.

Organic food (various)

There are many labels that indicate that a food product is organically produced. Organic farming in Europe is governed by EC regulation 2092/1991 and requires certification by an accredited organization. Within the United Kingdom, the body responsible for implementing this is the United Kingdom Register of Organic Food Standards (UKROFS). This body accredits independent organizations to inspect and certify farms and other producers and their products as organic.

There are many such independent organizations within the United Kingdom. A full list is available from DEFRA at www.defra.gov.uk/farm/organic.

Energy

There are several schemes applicable to electronic appliances and their energy profile.

European Energy Label

All European manufacturers and retailers are required by law to inform consumers of the energy efficiency of many types of appliances, particularly white goods. The European Energy Label rates appliances from A (most efficient) to G (least efficient). For more information, see www.mtprog.com.

Energy efficiency recommended

The Energy Saving Trust awards products with high energy efficiency. Various categories of appliance are eligible to be considered for the award, including white goods, light bulbs and fittings, loft insulation, cavity wall insulation and draught-proofing. For more information, see www.saveenergy.co.uk.

Energy Star

Energy Star is a voluntary labelling system that operates across the world. Its use is controlled by an agreement between the United States and the European Union. It indicates that the energy consumption of a product is below an agreed level when in 'stand-by' mode. Various products are eligible for the scheme, including computers, monitors, printers and fax machines. For more information, see www.energystar.gov.

The printing industry is the sixth largest industry in the UK, consuming vast resources of energy and raw materials including many powerful pollutants and possessing the potential to make a substantial negative impact on the environment. And yet it has the least enthusiastic adoption of environmental policies of any major industry.

It was against this background that a small East Sussex-based printing company, Beacon Press, set out to create a centre of environmental excellence within the UK printing industry.

A decade on, and belieing its SME status, Beacon is now acknowledged as one of the greenest companies operating in any sector in the country. Its environmental management programme, fully accredited to IS0 14001 and EMAS, has attracted 24 top UK and international awards, including a Queen's Award for Sustainability.

Beacon's environmental stance – which includes over 100 separate practical initiatives in favour of the environment – has pioneered and inspired the growth of 'green consciousness' within its own industry and attracted international interest.

Significant environmental benefits have been achieved and sustained within the company, especially by establishing a uniquely comprehensive programme of measures to tackle the root causes of environmental degradation within the printing industry – excessive solvent and chemical use, heavy energy consumption, paper and water wastage.

Beacon has adopted an unswerving cultural commitment to sustainability by exploring every avenue open to it to ensure that care for the environment is a key consideration in all the company's work practices, processes and methods of operation.

Much of its work is now directly attributable to its green reputation, with an increasing number of contracts coming from customers seeking to trade with ethically-based companies as part of their desire to create 'green supply chains.'

Beacon believes that this experience clearly shows the compatability of successful environmental management and commercial success.

Beacon Press, Bellbrook Park, Uckfield, East Sussex TN22 1PL
Telephone: 01825 768611   Fax: 01825 768042
Email: print@beaconpress.co.uk   www.beaconpress.co.uk

Founded in 1977, Calverts is a one-stop communications design and printing company. It is 100% employee-owned, and serves client organisations across the private, public and voluntary sectors.

A socially responsible firm and a class leader in sustainable design and print, Calverts holds the GreenMark and Inner City 100 awards, and is a level B1 signatory to the London Green Procurement Code.

Calverts works with agencies, consultancies and end-user clients to improve the social and environmental impacts of their print communications.

Services
- Professional graphic and publications design
- Illustration, photography, editing and copywriting
- Reprographics
- High quality colour litho printing
- Wide format and digital printing
- Full range of print finishes and binding styles
- Print mailing and UK or worldwide distribution
- Free samples, dummies and advice service

Products
- Newsletters and magazines
- Catalogues and brochures
- Flyers, leaflets and posters
- Business stationery
- Folders, packs and binders
- Display and point-of-sale materials
- Annual reports and books
- Full range of recycled and FSC accredited papers

Calverts environmental statement, client list and portfolio are available at www.calverts.coop

Calverts
9-10 The Oval, London E2 9DT
T: 020 7739 1474
F: 020 7739 0881
E: info@calverts.coop
www.calverts.coop

Calverts North Star Press Ltd is registered under the Industrial & Provident Societies Act 1965, Reg No 21946R

TREES DIRECT

TOTTERTON FARMHOUSE, LYDBURY NORTH, SHROPSHIRE SY7 8AN
Tel: 01588 680280   Fax: 01588 680696
Email: info@treesdirect.co.uk   Web:www.treesdirect.co.uk

It is now widely recognised that a good reputation, born of acting ethically in Trees Direct was born in 1998. We loved trees and were aware of the damage being done to the environment. Five years on we are proud to say that we are still growing and branching out.

Our aim is to encourage people to send trees as gifts. Trees can help to relieve the effect of carbon emissions and at the same time bring beauty, lasting pleasure and remembrance.

We feel we have done well in the private sector with more and more people of all ages responding as awareness grows. Our thanks go to the many environmentally aware magazines and newspapers which have backed us from the outset.

There have also been several innovative companies who have used us for promotions and Christmas gifts for clients. We sent out a thousand trees for one company as a form of advertising for their product. This is something that could be tried by businesses as a way of demonstrating their belief in the environment and a willingness to show awareness and a more forward thinking approach in helping to combat pollution.

Many more businesses, big and small could work in this way. We at Trees Direct are making a special thrust into the corporate gift market, and are happy to work with companies wishing to take a more ethical and environmental approach. We are able to advise what would be the best choice relative to the business, sending trees and shrubs with the logo and cards of the company and working round the budget of the company concerned.

By working together and thinking about the future, companies have a real and affordable opportunity to arrest some of the damage done in the name of progress while being viable and successful with a image of awareness and thought for the future.

Remember, send a tree and be remembered.

All our trees are sent potted, dressed in a hessian sack, tied with green garden string, message card and planting instructions.

FUTERRA

FUTERRA is a small but very dynamic communications consultancy. We work with business, NGOs, national and local government on the communication of social and environmental issues.

FUTERRA conducts training, dialogue and facilitation, provides consultancy and strategy, and sometimes plain and simple advice on how to communicate better. The calling card of the company is its "10 Rules of Sustainable Communication", a set of rules that FUTERRA uses in its own work. The Rules advocate a positive approach which makes people feel good about themselves and their ability to act.

Past clients of FUTERRA include BT, DEFRA, IDEA, the Ethical Tea Partnership, London Sustainability Exchange, the Department of Culture, Media and Sport, the New Opportunities Fund, and UNEP. FUTERRA has also initiated its own projects where it has felt that a problem exists, where more understanding is needed or where poor communication has caused problems.

The company has undergone a rapid expansion in the last year. FUTERRA's team now numbers nine people and continues to grow. Operating from a small and buzzing office in Brixton, South London, the team uses its increasing knowledge and experience for innovative projects. Most recently FUTERRA has been asked to write the UK's national strategy for government communications on climate change. In this, as with many projects, the team have been made to challenge their own assumptions about what will make a difference. This challenge is what makes FUTERRA tick.

We are a co-owned company and make decisions collectively about who to work with and what is important for us. However, we are always excited to hear about ideas for new projects and collaborations in all kinds of areas.

Our skills include:
- Training and Workshops
- Stakeholder Dialogue
- Facilitation
- Brokering Partnerships
- Media management and campaigns
- Running events, presentations and launches
- Qualitative research and surveys
- Corporate Responsibility Strategy
- Making films
- Creating games

FUTERRA
Shakespeare Business Centre
245a Coldharbour Lane
London SW9 8RR
T 020 7733 6363
E soli@futerra.org

'Talking the Walk'
Getting your message across

Why should you spend your time and energy trying to promote your efforts as a sustainable enterprise?

For large corporates who have embraced the sustainable development and corporate responsibility agenda there is a clear business case for communication, reputation and risk management. However, when your activities are unlikely to make it on to the front page of the *Financial Times*, other reasons must be found. I have learnt a lot from the multinationals we often work with – but as a small business entrepreneur myself, I know that our business is different. Different business models still make a big contribution to society. I hope you're not surprised to hear that small and medium sized businesses in the UK on average make an annual social contribution to the value of £3bn – almost 10 times that of larger companies. You are already likely to be practising corporate social responsibility, sustainable business practices and responsible enterprise, but as a business perhaps you just call it 'good business sense'.

So how do we advise companies to communicate or promote what is just good practice?

A very simple communication formula is to address the what, why, who, when and how!

What are you communicating?

Why are you communicating it, and to whom?

When will you do it and how?

These are all bread and butter questions for the professional communications industry.

What?
Are you 'doing' corporate social responsibility (CSR)? Companies of our size rarely even use the term 'CSR' and consider CSR-related activities to be an add-on and not an integral part of the business. 2001 research reveals that only one in six medium-sized businesses have any form of community or social policy, despite the fact that 84% of these businesses have discussed this type of issue in the last year.[1] We're doing it, we just don't use the jargon.

A report produced on behalf of the DTI entitled *Engaging SMEs in Community and Social Issues* said that while larger companies tend to be motivated by external factors, the most important part of any activity in

---

[1] Mazars Neville Russell research (2001) *Trends in corporate social responsibility among mid-corporates* [Available online] – http://www.bcconnections.org.uk/MazarsSurvey.pdf

smaller companies tends to be internally focused. "Staff are often the motivation, the catalyst and the focus of the activity and communication, and are also seen as the key beneficiaries."[2]

If you are going to communicate what you do as a sustainable enterprise you must first know what it is that you do! Review your commitments and audit your procedures/policies. Be clear about what you understand sustainable enterprise to be and what you are/should be doing to meet your own commitments.

Moral: As the Greeks used to say, 'know thyself', and work out what you want to say.

Why and Who?
Why should you talk about your efforts as a sustainable enterprise? Well, if the business case holds true, communicating your morals, values and honest reputation can never be a bad thing. If your main driver is to motivate and stimulate employees, it is important to ensure that you share with them what is on offer. Equally, your initiatives will never achieve the goal of improving your reputation or customer satisfaction if no one knows what you do.

According to the *Engaging SMEs in Community and Social Issues* survey:

> *Some [Small and Medium-sized Enterprises] communicated to large business customers because they had to, but the key communication was to employees. The quantitative research showed there is a lot of communication with employees (89% do), but it drops dramatically for external audiences, although over half of those with external shareholders do communicate to that audience as well. After that, SMEs are most likely to involve and inform customers and suppliers, with only 30% saying they have communicated at all with either government (central or local) or the media (trade, local or national).*

Moral: Be clear about *whom* you want to talk to – and *why*…don't waste your efforts.

When and How?
When should you do it? Do it now – start the dialogue and be transparent! Make it timely and appropriate.

Communications analysts Mantra and the specialist auditing consultancy Issues Analysis have undertaken a survey to compare the sustainable

---

[2] *Engaging SMEs in Community and Social Issues* February 2002 [Available online] *http://www.bitc.org.uk/docs/SMEs_1.pdf*

enterprise activities of small and large firms. The survey showed that 20% of smaller companies do not promote their socially responsible practices at all, and 50% say that they do it, but only in a limited way. You might want to talk about what you do, but are too busy doing it!

Before coming to the bit where I tell you HOW to communicate I need to attach a note or two of caution. Not all businesses are the same – they are all different shapes and sizes and their reasons for being are many and varied. There is no one way or language to use, and how you go about telling everyone what are you are doing will depend greatly on the 'why' and 'what', as well as your available resources, target audience and desired response.

Below is a list of ideas to get you started:

1. Ask yourself: "What are we actually doing?"
2. Make sure your communications match your needs – there's no point writing some big report if you want to reach your employees.
3. Use your social networks – talk with your family and friends. Let them know what you are doing and how it benefits your business as well as society. They can be your cheerleaders.
4. Start up a dialogue with the people immediately around you – local community, customers, suppliers etc. Make your dialogue two-way – that way you can learn from those people and improve your chances of benefiting financially too.
5. Market not only 'what' you do, i.e. your product/service offering, but also 'how' you do it, e.g. in a socially responsible way.
6. Use the local media to promote your involvement in local community activities.
7. Use the Internet – publish your CSR commitments on your website and network online with potential customers and other stakeholders.

My final moral – make any communications match your business.

Solitaire Townsend M.A, M.Prof. is co-founder and Managing Director of FUTERRA, the specialist sustainability communications company. Solitaire is a member of the United Nations Advisory Group on Advertising and Sustainable Development, the Institute of Public Relations Steering Group on Corporate Social Responsibility and the Forum for the Future Steering Group on Marketing and Sustainable Development.

strong language

Powerful communications for lasting change

Strong Language is a sustainable marketing consultancy combining leading edge branding, communications and design expertise with first hand knowledge of the opportunities of sustainability.

Building on past lives in brand consultancy, IT, journalism, NGO campaigning, and central and local government, the Strong Language team has a unique insight into the potential of a sustainable marketing approach.

To clients new to the issues, we offer up to the minute, insider knowledge of the debate, to create more sustainable products, services, and brands, benefiting society whilst maximizing competitive advantage.

And to clients already tackling challenges such as waste, transport, regeneration, and consumption, we bring the latest blue chip marketing techniques, fresh thinking and an all-important sense of humour.

Sustainable marketing is about change. It's about doing things better by doing things differently. So our work draws on the latest organisational change practices, particularly complexity theory and systems thinking. We have no formula, no rules, and no assumption that there is a 'right' way to do sustainable marketing. There are no easy answers. But we are working with clients to find out just how exciting, sexy, fun, meaningful and lucrative sustainable marketing can be.

Contact Esther Maughan, New Business Director

- Email: **esther.maughan@strong-language.co.uk**
- Telephone: **01237 470 143**

to find out more about our sustainable approach to the following services:

> Brand development
> Corporate social responsibility and business planning
> Graphic and website design
> Copywriting
> Public relations
> Events management
> Internal communications
> Training

Or sign up for our regular e-newsletter at **www.strong-language.co.uk**

Sustainable marketing: Crockerton's case study

So, as Tina Turner might have asked, what's marketing got to do with it? It's easy to see the benefits of sustainability to operations, HR, or finance, but marketing's role to date has been largely reactive, often limited to publishing environmental and social reports and rebuffing the accusations of greenwash that can follow.

Clearly sustainable development has a lot to gain from harnessing the creativity of business's greatest communicators. But what's in it for them? A marketing approach that rigorously explores its environmental and social impacts offers access to the growing number of ethical consumers looking beyond the label and putting their money where their values are. According to the Co-operative Bank's report 'Who are the ethical consumers?', ethical concerns are backed by over £8bn of UK consumers' money, a figure that chimes with findings by the Social Market Foundation that nearly one fifth of consumers are willing to pay more for ethical products and services.

But even if you take such surveys with a pinch of salt, it's clear that many of society's current preoccupations fall naturally under the sustainable development banner. If marketing is about understanding and responding to customer needs, emerging trends such as work/life balance, downshifting from city to country, stress, health and wellbeing and customization over mass production demonstrate how much consumers need sustainable responses from the marketing community.

And there's no greater preoccupation than food. From rising levels of obesity to GM and the state of British farming, what we eat has become a flash point for sustainable development as ethical concerns about organic food, animal welfare and farmers' livelihoods combine with personal concerns about our health. As a small indicator of a much larger trend, 2003 sales of products with the Fair Trade mark totalled over £92m, up 46% on 2002, and the great British public eat a third of a million Fairtrade bananas every day.

Crockerton's (www.crockertons.co.uk) is one food company already making the most of a sustainable marketing approach, assisted by specialist consultancy Strong Language. Based in Cardiff with plans for major expansion, Crockerton's is a delicatessen café and outside catering brand offering high quality local food in a relaxed, continental style. Sourcing a range of products from local Welsh producers and others who share the same responsible values further afield, Crockerton's offers some key insights for marketers wanting to adopt a sustainable marketing approach.

- **The sustainable message is not always enough**

As everyone knows, wearing your heart on your sleeve can lead to tears before bedtime. Crockerton's has developed a communications strategy which encompasses, but is not limited to, its sustainable ethos, under the brand positioning of 'Nouveau Welsh'. Tapping in to the wider renewal of Welsh identity, Crockerton's contemporary tone of voice (or rather voices, since everything's in Welsh and English) couldn't be further away from the wheedling, hair shirt guilt trips of the stereotypical greenie. Or the dragons and black chimney hats of olde Wales. With messages focused on product quality as well as lifestyle experience, Crockerton's has become a cool 'find' for Cardiff's hippest crowd, for whom sustainability comes second to fashionability.

- **Keep it mainstream (the niche market will find you anyway)**

The key to all good marketing is to keep it accessible. Whilst there is undoubtedly a growing niche market purchasing with their values first, deliberately alienating the mainstream would be fool-hardy. By opening outlets in funky areas such as Caroline Street, Cardiff's famous 'Chip Alley' takeaway mecca, Crockerton's has guaranteed high visibility and attracted customers beyond its natural constituencies of foodies and ethical consumers.

And it's a win win situation. Selling six packs to rugby fans on match day may seem surprising for an upmarket Welsh deli, but the greater the mass appeal, the more the business thrives to pass on benefits to its local suppliers and beyond into the community. The fans may even come back for some organic antipasti.

• Look good, do better

As fashion brands such as Howie's demonstrate, just because you're saving the world doesn't mean you can't wear a great Tshirt. Green marketing has traditionally relied on a hackneyed image bank of trees, globes and smiley children, a visual approach which now bores the committed and is simply ignored by the mainstream. In contrast, Crockerton's has created a modern brand identity centred around Snap, its funky crocodile icon, and its contemporary colour palette of red, black and ivory is consistently applied across signage and packaging to create maximum stand out. Even the furniture is on brand, made by local craftsman out of wood from a sustainable forest, but to a highly contemporary design.

• Tell the truth

Few marketers would admit they ever bend the truth, even slightly. But recent Food Standards Agency research suggests that the use of misleading words and phrases such as 'fresh', 'pure', 'natural', 'traditional', 'original', 'authentic', 'home-made' and 'farmhouse' are rife on packaging claims, and all sectors have their equivalent grey areas.

Crockerton's freely admits that, despite erroneous press claims, it's not a totally organic operation and not all its food is locally sourced (anyone seen a Welsh olive?) Admitting that you don't have all the answers may be an unsettling experience, but it's also a liberating one as it allows you to experiment creatively with new approaches. Then even Tina Turner might agree that you're 'simply the best'.

5

Waste and recycling

fones4safety

where recycling mobile phones can help save lives

fones4safety is an innovative "community safety mobile phone recycling scheme" providing businesses the opportunity to recycle their old mobile phones and simultaneously help protect the more vulnerable members of our communities.

Donated phones are reconfigured into personal safety alarms with instant access to 999 (Emergency Services) at the touch of a button. The phones also receive incoming calls for reassurance and are provided free of charge to 'at risk' individuals, such as victims of crime and harassment and those living in fear of crime, particularly domestic violence victims. Other vulnerable beneficiaries include the elderly, sick and disabled. Phones which cannot be re-used are responsibly recycled.

fones4safety presents an ideal opportunity for companies to "green" their waste disposal options of potentially hazardous waste and to engage staff in corporate social and environmental programmes. Organisations interested in donating old company or personal mobile phones can take advantage of the bulk collection service provided by fones4safety or use the FREEPOST facility for individual or small mobile phone donations.

The success of fones4safety is based on its strong partnership comprising CRISP (project co-ordinators) along with the London Metropolitan Police, Victim Support Southwark, and Shields Environmental (who operate Fonebak, the world's first national mobile phone recycling scheme compliant with current and forthcoming environmental legislation). Other major supporters to date include Southwark Council, Credit Suisse First Boston, T-Mobile and Media Strategy with seed funding provided by the government's Single Regeneration Budget (SRB) through the London Development Agency and Elephant Links Partnership.

Since its Launch by Harriet Harman QC MP in March 2003, fones4safety has been piloted in the Elephant and Castle in the London borough of Southwark and has continued to gather public support. It has also gained recognition as a best practice example of cross sector partnerships delivering social and environmental benefits.

The initiative is currently being expanded across London and the UK to support other areas of need and demand. To be a part of the growing network of organisations benefiting from and supporting fones4safety, please contact **Aterah Nusrat at CRISP on 020 7740 6533, e-mail aterah@crispej.org.uk** or **Debbie Belsham of Fonebak on 01708 683432.**

fones4safety

Donate Your Old Mobile Phone

to help protect vulnerable people

~ Donated mobile phones are reconfigured into personal safety alarms ~
Call 020 77406533 for business collections or send your old phone to:
CRISP, FREEPOST LON15948, LONDON SE17 1BR
A partnership scheme part funded by the London Development Agency

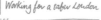

SEVERNSIDE
R E C Y C L I N G

 Complete Recycling and Waste Management Solutions

 Nationwide Coverage through Local Facilities

 Commitment to Invest in Recycling and Customer Care

 Quality Assured Service

 Fully Comprehensive Materials Recycling Audit of all sites

 Confidential data Collection and Destruction

Some of the UK's premier brands and well known organisations already benefit form our environmental approach to waste management, as well as thousands of local and regional businesse To find out how we can help your business contact our dedicated customer care team on ......

0800 7 831 83

You, Us and The Environment

click **www.severnside.com**
email **complete.services@severnside.com**

INVESTOR IN PEOPLE

Waste and recycling: introduction

Alistair Lamont, President, Chartered Institution of Wastes Management, 2004–05

All businesses produce waste. In the United Kingdom we're used to getting rid of it cheaply, and it's often an accepted or unnoticed cost. Now things are changing. The times ahead will be challenging for waste producers and waste managers alike.

The Chartered Institution of Wastes Management recognizes the new pressures on waste producers, and as its President I am delighted to present this introductory chapter to Part 5 of the book. I consider this part of the book, on waste and recycling, to be the most vital in this practitioners' guide.

Materials and energy costs are rising, and new EU waste law will make us all rethink what we use up and throw out. Traditional ways of managing our waste will be squeezed: we must recycle much more, recover energy from waste, landfill less or pre-process what we do send to landfill. The alternatives will cost more than we are used to – and capacity may lag behind demand for some waste treatment technologies in the medium term. Even where landfill remains acceptable, prices will rise. Landfill is the dominant and cheapest option in the United Kingdom at £10–£20 per tonne, plus tax, but in Ireland it already costs over £100 per tonne, plus tax, and rising.

More businesses will have to wake up to enhanced waste responsibilities. Many will have their wastes reclassified as 'Hazardous' in June 2005 – affecting nearly every business, large or small. Others will pick up 'extended producer responsibilities' for their products, such as cars, all manner of electrical goods and batteries. Any business taking corporate sustainable responsibility seriously will have to re-examine its practices and the skills of those of its employees who produce or manage its wastes.

If you're not already anticipating increased costs and more complex compliance with waste law – you will be. The next few years will bring a real waste wake-up call.

Waste and recycling: legal overview

Kathryn Mylrea, Simmons & Simmons

Waste management is an area that affects most businesses and that is highly affected by legislation. In many cases the laws can be difficult to apply. Much of the UK legislation and policy is derived from European legislation and case law, whose objective is to ensure that waste does not cause harm to health or the environment. The cost of waste disposal has increased significantly in recent years and can be expected to continue to increase in coming years.

Precisely what constitutes 'waste' for the purposes of the legislation can often be a difficult question, and an assumption that because something has economic value to someone else it is not waste would not be consistent with the legal position. There are several types of legislative requirement in the waste sector, some of the most notable being as follows:

- Waste permitting.
- Landfill tax, payable per tonne of waste deposited for disposal in a landfill, has been in place for several years, and government is committed to its remaining and continuing to increase.
- The United Kingdom is also in the process of implementing the requirements of the Landfill Directive. This has had serious ramifications for the use of landfill as a waste

management option since July 2004, especially for hazardous waste, and will require the achievement of very significant reductions in the amount of biodegradable municipal waste going to landfill.

■ The duty of care as respects waste has been a very successful provision of the Environmental Protection Act 1990, requiring all those in the waste-handling stream to do what is reasonable in the circumstances to ensure that waste is properly and lawfully handled.

■ 'Producer responsibility' legislation requires producers of waste materials to ensure levels of recycling or recovery. Packaging waste and waste electrical and electronic equipment are good examples of this.

It couldn't be easier to donate towards Scope's vital work and it's FREE!

Scope is a national disability charity. Scope's services include creating early years, education, housing and employment opportunities for people with cerebral palsy, a physical condition that affects movement. One of the ways we raise money for these services is through recycling mobile phones and toners.

How does the environment benefit?

You can minimise damage to the environment and raise money for Scope. With the lack of available landfill site and the chemicals and metals from waste seeping into the ground; it is becoming increasingly important to recycle.

- Every year four million used toner cartridges, both toner and inkjet, end up in landfill sites.
- Research suggests that there are over 40 million mobile phone users in the UK today, and an average user has at least one redundant mobile phone. Most of these phones are likely to end up in landfill when they become obsolete or damaged.

How does Scope benefit?

Just two inkjet cartridges could pay for an adapted can opener. Simple alterations to kitchen utensils can really give disabled people greater freedom by helping them to cook for themselves. Can you imagine not even being able to open a tin of soup?

And four mobile phones could pay for a starter word book, packed with brightly coloured illustrations, to help children begin to learn words and their meanings.

How do the schemes work?

Both the toner and mobile phone recycling schemes are incredibly simple and will not cost your office a penny. All you need to do is place a recycling box in your office and once it is full, call the number on the side of the box. It will be collected and replaced.

Simply call **020 7619 7105** to order your box or find out more!

*Scope also accepts chargers, mobile phone batteries. Scope shops can also accept phone and toner donations and there is a freepost address for smaller collections.

Waste management

Jon Foreman, Environment Agency

Throwing away waste costs the British economy at least £3 billion a year, and that cost is going to rise over the next few years. Every business creates waste, but many businesses have demonstrated that huge savings can be made by managing it better. Good management practices are also important to make sure you keep within the law, which is changing rapidly.

The expensive waste mountain

Businesses in England and Wales produce over 75 million tonnes of industrial and commercial waste a year, nearly three times as much as people put in their domestic rubbish bins. In some cases this is literally money (or at least value) down the drain. It is certainly a terrible waste of resources. Many companies have found that they can cut the amount of wasted materials by changing production practices, and can often reuse or sell waste that they currently pay contractors to take away.

That all adds up to lower costs, even before savings on waste disposal – which are going to become more significant. Most industrial and commercial waste is buried in landfill sites, but the cost of landfill is set to rise. The landfill tax in 2004 is £15 per tonne for general waste, but it is likely to rise over the coming years to £35 per tonne as a further incentive for businesses to reduce waste volumes. Under new regulations, waste will also have to pass waste acceptance procedures, and some will need pre-treatment before it can be landfilled, again adding to disposal costs.

Legal hazards

Currently, around 5 million tonnes of hazardous waste is generated each year in England and Wales, and disposal of this material is now being controlled more rigorously. The EU Landfill Directive bans (from July 2004) the previous practice of mixing hazardous and non-hazardous wastes. This will dramatically reduce the number of commercial landfill sites in the United Kingdom suitable for hazardous waste, from over 200 to less than a dozen. And these sites are not evenly distributed around the country: there are unlikely to be any in Wales or near London.

More waste will be classified as hazardous under new regulations that broaden the definition to include items previously discarded routinely, such as cars, fluorescent lighting tubes, computers and batteries. New controls will also require tighter monitoring of hazardous waste producers, and the separation of hazardous materials from other wastes.

Around 30,000 manufacturers and retailers will be subject to a new regulatory regime for electrical goods, which is due to come into force in stages from 2004 to 2006. The Waste Electrical and Electronic Equipment (WEEE) Directive covers more or less anything with a plug or battery, and is likely to be incorporated into UK law in 2005. Its purpose is to reduce the amount of electrical equipment that is just thrown away by promoting separate collection, introducing higher treatment standards and setting recycling targets.

For many manufacturers, the greatest challenge may come from related legislation restricting the use of certain hazardous substances (RoHS) in electrical and electronic equipment. Many companies will need to redesign their components or products before the July 2006 deadline in order to meet the agreed levels for the specified substances, which include heavy metals such as lead and cadmium and certain flame-retardant chemicals.

What should business do?

Businesses need to look closely at waste management practices and improve them to make sure they are not wasting money, and to meet the new regulations. Here are some key steps:

Check compliance

Make sure you know what is expected of you in respect of waste management. All producers and 'holders' of waste are subject to a legal duty of care. Waste is essentially anything you get rid of, so even if something is going to be recycled, the duty of care will still apply.

Every business should be able to answer these questions arising from this legal obligation:

■ How much waste do you produce and what kind of waste is it?
■ Is it stored safely?
■ Is it transferred to an 'authorized person' (eg someone registered with the Environment Agency)?
■ How is it managed after it leaves your premises?

Guidance on basic regulatory obligations is set out sector by sector on the NetRegs website, www.netregs.gov.uk. To find out more, refer to the Environment Agency's new guide,

Getting Your Site Right (available via the Environment Agency's customer service line, 08708 506 506). If you are in any doubt, seek independent advice.

Get free advice to help save money

All businesses can reduce either the amount of or the hazardous properties of the waste they produce, and recover value through recycling. The first step is to undertake a thorough waste management review. The Government's Envirowise programme offers small businesses a free 'Fastrack' waste minimization audit to get you started.

Envirowise also offers free and confidential advice on any environmental issues, including legislation. Its Environment and Energy Helpline is on Freephone 0800 585794, or information can be obtained via its website, www.envirowise.gov.uk.

Support your local community

Getting to grips with waste management can help enhance your image both locally and with your customers, while improving the local environment.

Increasing disposal costs may lead to an increase in fly-tipping, which can become a serious problem if action is not taken. By working with local communities, businesses can help put a stop to unlawful activities and at the same time improve their local environment.

Work with your suppliers

Work with suppliers to reduce waste and improve the recycling and reuse of materials. Working together will promote the exchange of best practice and shared solutions, so when you meet suppliers, consider sharing advice and guidance on waste management and minimization. Envirowise provides specific guidance in this area.

What is the Environment Agency doing?

The Environment Agency is responsible for implementing legislation to meet environmental objectives in the most effective way, as well as helping to develop new approaches. Our work includes:

- Regulating waste and environmental legislation to ensure a level playing field for waste producers.
- Influencing and working with government and other partners to develop policy and practice that promote sustainable waste management.
- Working with industry to minimize the amount of waste produced by installations regulated under the Pollution Prevention and Control regime.
- Running national campaigns to work with industry to develop solutions on key waste issues such as hazardous waste, tyres, construction waste and oils.
- Tackling fly-tipping, and helping to set up a new national fly-tipping database so that we know where illegal activity takes place. In partnership with local authorities we can then target enforcement activities.
- Publishing detailed waste production information on our website to help you to benchmark your performance on waste minimization against that of similar companies.

Where to find out more

The following websites will give you information on all aspects of waste management and regulations.

- Environment Agency – information on regulatory requirements, environmental information, tools and publications to help you to understand and meet environmental obligations: www.environment-agency.gov.uk.
- Netregs – offers small businesses clear regulatory and good practice advice on environmental issues tailored for their industry sector: www.netregs.gov.uk.
- Envirowise – for free advice and support on waste minimization techniques: www.envirowise.gov.uk.
- Department of Trade and Industry (DTI) – advice and information on producer responsibility initiatives, including WEEE and RoHS Directives: www.dti.gov.uk/sustainability/weee.
- Department of Environment, Food and Rural Affairs (Defra) – policy information, including details of government initiatives and consultations on waste management: www.defra.gov.uk/environment/waste/index.htm.
- Mini-Waste Faraday initiative – Mini-Waste is a partnership between industry and the science and technology base whose purpose is to undertake strategic research, training and technology transfer activities. Mini-Waste focuses on industrial waste minimization, particularly from the following sectors: electronics and battery manufacture; food processing; metals and metal finishing; construction; minerals and inorganics: www.mini-waste.com.
- WRAP (Waste and Resources Action Programme) – a not-for-profit company supported by government that works to promote sustainable waste management by creating stable and efficient markets for recycled materials and products: www.wrap.org.uk.
- The DTI Manufacturing Advisory Service – provides an integrated support service to industry in cooperation with the DTI Small Business Service network of business links. Includes assistance on lean manufacturing techniques: www.dti.gov.uk/manufacturing/mas/index.htm.
- Your local authority – for advice on local waste management and recycling services.
- LetsRecycle.com – for information on waste management and recycling services: www.letsrecycle.com/index.jsp.

By Jon Foreman, Industry Codes and Waste Minimization Adviser, Environment Agency. Jon has over 20 years of experience in waste management and regulation. Prior to the formation of the Environment Agency in 1996, he worked for the Hereford and Worcester Waste Regulation Authority and was responsible for the environmental management and regulation of the waste sector. He has specialized in hazardous waste management, and from the early 1990s became involved in industry waste minimization and resource efficiency programmes.

Your Money   ⟶   **Secure Distribution**
+   **+**
ENTRUST   **Effective Regulation**

*Looking for a company that has controlled over £700 Million of funds
through 2700 organisations to manage or regulate your funds?*

ENTRUST, your formula for success.

Dr Malcolm Cooper
mc@entrust.org.uk
0161 972 0044

The Landfill Tax Credit Scheme

Malcolm Cooper, ENTRUST

Introduction

There are many ways of interpreting sustainable development and many initiatives contributing towards the goals. Projects funded by the Landfill Tax Credit Scheme and other government schemes add value to many aspects of sustainable development. This chapter outlines how the scheme works and highlights some of the environmental projects that have benefited from this funding.

Outline of the scheme

The Landfill Tax Credit Scheme (LTCS) is a unique scheme introduced by the Treasury in 1996. It generates private funds innovatively by allowing Landfill Operators to give up a proportion of their tax to be used as credits. These funds must fulfil the requirements of the Landfill Tax Regulations 1996 (as amended in 2000 and 2003), which can be found in composite form in *Tolley's Environmental Taxes Handbook*. The LTCS encourages partnership throughout the United Kingdom and enables the waste industry to provide financial support for a great variety of environmental projects and activities undertaken by local communities. LTCS money provides welcome match funding for government grants and other public funds. It is estimated that LTCS funded projects have attracted an equivalent amount of additional funding from other such sources.

Role of ENTRUST

ENTRUST is the trading name of the Environmental Trust Scheme Regulatory Body, a private not-for-profit organization. ENTRUST regulates the LTCS under terms of approval from HM Customs & Excise, and also regulates and manages other government-funded schemes. The diverse organizations seeking funding under the LTCS either enrol as Environmental Bodies (EBs) direct with ENTRUST, or access funding through an EB, which distributes money and takes on the administration for them. ENTRUST's regulatory role is to scrutinize applications from organizations wishing to enrol as EBs, to register projects and to check that EBs spend their landfill tax money compliantly. ENTRUST also provides guidelines and information to help EBs meet their obligations under the LTCS. The ENTRUST website, www.entrust.org.uk, details advice for LTCS users, the role of the regulator and ENTRUST's other activities. There is also a dedicated website for LTCS users and those interested in the scheme at www.ltcs.org.uk.

To be enrolled by ENTRUST as an EB, an organization must be a not-for-profit corporate body (eg a company limited by guarantee), trust, charity or unincorporated association. It is also important that an EB has appropriate levels of corporate governance, which must be described in a written document such as a memorandum and articles of association, trust deed or constitution. As ENTRUST is charged with enrolling, monitoring and auditing organizations that have enrolled as EBs, ENTRUST provides guidance on these requirements. Another important role of ENTRUST is to provide information on the LTCS, which is done electronically and via newsletters. As there are over 3,000 active EBs, acting at both a local and a national level across the United Kingdom, these activities are quite demanding.

Landfill Tax Regulations

ENTRUST regulates the LTCS by ensuring that contributions from Landfill Operators support projects that fall within defined LTCS objects. These objects are defined in law by the Landfill Tax Regulations, and it is the role of ENTRUST to provide a consistent and fair interpretation of these objects and to monitor and verify project expenditure. The current objects of the Landfill Tax Regulations are categorized in Table 5.4.1.

Clearly, these objects are wide-ranging and include provision of public parks and nature reserves, the reclamation of brownfield sites through to restoration of historic buildings and churches. Biodiversity conservation can also benefit through object DA, introduced in April 2003, which organizations such as the Wildlife Trusts and RSPB use to help implement Biodiversity Action Plans. ENTRUST provides clear and consistent guidance on the boundaries of these objects through a telephone helpline. A strong web presence publicizing online publications such as the *EB Manual* also provides detailed support. The funding for new projects related to objects A, B, D, DA, E and F is expected to continue into the foreseeable future.

Table 5.4.1 Objects of the Landfill Tax Regulations

Object	Category
A	... activities to reclaim, remediate land and to bring it back into social, environmental or economic use. The proposed use must have been prevented or restricted by an activity that has now ceased. If the land was polluted, the polluter of the land must not benefit from the project.
B	... activities to reduce, mitigate or prevent pollution on land where the pollution has been caused by an activity that has now ceased. The polluter of the land must not benefit from the project.
D	... providing and maintaining public amenities and parks. Projects in this category must be located within the vicinity (usually within 10 miles) of a landfill site. The amenity must be open to the public, and not operated with a view to profit.
DA	... where it is for the protection of the environment, the conservation of biological diversity through the provision, conservation, restoration or enhancement of a natural habitat; or the maintenance or recovery of a species in its natural habitat, on land or in water situated in the vicinity of a landfill site (usually within 10 miles).
E	... restoring and repairing buildings and structures that are for religious worship or of architectural or historical interest. This includes work to places of worship for all faiths, ancient monuments and listed buildings. Projects in this category must be located within the vicinity (usually within 10 miles) of a landfill site. The building or structure must be open to the public, and not operated with a view to profit.
F	... the provision of administrative, financial or other similar services to environmental bodies enrolled with ENTRUST.

The Landfill Tax Regulation objects were amended on 1 April 2003, when the two objects in Table 5.4.2 were removed through revised Government legislation.

Although the funding for new projects related to objects C and CC has been halted, the nature of the LTCS is such that they frequently have lifetimes measured in years. Hence there are currently a large number of sustainable and recyclable waste management projects in the process of being delivered. These projects will continue to be monitored and regulated by ENTRUST until they have been completed.

Types and examples of projects

One of the great things about the scheme is that these are local projects for local people, covering local environmental improvements. These projects are delivered on the ground by

Table 5.4.2 Items removed on 1 April 2004 from the Landfill Tax Regulation list of objects

Object	Category
C	... research and education into sustainable waste management

a diverse cross-section of environmental groups ranging from small voluntary organizations (village hall groups, local conservation organizations, community self-help groups etc) to the regional and national charities (the National Trust, groundwork trusts, etc).

A typical example of the sort of community empowerment delivered by small LTCS projects (£5,000–£10,000) is the renovation and restoration of local village hall facilities. The LTCS funds for these projects tend to generate money from other sources. At the other extreme, many large national projects have been delivered. A prime example is the creation of a national cycle network across the United Kingdom, the National Byway, which has been aided by LTCS funding of over £1 million in a variety of projects. This has resulted not only in enhanced green transport links but also in the environmental improvements that go along with this, helping people of all ages and abilities to gain access to the countryside.

A good example of sustainable waste management in action is the Remade Partnerships between local and national governments, development agencies and industry. Here, LTCS funds are used to seed further funding into the development of markets for and products from waste. So successful has this approach been that there are a number of Remade iniatives across the United Kingdom (Remade Scotland, Remade London, etc).

Scheme e-systems and processes

ENTRUST has recently transformed the way it operates. Processes have been streamlined, with the closure of area offices and the introduction of home-based compliance inspectors. A greater proportion of time is now spent in the field, inspecting the projects funded by DEFRA and the devolved assemblies as well as EBs and LTCS projects. At the heart of this change has been a move from a paper-based administration system to electronic systems. This has been facilitated by the digitization of paper records, a process that has resulted in the scanning of some 800,000 documents. Web-based technology is in the process of being introduced, enabling EBs to undertake their own administration over the web since April 2004. This reduces the burden on those that ENTRUST regulates, helping to deliver the vision of a robust regulator with a light touch.

ENTRUST is currently collating Value for Money indicators, enabling the LTCS to be benchmarked against the United Kingdom's 'Quality of Life' sustainability indicators. This will demonstrate the delivery of the LTCS at a national, regional and local level in the areas of biodiversity, environmental improvement and recreational opportunities.

Scheme statistical highlights

One of the roles of ENTRUST, as regulator of the scheme, is to inform on the benefits that it provides. The new e-systems have sharpened information storage in the form of improved database management. All LTCS expenditure and project information can now be readily accessed through these ENTRUST systems. The following are a selection of national LTCS statistical highlights:

■ Over £700 million worth of LTCS funds has been generated.
■ £465 million worth of LTCS funds has been spent on environmental projects across the United Kingdom.

- ∎ £235 million worth of LTCS funds is currently being spent with environmental bodies.
- ∎ LTCS expenditure across different parts of the United Kingdom can be broken down as follows:

  - Northern Ireland, £9.5 million;
  - Wales, £19.7 million;
  - Scotland, £48.7 million;
  - England, £387.4 million.

- ∎ Over 25,000 projects have been registered to benefit for LTCS funding.

Readers may be interested to learn of the activities and environmental projects taking place in their locality – by region, county or local authority area. If you would like any further information, you can email helpline@entrust.org.uk with your request.

Other government scheme funds

ENTRUST is able to offer the skills and experience to manage other funds across the United Kingdom. Currently, such funds are being managed and distributed on behalf of DEFRA, the Scottish Executive, the Welsh Assembly Government and the Northern Ireland Environment and Heritage Service. This work is undertaken competitively as a result of economies of scale, utilizing systems capable of operating both regionally and United Kingdom-wide.

These funds have supported sustainable waste projects covering recycling, education and research and development. To provide some context, the recycling projects cover scrap stores to kerb-side recycling to composting. Educational projects encompass schoolchildren and the general public, through to the employment of waste minimization officers. Research and development projects range from bird control on landfill sites to controlling emissions on landfill sites.

The future

If we reflect on what has been achieved by the LTCS since its introduction, it should be remembered that prior to 1996 nothing of this sort existed, so the scheme is very young. Even so, scheme funds are currently oversubscribed by about three to one. It is gratifying to note that over £700 million worth of funds has been generated for environmental benefit. Looking forwards, here's to the Landfill Tax Credit Scheme becoming a billion-pound scheme!

Malcolm Cooper is Chief Executive Officer, ENTRUST.

www.entrust.org.uk
helpline@entrust.org.uk
www.itcs.org.uk

Recycling

Melanie Tyler-Thomas, Cleanaway Ltd

Where there's muck, there's a real opportunity to improve your bottom line!

The international community generally accepts that 'sustainability' is *ongoing development that meets the needs of the present without compromising the ability of future generations to do the same*. Broadly, this criterion covers four objectives: social, environmental, resource management, economic.

For the waste and environmental services industry, sustainability is an objective to be attained by working with and for its customers and local communities, researching and facilitating ways in which resources can be used and reused more efficiently, as well as minimizing the amount of material that is perceived as 'waste'.

The importance of the industry's contribution to sustainability is twofold. First, society currently consumes around 10 tonnes of raw materials to make just 1 tonne of consumables. Clearly, this pattern cannot be maintained, whether by those who source primary materials, manufacturers, intermediaries or, ultimately, by the world's financial markets. We must change the way we consume, what we consume and how we invest in that pattern of consumption. The solution is to reuse materials and reduce the amount of virgin resources that we expend.

But this is only half the issue. We must also find alternatives to the United Kingdom's traditional gravitation towards landfill as a disposal method – an option that still provides the final resting place for 77 per cent of total waste arisings and an option that is diminishing as we run out of both existing space and viable geological sites that could potentially provide more of that space. While the waste industry can invest in and implement new systems and operations, the responsibility for addressing these issues lies with each social and economic sector of society.

But can sound environmental practice complement running a business or commercial enterprise whose very *raison d'être* is to maximize its profit margin and minimize operating costs? Aren't profits and environmental sustainability mutually exclusive?

The hard drivers for change in the United Kingdom's pattern of consumption and disposal are the combination of new and imminent EU and UK legislation. Challenging waste recovery targets and landfill tax increases will quite simply make landfill disposal a highly expensive option. Each of these issues has the potential to impact on your bottom line.

Urban Mines is a not-for-profit environmental body that specializes in working with the private and public sectors to find practical solutions for resource management issues. It says that it is vitally important that businesses do not ignore the implications of current and upcoming waste legislation. If companies do nothing, their waste disposal bills are *guaranteed* to increase, whereas introducing segregation and recycling systems can potentially reduce medium-term costs. There are tangible monetary benefits to be had by businesses that are prepared to implement waste minimization procedures and increase recycling initiatives.

Although waste minimization will clearly reduce the costs incurred by the collection of general waste and from landfill disposal, opportunities for cost avoidance can best be identified by an external waste manager or consultant, because quite often firms fail to identify for themselves an existing waste stream that can be source segregated. The review that the waste specialist initiates will usually involve undertaking a comprehensive site analysis, examination, mapping and measurement of waste streams as well as advice on potential segregation and disposal methods and a final cost analysis.

Larger corporates that have a proactive segregation system that results in quantities of recyclable materials may even find financial rewards through the 'rebate' – a share of the market price for the clean, bulked recyclables as agreed with the waste handler. These initiatives have proved most successful for the top-end waste producers. The schemes are flexible and can be tailored to meet the individual needs of the customer. For example, the rebate may be offset against the costs of disposal or transportation.

Having a 'greener' conscience can also have an *indirect* impact on a company's bottom line. There is a massive public relations opportunity to enhance the company's community profile and emphasize fundamental social principles to the growing numbers of environmentally conscious consumers. And while, in theory, purchasers buy for both rational and emotional reasons, thanks to a growing awareness of one's environmental impact and responsibility, in 'green' issues rationality and emotions are increasingly linked.

Not surprisingly, waste and sustainability reviews are increasingly in demand. Urban Mines says that, among its private-sector clients, the objectives for a review are, initially, to ensure that they are complying with legal obligations; second, to identify areas where costs can be reduced; and third, related to environmental concerns.

Phil Hesford, Urban Mines' Project Director, says that increasing legislation is driving business towards addressing sustainability and forcing small and medium-sized enterprises (SMEs) to confront environmental issues. In doing so, they are obviously interested in whether doing so can also result in a lower cost base.

But if we are recycling more, at both a commercial and domestic level, how 'sustainable' is the market for recycled end products? Is society merely diverting resources into a business sector that can only ever be a market with a limited number of homogeneous products? Henry Ford – 'any colour so long as it's black' – would be highly amused at the 21st century's market for recycled toilet paper! Can the momentum of green production be maintained or is it short-lived?

In a recent speech, John Gummer MP stated that we, as a society, must move away from 'worthiness' in both the production and the consumption of recycled goods. To maintain the integrity of these goods in a free-market economy, we need to produce high-quality, viable and competitive products.

This opinion is supported by Bill Warnett, Director of Crystal Architectural Products (CAP), a Sheffield-based company that specializes in the manufacture of architectural products from recycled glass. Warnett and his colleagues – all previously holding senior posts in a large waste management company – cite using recycled materials as of prime importance when establishing CAP. Equally important to their business strategy was to build a company that was economically viable without subsidy or grant. This meant that their products had to be competitive with similar traditionally produced goods. (In fact, the quality and innovative features of the 'crystal' paving stones, tiles and cladding, together with the opportunity for the customer to have a bespoke creation, means that the product is priced at a premium compared to some of its alternatives.) Three years on, with a growing clientele, Warnett believes that a majority of CAP's customers buy for look and performance and that the sustainable aspect of the product is a 'nice to have' rather than integral to the choice and purchase.

One of Urban Mines' aspirations is that the consumer will ultimately 'purchase recycled' without realizing it, because the goods themselves will be perceived as indistinguishable in quality and design from the non-recycled alternatives. In order to attain this optimum purchasing position, firms using recyclables as part of their manufacturing operation need the same investment and infrastructure as any other. SMEs using secondary materials as a *raw* material are subject to the same economic criteria. They need investment. They need to have access to, or be located near, raw materials, workforce, land, buildings, plant and transport. They also need the same support services: R&D, IT, marketing.

One solution to meeting these needs is the 'sustainable growth park' (SGP), a unique concept from Urban Mines. This new initiative will combine a materials recovery facility plus reuse and repair centres with business and manufacturing units that will reprocess and recover the materials. Each of these purpose-built business parks will incorporate a Business Innovation and Incubation Centre that will provide opportunities for businesses to explore new markets and develop new ways in which materials can be reprocessed. To assist in this, as far as possible the sites will have links to the R&D facilities of regional universities and environmental organizations.

These parks will increase communities' propensity to sustainability by turning local waste into new or recovered products through encouraging new business and commerce, which in turn will revitalize regional economies and, by regenerating brownfield sites, use the existing workforce, local transport and communications infrastructures.

Waste management companies such as Cleanaway are increasingly acknowledging that their role in a sustainable future is to help develop and coordinate facilities like SGPs, investing in and providing a fully integrated service that will continue to increase society's ability and capacity to reuse and recycle.

Legislation. Research. Investment. Regeneration. Competition. Recovering yesterday's waste will become tomorrow's dynamic business. *That's sustainability!*

Melanie Tyler-Thomas is Marketing Manager, Cleanaway Ltd.

A Brambles Company

Cleanaway – Waste management and recycling

Cleanaway has over 100 years experience in waste management and recycling. The company can trace its history back to the beginning of the twentieth century when it was involved in the transfer of London's waste by barge on the River Thames. Since then, its growing range of operations has turned it into a major waste management company. Operating in 14 countries, it is now a wholly owned subsidiary of leading global support services group Brambles.

Cleanaway is a leader in all aspects of waste management, delivering environmentally responsible solutions around the globe. The company translates this experience into local solutions for resource management, recycling and recovery, treatment and disposal. Services to its 75,000 UK customers include integrated waste management solutions for all types of waste and waste producers, including municipal authorities as well as trade and industry.

The company employs 8,000 staff in the UK, and operates one of the largest collection services for industrial, commercial and trade waste through a specialist fleet of 1,700 vehicles. It also operates the most technologically advanced materials recovery facility, four landfill sites, a 70,000 t.p.a. composting operation, a nationwide network of service centres and a high-temperature hazardous waste incinerator – one of only two in the UK – with an annual capacity of more than 70,000 tonnes.

In addition, Cleanaway has contracts with local authorities to whom it provides a broad range of services covering waste management, recycling, street cleansing, grounds maintenance and a range of ancillary services.

Cleanaway will continue to work with the government, local authorities and business to form partnerships that will deliver legislative objectives, find solutions, and achieve results.

The future for recycled products...

One company which is putting forward an exciting and innovative approach to recycled products which are aimed at businesses, individuals and retailers is Remarkable.

Remarkable, which was set up in 1996 by Edward Douglas Miller, is already a multi award-winning British company which was set up to design and manufacture products made from recycled and sustainable sources.

The ethos behind the company is to produce UK-made products from UK waste materials to show the essence of 'closed loop recycling' in action.

The first product, the Remarkable Pencil, is a standard writing pencil yet it happens to be made from one recycled plastic vending cup.

The pencil writes and sharpens like a traditional pencil, but is recycled and contains no wood (hence also saving trees being cut down in the manufacturing process). The pencil was a winner of Invention of the Year in 1998, Recycled Product of the Year in 1999 and was one of the first accredited Millennium Products – showing that the pencil very quickly captured the imagination of designers, business leaders, individuals and politicians alike.

The pencils are supplied sharpened and printed with either Remarkable's branding or can also be bought personalised, which is ideal for companies which want to show their own environmental credentials through sourcing promotional recycled office products.

Remarkable has since grown its range and is now becoming recognised as a first point of call whenever companies are looking to source recycled products. Bespoke, as well as standard, office products are available and the Remarkable range always makes use of surprising recycled materials and pioneering manufacturing techniques.

Products in the range to date include: pencils made from recycled plastic cups, mouse mats, bookmarks and pencil cases made from recycled car tyres, rulers made from recycled polystyrene packaging, notepads made from 100% recycled paper, pens made from computer printers, mugs made from recycled plastic and much more.

Described by the Design Council as "one of the key innovators in British environmental design", when the company says it is turning junk into something Remarkable, it really is.

Remarkable (Pencils) Ltd
56 Glentham Road
London SW13 9JJ
Contact: Evan Lewis, Director of Marketing & Sales
T: +44 (0) 20 8741 1234   F: +44 (0) 20 8741 7615
E: sales@remarkable.co.uk   W: www.remarkable.co.uk

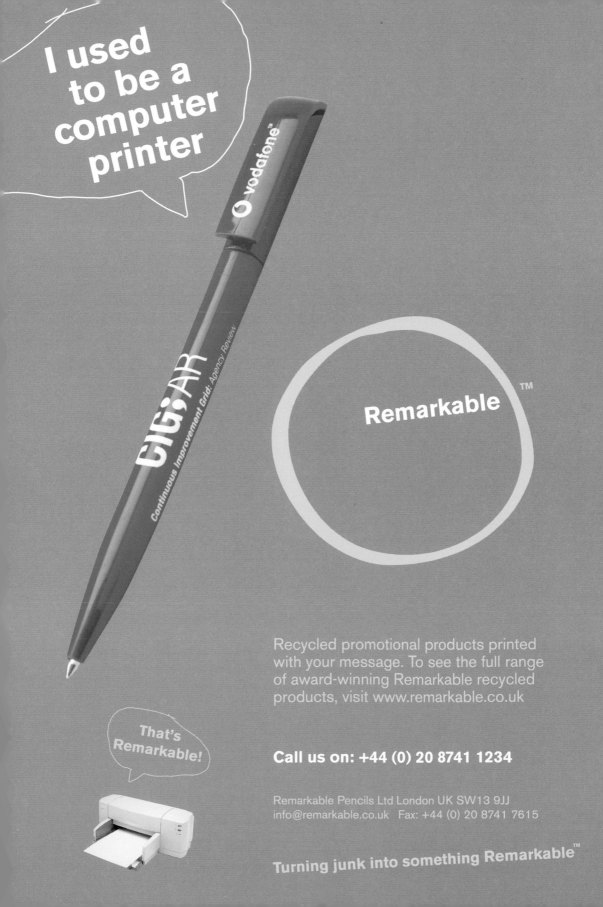

6

Emissions and contaminants

Emissions and contaminants: introduction

Department for the Environment, Food and Rural Affairs

Corporate social responsibility (CSR) is attracting an increasingly high profile in the business, NGO and government communities. CSR is not about philanthropy, but about the way business pursues its core activities and contributes to sustainable development – a key policy theme not only for DEFRA but also for other parts of government. As CSR becomes mainstream, the focus is more on how than on why.

The market is increasingly rewarding responsible behaviour, and regulation will remain a key policy tool to set the boundaries of that behaviour.

- The Government is committed to delivering cleaner air and has set out a framework for improving air quality through action at the international, national and local levels.
- Carbon offsets schemes can help raise public awareness of the scale of the climate-change challenge and the significance of present consumption patterns.
- The Carbon Trust was launched by government to take the lead on energy efficiency for business and the public sector, and to support the development of a low-carbon economy in the United Kingdom.
- Industry should continue to engage with government over chemicals of concern in the UK Chemicals Stakeholder Forum, including taking voluntary action to reduce risks associated with these chemicals.

■ In water the regulatory structure has worked well and continues to be able to accommodate changes and deliver improvements. The Water Framework Directive will be a key driver for the future in protecting and enhancing water quality.

CSR does not mean loading ever more responsibilities on to the corporate sector; it means businesses being accountable for its actions to their stakeholders and also playing their part in helping society to move towards a more sustainable pattern of consumption and production. Clearly, government has a continuing and important role, but there is much more that business can do. Working in partnership with governments and NGOs, business can make a massive contribution and be part of the solution in social progress, environmental protection, economic growth and employment.

Emissions and contaminants: legal overview

Kathryn Mylrea, Simmons & Simmons

There is great deal of legislation to control the release of contaminants into the environment, either by regulating the emissions themselves or by monitoring the quality of the receiving environment. At present there are a number of major pieces of legislation coming out of Europe that will have an important impact on the regulation of specific emissions and contaminants. Three of particular note are briefly described here as examples of three different approaches to improving emissions of contaminants into the environment.

One that has already gained a lot of attention, the EU Emissions Trading Scheme, is due to begin on 1 January 2005. It deals with emissions of greenhouse gases (and specifically CO_2 in the first instance). The scheme works on a 'cap and trade' basis, with member states' governments setting an emissions cap for every installation covered by the scheme. Installations will then be allocated allowances, the number of which is set out in the national allocation plan. The national allocation plan must show a commitment towards achieving national targets set under the Kyoto Protocol. The United Kingdom, which was one of the first countries to produce a draft national allocation plan, is one of very few member states to have set their cap beyond their Kyoto target.

In a major change to the control of chemicals, a new Registration, Evaluation and Authorization of Chemicals (REACH) scheme is now at the advanced proposal stage and looks set to become law within the next 12 months. The scheme is partly an attempt to bring under legislative control those chemicals that have escaped regulation because of the length of time they have been on the market. It requires, among other things, more testing and information for most chemical substances, and erases the distinction between existing and new chemicals.

In terms of contaminants in the receiving environment, the Water Framework Directive (Directive 2000/60/EC) establishing a framework for Community action in the field of water policy was finally adopted in October 2000. It is the most substantial piece of EU water legislation to have been produced, protecting all waters – rivers, lakes, coastal waters and groundwaters – and setting objectives that will ensure they meet 'good status' requirements by 2015. It also requires the reduction and control of pollution from all sources, including diffuse water pollution from agriculture. Regulations transposing the directive have been made in the United Kingdom.

Reducing the carbon emissions of your business

The Carbon Trust

Why should I read this chapter? Put simply, because your business could benefit financially.

Climate change is happening. It is the single biggest environmental threat we face and is primarily caused by the release of greenhouse gases produced as a result of things as simple as the heating and lighting in your business. The UK Government is committed to reducing greenhouse gases and is implementing a regulatory regime that will require businesses to cut their emissions. Those businesses that act now will benefit; those that don't will be penalized financially.

Why reduce carbon emissions?

The fundamentals of climate change have long been understood, because they involve the same basic physics that keep the earth habitable. Heat-trapping 'greenhouse gases' in the atmosphere (of which one of the most important is carbon dioxide, CO_2) let short-wave radiation through from the sun but absorb the long-wave radiation coming back from the earth's surface and re-radiate it. These gases act like a blanket – and keep the surface and the lower atmosphere about 33°C warmer than it would be without them. Primarily through the burning of fossil fuels and long-term deforestation, the concentration of CO_2 and other greenhouse gases has been increasing in the atmosphere since the industrial revolution began.

Surface warming in recent decades is established beyond doubt. Direct temperature records back to the middle of the 19th century establish that recent temperatures are warmer than any since direct measures began.

In addition, a number of other signs that the climate is changing are being observed. From the thawing of permafrost, the declines of some plant and animal populations, and the earlier flowering of trees, to an increase in the heavy rainfall that leads to flooding, the changes in surface temperature are having potentially far-reaching effects.

What could this mean for the environment?

Should global temperatures continue to rise as predicted, existing zones of vegetation and crops will migrate towards the poles, requiring farming practices and eco-systems to adapt. However, many species have limited scope to move. Currently it is estimated that about a quarter of the world's known animals and plants – more than a million species – will die out because of the warming projected in the next 50 years.

Combined with the probability of changing storm patterns, rising sea levels could have huge consequences for coastal cities; parts of Florida and delta regions such as the Nile Delta and lower Bangladesh may be impossible to protect. Other likely changes include more heat-related deaths and heat-related stresses on crops and livestock; more heavy rain, causing floods, landslides, avalanches, mudslides and soil erosion; drier summers and more droughts; and more intense tropical cyclones.

What could this mean for my business?

Driven by a scientific consensus that climate change needs to be addressed, governments around the world are putting in place policies to combat climate change. Virtually every UK business will be touched by the policy measures designed to reduce carbon, either through its fuel bill, its tax bill or, for example, through participation in a carbon trading programme or other measure.

Similarly, the investment community, customers and consumers have become increasingly sensitized to the impact of climate change. Investors are starting to factor in carbon risk and opportunities in their share dealings. Customers and consumers are increasingly looking to deal with companies with a strong social and environmental track record.

Finally, the need to reduce carbon emissions will also give businesses the chance to develop new products and services, and even new revenue. With the Government having accepted the aspiration to cut greenhouse gases by 60 per cent by 2050, carbon reduction will be a business opportunity no one can afford to miss.

The regulatory environment

The United Kingdom is a signatory to the 1997 Kyoto Protocol, an international agreement to reduce emissions of greenhouse gases. Six greenhouse gases are regulated under this agreement: carbon dioxide (CO_2), methane, nitrous oxide, hydrofluorocarbons, perfluorocarbons and sulphur hexafluoride.

However, the 2003 Energy White Paper placed climate change at the heart of UK environmental policy, and the UK Government aims to go beyond the reductions required under the Kyoto Protocol, with its own target of 20 per cent CO_2 emissions reduction by 2010, with a further step change reduction to 2020. This commitment has led to a number of regulatory changes designed to promote a low-carbon environment.

The Climate Change Levy

The Climate Change Levy came into effect on 1 April 2001. All parts of the non-domestic sector have to pay the levy, though it does not apply to fuel oil or fuel used for transport purposes. Energy supplied in small quantities is also exempt. The minimum energy thresholds are equivalent to the thresholds for paying the lower, 5 per cent rate of VAT on energy. Therefore, any organization that pays the 5 per cent rate of VAT on its energy bill is automatically exempt from the levy. Otherwise, it needs to pay in full – for example, 0.43 pence per kilowatt-hour for electricity and 0.15 pence per kilowatt-hour for gas.

Emissions trading

The UK Emissions Trading Scheme began with an auction in March 2002 in which companies and other organizations (known as 'Direct Participants') bid emission reductions over the five years 2002–06 in return for a share of funding from the Department for Environment, Food and Rural Affairs (DEFRA). The aims of the scheme have been to secure significant reductions in UK greenhouse gas emissions; to help UK firms learn about emissions trading and prepare for the EU Emissions Trading Scheme; and to establish the City of London and the United Kingdom as an international centre for emissions trading.

Building on this, the European Emissions Trading Scheme (EU ETS) will run from 2005. The largest emissions trading scheme in the world, the EU ETS will cover 46 per cent of European CO_2 emissions, and a total of 15,000 separate installations across five industrial sectors.

The new scheme will cover all 25 EU countries. Phase 1 of the scheme, running from 2005 to 2007, will set a cap on the emissions of all installations in selected energy-intensive sectors: power and heat generation, ferrous metals, oil refining, pulp and paper, and mineral products. The scope of the scheme may be extended to cover further carbon- and energy-intensive sectors, as well as other greenhouse gases, in phase 2, running from 2008 to 2012.

Companies involved in the scheme will be provided with a capped number of emissions 'allowances' (1 tonne of CO_2 per allowance) for each of their installations, which can be retained or sold across all countries within the scheme. As with the UK scheme, participants whose actual emissions exceed their allocated number of allowances can buy additional allowances in the market. Alternatively, a company can choose to reduce its actual emissions below its target, releasing emissions allowances to sell to other companies, or saving for use in future years.

However, the EU ETS will also affect companies not directly involved in the scheme. As a result of the scheme, and power generation companies' attempts to reduce carbon emissions in other ways, energy prices are likely to rise. The price rises could lead to an increase in costs for many businesses, and will make energy efficiency even more important in the future than it is today.

Additional regulations

The regulations described in this chapter will primarily impact on the energy-intensive industrial sectors. Potentially having a wider effect, particularly in the commercial sectors, will be the building energy efficiency regulations coming from the European Union's Energy Performance of Buildings Directive, due to be implemented by 2006. Under these regulations, new and refurbished buildings will be required to meet minimum energy performance standards. All buildings will be required to obtain an energy performance certificate whenever they are sold or let, and, in the case of public buildings, a certificate will have to be displayed.

Non-regulatory drivers

In addition to the direct impacts of the climate policy regime, the United Kingdom has also witnessed a rising level of attention to corporate social responsibility (CSR) over the past 10 years or more. This has been evidenced in negative ways (boycotts, protests, denial of site permits) and in positive ways (preferred supplier programmes, socially responsible investment funds, higher margins on 'sustainable' products, etc). As climate change has become an increasingly prominent issue in the United Kingdom, businesses with a significant public exposure (such as brand-name household goods, quality retailers, retail financial service companies) have sought to increase their brand value by adopting a proactive stance in relation to climate protection.

In addition, the investment community has become increasingly sensitized to the impact that carbon policy will have on net income and share prices. As a result, many investment houses are scrutinizing the carbon management approaches of their portfolio companies to evaluate the prudence with which they are managing regulatory risk. This in turn affects companies' cost of capital.

What's more, an increasing number of investors and customers are positively discriminating in favour of 'green' organizations. Improving emissions management can lead to an enhanced reputation for a company or brand, improving its relations with the community, helping it to attract and retain staff, and attracting new customers.

Reducing carbon emissions in my business?

The best way for individual businesses to tackle climate change right now is through energy efficiency. Energy efficiency reduces emissions but in addition it can deliver significant cost savings. A 20 per cent saving in energy consumption – easily achieved by many businesses – can have the same positive effect as a 5 per cent increase in sales, and by reducing your overheads you automatically improve the competitiveness of your products or services. Some companies even have the potential to save up to 50 per cent on day-to-day costs such as heating and lighting through energy efficiency.

Each year the Carbon Trust works with thousands of UK companies to help them reduce their energy bills, and has developed a simple list of the easiest ways to cut carbon, which have proved to be effective whatever the business's size or sector:

■ Check regularly on your consumption of electricity, gas and oil and check that your bills relate to what you actually use, rather than being an estimate.
■ Turn off lights in empty rooms and corridors – especially at the end of the day. This can save up to 15 per cent of your energy bill.
■ Keep windows closed in cold weather. If staff are too warm, turn the heating down instead.
■ Use just the light you need. If the lights in your corridors are too bright, remove or switch off alternate fittings. Use daylight. It's free – so keep windows and skylights clean and clear.
■ Clean light fittings annually. Dirt reduces lighting efficiency, encouraging people to switch more lights on.
■ Set the thermostat at 19°C; costs rise by 8 per cent for every 1°C increase.
■ Don't heat unused space. Storerooms, corridors and areas where there's heavy physical work being done can be set to lower temperatures. Reduce heating during holidays and at weekends.
■ Check that thermostats are sited out of draughts and away from either cold or hot spots.
■ Don't block radiators with furniture; it reduces efficiency and output.
■ Ask your colleagues where they think energy is being wasted and for their ideas about saving energy.

Are there any 'added value' opportunities?

Carbon reduction and regulation going forward will be not just about opportunities to cut costs, but about opportunities to actively generate revenue as well. Through emissions trading schemes, larger companies will have an opportunity to open up revenue streams through selling on unused emissions allowances, but companies of all sizes that are on the front foot now will have a wealth of opportunities in the future.

With the Government keen to develop a low-carbon economy, new products and services will be needed to support this. Whether developing new energy technologies or advising on cutting carbon emissions, there are potentially many areas for business growth in the future.

Where can I go for help?

The Carbon Trust is an independent company funded by government. Its role is to help the UK move to a low-carbon economy by encouraging business and the public sector to reduce carbon emissions now and capture the commercial opportunities offered by low-carbon technologies.

In order to meet these aims, the Carbon Trust develops and implements a range of programmes, including:

■ providing independent information and advice on energy efficiency and carbon management to the business and public sector, through schemes such as Action Energy and the Carbon Management scheme;
■ promoting the Government's Enhanced Capital Allowances Scheme to encourage investment by business in qualifying energy-saving technologies;
■ investing in the development of low-carbon technologies in the United Kingdom.

For more information on the Carbon Trust, and to find out what help is available for your business to reduce its carbon emissions, visit www.thecarbontrust.co.uk.

Trading greenhouse gases

Alan Sweeting, Environment Agency

From the beginning of 2005, about 1,100 UK sites will be part of the European Union's Emission Trading Scheme (ETS), along with up to 20,000 sites on the Continent.

The ETS is a key tool to deliver the reductions in carbon dioxide emissions that are essential to combat global warming. It will help the United Kingdom achieve its legal obligations under the Kyoto Protocol and the Government's 2010 target of emissions of 20 per cent below 1990 levels. The aim of emissions trading is to allow the reduction targets to be met in the most cost-effective manner. It works by setting an overall cap, which is then carved up into allowances for participating sites. At the end of each year, participants in the trading scheme must hold allowances equal to all of their emissions.

How trading will work

The installations covered by the scheme are:

- combustion processes (with a minimum thermal input of 20 megawatts);
- production and processing of ferrous metals;
- production of cement clinker or lime;
- manufacture of glass and glass fibre;
- manufacture of ceramic bricks;
- production of pulp from timber or other fibrous materials;
- manufacture of paper and board.

(For the full definition of installations, see Schedule 1 on page 194.)

Businesses in these sectors should have applied for a permit to release carbon dioxide into the atmosphere, and will be given an allocation by the Government that defines a target level of emissions. Permits that will allow businesses to participate in the scheme were to be issued by the end of March 2004. Emission allocations will be based on the Government's decision on the national cap for carbon dioxide emissions, and how it will be divided among sectors. The allocations will be finalized after public consultation and approval by the European Commission, which will be no later than 21 February 2005. Following the proposed amendments to the United Kingdom's draft National Allocation Plan, total emissions of carbon dioxide of 563 million tonnes are expected by installations covered by the scheme between 2005 and 2007. The Government will allocate 756.1 million allowances for the period 2005–07; this alocation is 5.2 per cent below projections of business as usual in the UK. A small propertion of the total allowances are reserved for new plants that come into operation after 2003.

From March 2005, businesses in the scheme will be able to buy or sell emission allowances, which provides an opportunity to make profits from trading. Companies that can limit emissions below their allocation will be in a position to sell the surplus allowances. Other companies will have to judge whether it will be cheaper to buy allowances or to invest in emission reductions. (The price of a tonne of carbon in the futures market early in 2004 was around 12.5 euros.)

At the end of each period (the first deadline being 30 April 2006), participants in the trading scheme must hold allowances equal to all of their emissions during the period. Those allowances are then surrendered. This is how the scheme delivers the most cost-effective emission reductions. Firms will choose to buy allowances from other participants if doing so costs less than other means of staying within their allocation. On the other hand, firms that can reduce emissions relatively cheaply will do so, putting them in a position to sell surplus allowances. The desired environmental result will be achieved because the overall allocation of carbon dioxide allowances is fixed, but trading will make possible the most cost-effective route to the required reductions.

Example

A company that currently emits 100,000 tonnes equivalent receives allowances of only 90,000. If allowances were trading at 20 euros, it would cost 200,000 euros to bridge the gap (10,000 tonnes equivalent at 20 euros per tonne equivalent).

Table 6.4.1 Key dates for emissions trading

10/11/2003 – 31/01/2004	Operators apply for permits
01/01/2004 – 31/03/04	Competent authorities (the Environment Agency in England and Wales) to issue permits
31/03/2004	Operators required to hold a greenhouse gas trading permit to be included in the National Allocation Plan (NAP) and receive an indicative allocation
31/09/2004	Submission of draft NAP for approval by the European Commission
10/11/2004	Submission of proposed amendments to NAP to European Commission
01/01/2005	Start of the scheme – all operators required to hold a greenhouse gas trading permit to emit carbon dioxide
21/02/2005	Final decision on allocation of allowances
28/02/2005	Allowances allocated to operators for first year of scheme
30/04/2006	All installations to have surrendered allowances equal to their verified emissions in the first year of the scheme

If it would cost more than 200,000 euros to bring emissions within the ceiling, then it would be worth buying the extra allowances. But if emissions could be cut for less than 200,000 euros, that would be the better option.

Monitoring and verification

National targets will only be achieved if emissions are properly monitored and controlled. Operators will have to report their annual emissions, which must be verified by a competent independent verifier. All emissions of carbon dioxide from all sources belonging to regulated activities must be included, and operators will need to specify their monitoring methodology. Operators must submit a verified report to the Regulator (in England and Wales, the Environment Agency) for the preceding calendar year by 31 March, beginning in 2006.

The European Union has adopted monitoring and reporting guidelines that offer a choice between direct measurement and calculation of emissions. They present a range of 'tiered' methodologies, based on the level of accuracy, for each industry sector. Operators will be expected to use the highest (most accurate) tier unless that is not technically feasible or will lead to unreasonably high costs. There is limited provision within the guidelines to apply less stringent standards to minor sources within sites, namely sources that contribute less than 5 per cent of total emissions from that site.

Biomass fuels, although included in the scheme, will be zero rated, and the following fuels are carbon neutral for the purposes of the scheme:

- wood wastes;
- sewage sludge;
- bio-fuels;
- landfill gas;
- biomass fractions of paper, cardboard, municipal waste, and cardboard waste.

Penalties

Penalties will apply for failing to hold a valid permit, failing to comply with monitoring and reporting conditions, or failing to have surrendered sufficient allowances (which is equivalent to producing excessive emissions).

During the first phase of the scheme, to the end of 2007, failure to have surrendered enough allowances will incur a fine of 40 euros for each excess tonne. Our example company with annual carbon dioxide emissions of 100,000 tonnes equivalent but with allowances of only 90,000 tonnes equivalent could be liable for a fine of 400,000 euros if it does not balance the books either by reducing emissions or by purchasing more allowances.

The second phase

The second phase of the scheme will run from 2008 to 2012. In this period, other greenhouse gases will be included: methane, nitrous oxide, hydrofluorocarbons, perfluorocarbons and sulphur hexafluoride.

During this phase the scheme is likely to be extended to include the chemicals, aluminium and transport sectors. Also, the fine for failing to retire sufficient allowances will rise from 40 euros to 100 euros.

Further information

For further information and guidance on policy issues, visit the Defra website at http://www.defra.gov.uk/environment/climatechange/trading/eu/index.htm. For further information and guidance on the EU ETS, including applying for an EU ETS permit in England and Wales, visit the Environment Agency website at http://environment-agency.gov.uk/emissionstrading.

Schedule 1: Installations covered by the EU Emissions Trading Scheme

The first phase will cover installations that carry out any of the activities in Annex I of the EU Emissions Trading Directive – listed below. For the first phase (2005–07), the scheme will cover emissions of carbon dioxide only.

The way in which the UK Government has interpreted 'energy activities' within the combustion installation criteria is shown in Table 6.4.2.

Table 6.4.2 'Energy activities' within the combustion installation criteria

Included	Excluded
Electricity generators	Ovens
Boilers	Reactors
CHP	Dryers
	Furnaces
	Non-ferrous metal production
	Incinerators

Energy activities

- Combustion installations with a rated thermal input exceeding 20 MW (excepting hazardous or municipal waste installations).
- Mineral oil refineries.
- Coke ovens.

Production and processing of ferrous metals

- Metal ore (including sulphide ore) roasting or sintering installations.
- Installations for the production of pig iron or steel (primary or secondary fusion) including continuous casting, with a capacity exceeding 2.5 tonnes per hour.

Mineral industry

∎ Installations for the production of cement clinker in rotary kilns with a production capacity exceeding 500 tonnes per day or lime in rotary kilns with a production capacity exceeding 50 tonnes per day or in other furnaces with a production capacity exceeding 50 tonnes per day.
∎ Installations for the manufacture of glass including glass fibre with a melting capacity exceeding 20 tonnes per day.
∎ Installations for the manufacture of ceramic bricks by firing, in particular roofing tiles, bricks, refractory bricks, tiles, stoneware or porcelain, with a production capacity exceeding 75 tonnes per day, and/or with a kiln capacity exceeding 4 cubic metres and with a setting density per kiln exceeding 300 kilograms per cubic metre.

Other activities

Industrial plants for the production of:

∎ pulp from timber or other fibrous materials;
∎ paper and board with a production capacity exceeding 20 tonnes per day.

Note: The threshold values given above generally refer to production capacities or outputs. Where one operator carries out several activities falling under the same subheading in the same installation or on the same site, the capacities of such activities are added together.

Alan Sweeting is a member of the Environment Agency's greenhouse gas emissions trading team, and has responsibility for external communications and business planning for the project. He has worked for the Environment Agency in environmental impact assessment and research management, as well as in project management in the private and not-for-profit sectors. He is currently seconded to the Environment Agency from AEA Technology.

Carbon offsets

Tom Morton, Climate Care

Introduction

How does your company measure up when it comes to the environment? If you are starting from scratch, then high on your list of priorities will be investigating your contribution to global warming. All businesses rely to a greater or lesser degree on energy, and in most cases this comes from fossil fuels. The by-product is carbon dioxide, the main gas responsible for global warming.

'Global warming' sounds rather benign; 'global climate disruption' is probably a better description of what is happening to our climate. We are seeing the consequences of severe weather events affecting businesses and societies closer and closer to home on a more and more frequent basis. Global warming isn't something that just happens to people in other countries; it will affect us in the United Kingdom too, not to mention the international arms of companies around the world.

It would be excellent if we could all switch to renewable energy tomorrow, thereby cutting out emissions at a stroke and putting the brakes on climate change. However, this is not going to happen. What we need to do is switch to low-carbon fuels wherever possible and reduce our emissions by using energy more efficiently. Even so, there will still be emissions that we cannot cut out, which is where carbon offsets have a role.

Carbon offsets

Carbon offsets balance out your emissions by making an emissions reduction elsewhere on your behalf. In effect, your emissions are cancelled out by the reductions, making the original activity climate neutral.

The first step in the process is to determine what your company's emissions are. This may be from its entire operation, or it may be from a particular part, such as air travel, the car fleet or energy use. This needn't be an onerous task, particularly if you have records of your travel and energy use. The energy used by these processes is converted into a carbon dioxide (CO_2) figure – normally measured in tonnes.

Carbon dioxide is a gas – so how can it weigh a tonne? This is a question that is often asked. Think of a lump of coal in your hand; it feels heavy and is made from solid carbon. If you burn it, the carbon atoms still exist; they have just spread out and combined with oxygen to form a gas. As a visual guide, CO_2 occupying the volume of a hot air balloon would weigh about 4 tonnes.

So, it's all about planting trees...?

When carbon offsets are mentioned, most people think of planting trees, otherwise known as 'carbon sequestration'. This is fair enough. Most people remember from their schooldays that trees 'breathe in' CO_2 from the atmosphere, 'breathe out' the oxygen and store the carbon as wood. As trees grow, more carbon is locked up and is stored over the long term.

Trees are a great communication tool, but they are not going to save the planet from global warming. Society cannot go on taking oil and coal from underground and try to store its pollution in a thin layer of trees on the earth's surface. One problem is that trees can burn down and, if this happens, you are back where you started, with the CO_2 being returned into the atmosphere. What we need to do is look for a more permanent approach, which is to try to leave the fossil fuels in the ground.

Technology projects

This leads us on to the second type of carbon-offset project. Rather than try to soak up emissions in trees, you pay to reduce somebody else's fossil fuel use. This could be a renewable energy project that means less coal is burnt. Alternatively, it could be an energy efficiency project that means less electricity is used. Electricity is mostly generated from fossil fuels, so using it more efficiently means that CO_2 emissions are reduced.

The main aim of an offset project must be to reduce the amount of greenhouse gases in the atmosphere. However, the projects usually have other positive benefits such as saving on energy costs, improving air quality or general development in the host community. Sequestration projects also have significant social benefits in terms of employment and ecological benefits for wildlife. All these aspects can add to the story that you are telling stakeholders.

What can I offset?

There are two main ways to go. Either you can offset the emissions from your operations or you can do an offset on behalf of your customers – because the product you are selling them emits CO_2.

Organizational offsets

Some companies are able to offset the entire CO_2 impact of their operations. This is often possible for service companies or those that don't have large energy bills. An alternative is to pick one area of operations, such as company air travel or the company car fleet.

Companies often use offsets as part of a wider package of measures. For example, at Climate Care we are currently talking to a company that spends of the order of £4 million a year on air travel. The company has a strategy to reduce its air travel by 10 per cent on both cost and environmental grounds – leaving total emissions of around 2,500 tonnes of CO_2 per annum from air travel. The company is considering offsetting these emissions through the Climate Care scheme. The cost of doing so is just 0.5 per cent of the current air travel budget.

Offsets for customers

A number of companies do a carbon offset on behalf of their customers. Once again, a good example would be that of air travel. Increasingly, companies are seeing the irony in selling holidays that are based on a pristine environment when customers have to get in an aeroplane to get there – emitting literally tonnes of CO_2 in the process. A number of travel companies now either offset these emissions from their customers' flights or give them the chance of doing it as an extra.

The Co-operative Bank has built its reputation on its ethical and environmental standards. When it re-entered the mortgage market in 2000, it wanted something that would make its mortgages stand out from the rest. Interest rates are boring; the bank wanted something else to talk to customers about and Climate Care fitted its profile well. The Co-operative Bank now offsets 1 tonne of CO_2 emissions for each of its customers every year for the life of their mortgages. This amounts to 20 per cent of the emissions from the average household's gas and electricity. The bank can now talk to customers about the projects that it has funded around the world, as well as the more mundane subjects that surround mortgages.

High-quality offsets

Carbon offsets are voluntary; to this end, companies cannot use them to fulfil other emissions reductions liabilities. As they are voluntary, they are all about doing something extra. This is where the concept of 'additionality' comes in. It is essential that the carbon-offset projects that you are investing in are doing something new – over and above what would have happened without your investment. There is no point in paying for a CO_2 reduction that would have happened anyway. There are no hard-and-fast rules when making the judgement about additionality, but you should ask you carbon offset provider to prove that its projects are additional.

Following on from this theme, you need to ask where the project is being done. At Climate Care we are often asked if we are doing any projects in the United Kingdom, but the answer is no. The main reason for this is that the United Kingdom has undertaken to meet targets on emissions reductions that will become legally binding when the Kyoto Protocol comes into force. If we did projects in the United Kingdom, we would be helping the Government reach its targets, meaning that it would have to do less elsewhere. When we do projects in developing countries, this is not the case, as their governments do not have legally binding targets.

A final point to be aware of is the monitoring of projects. The savings are based on a counter-factual situation: what would the emissions have been without this project? So you need to be very sure that real emissions reductions are being made. This will normally involve a third-party report that the offset provider should be able to make available for each of its projects.

Conclusions

High-quality carbon offsets give companies the opportunity to repair their contribution to global warming – either from their operations or on behalf of their clients. The main benefit as far as the climate is concerned is the reduction in carbon dioxide. From the company's point of view, just 'doing the right thing' is not usually enough; there needs to be a commercial driver before funds are committed. The driver may be a need to communicate a new message with customers or simply to raise the company's corporate social responsibility profile. Alternatively, offsets can be used as part of a wider strategy to promote climate change issues to staff within an organization.

As an issue, climate change is continuing to climb the corporate agenda. Companies must take steps to reduce the direct greenhouse gas emissions from their operations. However, there will also be emissions that cannot be cut out, and this is where high-quality carbon offsets have a role to play. Offset projects not only stimulate CO_2 reductions, but often run in parallel with the wider aims of sustainable development – giving companies a powerful story to communicate to stakeholders.

Tom Morton is Director of Climate Care.

Air pollution

James Mills, Air Monitors

Introduction

Ever since humans learnt to make fire, we have been polluting the air on which we rely to survive. Today it is difficult to imagine many anthropogenic activities that do not have some impact on air quality, so it is essential that we do whatever we can to minimize the impact on the atmosphere and to ensure that we can all continue to exercise our fundamental right to breathe clean air.

Air pollution in the 21st century is perhaps not as obvious a problem as in the 19th and 20th centuries; it arguably reached its peak during the industrial revolution. The nature of pollution has changed, with less coming from the burning of coal and wood and more from oil and gas, which are generally regarded as cleaner fuels and, if used with care, would tend to reduce air pollution. However, we are using much larger quantities of fuel today than ever before, further driving up CO_2 emissions, and many experts predict that if we stay on this course we face catastrophe through global warming.

Health effects due to air pollution have changed too. Gone are the acute respiratory epidemics caused by the infamous London smogs of the 1940s and 50s, and in their place have come more subtle but nevertheless serious health effects such as an increase in the incidence of asthma in many of our children, which may be caused or at least aggravated by relatively low levels of human-made airborne pollutants.

Air pollution cannot be eradicated completely, at least not without reverting to a pre-cave dweller existence, so must we resign ourselves to an ever-worsening situation, or are there things we can do individually or collectively to manage the problem in a sustainable manner?

Working towards sustainable improvements in air quality, as with any other pursuit, will very much depend on our knowledge of the current situation and our ability to measure the effectiveness of measures we take towards our goal. It follows therefore that we must gather robust information on current levels of pollution or emissions, relate this to historical data where available, and use computer-based modelling technology to project forward. There is little point in taking action if there is no way of measuring how effective that action might be, so research, monitoring and modelling all play a vital part in ensuring that the most appropriate actions are taken and that they continue to be effective. There is an old Irish saying, 'If you want to get to there, I wouldn't start from here.' As with many decisions in business, we rarely get to choose our starting point, but if we are to make progress towards clean air, we must at least understand the facts of where we are at any point in time in order to improve the likelihood of arriving at a successful and sustainable outcome.

A brief history of air-quality legislation and practice

National legislation aimed at reducing the effects of air pollution has been around for a surprisingly long time. Restrictions on certain types of coal use were introduced as early as the 13th and 14th centuries. It was, however, the notorious London smogs of 1952 that led to the introduction of the first Clean Air Act in 1956, which was revised in 1968. Since the 1970s, air pollution legislation has been dealt with at a European level, with directives having been issued in an attempt to control a range of pollutant substances such as ozone, sulphur dioxide, nitrogen oxides, carbon monoxide, particulate matter (PM), lead and certain volatile organic compounds (VOCs). In response to these directives, the UK Government introduced the Environmental Protection Act of 1990 and the Environment Act of 1995, which transferred the responsibility for pollution control of smaller industries to local authorities, leaving the Environment Agency to deal with the larger processes. In 1997 the Department for Environment, Food and Rural Affairs (Defra) published the National Air Quality Strategy, which set ambient air quality standards for the pollutants of most concern.

Legislation controlling industrial pollution is much tighter today than at any time in the past and is more rigorously enforced by government agencies at a national and local level. The effectiveness of these measures can only be determined by the monitoring of ambient air quality across the country, and the keeping of a National Atmospheric Emissions Inventory (NAEI). Across Europe, air-quality networks monitor ambient air quality 24 hours a day, and these data are used along with computer modelling to guide air-quality management strategies. In the United Kingdom, Defra runs the Automated Urban and Rural Network (AURN), and data are available at http://www.air-quality.co.uk. The monitoring sites are a requirement of the European air quality directives, and these 'statutory' sites are designed to satisfy the United Kingdom's obligations under the directives. Many local authorities in the United Kingdom also have monitoring programmes, and an estimated 500 or more sites provide valuable background information to complement the national sites.

The NAEI is managed and published by DEFRA and provides information on the total emission of each of the controlled pollutants on a national basis. Current trends for most species are down and in line with targets to reduce levels further to below the levels required in the EU National Emission Ceilings Directive by 2010. Details on the NAIE are available at http://www.defra.gov.uk/environment/statistics/airqual/whatsnew.htm.

Current legislation

At the present time, processes in the United Kingdom are overseen either by the Environment Agency or by local authorities, depending on their size and type. The larger processes (Part A) are dealt with directly by the Agency and the smaller (Part B) processes by the local authorities. Conditions of operation can be imposed by these government bodies, and monitoring to ensure compliance with the authorization conditions is often required. Information about each individual process is placed on the public register and is open to scrutiny by interested parties and the public at large. In addition, new processes usually require an environmental impact assessment (EIA) to be carried out, and in July 2004 a new European directive on strategic environmental assessment (SEA) took effect in the United Kingdom. The Commission website on SEA states:

> The purpose of the SEA-Directive is to ensure that environmental consequences of certain plans and programmes are identified and assessed during their preparation and before their adoption. The public and environmental authorities can give their opinion and all results are integrated and taken into account in the course of the planning procedure. After the adoption of the plan or programme the public is informed about the decision and the way in which it was made. In the case of likely transboundary significant effects the affected Member State and its public are informed and have the possibility to make comments which are also integrated into the national decision making process.
>
> SEA will contribute to more transparent planning by involving the public and by integrating environmental considerations. This will help to achieve the goal of sustainable development.

Further information is available at http://europa.eu.int/comm/environment/eia/sea-legalcontext.htm and at the UK Government site http://www.odpm.gov.uk/stellent/groups/odpm_planning/documents/page/odpm_plan_026662.hcsp.

What can be done?

Air pollution has no respect for national or regional boundaries, and may have quite different effects on local air quality from those it has regionally and globally. Relatively small changes in practice locally can and do make a significant difference on a global scale. This fact is acknowledged by the United Nations and has been gaining momentum since the call in 1989 for a United Nations Conference on Environment and Development. The subsequent publication of Agenda 21 sets out the aims, objectives and methodology to be adopted by governments if we are to make progress on the path to sustainable development. Chapter 9 of Agenda 21 deals with air pollution and atmospheric protection, and the remainder of this chapter will attempt to highlight ways in which we as company directors, managers and individuals can contribute.

There are four main areas to consider:

■ information gathering – to form the basis of good decision-making;
■ reduction of energy consumption, alternative fuels and/or renewable energy sources;
■ improved production, abatement and waste management technologies;
■ ongoing monitoring to ensure compliance and monitor progress.

Information gathering

Before making changes to current practice it is wise to gather robust information about the true levels of emissions from and ambient air quality around the plant or process. This can be done by mass balance calculations, monitoring and modelling. Usually the right combination of all three yields the most valuable results. Many companies cut corners at this early stage in the process and end up regretting it later. Modern-day tools for monitoring levels of emissions to air at source and in the general environment are often highly sophisticated and can be overwhelming for non-technical company directors.

To assist in the selection of the proper technology for air and emissions monitoring, the Environment Agency introduced the MCERTS scheme (http://www.environment-agency.gov.uk/mcerts), under which equipment can be awarded certification for use in appropriate applications. Although not yet able to cover all eventualities, the scheme does help to avoid major mistakes and can ensure that any capital investment is well founded and that the quality of resultant information is worthy of the decisions that may inevitably flow from it.

The scheme has recently been extended to cover the certification of environmental professionals engaged in monitoring activities, providing further peace of mind for anyone seeking assistance with a monitoring project. Further help and advice can be obtained from the Source Testing Association (STA) (http://www.s-t-a.org.uk), a trade organization with a comprehensive membership of technology providers and service companies engaged in all aspects of air-quality monitoring.

The Government also provides a wealth of information on both European and national air quality issues at the DEFRA website http://www.defra.gov.uk/airquality and the Environment Agency site at http://www.environment-agency.gov.uk/subjects/airquality/. The latter includes information on the National Atmospheric Emissions Inventory (NAEI) and local and national air pollution trends.

Energy and the environment

Alternative energy sources, reduction in consumption and renewable sources are dealt with elsewhere in this book. The Department of Trade and Industry (DTI) has an energy group that has provided resources on its website dealing with environment-related issues including air quality: http://www.dti.gov.uk/energy/environment/index.shtml.

Improvements to production, abatement and waste reduction technologies

Sometimes the emission of airborne pollutants can be reduced or eliminated by careful attention to basic process conditions, procedures and fuel choices. More often, it is necessary to employ some sort of 'clean-up' after the process and before emission to atmosphere. These 'abatement' technologies vary widely in their complexity and principle, but for instance include trapping, absorption, adsorption, conversion and dissolution of the offending pollutants. Although many are effective at removal of substances from air, they can result in simply moving the problem elsewhere. For example, dissolving a noxious gas or vapour in water can be an effective way of removing it from air, but in turn may create an equally nasty liquid-based pollutant that may have to be further treated before being disposed of. A holistic approach is therefore required before one can really claim to have improved the overall environmental burden. IPPC legislation is designed to encourage holistic thinking when investing in process improvements and there are useful resources on the subject at http://europa.eu.int/comm/environment/ippc/.

When selecting an improvement strategy, one should consider carefully how the efficiency of the strategy will be determined and maintained. Mass balance calculations, monitoring and modelling again will all play a part in ensuring that whatever investment is made is worthwhile. Many abatement technologies work better on paper than they do in the real world, so seek data from the supplier on the removal efficiency in a process as similar to the one concerned as possible and carefully specify performance criteria that can be measured to ensure that the system is truly fit for purpose. It is also important to measure ongoing performance, as some abatement processes can deteriorate over time, and if not properly maintained can become ineffective and may not maintain compliance within your authorization limits.

Think also about the possible by-products of abatement systems and the cost of disposal of waste products. There is little point in solving your air pollution problems only to create a different problem with the disposal of liquid or solid waste.

Ongoing monitoring to ensure compliance with legislation and monitor progress

Once you have decided on the appropriate course of action to improve your emissions to atmosphere, it will pay you to consider how to ensure that the system continues to operate within the specification. You may be required to do this as part of your authorization permit in any case, but it usually pays to ensure that the critical parameters affecting the performance of the abatement system are monitored and maintained.

Summary

The effects of air pollution, unlike those of any other kind of pollution, cannot be avoided by the general population. We can choose when, where and what we eat and drink but we cannot choose whether or not to breathe the air around us. For this reason, air pollution is an issue that should be of fundamental importance to all. Companies that work to minimize the effects of their activities on the quality of our air create goodwill and develop strong ecological reputations. In contrast, those that do not take the issue seriously invite hostility from local residents, possible legal action over nuisance complaints, or lawsuits arising out of human health effects. If sustainable development is our goal, then air-quality management should be at the very heart of everything we do along the way.

We're proud to work with our business customers – big, small and wherever they are. We work to save them money, protect the environment and preserve our Earth's most precious resource – water.

Thames Water was recently named "Welsh Employer of the Year" in the National Business Awards. In Cardiff we work in partnership with Dwr Cymru Welsh Water to provide meter readings, billing plus contact and credit management services to customers across Wales. In Scotland, Thames Water is a member of the Scottish Water Solutions Joint Venture helping to deliver Scottish Water's £1.8 Billion capital investment programme.

We are also operating treatment works in and around Edinburgh. Our asset management and operational expertise is in demand far beyond the Thames Valley.

For more information contact us at www.thameswateruk.co.uk

 Group

Thames Water Utilities Ltd Clearwater Court Vastern Road Reading RG1 8DB
T +44 (0)845 9200 800

Water

Ed Mitchell, Thames Water

Though rain falls freely from the sky, water is precious, and far too many of us take it for granted. We shouldn't. While taps don't run dry in the United Kingdom, water is a real priority issue. Although the popular view is that it is always raining in England, the south-east of the country is in fact relatively dry. London, for example, receives less rainfall than either Rome or Istanbul.

Yet demand for water continues to grow, as a result of changes in lifestyle and movements of population. Current demand in the Thames Water area is about 160 litres per head per day, but the latest forecasts see this rising by more than 9 per cent by 2030 to about 175 litres per head per day. Furthermore, it is estimated that there will be approximately 1 million more customers in the region by 2016. London alone is set to grow by 800,000 people in the next 12 years – the equivalent of the current population of Leeds moving to the capital.

Assuming that the current nature and pattern of rainfall do not change markedly in the foreseeable future, the growth in water consumption means that we need both to protect our water sources from pollution by disposing of wastewater properly, and to ensure that we use water more wisely. This twin-track approach should ensure a more sustainable use of our limited water resources into the future.

Protecting our resources

As a result of improved sewage treatment standards, the River Thames today is cleaner than it has been since pre-industrial times; indeed, it is one of the cleanest metropolitan rivers in the world. Water companies also work with industry to minimize pollution, through trade effluent discharge consents and by the provision of advice. This has undoubtedly helped to reduce the amounts of contaminants such as heavy metals and other non-biodegradable compounds arriving at wastewater treatment works directly from industrial sources. It is a system that works.

Most pollution prevention can be described as common sense – often requiring only minor and inexpensive modifications, which can considerably reduce risk on a site. There is a surprising lack of awareness of the environmental consequences of seemingly innocent activities such as washing down spillages, and of everyday products such as milk and sugar that are extremely polluting if they enter a watercourse. There is also a genuine and widespread ignorance of the fact that there are three types of sewerage system (foul, surface and combined), and discharging the same effluent to each one will have very different environmental consequences. Companies should get to know their systems – where their wastewater and surface water goes – and then ensure that each is connected to the right system.

Polluting substances discharged to a surface water drain, designed to deal with run-off from roads, roofs, etc, will usually flow direct to a watercourse. The same discharge to a foul drain will also flow to a watercourse but via a sewage treatment works, where it will be treated to minimize risks to the environment.

Rules governing discharges

There are strict rules governing discharges:

- Trade effluent discharges to surface water sewers are not permitted other than in exceptional circumstances.
- Surface water sewers should be regarded as culverted streams and treated accordingly.
- Discharges to the surface water system are prohibited other than those consistent with normal road, roof or vehicle park run-off without the potential for contamination.
- Contaminated surface water must normally be diverted to the foul sewerage system.
- Areas of actual or potential contamination should be separated and minimized.

Misconnected drains – equipment that is incorrectly plumbed into surface water sewers rather than into foul sewers – pose a real environmental threat to streams and rivers. For example, it is estimated that in London at least 1 in 10 properties contribute to the problem. In the worst-affected boroughs the figure is closer to 1 in 3. Thames Water is working with the Environment Agency to provide practical advice on how to carry out simple visual checks to ensure that drains are not misconnected.

Reducing the pollutant load

Companies should look at drainage from areas of hardstanding where spills might happen as a result of the handling of chemicals in storage areas or loading bays. These should be bunded and/or roofed over, and there should be emergency plans in place to cope with a spillage. Oil interceptors should also be fitted to handle run-off from car parking areas.

They should also check whether reducing the pollution load could have financial benefits by saving discharge fees and potentially allowing the recycling of water and expensive raw materials. Businesses with a trade effluent consent need to ensure that they minimize the risk of breaching the consent as a result of operational failures or materials handling problems. This will require a review of operating procedures and infrastructure such as storage facilities and bunding.

In many industries, waste minimization and pollution prevention are two sides of the same coin. Waste that isn't produced can't pollute the environment – and can save you money. Pollution prevention pays. *But so can water conservation.*

Using water efficiently

As a business, making sure you use only the water you need is one way of demonstrating the importance your organization attaches to caring for the environment. This is something that investors are paying increasing attention to. But more pragmatically, it can potentially reduce the size of your water bill.

The best place to start is with a water audit to find out where most water is being used. This allows reduction measures to be targeted most effectively.

For manufacturing industries, operational water use is likely to represent the greatest area of consumption. Options for reducing operational water use include revising operating procedures – especially washing activities – and the introduction of control measures and devices. The financial savings these activities can make are likely to be enough to make this exercise worthwhile.

Most companies today, however, aren't involved in manufacturing, yet nonetheless use a considerable amount of water on day-to-day essentials such as catering and washrooms. The amount used can often be reduced with minimal investment.

A recent study into office water use discovered four factors that had the most effect on consumption:

∎ office size (floor space);
∎ number of employees;
∎ catering facilities;
∎ how efficiently water is used.

Not many surprises there. But the study also found that three-quarters of offices are probably using more water per employee than they need to and, as a consequence, are pouring money down the drain.

It is believed that about half of all offices could cut at least 25 per cent off their water bills by implementing some simple water-saving measures. Table 6.7.1 shows the amount of water you could expect to be using if your office were truly water efficient.

As with manufacturing, it is a good idea to start by carrying out a basic audit of your office's water use to pinpoint areas for improvement. This should identify some 'quick wins' for saving water simply and efficiently. There are also other measures worth taking that will pay back over the longer term.

Here are some of the things to look at:

Table 6.7.1 Target water usage for a water-efficient office

Size of office	Target water usage per employee per annum (m3)
Small (under 1,000 m2)	4.4
Small (under 1,000 m2) with catering	5.9
Larger	6.8
Larger with catering	8.3

1. **Monitoring water consumption.** This should always be the first step towards effective water management, and it's easy to do. Water bills provide valuable information about patterns of water use and can help identify potential problems. Plot on a graph your annual water use over three or four years to see if there is an increasing trend. This could indicate a leak in your underground supply pipe. Clearing this up will save water and money.
2. **Public washrooms**. It's important to make sure all water fixtures are regularly maintained. Dripping taps and overflowing cisterns can be a constant drain on resources. A range of water-efficient devices are available to reduce unnecessary wastage – for example, percussion taps that turn themselves off after a fixed length of time.
3. **Toilets**. Any toilet cistern installed before 1993 may well be using more water than it needs to. Installing a simple cistern displacement device can save up to 3 litres per flush. Multiply this by the number of daily flushes and it soon mounts up. Displacement devices such as 'Hippos' are easy to fit and widely available – indeed, Thames Water can supply up to 100 of them free of charge.
4. **Urinals**. Automatic flushing in men's toilets is a common source of wasted water because it continues even when urinals are not in use, for instance during the night. Make flushing more cost-effective by installing automatic flush control systems that only allow flushing when it's needed.
5. **Catering areas.** If your company has a restaurant or catering area, then there's even more opportunity to minimize water use. Considerable savings can be made by making staff aware of the efficient use of water – for instance, by making sure taps are not left running and by encouraging good practice. Why not give a briefing session or put up some posters as a reminder? Tap controllers, which stop water flow automatically, can also help.

Sources of information

This chapter is written by Thames Water. For more information, contact us at www.thameswateruk.co.uk.

Every UK water company will provide advice on reducing water usage and preventing pollution. Thames Water, for example, has a guide called *Saving Money by Saving Water*, which offers practical advice to businesses. The guide is available through the website www.thameswateruk.co.uk/waterwise, which offers additional advice on how to conserve water and reduce costs.

The Environment Agency has also produced a guide to developing and implementing a water management plan. This can be downloaded from its website, www.environment-agency.gov.uk.

Confidential advice and support on practical ways to increase profits, minimize waste and reduce environmental impact is available from Envirowise at www.envirowise.gov.uk. Its big-splash campaign, which is funded by the DTI and Defra, is intended to help companies across the United Kingdom to make money by saving water. Envirowise will provide free, hands-on advice to help you understand how much water your business currently uses, simple ways this can be reduced and how to measure the cost savings. The Envirowise site also tells you how you can save money on your tax as well as water bills by purchasing products from the Water Technology List, an initiative developed by DEFRA, the Inland Revenue and Envirowise to encourage more efficient water use.

Businesses investing in the products on the Water Technology List can claim tax relief through the Enhanced Capital Allowance (ECA) scheme, which may provide a cash flow boost as well as an ongoing cost saving on water bills. Businesses can offset 100 per cent of the cost of products on the Water Technology List against their taxable profits. All businesses that pay corporation and income tax in the United Kingdom are eligible for the tax allowance.

Conclusion

Preventing pollution and using water efficiently require you to be in control of what you are doing, and in possession of the right systems and procedures. But that should be the case for all aspects of your business. It is therefore no surprise that the management of environmental issues, including water and wastewater, is increasingly being seen as a mark of a well-managed business.

Ed Mitchell is Corporate Social Responsibility Director for Thames Water.

Chemicals: Responsible Care and a sustainable enterprise

Colin Chambers, Chemical Industries Association

Introduction

Society has become more risk adverse and intolerant of the burden, both social and environmental, caused by industry. With particular regard to 'chemicals' and the chemical industry, they have been seen as part of the 'problem' rather than part of the 'solution'. In response to this changing business environment, both industry and government are devising ways towards a more socially and ecologically responsible way of doing business that also supports the principle of 'sustainable development'.

A competitive and economically sustainable industry must adopt innovative business solutions that help satisfy society's needs while optimizing the use of resources and ensuring that we have taken all reasonable steps to prevent harm to human health and the environment. It is also essential to demonstrate good practice in ethical behaviour, respect the culture and rights of individuals, and adopt the highest standards of corporate governance and accountability.

Having a vision

Back in November 2000 the Chemical Industries Association (CIA) launched its Leadership Statement on Sustainable Development as the first step in its sustainable development strategy. In the statement the CIA committed itself to making every effort to deliver a major contribution to sustainable development through the continuing success of the UK chemical industry, whose products are essential for economic, social and environmental progress.

The Chemical Industries Association's vision of a sustainable chemical industry, developed from this statement, may be summarized as 'Meeting Needs and Expectations':

a competitive and economically sustainable industry, adopting innovative business solutions that help satisfy society's needs while:

- optimizing the use of resources;
- ensuring that we have taken all reasonable steps to prevent harm to human health and the environment;
- demonstrating good practice in ethical behaviour;
- respecting the culture and rights of individuals;
- adopting the highest standards of corporate governance and accountability.

Making the vision a reality

To support this vision the CIA made a public commitment to develop an integrated set of economic, social and environmental goals for sustainable development by mid-2004. These goals and the 'Guiding Principles for Sustainable Business Practice' derive from and support 'Meeting Needs and Expectations', the CIA's declared vision for a sustainable chemical industry.

As part of its development of a full set of sustainable development goals, the CIA set its first Responsible Care performance goals on Health and Safety in January 2003 and completed the set in January 2004 by agreeing on environmental and product goals. Responsible Care is a self-imposed commitment by chemical companies worldwide under the auspices of the International Council of Chemical Associations (ICCA) designed to help companies continuously improve the health, safety and environmental performance of their operations and products. In the United Kingdom, where the Responsible Care initiative has been in operation for around 15 years, compliance with the guiding principles of Responsible Care and self-assessment of Responsible Care management systems are mandatory for all CIA members.

Demonstrating our commitment to an economically sustainable industry operating within the context of good ethical practices will represent a major communications challenge for the industry. We have to begin to understand why what we say, or what we mean to say, is not always what our audiences hear. And then, of course, we have to learn how to say the right things in the right way. We have to learn a new language, and a new set of behaviours, if we are to succeed in getting our message across, which is essential for the chemical industry's future success as part of today's society.

Responsible Care

Responsible Care is the international chemical industry's commitment to continuous improvement in its safety, health and environmental (SHE) performance, and openness and transparency with stakeholders. It began in Canada in 1985, was adopted in the United Kingdom in 1989, and by the middle of 2004 had spread to no fewer than 47 countries worldwide, including 23 in Europe.

Responsible Care is also an attitude of mind that puts the chemical industry in the lead on progress in industrial SHE performance. And it is a brand whose strength confers moral authority and helps ensure public and official recognition of the industry's achievements.

Responsible Care provides a practical approach for organizations to demonstrate to external stakeholders that all reasonable means have been taken to deliver continuous improvement in health, safety and environmental performance over and above that required by legal compliance. Responsible Care helps an organization to:

- meet statutory requirements and industry goals and targets;
- maintain control of activities, people, equipment and materials;
- achieve continual improvement;
- assemble and retain Responsible Care knowledge and good practice;
- provide education and training for its employees and contractors;
- provide transparency of information and demonstration of improvement for its stakeholders.

Measuring and reporting our performance

As part of the CIA's Responsible Care initiative, the industry's SHE performance has been reported in the annual indicators of performance (IoPs) since 1991. The most recent set of indicators, that for 2003, was published in July 2004.

Working to spread Responsible Care principles

As the supplier of chemical building blocks to customers and consumers down the supply chain, the chemical industry has sought to encourage and foster the adoption of the Responsible Care principles with user industries. In July 2000 the CIA and the British Coatings Federation (BCF) signed a memorandum of understanding confirming the commitment to BCF's sister programme, Coatings Care, becoming mandatory for membership of the BCF, extending the BCF's existing voluntary support for the Responsible Care initiative. This followed the adoption of mandatory commitment to the Responsible Care initiative by the British Chemical Distributors and Traders Association (BCDTA) earlier in the same year.

Managing risks in the supply chain

Product stewardship was highlighted at an early stage as an important aspect of Responsible Care; however, its achievement has proved something of an intractable problem, as one of the key routes down through the supply chain is through sales forces. To meet this challenge, in 2003 the CIA launched a training package aimed specifically at sales forces, to explain the concept of product stewardship and the role of sales forces.

The industry has also sought to respond to all its stakeholders in its approach to Responsible Care. While focusing initially on performance within their own plants and manufacturing sites, chemical companies have found increasingly that stakeholder concerns have shifted away from production to products, matched by calls for a better way of presenting the levels of improvement that the industry has achieved.

Greater scrutiny of how the retail sector sources products from across the globe is driving it to explore the concept of 'corporate responsibility', demonstrating to its stakeholders that it is actively managing the social and environmental 'footprint' of its supply chains and the products they produce. Chemicals are present in virtually every consumer product that retailers sell, and therefore need to be addressed within their commitments on corporate social responsibility. As a response, in early 2004 the CIA and the British Retail Consortium formed the Supply Chain Leadership Group (SCLG) to draw together chemical companies and retailers to determine how chemicals are used in supply chains.

Retailers and chemical companies can be seen to represent the beginning and end of the supply chain. As the SCLG evolves, it is hoped to engage all those companies and organizations that operate within the supply in order that they become involved and engaged in its work and the solutions it develops. We also wish other stakeholders, including pressure groups and regulators, to play an important positive role in shaping the work of the SCLG. This alliance with the retailers, against the backdrop of the all-encompassing EU chemicals policy, gives the chemical industry an invaluable chance to understand the new realities bottom-up, from the perspective of the everyday customer and his or her concerns about the products of the chemical industry.

Listening to our stakeholders

A critical aspect to operating as a sustainable enterprise is listening to your stakeholders and understanding their needs and expectations. For example, the chemical industry continues to engage with government over chemicals of concern in the UK Chemicals Stakeholder Forum, including taking voluntary action to reduce risks associated with these chemicals.

In the area of performance, our stakeholders told us, 'This is all very good, but what we really want to know are your future goals and targets, not where you are coming from.' The industry failed to hear this message for many years and chose to continue on its agreed path of focusing on the past performance. It did not take account of stakeholders' views until around three years ago, when it was recognized that to move forward we needed to align our thinking with that of the stakeholders.

To be a sustainable enterprise requires a good reputation. However, reputation is a function of performance; performance improvement has to come before reputation improvement. But as an industry we can't be selective about the areas where we improve our performance. It has to be across the board – in all aspects of our business performance and in some of the softer areas too through:

■　better listening and empathy with public concerns;
■　showing by our actions that we mean what we say;

- being consistent;
- being prepared to communicate – and not seeking to limit the agenda.

It means understanding future market needs better, and providing solutions to those needs and expectations – and *not* defending products and processes that are clearly not defendable. Most important of all, it means talking about the positive benefits of our industry – particularly the products of our industry – not persistently focusing on defending the negative impacts.

We now characterize our old behaviour as decide–announce–defend:

- decide what we want to do;
- tell everyone we're going to do it; and then
- defend our position unwaveringly when people question or criticize our decisions.

The new behaviour means a new process, one that requires us to listen first, take time to understand and be sure that we know what's being asked of us. Only then should we respond and deliver – but we can do so with enthusiasm about the positive benefits of our industry.

Goals and targets for continual improvement

While IoPs indicate progress that has been achieved, more recently stakeholders have called for the industry to set itself challenging targets. Through a series of discussions held during 2002, a wide range of stakeholders, including regulators, employee representatives, environmental groups and other non-governmental organizations (NGOs), contributed their thoughts on how a set of targets might be generated. These contributions were constructive and included key messages, such as that goals should be based on an overarching vision statement; there should be more interest in product than operational goals; and more interest in sustainable development than just SHE goals. There was much support for a step-by-step approach, without undue criticism if the industry failed to meet challenging goals.

These suggestions helped to direct CIA thinking, and in January 2003 an initial set of performance goals was launched (see Table 6.8.1).

All the goals listed are for the period 2000–10 and relate to the aggregate performance of the CIA membership. Progress towards the goals will be measured and reported annually.

This initial set of goals was further developed into a complete set of SHE goals by adding goals on environmental impact and products. They represented the first step in the CIA working to establish a chemical industry vision for sustainability, which provided the framework for the full set of sustainable development goals launched in July 2004. These goals also included social and economic aspects.

Legal compliance

Organizations should have a process for identifying and maintaining a list of legal and other requirements that are applicable to its activities, products and services. Once a list of these requirements has been generated, the regulatory part can be maintained by using one

Table 6.8.1 Initial set of targets for hazard reduction

	Type of Hazard	Target
Health and Safety	Lost time injuries	50% reduction
	Reportable diseases	30% reduction
Incidents	COMAH incidents reportable to the EU	Zero
	Distribution incidents	50% reduction
Resource Use	Energy usage	11% reduction
	Water usage/tonnage production	20% reduction
	Hazardous waste/tonnage production	25% reduction

of the commercially available index services. These can often provide access to copies of the relevant documents using files based on software or microfiche. Systems should be established to ensure that those individuals appointed as accountable for implementations of requirements are notified.

The applicable requirements include:

■ Legal requirements, including all relevant regulations, as well as product notifications and authorizations, limit values, conditions or improvement plans, requirements of consents, licences and other operating permits.

■ Codes of practice. Consideration should be given to relevant codes to which the organization subscribes, eg Responsible Care guidance. Criteria or guidance published by competent authorities (eg the Environment Agency, the Health and Safety Executive, the Department of Trade and Industry (DTI), the Department for Environment, Food and Rural Affairs (DEFRA)) may be relevant.

■ Relevant technical standards.

■ The views of other stakeholders. Objective evidence of these views could include, but not be limited to, views of employees, letters from the public or from environmental organizations, shareholders' comments, insurance audit reports and surveys and questionnaires, or requirements from customers.

Each of the applicable requirements should be reviewed to identify duties of and prohibitions on the business, and to reference where in the management system this requirement is to be managed and how – for example, what procedure is to be followed and who will be responsible for it. This enables the business to manage and periodically audit all its applicable requirements.

Managing risks and improvement programmes

Good management systems are required to drive long-term continual improvement, and third-party verification provides another means to meet the concerns of stakeholders who are sceptical about industry's claims.

In 1998, Responsible Care Management System (RCMS) guidance on how companies could enhance their business management systems to incorporate and deliver on their

Responsible Care commitment was introduced. The RCMS is based on the Deming management cycle (plan–do–check–act), which seeks to support demonstrable and continuous improvements in SHE performance through the identification, management and control of all significant risks associated with a company's activities.

In 1998 the CIA also introduced processes for members to verify their implementation through self-assessment and for independent third-party verification against the CIA Responsible Care Management System as a means to improve trust and credibility with stakeholders.

A responsible approach to a sustainable future

As a member of the International Council of Chemical Associations, the CIA is thus seeking to improve awareness and initiate new dialogues with stakeholder groups. We want to work with these groups in ways that will further improve our performance, help us achieve sustainable growth, and improve people's knowledge and understanding of the business of chemistry under the successful banner of Responsible Care.

The chemical industry in the United Kingdom employs 230,000 highly skilled people nationwide and accounts for 2 per cent of GDP and 10 per cent of manufacturing industry's gross value added. The industry invests more than £2 billion annually, representing 14 per cent of total manufacturing investment, with a further £3.5 billion being spent on R&D. It is the United Kingdom's top manufacturing export earner, with an annual trade surplus of nearly £5 billion on sales of £33 billion, of which £29 billion is accounted for by exports, with a large proportion going to other countries in the European Union. Thus, it can be seen that the industry makes a vital contribution to modern life on a worldwide scale while seeking to operate as a responsible and sustainable enterprise.

The UK chemical industry has chosen to adopt sustainable development as the vehicle through which to deliver this culture change. It's an enormous challenge we've taken on, but we have heard the messages from our stakeholders. It's a great opportunity to be part of the solution rather than the problem, and we are trying to respond. The industry is mobilized and we feel that we have arrived at the root of the issue at last. Success can't be guaranteed, but we hope that we will be successful – because the future of this industry depends upon it. In fact, the route to sustainability – of the planet, not just the industry – depends on it.

Colin Chambers is Head of Group – Operations and Assurance, Chemical Industries Association, United Kingdom.

Tel and fax: 01928 732941
Mobile: 077660 234532
http://www.cia.org.uk/

Air Monitors is a monitoring technology company specialising in air quality sampling and measurement. The company is the UK's exclusive distributor of the industry leading R&P range of products and are able to provide the very best advice and support to clients involved in all types of monitoring applications. Whether your interest lies in source emissions, ambient air quality, intentional release monitoring for chemical, biological or radiological contaminants, personal dust monitoring or dust characterisation the company can assist. In dealing with our industrial clients our aim is to provide monitoring solutions which not only help with compliance but add value wherever possible. The company's approach is based on best value and best practice which although not always the lowest up front cost, inevitably returns the best investment over time. Air Monitors offers equipment for sale or hire and can provide a full monitoring services option where they will plan, deploy and manage the equipment throughout the life of the project providing validated data to clients who prefer not to get directly involved in field operations.

Contact details:

Air Monitors Limited
Unit 2a The Hawthorns
Pillows Green Road
Staunton, Glos. GL19 3NY
T   +44 (0)1452 849111
F   +44 (0)1452 849112
E   enquire@airmonitors.co.uk
W www.airmonitors.co.uk

Jim Mills
Managing Director
E   jim@airmonitors.co.uk
M 07973 661931

CARBON TRUST

Making business sense
of climate change

The Carbon Trust is an independent company funded by Government. Their role is to help the UK move to a low carbon economy by encouraging business and the public sector to reduce carbon emissions now and capture the commercial opportunities of low carbon technologies.

The Carbon Trust is focused on reducing carbon emissions in the short and medium term through energy efficiency and Carbon Management and in the medium and long-term through investment in low carbon technologies.

The objectives of the Carbon Trust are:

- To ensure that UK business and public sector meet ongoing targets for CO_2 emissions;

- To improve the competitiveness of UK business through resources efficiency; and

- To support the development of a UK industry sector that capitalises on the innovation and commercial value of low carbon technologies.

In order to meet these, the Carbon Trust is developing and implementing a range of programmes, including:

- Delivering independent information and impartial advice on energy efficiency and carbon management to the business and public sector, through schemes such as the Action Energy programme and Carbon Management;

- Promoting the Government's Enhanced Capital Allowances Scheme to encourage investment by business in qualifying energy saving technologies;

- Investing in the development of low carbon technologies in the UK – whether through research and development funding, technology acceleration and direct support for pre-commercial and commercial organisations

For more information on the Carbon Trust, and to find out what help is available for your business to reduce its carbon emissions, visit **www.thecarbontrust.co.uk**

CHEMICAL INDUSTRIES
ASSOCIATION

The UK chemical industry & The Chemical Industries Association: A credentials statement

Chemicals' Contribution to Society: the industry's products form the basis for every manufacturing activity, underpinning transport, healthcare, food and drink, construction, textiles, IT - and indeed all other sectors of the economy. It is impossible to divorce a successful and responsible chemical industry from the colourful, diverse, clean and safe environment and high standard of living that we have come to take for granted.

In particular, industrial chemicals can proudly claim a major role in increasing human longevity and the quality of life - life expectancy at birth doubled in the 20th century. Not only can this be attributed to such recognisably chemically derived products as drugs and antibiotics but improved water treatment, detergents and pesticides have all played their part.

Key Contribution to the British Economy & Employment: the chemical industry in the UK employs 230,000 directly nationwide, and accounts for 2% of UK GDP and 11% of manufacturing industry's gross value added. (Within the EU as a whole, the chemical sector employs 1.7 million people).

It invests over £2 billion annually (plus £3.5 billion on R&D) and is the UK's top manufacturing export earner, with an annual trade surplus of nearly £5 billion on a gross output of £46 billion. It also provides a tax and national insurance contribution of nearly £5 billion a year to the UK national government and local authorities. The sector also invests approximately £400m a year on training and, on average, full-time employee hourly earnings are 29% higher than in manufacturing generally.

Industry and the Environment: in 2001, the chemical sector spent more money on environmental protection than any other comparable British sector. An independent report for Defra estimates that the UK chemical industry spent a massive £713m on environmental protection during 2001 or 18% of the £3.9 billion spent by the whole of UK industry.

This level of expenditure is indicative of the importance that the chemical sector places on protection of the UK's air, water and soil environments and, as such, is also a tribute to the success of the CIA's part in the global "Responsible Care" programme that commits all its members to continual improvement in all aspects of health, safety and environmental performance.

CLIMATE CARE

Climate Care raises funds by selling greenhouse gas emissions reductions (referred to as CO_2 offsets). It then develops projects that reduce emissions, ensuring that the total reductions achieved match the amounts sold.

Examples of the projects that Climate Care is funding include:

- Efficient coffee drying in Costa Rica – coffee farmers currently supplement their dryers with wood cut unsustainably from local forests. Climate Care is providing the equity to install efficient burners that eliminate the need for the wood

- Low energy lighting in low income households in South Africa – as electricity is generated from coal saving electricity reduces CO_2 emissions, as well as reducing bills for householders

- Reforestation in Uganda – substantial parts of Kibale National Park in Uganda were cut down in the 1970s. Climate Care is contributing to the replanting of the area with native tree species. As well as sequestering CO_2 the project provides local employment and is a valuable wildlife habitat.

Climate Care is involved in a number of other projects and is able to fund a growing number of new ones each year. In 2005 we expect to take on a liability to reduce CO_2 in the atmosphere by 100,000 tonnes.

Climate Care has a wide client base – from large corporates to SMEs and individuals. Clients tend to offset the emissions from their flying, driving or processes. Alternatively they offset emissions on behalf of their customers and stakeholders for promotional reasons.

Whether your interest is in reducing your global warming or becoming involved in sustainable development projects, Climate Care can help.

**For further details see www.climatecare.org
or contact tom.morton@climatecare.org**

Clean water is something we can take for granted but over a billion people in the world don't have it, and over two and a half billion people lack basic sanitation. As a result a child dies every 15 seconds from water-related diseases.

Without safe water and sanitation nearby people find it impossible to escape the downward spiral of poverty and disease. Many women and children in developing countries spend hours each day walking miles to collect water, taking up valuable time and energy, preventing women from working and stopping children from going to school. The water they walk so far to collect is usually dirty and unsafe, but they have no alternative.

WaterAid is the UK's only major charity dedicated exclusively to the provision of safe domestic water, sanitation and hygiene education to the world's poorest people. Established in 1981 WaterAid now helps over 500,000 people every year in 15 counties in Africa and Asia. With local organisations WaterAid helps to set up low cost, sustainable projects using appropriate technology. The local community is empowered to plan, construct, manage and maintain their own projects so that they last long into the future.

WaterAid also seeks to influence water and sanitation policies at a national and international level to ensure that more of the world's poorest people gain access to these basic needs.

As an independent charity WaterAid needs support to carry out this vital work. WaterAid can work with companies and individuals in a range of ways from high profile events, to long-term strategic partnerships or employee involvement.

Your support today will help expand our work to help more of world's poorest people gain access to safe water and a better quality of life.

Call 020 7793 4500 or visit www.wateraid.org to find out more.
Charity registration number 288701.

7

Land use

LAND USE

East Yorkshire has some of the highest rates of coastal erosion in north-west Europe. The area's holiday industry is worth £92 million a year to the local economy, but with an average of two metres of land per year disappearing into the sea, caravan and holiday home parks currently overlooking the coast are in danger of literally falling into the North Sea.

Yorkshire Forward is working with East Riding of Yorkshire Council on the Roll-Back Initiative, a project designed to address the problem by encouraging site owners to identify and move to new parks outside of the risk zone. This will provide a sustainable solution by minimising the economic impact of coastal erosion and enabling the owners to stay in business and contribute to the local economy.

Alex Smith, principal sustainable development officer, East Riding of Yorkshire Council, said: "Roll-Back is part of a wider programme, Integrated Coastal Zone Management, a sustainable development approach to managing the competing demands in a coastal area.

"ICZM seeks to integrate inshore marine plans and policies with terrestrial counterparts, an ensuring that human activities driven by market forces complement and consider environmental demands and in turn enhance social well being.

"Abandoned sites have historically been left to deteriorate and fall to the mercy of the waves, leaving the local authority to pick up the cost of cleaning up.

"Yorkshire Forward's funding seeks to tip the balance in favour of relocation and protect the industry and landscape."

The new Rolled-Back sites will be developed with minimum impact on the landscape. English Nature has funded a guide to ensure that the vacated site, which will become public land, will be cleared to high standards that benefit coastal biodiversity and public access.

Land use: introduction

Office of the Deputy Prime Minister

The Government aims to create sustainable communities – places where people want to live – that promote opportunity and a better quality of life for all. Sustainable communities address the three pillars of sustainable development: they promote economic growth, social progress and environmental protection; and there is a place for the private sector in all those key areas.

The Office of the Deputy Prime Minister (ODPM) is the focal point for delivery of sustainable communities, and the action plan set out in *Sustainable Communities: Building for the future* will be taken forward with a range of partners from private housebuilders through to regional planning bodies. Local strategic partnerships are central to the delivery of the strategy, and the Government's long-term commitment to revitalizing our most deprived neighbourhoods is an integral part of its efforts to promote sustainable development and sustainable communities.

The Government is committed to maintaining the target that 60 per cent of additional homes should be on previously developed land; and through the Regional Development Agencies (RDAs) and English Partnerships, we will remediate brownfield land at a rate of over 1,400 hectares per year for economic, commercial, residential and leisure use. This is an area the size of the London Borough of Islington. In addition, we will ensure that every local authority has undertaken an urban capacity study (as set out in PPG3) to identify the full potential for using previously developed land and conversions.

ODPM and English Partnerships are developing a comprehensive national strategy for brownfield land. This started from a detailed understanding of what brownfield land is available, making full use of the National Land Use Database (NLUD), which identifies

66,000 hectares of previously used land capable of redevelopment. A quarter of this has lain dormant or derelict for 10 or more years. The strategy will cover how best to bring sites back into use, especially in the growth areas.

English Partnerships' The RDAs will develop national strategy in more detail to produce Brownfield Land Action Plans in cooperation with local authorities and other relevant agencies and statutory bodies. These plans will fit closely with the Regional Economic Strategies and Regional Housing Strategies.

The Government has a package of fiscal measures to support regeneration. These include:

- *Stamp duty exemption* for residential property transactions up to £150,000 and for all non-residential property transactions in the 'enterprise areas'.
- *VAT reductions* to encourage better use of existing housing stock and reuse of empty homes. VAT has been reduced to 5 per cent for the cost of converting residential properties into a different number of dwellings or into residential communal homes, and for the renovation of homes empty for 3 years or longer. In addition, there is VAT relief for the sale of renovated houses that have been empty for 10 years or more.
- *Contaminated land tax credit* to encourage reuse of contaminated land.
- *One hundred per cent capital allowance* for the development of flats over shops.
- A *tax incentive* to encourage business donations to the running costs of urban regeneration companies (URCs).

In addition, the 2003 Pre-Budget Report (PBR) and 2004 Budget announced the Government's intention to introduce a *Business Premises Renovation Allowance* in the enterprise areas. Subject to State Aids approval, the scheme will be introduced in 2005, and draft legislation will be published shortly.

Further, in line with the recommendations of the Barker Review and the statement in the Pre-Budget Report, the Budget announced that the Government is looking to extend the contaminated land tax credit to land that is *long-term derelict*. The Government continues to examine the effectiveness of this proposal, and will take into consideration the planned evaluation of the contaminated land tax credit.

Land use: legal overview

Kathryn Mylrea, Simmons & Simmons

The land-use planning system in the United Kingdom dates back to 1949 and has provided the framework for determining the acceptability of development. Development may be anything from a building or installation on a greenfield site to a change of use of an existing development, or an engineering operation such as an infrastructure project. The Government is currently in the process of reforming the planning system, with the aim of increasing flexibility and reducing bureaucracy. The Planning and Compulsory Purchase Act, which received royal assent on 13 May 2004, is the first step in this reform and it is being implemented in stages. Although it does not change the fundamental concepts underlying the system of planning permission, it does make changes to the wider development planning process. The Act includes a specific provision requiring persons who exercise functions in relation to regional spatial planning and local development documentation to exercise the function with the objective of contributing to the achievement of sustainable development.

The planning system is inextricably linked with environmental issues. For example, the EU Environmental Impact Assessment (EIA) Directive (Directive 85/33/EEC as amended by 97/11/EC), implemented in the United Kingdom through the planning system as part of the planning application process, prescribes a procedure that must be followed for certain types of development before they are granted development consent. EIA requires that a developer compile an environmental statement (ES) describing the likely significant effects of the development on the environment and any proposed mitigation measures. The ES must be circulated to statutory consultation bodies and made available to the public for comment. Its contents, together with any comments, must be taken into account by the competent authority (eg local planning authority) before it may grant consent. The EIA also applies to development for which planning permission is not needed, and there is specific legislation covering those situations.

Other environmental controls are implemented through the planning system. For example, Directive 96/82/EC (the Seveso II Directive) on the control of major accident hazards involving dangerous substances requires member states to ensure that the objectives of preventing major accidents and limiting the consequences of such accidents are taken into account in their land-use policies. These obligations have been implemented through the Planning (Hazardous Substances) Act 1990 and Regulations made under the Act, which include the Planning (Control of Major-Accident Hazards) Regulations 1999 (the COMAH Regulations).

Land-use planning also plays a major role in securing remediation of contaminated land. Local planning authorities must take account of contamination or the potential for contamination in preparing development plans setting out the policies and proposals for future land use and development within their area, and in determining individual applications for planning permission. There is also a raft of non-statutory mechanisms to support the regeneration of contaminated land – for example, the development of a single remediation permit, remediation tax relief and landfill tax credits.

Contaminated land

Peter Ord, Environment Agency

Buying or selling land that is contaminated in some way should only be done with full knowledge of the facts and the potential consequences. Contamination need not break the deal, but it is an important factor in considering the end use of a site. The extra time and money required for cleaning up the site also need to be considered.

If you own or buy land, you should make sure you are aware of any existing contamination. An audit will reveal any problems and what the associated risks are. If you cause or knowingly permit land to be contaminated, or if you own or occupy land that is contaminated, then the regime introduced in the 1990 Environmental Protection Act (EPA) may require you to investigate and clean it up.

If you redevelop land, any existing contamination will be regarded as a 'material planning consideration' for planning purposes. The planning authority will normally require investigation and clean-up as a condition of granting planning permission.

Who pays?

In accordance with the principle of 'the polluter pays', whoever caused or knowingly permitted the contamination will be liable. If the polluter cannot be found (the person may have died, or the company may have gone into liquidation), the enforcing authority itself may undertake the work. Alternatively, the owner or occupier may be liable.

What is contamination?

There are thousands of sites in the United Kingdom that have been contaminated by industrial, mining or waste disposal activities. They may pose a risk to the environment or human health. Contamination may inhibit the redevelopment of derelict industrial sites and increase development pressures on greenfield sites.

Contaminated land is defined in Part IIA of the EPA as land having substances in, on or under it that a local authority believes are polluting (or are likely to pollute) rivers, lakes or other 'controlled' water, or are causing (or are likely to cause) harm in other ways. The term 'harm' is used in relation to:

- human beings;
- ecological systems or living organisms;
- crops, produce and livestock;
- buildings.

In certain cases, contaminated land may also be designated as a 'special site'. This applies to land causing certain kinds of water pollution, land contaminated by waste acid tars, land used for refining oil or manufacturing explosives, and nuclear and Ministry of Defence sites. 'Special sites' are regulated by the Environment Agency (in England and Wales) or the Scottish Environment Protection Agency (SEPA – in Scotland) instead of the local authority.

Cleaning up

The Government has set a target of 60 per cent of new housing to be built on previously developed or brownfield land. Some brownfield land may also be affected by contamination. Government encourages voluntary clean-up where contamination is found, wherever possible, rather than regulatory action.

Where enforcement is needed, it comes through:

- conditions of planning permission from the local authority under the Town and Country Planning Act when a site is redeveloped; or
- the regime introduced under Part IIA of the EPA, which provides a framework for the identification and clean-up of contaminated land. (In Northern Ireland, regulations are not yet in force but are provisionally scheduled to be in operation by 2006.)

The Part IIA regime is clearer and more consistent than previous legislation. It should allow businesses that may have liabilities to assess the likely requirements and plan their own investment programmes to clean up sites voluntarily, instead of waiting for regulatory action.

Enforcement

Local authorities are the primary enforcers in England, Wales and Scotland, except in the case of 'special sites', as described previously. Every local authority has a duty to ensure that its area is inspected from time to time, to identify contaminated land and to enable the local authority to decide whether any such land should be designated as a 'special site'.

Where a local authority has identified land as contaminated, it is required to notify:

- the Environment Agency or (in Scotland) SEPA;
- the owner of the land;
- anyone who occupies all or part of the land;
- any other appropriate person.

The authority must also determine what needs to be done by way of clean-up, and serve a 'remediation notice' on each appropriate person (any of the people identified above) that states how and by when the condition of the land must be improved.

Further information

Before dealing with any contaminated land, obtain accurate information on its condition so that any risks or liabilities can be managed appropriately. Useful websites include:

www.environment-agency.gov.uk
www.sepa.org.uk
www.defra.gov.uk
www.ciria.org.uk

Peter Ord is a Policy Adviser in the Land Quality section of the Environment Agency's Head Office at Bristol. He deals primarily with issues relating to the clean-up of land contamination within the town and country planning regime. He has worked for the Environment Agency and previously the National Rivers Authority for nine years and has also worked in local government and the private sector.

Planning and consents

William Tew, Royal Institution of Chartered Surveyors

As with almost all areas of business, consumer expectations of corporate behaviour are rapidly changing and businesses are having to adapt their practice accordingly. The consumer of today takes a far greater interest in how businesses conduct themselves and whether they trade in an ethical manner. This should not suggest that there are no benefits of corporate social responsibility (CSR) for the business itself. On the contrary, trading responsibly has shown real benefits for productivity and financial sustainability.

Responsible business planning involves incorporating ethical and environmental issues into all aspects of the company's development. This is especially important when investing resources in the workforce, the financial market and building capital; these areas should be carefully planned so that their productivity is sustainable for years to come.

Because of the influential nature of the planning process and its huge scope to impact upon the very fabric of society, the planning system has an almost unique ability to actively promote civic renewal within the community. It is this ability to cooperate with the community that offers the property sector a great opportunity both to help achieve the long-term aims of CSR and to enjoy the real business benefits that it brings.

Richard Roberts (2003), writing in *RICS Business*, highlighted the four main benefits for a company when it incorporates CSR into its business planning. These benefits are:

■ *Compliance and risk management*. Companies are currently forced to comply with a vast array of legislation around workplace practice and planning issues. As a result of this, it is far more productive for them to have considered and planned for responsible working in the first place than to face a claim for malpractice and the subsequent fundamental changes to their working that are necessary to avoid further claims. This area is especially important in today's culture of blame and litigation.

■ *Competitiveness and operational efficiency*. Consumers and investors are now in the powerful position of being able to choose between a vast number of companies when making their business decisions. Companies practising in a responsible manner are in the advantageous position of being able to attract the business of the growing number of ethically minded users. Also, operating responsibly increases the overall efficiency, so that more financial resources are available for re-investment into the business.

■ *Reputation management*. There are a considerable number of bodies ready to criticize business if its decisions are considered mercenary and unethical. It is essential for companies to work with, rather than against, such sectors by being transparent and honest about their working practices. The business can then hope to develop a reputation for responsible planning and resource management.

■ *Market differentiation*. This benefit incorporates elements from all the above areas. Working responsibly and efficiently frees up resources for internal investment, and building a solid reputation allows a company to outshine its rivals in the competitive business market. These forces result in a company that stands out in terms of its ethical reputation as an employer, an investor and a service provider. A company that is dedicated to CSR could be expected to surpass its rivals and excel in the marketplace.

As a business, how would you go about introducing CSR into your practice?

It is important to accept that change is a gradual process that begins with the adoption of new thinking practices and priorities. Responsible working is likely to begin at a senior level, where new plans are devised and ultimately roll down to the delivering of staff training that instils the ethos down to project level.

With the sustainability of new developments now a matter of growing relevance to the property sector, many companies have begun to establish working groups to address CSR issues, and to ascertain how their practice impacts upon the individual, society and the environment. These working groups can identify and utilize environmental friendly technologies that actively promote sustainability – for example, eco homes, energy-efficient appliances, thermal efficiency, photovoltaic panels, solar heating or sustainable urban drainage systems (SUDS).

As well as the implementation of CSR, it is also important that the business incorporate measures that monitor its performance in terms of CSR issues, including the energy effectiveness of its buildings and the impact of its health and safety policies, allowing for areas of poor performance to be addressed and rectified.

It is also just as important for it to ensure that its published documents reflect its ethical policies and attention to current issues, such as human rights, environment and biodiversity. Doing so will allow consumers and investors to become familiar with its policies and differentiate it from its competitors. The company should also actively invest in the local community. As well as enhancing its reputation, such investment will help to sustain its workforce both currently and in the future.

The Government's new agenda for planning legislation serves to help businesses to incorporate CSR into their planning. In December 2001 the Government released the Planning Green Paper, which detailed a major programme to reform the planning system in England by making it more flexible and responsive. Having gained Royal Assent in May

2004 and in place in early summer 2004, the new Planning and Compulsory Purchase Act places a huge emphasis on community involvement within the planning system. The Act is creating significant changes at all levels of the planning system: regional planning, local planning and the handling of planning applications. These changes are designed to allow people to access information more easily and to participate more readily in the decision-making process.

When organizations make information available about their plans and planning applications, individuals can take advantage of their right to make representations on these applications, which allows, where appropriate, the individuals' views to influence independent examinations and inquiries. This process of empowering individuals serves to enrich the life of the local community as well as promoting the organization's sustainability.

The new provisions within the EU Strategic Environmental Assessment (SEA) will ensure that any significant environmental effects are assessed at an earlier stage in the preparation of plans and programmes, and before decisions on key issues such as alternative sites have been taken. The new Environmental Assessment of Plans and Programmes Regulations 2004 requires environmental assessment to be carried out in a number of sectors, including agriculture, energy, industry, transport, waste management, tourism, and town and country planning. The authorities responsible for preparing the plan or programme have to compile an environmental report, which must evaluate the likely significant environmental effects of implementation and of reasonable alternatives.

In many ways the planning system, in its current form, already provides numerous opportunities for the local community to participate in key decisions throughout the planning process. Nevertheless, it can also be recognized that there remains a need for a more transparent and accessible system, if the Government is to engage with local people and deliver the objective of creating an inclusive, accessible and sustainable environment.

Regeneration

English Partnerships

Regenerating previously developed land: the role of English Partnerships

English Partnerships is the national regeneration agency supporting high-quality, sustainable growth across the country. One of our core business areas is to act as the Government's specialist adviser on brownfield, or previously developed, land (PDL). We are also a key delivery vehicle for the urban renaissance and the Deputy Prime Minister's Sustainable Communities Plan.

One of the main aspects of this plan is to ensure that we are making best use of the nation's scarce supply of land. It outlined a strategic role for English Partnerships to search out and assemble land, especially brownfield and publicly owned land, for sustainable development. We are responsible for producing and maintaining a National Brownfield strategy on behalf of the Office of the Deputy Prime Minister (ODPM) to ensure that as much new development as possible is accommodated on previously developed land. The Strategy will provide a coherent vision for the future development of brownfield land in a way that underpins national, regional and local development aspirations.

English Partnerships' *Towards a National Brownfield Strategy*, published in November 2003, is the most comprehensive study ever undertaken to assess the state of England's brownfield land supply. The findings, along with a series of recommendations, were presented to the Housing and Planning Minister, Keith Hill. The study highlights the huge potential to recycle brownfield land to meet Government housing growth targets, while reducing the pressure to develop on our countryside.

The report concludes that more than 20,000 hectares of brownfield or previously developed land (nearly one-third of the total) has been identified as being unconstrained and therefore available for redevelopment. In addition, almost one-third of the brownfield land identified is contained within the key 'growth area' regions of Greater London and the South East and East of England.

The National Brownfield Strategy is being taken forward by ODPM and English Partnerships through a joint-project team. It is expected that the strategy will be published in summer 2005 and will serve as both a best-practice guide and a toolkit for those involved in the reuse of previously developed land.

We are supporting Regional Development Agencies (RDAs) in the creation of their Brownfield Action Plans aimed at speeding up brownfield delivery, especially in the four major growth areas. The plans will propose methods of making better use of brownfield land to deliver regional economic and housing strategies as well as identifying new development opportunities and different ways to tackle the blight caused by long-term dereliction.

Two pilot sub-regional action plans have been undertaken in the North West: one in east Lancashire, one in part of Greater Manchester. It is intended that these plans will form a basis of best practice for other RDAs.

English Partnerships is looking at mechanisms to bring previously developed land back into productive use. The National Land Use Database (NLUD), which we helped to create, contains information about previously developed vacant and derelict land and buildings. It is the first countrywide source of statistics on the number, type and planning status of previously developed sites. NLUD is a vital source of data for the production of the National Brownfield Strategy.

Not all previously developed land is suitable for recycling as plots for housing or commercial development, owing to factors such as contamination, ground conditions or location. However, many do have huge potential as safe 'green amenity' sites such as woodland, parks, commons, nature areas and other public open spaces. The Land Restoration Trust (LRT) was established in 2004 to restore and manage brownfield land for use as public green space. The LRT is a partnership of English Partnerships, Groundwork, the Forestry Commission and the Environment Agency, and has the backing of ODPM through the Sustainable Communities Plan.

One of our most successful countrywide projects to regenerate previously developed land is the 10-year £385 million National Coalfields Programme. Since the programme began in 1996, significant progress has been made in addressing economic, environmental and social issues in former coalfield communities, which were characterized by huge job losses, contamination and dereliction following the pit closures of the 1980s and 1990s. The programme will help to create new uses for around 4,000 hectares of former colliery or coking works land. In addition, 27 sites from the National Coalfields Programme will eventually be reassigned to the Land Restoration Trust to be transformed into sustainable green spaces with social, economic and environmental benefits.

We have also been responsible for cleaning up heavily contaminated sites on the Greenwich Peninsula in London and Middlehaven in Middlesbrough. In 1997, English Partnerships began the task of transforming the Greenwich Peninsula – formerly the site of the largest gasworks in Europe – into a thriving, 21st-century community. The Greenwich Peninsula is the largest development site in London and one of Europe's biggest regeneration projects. We have invested over £200 million in acquiring, reclaiming and developing the Peninsula site and received an environmental award in recognition of our work.

At the other end of the country, English Partnerships is working with Middlesbrough Council, One NorthEast and Tees Valley Regeneration to regenerate Middlehaven, an 80-acre former docks adjacent to Middlesbrough town centre. Following the recent completion of an £18 million reclamation and restoration contract for the dock basin and surrounding land, a regeneration site covering over 15 hectares has been prepared for commercial and residential development. The initial phase of the project is expected to comprise a new business park, an exclusive waterside residential development and a range of community and leisure facilities.

As well as being involved in physical regeneration, we support organizations such as CL:AIRE (Contaminated Land: Applications in Real Environments), a public–private partnership devoted to finding innovative solutions for dealing with contaminated land. Enabling cost-effective land remediation techniques to be tested under real site conditions, it acts as an important link for the United Kingdom's main players in contaminated land reclamation. Through stimulating new partnerships and projects and matching them with suitable sites, CL:AIRE can then achieve environmental objectives in its development and reuse of derelict, contaminated sites. In this way, UK expertise and contaminated land technologies are brought to the fore.

Part of English Partnerships' role as the national regeneration agency is to disseminate the lessons learnt from our initiatives to inspire a better way of life for the communities we serve. By sharing our experiences of best practice in land decontamination and remediation, we aim to limit the impact of building much-needed housing on the countryside and make England a better place to live.

For further information please contact Professor Paul Syms, Project Director for National Brownfield Strategy and Strategic Joint Ventures, English Partnerships.

8

Energy use

Energy use: introduction

The Carbon Trust

Saving energy is not just good for the environment – it's good for business.

In the United Kingdom, businesses waste an average of 30 per cent of the energy that they buy. In 2003 alone, as a whole this added up to a staggering loss of £12 billion. Yet most businesses could easily cut their heating, lighting and power bills by up to 20 per cent without any capital investment, with some companies being able to save even more. By cutting these bills and reducing energy costs, businesses can generate immediate savings to the bottom line, increasing profitability. For example, a 20 per cent saving in energy consumption – which, as already stated, is easily achieved by many businesses – can have the same positive effect as a 5 per cent increase in sales.

Improving energy efficiency encompasses everything from simple measures such as turning off lights and turning down thermostats, to full audits of how energy is used in every aspect of an organization, or looking at building design to make it as environmentally sound as possible. There's a wealth of free help and advice available out there to businesses wanting to make improvements, and even financial help to offset any initial cash outlays.

By reducing overheads, businesses automatically improve the competitiveness of their products or services, and with more and more investors and customers positively discriminating in favour of 'green' companies or organizations, it's an issue no business can afford to ignore.

For more information about saving energy for your business, call the free Action Energy helpline on 0800 57 58 94, or visit www.actionenergy.org.uk.

Energy use: legal overview

Kathryn Mylrea, Simmons & Simmons

There has been a great deal of new legislation in the field of energy and the environment, particularly in relation to greenhouse gas emissions and renewable energy sources. As well as energy-specific regulation, the environmental impacts of energy production are also taken into account within other regulatory regimes – for example, pollution prevention and control (PPC) requires that the best available techniques are used in connection with emissions and operations for many energy production and combustion processes, and requires energy efficiency measures for other energy-intensive installations.

Many of the drivers for change in the approach to energy issues come from the European Union. For example, the Renewables Directive (2001/77/EC) was adopted in September 2001, and member states had until October 2003 to implement it. The recitals to the directive state that the Community recognizes the need to promote renewable energy sources as a priority measure, given that their exploitation contributes to environmental protection and sustainable development. The directive required member states to adopt national indicative targets, compatible with their Kyoto targets, for future consumption of electricity from renewable sources. Member states were also required to provide an outline of the measures taken or planned to achieve those targets, including a system of guarantees of origin of electricity produced from renewable energy sources, which had to be put in place and supervised by a competent body.

In the United Kingdom a 'Renewables Obligation' (RO) was imposed on licensed electricity suppliers on 1 April 2002, creating a unified United Kingdom-wide system of tradable green certificates known as ROCs. The intention of the RO is to provide a stable market, which will in turn encourage investment in new renewable electricity generating capacity, helping the United Kingdom achieve its 10 per cent renewable energy target by 2010, and whatever targets are set thereafter until 2027.

Directive 2002/91/EC on the energy performance of buildings requires implementation by 2006. The objective is to improve the energy performance of buildings within the Community, with member states required to set minimum energy performance requirements for all buildings, subject to specified exemptions. When buildings are constructed, sold or rented out, an energy performance certificate must be made available, allowing consumers to compare the energy performance of different buildings.

Another important element in the UK Government's new energy policy, as set out in the Energy White Paper, is cogeneration, or combined heat and power (CHP). CHP is a fuel-efficient energy technology that, unlike conventional forms of power generation, puts to use the by-product heat that is normally wasted to the environment. In this way, CHP can increase the overall efficiency of fuel use to more than 75 per cent (compared with around 40 per cent from conventional electricity generation). Furthermore, because it often supplies electricity locally, CHP can also avoid transmission and distribution losses.

Energy efficiency

Tim Ashmore, London Energy

Meeting the energy challenges ahead

The combined effect of the Climate Change Levy and the target for reducing CO_2 emissions by 2010 has been that UK industry is coming under increasing pressure to improve the environmental performance and cost-effectiveness of its processes and buildings. However, unpredictable consumption patterns and the apparent difficulties of devising energy efficiency programmes for commercial sites dissuade many firms from trying to implement energy-saving measures.

The low price of energy over the past few years has done little to encourage energy efficiency initiatives, especially as cost savings could be more easily made by reducing the unit cost of electricity. However, it is clear that a huge amount of energy is now being wasted through a lack of action on the part of energy users. Action Energy, part of the Government-funded Carbon Trust, estimates that every year £12 billion of energy is wasted across the United Kingdom. This represents a staggering 30 per cent of the country's consumption, with UK businesses losing up to £400 million per year just by neglecting to implement energy efficiency measures. In the past year, energy costs have risen significantly, and if they continue to rise over the next few years, the current level of energy wastage will cost UK industry more and more. Of course, this rise in the base rate also means that the payback period for efficiency measures already taken will begin to shorten, thereby rewarding organizations that are addressing energy conservation.

Public pressure

With soaring oil prices and a renewed debate over climate change and security of supply, energy has been high on the news agenda. Public concern over energy efficiency and global warming is increasing. There is also a growing demand for 'corporate greenness' that seems unrelenting, and companies are faced with an increased public awareness of corporate social responsibility. Reducing energy consumption offers a fast and politically acceptable alternative to traditional areas of cost cutting. And these savings are sustainable. But it's not just about cost control. Reducing energy consumption offers relief from these growing environmental pressures on business.

Government action

In addition to the financial burden arising from the increase in energy costs, industrial users may also find themselves liable for penalties imposed by the Government on wasteful users. In February 2003 the Government published the Energy White Paper, confirming its views regarding Britain in a low-carbon future. The paper strongly stated the need for more renewable energy and greater energy efficiency, and outlined demanding goals for reductions in CO_2 emissions, with targets or 'ambitions' set for 2010, 2020 and 2050. The Government aims to cut the level of carbon emitted over the next 50 years by 60 per cent.

In April 2004 the Environment Secretary, Margaret Beckett, unveiled the Government's implementation plan, which outlined how it will deliver the strategy set out in the Energy White Paper. *Energy Efficiency: The Government's plan for action* sets out how the Government aims to tackle climate change, cutting carbon emissions by an extra 12 million tonnes through energy efficiency within the next six years, and saving more than £3 billion a year on energy costs. The strategy includes a range of measures, such as changes to the building regulations to raise energy efficiency standards, doubling the level of Energy Efficiency Commitment activity from 2005 to 2011, and new energy service pilot schemes through which energy suppliers can offer energy-efficient packages to customers.

Renewable energy

Actions aimed at limiting carbon emissions are already under way in the form of the Climate Change Levy (CCL) and the Renewables Obligation, which requires electricity suppliers to sell a defined, and annually increasing, percentage of renewable electricity. The EU Directive on Fuel Labelling, which came into effect at the end of July 2004, gives suppliers one year in which to comply with new regulations. Suppliers are obliged to state clearly where their energy is sourced from and the percentages from each source. The government wants to see 10 per cent of the country's electricity power derived from renewable sources by 2010 and 20 per cent by 2020.

As renewable energy sources are currently relatively scarce yet high in demand, renewable energy commands a premium. Organizations looking to improve their environmental performance with renewable energy should plan ahead and communicate their needs to their energy supplier sooner rather than later to secure the volume they require.

While the cost of renewable energy is expected to fall as supply increases, the Government itself estimates that the various measures proposed in its White Paper will add between 10 and 25 per cent to industrial electricity prices. This implies that if UK firms are to avoid a large financial burden, they need to act soon to get energy efficiency measures in place.

Measuring and monitoring energy wastage

As these measures continue to take effect, UK industry is realizing that there is a growing cost implication for firms neglecting to properly address their energy wastage. The CCL and the Renewables Obligation, coupled with the current short supply of energy from renewable sources, have contributed to increasing energy costs, which coincide with the current rise in the electricity base rate.

The key to avoiding unnecessary cost is to know how much energy is used and where, so that wastage can be identified and eliminated. Of course, those organizations already involved with CCL agreements are familiar with the need to monitor and record their energy consumption, to be sure of meeting their CCL agreement targets. Measurement can itself be seen as a cost, but given that it can help firms fulfil their CCL obligations and also address energy wastage across the whole organization, use of such a measurement system is extremely beneficial.

Certain products are available that can aggregate and analyse energy consumption data. One example is London Energy's Energy Performance Reporting service. Via products such as this, changes in consumption can easily be delineated and linked to a wide range of variables, helping firms measure the effectiveness of any energy efficiency initiatives that have been implemented. Such monitoring and analysis can even be done over multiple sites, making it suitable for comparing their energy performance.

Implementing energy efficiency

Energy efficiency measures often fall at the first hurdle, owing to the perceived high cost of implementing and maintaining such initiatives. Many organizations tend to view energy as an uncontrollable overhead, but this is far from true. There are several simple measures firms can take to cut energy wastage, many of which are free.

Of course, the cheapest unit of energy is the unit not used, and staff awareness of simple energy-saving measures can save an organization a considerable amount of money. Even a small business can substantially cut its energy costs by merely turning off computers, monitors, photocopiers and televisions overnight, rather than leaving them on standby. Imagine the energy wasted, and hence the cost generated, by a large organization that left all its computers and monitors on standby over the Christmas holiday. Lighting often accounts for around half of all energy used, so turning off lights, especially high-powered task lighting, is a very effective form of energy efficiency.

London Energy offers free posters to its customers showing ways in which they can use less energy, thereby raising awareness of the importance of energy-saving measures 'on the shop floor'. Recent research carried out by London Energy has revealed that it may be possible to persuade staff to apply simple energy-saving measures. The survey found that almost 80 per cent of companies believed that staff are responsive to simple energy-efficient policies such as turning off computers and photocopiers overnight, given suitable encouragement.

The second stage of improving energy efficiency is to ensure that energy-using equipment is maintained correctly and regularly. This applies also to control systems for heating, air-conditioning, etc. Poorly maintained plant and controls will almost always use more energy than necessary, and often the cost of maintenance can be more than balanced by the savings from the consequent reduction in energy consumption.

While these simple measures are a very good starting point, other routes to energy efficiency, and hence cost savings, do require some initial investment. In terms of premises, buildings should be well insulated and have draught-proof doors and windows. Heating and air-conditioning units should be regularly serviced and well maintained. As 25 per cent of the United Kingdom's carbon dioxide emissions come from lost heat emitted from buildings, improved energy efficiency is a primary element of the UK Climate Change Programme set out by the Office of the Deputy Prime Minister. Saving heat reduces energy bills and lowers harmful emissions. Recent amendments to building regulations together with the forthcoming EU Directive on Energy Performance of Buildings will oblige companies to maintain energy-efficient buildings.

Companies that have energy-intensive core processes need to undertake a cost–benefit analysis to ensure that old or poorly maintained equipment is not costing them more in the long term than the up-front cost of upgrading to more energy-efficient machinery now. The efficiency of high-energy-use machinery is absolutely vital when tackling energy wastage. While these measures can require a large initial outlay, the consequent savings in energy usage are immediate and ongoing, especially when the rising cost of energy is factored into the equation. Of course, these measures also have knock-on benefits for the environment.

Performance partnerships

Many businesses are looking for new solutions that improve their position over the long term. One example is a joint venture by London Energy and Dalkia, which offers a fully integrated solution that tackles both cost and environmental pressures. 'Performance Partnerships' is a packaged solution that bundles together the three key interdependent elements that comprise a business's total energy cost:

■ competitively priced electricity and gas supply;
■ energy management practices;
■ building services maintenance.

A single contract to encompass both energy supply and energy management services guarantees a reduction in total energy costs against anticipated levels over the contract period. This also provides the business with protection from inflation and fuel price increases, and the environment benefits through an absolute reduction in greenhouse gas emissions – a direct contribution to global environment protection.

Conclusion

Sustainable energy savings are not a quick fix. Therefore, businesses need to take action now to improve their energy performance and optimize future energy budgets. Energy management has been too low on the priority scale for many businesses for too long. Upward pressures on the cost of energy should encourage them to begin using it more efficiently. Reducing consumption is not as difficult as it may seem, and there are many solutions on the market that can help UK industry improve its performance. It simply needs to take the initiative.

Tim Ashmore is Energy Services Manager at London Energy.

Renewables

Richard Hussey, Good Energy

How to buy green electricity for your business

Green consumerism is becoming increasingly important. Large and small businesses alike are expected by customers, investors and other stakeholders to have an appropriate environmental policy and standard.

At present, the biggest source of carbon dioxide emissions is power stations, accounting for some 29 per cent of the total.[1] If your electricity supply is generated from entirely renewable sources, you can be sure that however much electricity you use, no additional carbon dioxide will be released into the atmosphere from its generation.

In fact, according to *The GOOD Energy Guide*, published by the Ethical Marketing Group, 'Any company, small or large, that claims "corporate social responsibility" that has not yet switched to a renewable energy supply should think again!'

Renewable electricity doesn't cost the earth

As a new technology, it is currently more expensive to supply electricity from renewable technologies than from conventional fossil fuels, although some of the premium will be off-set by an exemption from the Climate Change Levy. Most companies are prepared to pay a 10 per cent premium for the environmental benefits of renewable electricity. The actual difference in cost can vary greatly, depending on your usage and current supplier. Some companies have even reduced their energy costs by switching to renewable energy.

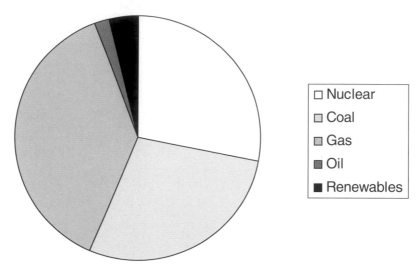

Figure 8.4.1   Sources of electricity: UK national average, 2001

Choosing a renewable electricity supplier

Your choice of green electricity will determine your level of support of renewable energy and affect the credibility of your environmental policy. Many electricity suppliers offer a 'green' tariff to their customers. However, this often does not exceed or even match the Government obligation that a small percentage of their energy comes from renewable sources. In this case, no extra demand for renewable energy is created.

Ask the right questions before you buy your electricity:

1. *Where does your supplier's electricity come from?* In July 2004 new legislation was implemented requiring all electricity companies in the United Kingdom and across Europe to provide information to customers about the fuel sources that they use to generate the electricity supplied to their customers. This disclosure requirement allows customers to know where their suppliers have bought power from, and therefore what type of generation they are supporting by buying electricity from that supplier. Figure 8.4.1 shows the UK national average for sources of electricity supply in 2001, and Figure 8.4.2 represents the comparison for Good energy.

2. *Will you be making a difference?* Every electricity supplier is required by the Government to source a small percentage of electricity from renewable sources. If you want to make a difference, you need to ensure that the green electricity tariff you choose creates additional demand for renewable generation and does not simply contribute to that supplier's obligation.

3. *Is this verified by an independent audit?* There is currently no independent accreditation body for green electricity tariffs. Ask your electricity supplier if it has an independent audit procedure to verify that it is delivering on its environmental claims. The *GOOD Shopping Guide* and organizations such as Friends of the Earth have compiled their own ratings of green electricity supply.

Simple

Cut your pollution at work or home.

Simply switch electricity to Good Energy 100% renewable electricity.

To get a quote or to switch, phone us on 0845 456 1640 or visit www.good-energy.co.uk

Good Energy ○
100% renewable electricity

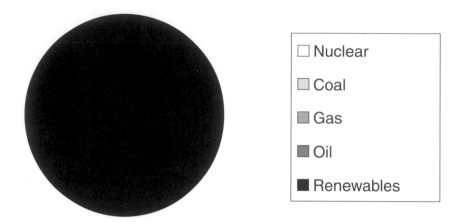

Figure 8.4.2   Sources of electricity: GOOD Energy supply, 2002

4. *How green are your electricity supplier's renewable sources?* Wind power, small-scale hydroelectric (eg water mills) and solar generation produce no carbon dioxide when they generate electricity, whereas biomass and landfill do.
5. *Is it an ethical company?* Request a copy of the company's environmental report and check its ethical rating with the Ethical Consumer Research Association's findings in the *GOOD Energy Guide*, which looks at the ultimate holding company as well as the tariffs themselves.
6. *What if we want to generate renewable electricity ourselves?* If you are interested in going one step further and installing renewable generation on site, some suppliers have schemes specifically designed for supporting small-scale generators.
7. *Are there any additional benefits?* Will your supplier offer further business benefits such as PR and marketing support to help you communicate your environmental commitment to your customers?

More information

If you would like more information about switching your business to renewable electricity, Good Energy, a supplier dedicated to supplying only 100 per cent renewable electricity, can provide a personalized quote to show how much CO_2 you can save, as well as how much it would cost. Simply fax a recent electricity bill to 01249 766091 or call them on 0845 456 1640.

Useful contacts

■ Green electricity suppliers recommended by Friends of the Earth: www.foe.co.uk/campaigns/climate/press_for_change/choose_green_energy.
■ Suppliers recommended by *The GOOD Shopping Guide*: www.thegoodshoppingguide.co.uk.

■   The Ethical Company Organisation ethical company accreditation scheme illustrates which companies are, overall, most responsible towards the environment, people and animals: www.ethical-company-organisation.org.

■   The Energy Savings Trust for advice on Energy Efficiency and generating your own renewable electricity: www.est.org.uk.

Note

1   DTI Report (2003) Energy: Its Impact on the Environment and Society – 2003 update, www.dti.gov.UK/energy/environment/energy-impact/2003 update.pdf

Combined heat and power

David Green, Combined Heat and Power Association

Cutting energy costs with combined heat and power

The rate of adoption of new, high-efficiency combined heat and power (CHP) plants has been slow in the past two or three years, due to a number of factors. But this is about to change for many types of CHP schemes, as electricity prices have already begun to climb again from the artificially low levels resulting from the adoption of new electricity trading arrangements (NETA) a few years ago.

Indeed, the fundamentally sound economic and environmental case for CHP is unaltered: a well-designed CHP plant operating at a site with suitable heat and power loads can significantly reduce both energy bills and carbon dioxide emissions to the atmosphere. A technology that converts 80–90 per cent of the energy contained in fuel into useful energy, rather than discarding half of it, as conventional, power-only stations do, will always be a better bet in economic and emissions terms.

A third advantage is that on-site CHP can also ensure that energy loads remain supplied during periods of interruption to main gas and/or electricity supplies. This can make the difference between a company remaining open for business during a power cut, or closing.

CHP exists in well-proven technology forms able to serve sites from as small as 6 kWe up to large industrial sites and even whole towns. The development of new technologies, including new ultra-low-emissions microturbines, domestic-scale CHP and fuel cells, means that many more energy users across the range will be able to benefit. Energy users can access CHP and its benefits either by investing in their own on-site scheme or by asking a member company of the Combined Heat and Power Association to build, and operate, a plant for them – often at no capital cost.

The economic case for CHP has also been helped by the full exemption of CHP from the Government's Climate Change Levy (CCL), which came into force in April 2003. Previously, CHP had enjoyed only a partial exemption from the levy charge, which is designed to persuade energy users to switch to greener supplies. Fuel supplied to the CHP plant was levy exempt, but power exported off-site by the CHP was not. Now, energy used at the site of the CHP plant, as well as energy sent to neighbouring sites using dedicated wires, and energy bought on the open market from remote CHP plants, are all exempt from levy charges.

A further economic advantage flows from CHP plants being eligible for 'enhanced capital allowances' under the Climate Change Levy package. Customers investing in CHP are able to write off the whole cost of their investment in CHP during the first year of its operation. The allowance can be seen as equivalent to a small but significant cut in the capital cost of new qualifying energy efficiency equipment.

The Government is committed to CHP as a means of achieving a significant part of its carbon dioxide emissions reduction target. In the 2003 Energy White Paper the Government recommitted itself to its target of achieving at least 10 GWe of CHP by 2010 – roughly doubling the amount in use today. The Government also published its CHP Strategy in May 2004.

However, the latest research suggests that the target is likely to be missed, and the CHP Association is campaigning for the adoption by the Government and regulator, of certain measures designed to put CHP back into strong growth. The main changes we would like to see are:

- the positive promotion of CHP under the EU Emissions Trading Scheme;
- an exemption for CHP power exports from the Government's Renewables Obligation;
- a tilting of the power stations consent procedure, which continues to allow low-efficiency power stations to be built;
- tackling the adverse effects of NETA.

Created in 2001, new electricity trading arrangements have not helped the case for small, green generation plant such as CHP. NETA has created a complex trading mechanism that penalizes generators such as renewable energy and CHP plant operators for the sometimes unpredictable output of their plants to the grid. The CHPA continues to campaign for fair treatment for CHP and other distributed generators under NETA, so that users are not prevented from switching their own energy supplies over to lower-carbon forms of generation.

Current energy market conditions in the United Kingdom have tended to mask the very powerful economic and environmental advantages of CHP, which can make it the most cost-effective solution for businesses with substantial heat and power loads and long working hours. This is particularly the case for smaller CHP schemes that do not plan to export excess power to the grid, and for users requiring a secure, high-quality local power supply.

As electricity prices rise again and with the backing of a Government keen to see its carbon-saving potential realized in full, CHP remains a vital, green and well-proven technology. Now is the time to re-examine the case for CHP as a way of cutting costs and improving environmental performance at your site.

CHP technology

CHP – sometimes known as cogeneration – is a family of technologies rather than a particular type of plant, and can be used at an enormous range of sizes, from as small as a factory-assembled domestic-scale unit, through engine- or microturbine-based plants serving a commercial building, to custom-built plant from many tens to a few hundred megawatts in size used in an industrial setting. Small-scale cogeneration usually comprises factory-assembled units with an electrical output of less than 1 MWe or 2 MWe, while larger installations tend to be custom-designed and built.

CHP is also used as the energy source for 'district energy' schemes whereby heat and power produced in a central plant are distributed to a group of homes and buildings within a district, town or area of a city. Social housing in many parts of Britain has traditionally been supplied by heating-only 'district heating' schemes; in some cases these are being extended, with the addition of cogeneration plant, to supply electricity as well. A Government support programme, the Community Energy Programme, has helped to stimulate this sector in recent years.

In the United Kingdom, CHP technology based on gas engines, gas turbines and waste heat boilers is fast replacing plants based on coal and steam turbines. While fuelled principally by natural gas, many such systems also burn gas oil from time to time. In addition, a range of renewable fuels may be used. Perhaps the most commonly employed are waste gases from landfill sites and sewage treatment works, along with solid agricultural and forestry wastes.

New, advanced technology for use with CHP is also coming on to the market. The most exciting development is perhaps the fuel cell, which combines hydrogen and oxygen to generate heat and power, the only by-product being water. Several packaged fuel cell cogeneration units are already at work across Europe and in the United States and Japan.

Meanwhile, the use of microturbine technology has been demonstrated in several countries. Even smaller units, designed to provide energy to a single home, are also becoming available. As they are taken up, these new technologies may well boost the use of CHP to new levels.

Energy-intensive industrial processes give cogeneration the best opportunity to make significant cuts to energy bills, and many industries have heat and power loads that are particularly well suited to cogeneration, including the chemicals, pharmaceuticals, refineries (often fuelled by valuable waste gases produced at the refinery), paper and board manufacturing, food and drink, and iron and steel industries.

For purchased plant, typical payback periods can be from 3 to 7 years, with the CHP plant continuing to generate energy cost savings for its economic life, a further 15–20 years. Alternatively, the energy services approach allows consumers to benefit without making any capital payment.

Trigeneration is the extension of CHP to include cooling. The key to cooling is an extra device, an absorption chiller, which generates cooling from the heat produced by the cogeneration unit. Cooling is normally used to chill water for air-conditioning.

Where a mixture of heating and cooling is needed – for instance, winter heating and summertime cooling, or simultaneous heating and cooling – a trigeneration plant is a particularly economic solution. But the benefits go much further. Adding an absorption chiller to the system designed for a building allows installation of a cogeneration plant larger than one dictated purely by the heat load, or for the cogeneration plant to run for longer; improves the performance and benefits delivered by the plant. The absorption chiller is effectively running on 'waste' heat, rather than the electricity that conventional chillers require.

David Green is the Director of the Combined Heat and Power Association. Tel: 020 7828 4077, or visit the website at www.chpa.co.uk.

THE BRITISH
WIND ENERGY
ASSOCIATION

The British Wind Energy Association (BWEA) is at the heart of the wind energy activity in the UK.

Established 26 years ago, BWEA is the trade and professional association for the wind industry, representing some 330 companies active in the sector with membership interests ranging from wind energy research, consultancy, manufacture, development, operation and associated services.

The UK's largest renewable energy body, BWEA represents the wind industry at home and abroad, to Government, regional bodies and local authorities throughout the UK and to the business community, the media and the public. BWEA co-ordinates statistics and intelligence on every aspect of the industry, acting as a forum for members and a central point of information for all.

With a recognized voice in lobbying on behalf of the wind industry, BWEA recently expanded its mission to champion marine renewables, with many companies amongst its existing membership already having strong interests in this sector.

There is wide agreement that marine renewable technologies are is in the position that wind power was several years ago, and that it is likely to experience the same rapid growth over the next few years. This expansion of BWEA's remit will establish the platform which will allow industry players to share experiences and learn from the lessons of the wind sector and its move offshore.

Wind power, both on and offshore, will be meeting some 8% of UK electricity supply by 2010, while this country's wave and tidal resources have the potential to provide a considerable percentage of power in the future.

BWEA is at the forefront of ensuring that the necessary policies and infrastructures are in place to allow these technologies to play their rightful role in meeting challenging targets on climate change, generating not just a secure energy supply but also a new industry for Britain.

Harnessing the power of the wind is as old as the hills. Today's modern wind turbine technology generates clean green electricity from one of the world's most abundant natural resources and does so without any harmful waste products or emissions.

Wind power can be utilised practically anywhere, traditionally on agricultural land in 'wind farms', but can be equally readily installed on industrial or brownfield sites, or even in the car parks of supermarkets. The UK is after all the windiest country in Europe and there are very few places in the UK which do not have some capability for wind generation.

And wind power is an attractive business option. 'Doing your bit' to save the environment can have its own reward, but a number of new policy measures now mean that wind power makes good economic as well as environmental sense.

The Climate Change Levy is a tax on energy use by both business and public sectors with the aim of encouraging greater energy efficiency. The Levy on electricity is set at 0.43 pence per unit, and relevant bills have increased by an average 8-10%. The simplest way to be exempt from the Levy is to be wholly or part-supplied with accredited renewable electricity, and wind power is eminently eligible and one of the cheapest renewables available. If more of an incentive to invest is required, then the Renewables Obligation effectively sets a value on the greenness of electricity at 3.51 pence per unit, over and above any value attached to the price of power itself.

And so on-site generation is a new feature for many businesses, most recently for Ford at their Dagenham factory in East London. Two 1.8 MW turbines installed in April this year at what is Europe's first city-based wind farm generate 100% of the electricity requirements of Ford's new Clean Room Assembly Hall, meaning that all Ford's diesel engines will be produced by wind power. Sainsburys led the way in 2001 when they installed a single 600 kW wind turbine at one of their distribution depots in East Kilbride in Scotland which powers at least 1/3 of the electricity required by the cold storage depot, and then added innovative hybrid wind-photovoltaic systems in the car parks of two of their London supermarkets. Other examples include a dairy in Yorkshire, a hospital in Northumberland, a make-up factory in Wales, a quarry, a steel mill…the list goes on, demonstrating how simple it is to switch on to the power of the wind.

Nor are businesses the only ones to benefit – schools and householders too have been joining the renewables revolution. Ladygrove Primary School in Telford, West Midlands, has just installed a Proven 2.5kW turbine costing £12,000, and estimated to save the school around £400 a year in electricity bills, while over in North Yorkshire, the 20 kW Gazelle turbine at Nidderdale High School and Community College, funded by npower renewables and the Lottery Fundís Seed Challenge-programme, produces over 50,000 units of electricity each year, making substantial savings in the school's electricity bills.

Meanwhile many homes are turning their back gardens into mini power stations, with the added bonus that power companies will buy back surplus electricity from domestic generation, such as Good Energy, who will pay Home Generation customers for every unit of renewable electricity they generate on their own premises, including the units that are used on site – a cottage industry indeed!

Wind turbines large and small, commercial or domestic, all are contributing to combating global climate change and helping to keep the green lights on in Britain.

More information at **www.bwea.com**

Transport

Transport: introduction

Tony McNulty MP, Department for Transport

Transport has a vital role to play in supporting a vibrant and prosperous economy. But improvement must be achieved in a way that minimizes environmental impacts and enhances social benefits – balancing the need to travel with the need to improve quality of life.

Clearly, the Government plays an important role: providing sustained investment, improving the management of the existing system, and planning ahead. But to enable a truly sustainable transport system to be delivered, business must play its part too.

The Department for Transport (DTI) sponsors a number of initiatives to help businesses do this, including:

■ Promoting workplace travel plans. These help to reduce the demand for car parking spaces, with consequent savings. And by improving accessibility, workplace travel plans can make it easier for employers to recruit new staff.
■ Helping hauliers to save on fuel bills by adopting more fuel-efficient driving and operating practices.
■ Promoting alternative fuel use in fleets. The company car tax and vehicle excise duty regimes have been radically reformed, providing incentives for the purchase of clean, fuel-efficient vehicles.
■ Offering grants to operators to help towards the additional purchase costs of environmentally friendly vehicles as part of the Powering Future Vehicles strategy. Details are available at www.transportenergy.org.uk.

There is good news. Notably, there has been considerable improvement in air quality over the past decade, particularly as a result of action to reduce road transport emissions.

But there is more to be done. It makes sense from a commercial and an environmental perspective to make the most of the support that is available.

This part of *The Sustainable Enterprise*, Part 9, provides further advice on what business can do to help deliver more sustainable transport.

Transport: legal overview

Kathryn Mylrea, Simmons & Simmons

Transport is increasingly being recognized as a critical issue in the sustainability debate, and there are numerous initiatives designed both to change transport patterns and to reduce the impacts associated with transport.

For example, the EC Directive on the use of biofuels and other renewable fuels for transport has as one of its main objectives the reduction of life-cycle emissions of carbon dioxide from transport across Europe. The directive requires member states to set indicative targets for 2005 and then 2010 for the use of biofuels or other renewable fuels as a substitute for petrol or diesel used in transport. In the United Kingdom, tax relief already exists to encourage the use of certain environmentally less damaging fuels. In 2002 a new duty rate for biodiesel was introduced at 20 pence per litre below the rate for ultra-low-sulphur diesel (ULSD). Until then, biodiesel for road use was taxed at the same rate as ULSD. The 2003 Pre-Budget Report also announced that the duty incentive for LPG would be decreased over time to a level more commensurate with its environmental benefits. The 2004 Budget confirmed that the LPG incentive relative to the main road fuels would be decreased by the equivalent of 1 penny per litre in 2004/05, and by a further 1 penny per litre in both 2005/06 and 2006/07. Transport is also widely expected to feature in the second phase of the EU Emissions Trading Scheme, which would have an impact on the sector – in particular, on aviation.

Local authorities have statutory duties for local air quality management (LAQM) under the Environment Act 1995. They are required to carry out regular reviews and assessments of air quality in their area against standards and objectives in the national Air Quality Strategy, and where these are unlikely to be met, authorities must designate air quality management areas (AQMAs) and prepare and implement remedial action plans to tackle the problem. Monitoring undertaken by the local authorities includes monitoring of nitrogen dioxide, nitrogen oxides and particles (PM10) at locations near to roads throughout the United Kingdom.

The London Congestion Charging Scheme commenced charging on 17 February 2003 following the approval by the Mayor of London of orders made by Transport for London. Article 3 of the Order designates the roads within the charging area (Greater London) in respect of which charges are imposed. The zone essentially comprises all publicly maintainable and Crown roads within the central zone, and there are controversial proposals to extend the charging area. Annexes to the order sets out the classes of non-chargeable vehicles and reduced-rate vehicles (including some alternative fuel vehicles), and the reduction for residents of the central zone. An amount (currently £5) is payable for a single-day licence if the charge is paid before 10 pm, rising to £10 if paid between 10 pm and midnight. The scheme is reported to have reduced traffic in the central zone during the charging periods, although negative effects on businesses located in the charging area have also been reported.

Alternative fuels and fleet management

Larry Parker, Travelwise

Crude oil not looking so slick

Road transport is a big problem. Not only does it account for in excess of 24,000 deaths per year, but it is also the third largest and fastest-rising emitter of greenhouse gas emissions. Never mind the fact that the world is running out of supply oil.

Until recently, local emissions were the biggest concern with regard to transport pollution. Now, however, another villain rears its ugly head: that of climate change and its pernicious consequences. Air quality is still a major issue, and a lot of the legislation and incentives are focused on this area. But the tide is turning – and has to – to a low-carbon focus for the United Kingdom's transportation sector.

Transport for London (TfL), along with the Association of London Government (ALG) and Sustainable Energy Action (an environmental non-governmental organization), held a conference addressing these changes in the field of alternative fuels, 'Alternative Fuels: A practical guide for fleet managers', on 6 July 2004. The rest of this chapter refers to the findings of this landmark conference bringing public and private fleet managers, local borough policy-makers and officers, councillors, government and European officials together to take seriously the need for progress and direction in the area of alternative fuels. The conference did not look at all possible alternative fuels, as they are numerous and each has its own cavalier protagonists, but concentrated on awareness-raising concerning those fuels that have potential today, and some that may have been overlooked to date.

The ALG had recently instigated a fleet survey of all the London boroughs to investigate to what degree fleet efficiency and emissions could be improved in the capital. It found a distinct lack of coordination between council fleets and in some cases within the fleets themselves, although many of the fleets had initiated the introduction of alternative fuels, motivated mainly by the cost incentives of the Powershift scheme. It appears evident that more complete management is necessary in particular with regard to fuel logging and accounting. Malcolm Noyle of LloydsTSB autolease management is in possibly the best position to comment on alternative fuels, as he is currently the green fleet development manager for the largest private fleet in the United Kingdom. His verdict was that a clean fleet strategy will save a company money and underline environmental corporate responsibility, and that fleets must accept and embrace change.

The discussion of the conference made a swift switch from the LPG champions to those of the biofuel industry. Biofuels' main advantage is that they can be used up to certain blends with conventional fuels in unmodified vehicles. This was swiftly followed by an update from a hybrid vehicle manufacturer concerning the supply status of hybrid and fuel cell vehicles. It appears that progress is being made in this area, but costs are still a significant barrier. A few years, however, should see a real market penetration of hybrid vehicles.

For effective medium-term decision-making, it is imperative that fleet managers and operators are aware of the legislation, taxation, grants and concessions that will be available in the next decade. TfL spoke on congestion charge exemptions for fleets, the Department for Transport (DfT) on its future taxation and strategy, and the European Union on its road fuel strategy.

It is becoming clear that, with the exception of the Mayor of London's policies, which understandably are focused on air quality, sustainability is becoming the major driver towards UK transportation strategy. In this capacity, biofuels are without doubt seen to be the fuel of the medium-term future – so much so, that it seems quite amazing that until the passing of the EU Biofuel Directive in 2003, most people in the United Kingdom had no understanding of the fuel. The London borough fleet managers will now go away and contemplate their attitude towards biofuels and whether it may be wise for them to start using them as a vital part of their fleet management. CNG was also mentioned as part of the EU road fuel strategy, but the general feeling among fleets is that it is a big, expensive switch with limited emissions benefits. For London, it seems that liquefied petroleum gas (LPG), compressed natural gas (CNG) and electric will still play an important part, as fuel concessions, grants and congestion-charge exemptions make them financially very attractive. Biofuels, though, appear to be close on their heels, with TfL considering broadening congestion charge exemptions to include biofuels for fleets if a way to account for them can be developed.

The day as a whole was aimed to give fleet managers and decision-makers a clearer picture, or at least make a start to that goal. Much help is available from 'Transportenergy Motorvate' and Best Practice schemes, which are focused on fleet efficiency. Sustainable Energy Action spoke on fuel policy as a means for councils and companies to green their fleet in a sensible and transparent fashion, and offer their services to any interested organizations.

The next challenge is to get the measures of fleet efficiency management and clean technologies introduced at council level and then see engagement of the private fleets. Oil prices are only going one way. It is in all fleets' interests to consider seriously what was discussed at this landmark conference, pick up the gauntlet and drive to a sustainable future – not off the cliff of finite fossil fuel consumption.

Improving London's Air Quality – Fuel Cell Buses

The situation today

Clean air is important to all of us. It is estimated that up to 1,600 people can die prematurely each year, due to health problems caused by breathing London's polluted air. The most vulnerable people are children, older people and those with heart and lung problems.

London's air has long been polluted. As recently as the 1950s the capital was frequently engulfed in smogs. Since then, government clean air regulations, the closure of coal-fired power stations and increasing use of central heating rather than coal to warm our homes, has ensured that smogs are no longer a problem in London.

Pollution is now less visible, but is still damaging our health. Today, most pollution in London comes from road traffic. London is a busy city, with 11 million car journeys made every day. Transport is essential to the capital, and we need to enable people and goods to travel freely, but we also need to improve air quality.

London leading the way

London Buses already run the UK's cleanest bus fleet, but as part of the Mayors commitment to clean air and improving environmental conditions in London, continues to look at ways of reducing its environmental impact.

One of the ways we are doing this is taking part in a pioneering project to reduce air pollution and noise by testing the first generation of zero emission fuel cell buses. This important initiative is a key part of the Mayor's Transport and Air Quality Strategies, which are designed to help give Londoners a cleaner and healthier future. Not only is the fuel cell bus trial a significant step towards achieving that goal, it also demonstrates that London is leading the way in alternative forms of public transport.

Nine cities in Europe are taking part in the Clean Urban Transport for Europe (CUTE) fuel cell bus trial, making it the largest project of its type anywhere in the world. The reason it's so important is because of greenhouse gas emissions, harmful exhaust fumes and inner city noise levels which are a major source of complaint. The project brings together over 40 organisations including the bus manufacturer, operating companies, hydrogen suppliers, fuelling and storage facilities, and universities. It is part of the ongoing development of clean urban transport systems that combine energy efficiency with cost-effectiveness.

The CUTE project started in November 2001. It was initiated by DaimlerChrysler/Evobus and is supported by the EU. The nine European cities taking part in the CUTE project are Amsterdam, Barcelona, Hamburg, London, Luxembourg, Madrid, Porto, Stockholm, and Stuttgart (Reykjavik and Perth (Australia) have since joined the trial). Chosen out of a much larger number of interested cities, the choice fell on these nine candidates based on their geographical and topographical diversity, as well as on their technical ability to tackle such a technologically advanced project. Each of these cities has bought 3 DaimlerChrysler/Evobus Citaro buses with Ballard fuel cells.

The CUTE experience so far

Up till April 30th 2004, the 30 buses have seen an average service life of 5.6 months in normal passenger service, during which time the buses have covered a total of 190,000 km, and the time in service amounts to 15,000 hours.

The daily running time of the buses is 10.3 hours on average, ranging from 8 hours to a maximum of 15 hours. The scheduled mileage is 120 km average with extremes of 80 km and 171 km. The main conclusion from these figures is that the use of Fuel Cells is not the limiting factor in running time, but rather the availability of skilled service personnel.

Bus reliability has been very high, with few instances of breakdowns, or long (5 day+) out of service incidents. Where these have occurred it is more likely to be issues around the re-fueling stations or spare parts availability rather than any problems relating to the fuel cell technology itself.

Confidence in the reliability of the buses is shown by the fact that in half the cities the CUTE buses replace a conventional bus in service, while in the other the fuel cell buses run in between two normally scheduled conventional buses.

The future for fuel cell buses looks good, as 80% of the cities see the fuel cell bus as an option for future procurement and 70% seeing it as a possibility to solve future energy problems. This result alone seems to be a very positive assessment of the quality and reliability of the CUTE buses in the various cities.

Working in partnership

To successfully introduce Fuel Cell buses to London, a number of key partners have been involved, each with different responsibilities and expertise.

London Buses is part of Transport for London, and is responsible for achieving environmental targets and standards for the whole of London's bus fleet, as required by the Mayor's Air Quality Strategy.

First operates around one sixth of the London bus network. Their experience, support and expertise in transit management is crucial in ensuring the trial is conducted and assessed to rigorous standards.

BP is providing the hydrogen-refueling facilities for the fuel cell buses. BP is an infrastructure partner in five of the nine CUTE cities and is demonstrating a range of different hydrogen technologies in each location.

Energy Saving Trust is supporting the project through grant funding from its New Vehicle Technology Fund programme.

Daimler Chrysler has developed and manufactured the buses and will provide technical support during the trial.

The **European Union** has co-financed the trial, with the support of the European Commission Directorate-General for Energy and Transport.

Without these partners, and funding from the Energy Saving Trust and European Union, it is unlikely that the Fuel Cell bus project would have been implemented as soon as it has.

In time however the costs of fuel cells will come down, with the last few years already having seen a dramatic drop in prices. As this occurs, and with the practical experience gained during the CUTE project, fuel cell technology is likely to become more widespread throughout the UK. Provided the EU and UK government continues to support the development of fuel cell technology, this could prove to be a viable alternative to traditional fossil-based transport fuels, in the longer term.

For further information on London Buses involvement in the Fuel Cell bus project, please contact Anna Rickard (Environmental Manager) at:

London Buses
200 Buckingham Palace Road
London
SW1W 9TN

Alternative fleet and dispatch

Andrea Casalotti, ZERO

Mention the words 'work' and 'bike' to many people and they will evoke a homely image of wartime boneshakers bearing a basketful of grocer's wares. To the well travelled, the words may conjure up colourful rickshaws rattling through busy Asian streets on their way to market, or trendy pedicabs transporting tourists in downtown New York.

But workbikes are much more than a post-war relic or passing gimmick. They have become lean, green machines that offer a real business advantage. This is only partly because workbikes embody the environmentally responsible image that so benefits almost any corporate image. Workbikes also **save time and money**. At a time when decision-makers are presented with a proliferation of new high-tech choices, no other reasons can explain why so many are opting for workbikes. Sales show a year-on-year increase.

Despite this impressive trend, no one is suggesting that the workbike can completely replace the work van or car. Their uses overlap, but each has its own unique business benefits. A powerful computer is a sophisticated and indispensable tool but no good to a journalist in a media scrum; a work van is a powerful machine but an encumbrance in a congested city centre.

A work van needs no definition. But what, precisely, is a 'workbike'? It can be any pedal-powered vehicle, ranging from a simple two-wheeler with a sturdy rack to a capacious three- or four-wheeler with enough covered storage room for safe carriage of heavy and/or delicate items. The first can be used by, say, a telephone engineer with a limited and predictable range of equipment, the second for substantial bulk goods.

While not always in direct competition with cars and vans, workbikes can often substitute for them. They are successfully used as a reliable delivery option for private or public companies, to serve cycle courier companies or as a convenient way for support staff to travel. They work equally well in public parks, city streets, the campuses of global enterprises or on the factory floor.

The low initial investment cost is a definite attraction to small enterprises. But despite their cottage industry image, the appeal of workbikes goes beyond this. Companies such as Texaco, General Motors, DHL and national post offices have all exploited the unique contribution of the workbike to increased corporate responsibility as well as profit margins.

Financially, it is **not just the initial cost of the vehicles** (around £10,000 less than a van even for a top-of-the-range workbike) **that makes them attractive**. Insurance, at around £50 per vehicle, is lower. Parking fees and fines, such as road tax and vehicle licence costs, are eradicated. Maintenance costs average £30–£40 per vehicle per year. There is no congestion charge, and, even for the bigger load-carrying bikes, storage costs are a fifth of those for vans.

Fuel overheads, of course, are negligible: a bicycle can travel over 2,000 kilometres on the energy equivalent of 5 litres of petrol (and unless you are subsidizing the riders' food, this is not a cost the company will carry!). All said, a workbike doing a multi-drop run of 30 consignments will cost less than half the same run done with a van – without adjusting for the money saved in quicker delivery times.

Their **durability** is the icing on the cost-saving cake. With far lower depreciation and risk of accidents, these vehicles can last decades – a fact lamented by the vice-president of the New York Worksman workbike manufacturer, as he sells fewer – but warmly welcomed by any buyers.

The same qualities that make workbikes economical also make them versatile. Although they cannot compete with vans or trains over long distances, they can complement them to ensure sustainability and economy. DHL operates 11 bikes to support its services out of three London hubs. They can handle 200 consignments of up to 150 kilos a day. Efficiency of this side of DHL's business has increased by 50 per cent since it introduced workbikes. This is where pen and paper supplement the computer, as it were. Conventional transport systems can cover the gross distance, but bikes get around cities much faster than anything with four doors and an engine, especially in the rush hour. Time-sensitive deliveries with multiple drop-off points benefit most. *Evening Standard* newspapers took advantage of this 'combination carriage' by using its vans to deliver the papers to central London pick-up points, from where ZERO cycle couriers would disperse them concurrently in multiple directions around the congested areas.

Nothing is more time sensitive than medical emergencies, and this has formed the backbone of Moves, a courier company serving many practitioners in Harley Street. On a much larger scale, the National Health Service (NHS) has started using bicycles for paramedics: where an ambulance isn't necessary to transport a patient, a cyclist can arrive on the scene more quickly, even carrying 40 kilos of equipment.

Also in a daily race against time, the Danish postal service uses 40 Christiania workbikes for large consignments. With 35,000 two-wheelers already in service, the British Royal Mail may yet follow its lead. Other possible users are meter readers, police officers and parking wardens, to name but a few.

Since 1999 the Government has committed itself both to sustainable distribution policies and to a substantial increase in cycle journeys. With greater use of workbikes by
Government agencies, enabling legislation is likely to follow. A successful Dutch system of
tax breaks for employers that buy company bikes instead of cars could well catch on in the
United Kingdom.

So much for the vehicles. But what about their riders? Does the initial novelty value of
a workbike wear thin with employees? Experience suggests not. Indeed, suppliers have
found that the bikes take on a cult status. One sceptical 50-something employee at a refuse
collection company renounced his initial doubts about bike transport after a few weeks in
the saddle, and his enthusiasm soon spread to his co-workers.

In the case of couriers, this enthusiasm rubs off on clients. ZERO says that customers
report better relations with cycle couriers, perhaps because, arriving less stressed and more
energized, they interact more positively on the doorstep.

Although they cycle in all weathers and terrains, even experienced couriers have their
physical limitations. The strongest bikes may carry up to 300 kilograms, but you can't
always expect hardened messengers, let alone corporate employees, to supply the corre-
sponding muscle and lung power. Where this is lacking, **electric assist** is an expedient
substitute. This is optional battery back-up that operates when pedal-pushing powers are
tested most: from a standing start, up a hill, into a wind or with an exceptionally heavy
load. It is used to good effect by La Petite Reine, the Parisian courier whose 'transship-
ment' system has attracted the custom of FedEx and DHL and enabled it to double its customer base in the space of a year. It now handles over 5,000 packages a month, covering
40 kilometres per bike each day.

The absence of an engine can be a positive attribute: safety considerations on the plant
floor of petrochemical companies, for example, have made workbikes the in-house vehicle
of choice for several multinationals.

But what about the rider's safety? The record at both ZERO and Cyclone Couriers, a
similar outfit working in York, is probably not untypical: just one minor accident per year.
The enhanced visibility of workbikes is doubtless a protective factor – and can provide a
free advertising space into the bargain.

Despite all their benefits, there is a question that, left unanswered, may deter many
businesses from trying out workbikes: the weather. Although workbikes are widely used
in Switzerland, the Netherlands and Denmark – hardly fair-weather countries – a residual
fear of rain may dampen the enthusiasm of many a prospective buyer. To which the work-
bikers reply, 'There is no such thing as bad weather, only inappropriate clothing.'

Perhaps there is no such thing as the perfect vehicle; only one that suits the job at hand.
Workbikes can often be just that vehicle.

For more information please visit www.workbike.org.

Congestion charging

Transport for London

Introduction

This chapter is about congestion charging in central London and the scheme that is currently operating in the charging zone. The chapter explains the aims of congestion charging and the operation of the current scheme. It also discusses the monitoring of the scheme and the results that highlight the benefits it delivers to businesses and the community.

Congestion charging in central London

The form of congestion charging employed in central London is a system based on camera enforcement using automatic number plate readers. This system was chosen because it had been proven to work. Presently this system is a means of enforcement and is not used to administer the charge.

The aims of congestion charging in central London

Congestion charging's primary aim is to reduce traffic congestion. In addition, it also addresses three other mayoral transport objectives:

- to make radical improvements to bus services;
- to improve journey time reliability for car users;
- to make the distribution of goods and services more reliable, sustainable and efficient.

Congestion charging is part of an integrated package

Congestion charging is not a stand-alone policy for reducing traffic congestion, but is part of an integrated package of measures to tackle congestion in central London. Such a package of measures is crucial to supporting alternative travel options and to managing related economic, social and environmental impacts. These measures include:

- improvements in public and social transport;
- better enforcement of traffic and parking regulations;
- improved maintenance and management of the main road network to ensure smoother traffic flow and more reliable journey times.

Working with London boroughs

Transport for London (TfL) has worked with London boroughs to ensure that measures complementary to congestion charging are implemented. These have included increased bus services and associated bus priority measures, environmental traffic management schemes and controlled parking zones in areas adjacent to the congestion charging zone to prevent 'rat-running' and displaced parking in sensitive areas.

Working with business

TfL has set up a series of measures to combat traffic congestion with the intention of enabling businesses to operate more efficiently across the capital. These include:

- coordinating street works by utility companies and highway authorities to avoid roads being constantly dug up;
- reviewing the London Lorry Ban's exempt network and access routes to it;
- setting up a London Sustainable Distribution Partnership so that the business voice is clearly heard when transport proposals are being developed.

With traffic down by some 15 per cent inside the charging zone, businesses are benefiting from the scheme in terms of more reliable deliveries and easier business and taxi travel. Employees of businesses within the charging zone also benefit from public transport improvements arising from more reliable bus operations and the investment of the net revenues in further transport improvements.

The congestion charge in central London operates on a camera system, which enforces payment. Options to pay are by retail, the web, telephone, text and by post. Drivers have to inform TfL of the day they wish to travel. TfL has recognized the administrative burden this could pose for businesses operating in London and therefore has devised two fleet schemes.

Automated scheme

The automated scheme applies to lorries, light trucks and vans (not cars). All vehicles entering the zone are registered. The appropriate charge is then deducted from the fleet operator's holding account at the end of the month based on the number of fleet vehicles captured by the camera network within the congestion charging zone.

Notification scheme

The notification scheme is for cars and lorries. At the end of each month, the fleet operator must notify TfL of all vehicles that have entered the congestion charging zone during that month. This notification is validated against evidence from the camera network, and the appropriate charge is then deducted from the fleet operator's holding account.

Impacts of congestion charging on the community

It is recognized that congestion charging will have different impacts on different groups in society, some of which will be more disadvantaged. To prevent disadvantaging certain vulnerable, or essential, sectors of society, congestion charging offers a range of exemptions and discounts. The following classes of vehicles are *exempt*:

- emergency vehicles;
- licensed buses with nine or more seats;
- London-licensed taxis and minicabs;
- motorbikes, mopeds and bicycles;
- certain operational vehicles used by emergency services.

The following receive *100% discount*:

- disabled blue badge holders;
- electrically propelled vehicles and certain vehicles powered by alternative fuels;
- certain journeys undertaken by firefighters, NHS staff and certain NHS patients.

The following receive *90% discount*:

- residents of the zone.

Discounts and exemptions of the congestion charging are subject to review. If the number of discounts and exemptions were found to jeopardize the impact of the scheme in terms of reducing congestion, revisions would be considered.

Benefits for the community

The benefits the community receives are as follows:

- There is reduced traffic and congestion in the central zone, making essential journeys across the zone quicker and perceptibly safer, and making it easier to move around the zone as a pedestrian or cyclist.
- There has been an increase in bus services and bus reliability.

- There has been a greater reduction in the number of accidents inside the zone than in other areas of Greater London.
- Money generated by congestion charging is to be used to further improve transport in London.

Congestion charging is delivering net transport benefits of some £50 million per year and net revenues of some £80 million per year to London.

Commitment to monitoring

From its inception, it has been recognized that congestion charging is not just about traffic impacts. TfL has established a comprehensive five-year monitoring programme examining the economic, environmental, social and wider transport impacts of the scheme. Some of these impacts, such as that on air quality, can only be credibly assessed in the medium and long term, hence the five-year length of the programme.

The monitoring programme is concentrated around a programme of specifically designed TfL surveys to assess changes in, for example, congestion levels, traffic patterns, public transport passenger levels, business activity, public attitudes and behavioural changes. It has also been designed with the ability to explore particular issues of concern that arose before or after charging commenced.

Success of congestion charging

Since its inception on 17 February 2003, congestion charging in central London has achieved its primary objective of reducing traffic congestion. Monitoring of the scheme prior to and throughout its first year has delivered the following results.

- Traffic circulating inside the zone has been reduced by 15%.
- Overall congestion has been reduced by 30%.
- There have been no adverse traffic impacts outside the zone.
- Bus reliability and journey times have improved.

As has been mentioned, a five-year monitoring programme will continue to deliver statistics and conclusions on the effectiveness and impacts of the congestion charge.

The future of congestion charging in central London

With the success of congestion charging in its first year, TfL has begun to look at ways it can be improved and extended. Work is currently being carried out to look at:

- developing and consulting upon an extension to the zone where there is traffic congestion, within the capabilities of the technology;
- trialling potential new charging technologies for London;
- how, in general terms, road-user charging might be employed in the pursuit of a wider range of objectives in London in the light of a potential national scheme.

Congestion charging and corporate social responsibility

Congestion charging is still a very young project, and its full benefits will not be fully understood for another couple of years. However, it has clearly demonstrated that it can reduce congestion. This in itself provides benefits by improving journey times and reliability for public transport and individuals. Alongside this benefit, the measures introduced have impacted on road safety and fuel emissions, making London a pleasanter place to live in, work in or visit.

CLIMATE CHANGE AND EMISSIONS TRADING
By Mike Clasper, BAA Chief Executive

Climate change is arguably the biggest issue on the environmental agenda of societies and Governments across the world. And for those nations which have opted into the Kyoto Protocol, cutting greenhouse gas emissions has become the number one environmental priority.

Air travel currently causes around three per cent of global greenhouse gas effects, a figure which is dwarfed by the share caused by motor vehicles, energy generation and industry.

But aviation's emissions are going to increase, both absolutely and proportionately, as air travel grows faster than the technology to improve emissions performance. The Intergovernmental Panel on Climate Change believes that aviation could account for six per cent of global emissions by 2050.

A significant number of stakeholders in the environmental lobby, in Parliament and in Europe believe that the best way to tackle aviation emissions is by imposing punitive levels of taxation to discourage people from flying. But this would be a mistake: not just for aviation, but for the businesses and wider economy which depend on it.

BAA recognises that aviation should pay its environmental costs, but should do so in a way which tackles the impacts. Where economic instruments are deployed, we believe that they should be applied proportionately to the environmental costs, and that any revenue raised should be used to reduce the impacts.

There is no prospect, in the next 50 years, of an alternative to burning kerosene. So aviation needs a different approach if it is to meet its climate change obligations. I believe that the best approach is emissions trading.

Emissions trading is a market mechanism for directing funds at reducing emissions where they can be cut most quickly and cheaply. Within an overall emissions cap, companies are set limits on their allowable emissions, and if they wish to exceed their limit they have to buy permits representing compensating cuts made by other companies. This way, a nation's total emissions can fall, even though some industries may actually increase their emissions.

This is a fitting solution, because the trade creates economic incentives for industries which can cut emissions to do so, because they can sell their surplus permits to other industries. And it works, as a national sulphur dioxide emissions trading scheme has already proved in the USA.

UK aviation and the UK government are ahead of the rest of the world on this issue. We have already been working on it for at least three years, and BAA has led a process of stakeholder engagement, involving industry, Government, academics, NGOs and others, to work out how aviation can be part of an emissions trading scheme.

Following strong lobbying from UK aviation, the Government gave public support to aviation emissions trading in *The Future of Air Transport* White Paper. It is publicly committed to using its 2005 Presidency of the EU to make international progress on this.

BAA, BA and the UK government are now working to persuade European airports, airlines and national Governments that it is in all of our interests for aviation to be included in the European Union Emissions Trading Scheme (EU ETS) by 2008. Meanwhile, the European Commission is appointing consultants to work at how aviation can be grafted onto the EU ETS, with our full support.

But this is by no means a done deal. The European Commission is keeping open the alternative options of taxes and charges. If the attempt to integrate aviation into the EU ETS fails, then pressure to impose taxes and charges, either EU-wide or by national governments unilaterally, will grow.

BAA has made this a priority issue because it is good business sense. Although this is not strictly an airport issue, as the emissions are made by aircraft in flight, policy measures such as taxes, charges or the capping of capacity, if imposed, would lead to a stifling of aviation growth, and that would directly affect our bottom line.

So it is in our business interests to provide leadership on this issue, by raising the debate, investing senior staff time in thinking through the solution, being an 'honest broker' between different stakeholders and lobbying hard within and outside the industry.

The environment has been called "the sleeping giant on the political landscape." It's an unwise business that refuses to acknowledge that the giant is rising from its slumbers.

SUSTAINABLE DEVELOPMENT – AT THE CORE OF BAA'S BUSINESS

Aviation is a key driver of the UK economy and plays a vital part in supporting hundreds of thousands of jobs, supporting business, boosting trade and inward investment and fulfilling people's desire to travel.

But like all forms of public transport, aviation has environmental consequences which must be addressed if the industry is going to be allowed to grow.

However, sustainable development is not and should not be simply "tacked on" to business as usual. At BAA our sustainable development policy is applied throughout our business, providing a framework for operating and developing our airports and an approach to building new capacity.

We work within the UK Government's policy, which sets four criteria to meet sustainability objectives:
- Social progress that recognises the needs of everyone
- The effective protection of the environment
- Prudent use of natural resources
- The maintenance of high and stable levels of economic growth and employment.

We firmly believe that we can contribute to global, national and regional sustainable development strategies, through our industry, in five key ways:
1. By minimising negative impacts such as noise, air quality, climate change, waste and road congestion
2. By promoting a vision for a cleaner, smarter growth in aviation to maximise the positive benefits for society, facilitating prosperity, regeneration and the UK's regional and national competitiveness
3. By facilitating the UK's promotion of the knowledge-driven economy which relies on strong and competitive international connections
4. By making the best use of existing capacity and by facilitating the uptake of sustainable new technologies in the economy
5. By contributing to the broader global benefits of cultural exchange, inter-governmental communications and social inclusion, through making travel available to the widest number of people.

We cannot do this alone, so the engagement of our stakeholders lies at the heart of our sustainable development policy. Local communities, businesses, business partners, Government and local authorities all play a fundamental role in determining how we operate and grow our business, responsibly, safely and securely within the framework of a sustainable development policy.

ZERO – Leaders in workbikes

Zero Emissions Real Options Ltd. specialises in freight cycles.

We offer for sale or rental a wide range of vehicles, from bicycles designed for speedy deliveries of parcels, lunches, etc. to large tricycles with electric assist able to transport up to 300kg without putting strain to the rider.

We run a successful delivery service in London, and all the vehicles we offer have been thoroughly tested by our riders. We are confident that our portfolio includes the best vehicles in each class.

Many businesses can benefit from including freight cycles in their vehicle fleet. A few examples:

- **Companies with field engineers.** In dense urban areas, a service engineer can reach customers more quickly by a well-equipped bicycle fitted with detachable tool-box.
- **Companies with several offices in the same city**. Internal mail will be delivered more efficiently and much more cost-effectively by Post-trike.
- **Delivery companies.** Whenever time is critical, one needs a mode of transport that is absolutely reliable. Our delivery bicycles are fast and extremely sturdy; most importantly, they don't get stuck in traffic
- **Companies that operate in traffic free areas.** Managing parks and gardens, shopping malls and railway stations, often requires transporting heavy goods: our workbikes are the ideal vehicles to accomplish jobs without disturbing the general public.

Workbikes are fantastic value for money. Not only are they cheaper to buy than conventional motorised vehicles, but they have no running costs, minimal maintenance costs... and you don't get parking tickets. Moreover they are moving billboards, generating invaluable free publicity.

ZERO also publishes the online guide **www.workbike.org**. Feel free to peruse it for additional information, and call us if you would like to arrange a test ride.

Tel: **020 7486 0379**
E-mail: **zero@workbike.org**
Website: **www.zeroisbest.com**

Health and safety

Health and safety: introduction

Tony Connell and Clive Stallwood, BSI

The risks faced by people in the modern British workplace are far smaller than those faced by previous generations – a reflection of the increasing value placed on life and health by an increasingly prosperous society. Successive enhancements to regulatory and legislative frameworks have emphasized the responsibilities now shared by employers and employees.

During the 20th century great strides were made to reduce mortality rates within the manufacturing sector, as a result of the adoption of safer working practices and technological improvements. Accident rates in labour-intensive industries such as construction and agriculture remain a perennial cause for concern, whereas risks of physical injury in the ever-expanding services sector are relatively low.

Health and safety professionals now focus on quality of life rather than just its preservation. We have a far better understanding of the linkages between debilitating injuries and illnesses and their causal factors, including long-term exposure to dust, carcinogens, vibration or repetitive tasks. We also have a growing understanding of the economic as well as the social consequences of illness or injury.

Part 10 of the book explores the business case for strong occupational health and safety before considering the attitudes of legislators, employers, employees and investors. It concludes by examining specific issues and solutions in the context of noise, stress and the food industry.

Health and safety: legal overview

Kathryn Mylrea, Simmons & Simmons

Health and safety is an area in which there is a long-established legislative regime: the Health and Safety at Work Act 1974 and the numerous regulations and approved codes of practice. Some, but not all, of the legislation is derived from European legislation. The Health and Safety Commission Business Plan for 2003–04 contains four main blocks:

- priority programmes (which cover falls from heights, workplace transport, musculoskeletal disorders, work-related stress, construction, slips and trips);
- major hazards (including a national target);
- securing compliance (inspections, accident and complaint investigation, formal enforcement action, improving standards with poorly performing duty holders, and coordination with multi-site organizations);
- mandatory activities (modernizing and simplifying the regulatory framework, providing information and advice on health and safety, science and innovation).

The Health and Safety Commission (HSC) is also working to develop a new strategy for 2004–10 and will be consulting on this. Stakeholder engagement and communication is a major part of the delivery of improved health and safety.

Much attention is paid to prosecutions and the levels of fines that can be, and are in practice, imposed. A private member's Bill to increase health and safety fines to levels comparable with environmental and food safety legislation has considerable support. The Bill would include the power to impose custodial sentences on directors or managers who are found to be responsible for the company's failure. There are long-standing provisions for legislation that would create a new offence of corporate killing, which followed some of the large-scale disasters that have occurred. To date, no time in the legislative calendar has been found for a Bill on this, but the commitment of the HSC and Health and Safety Executive (HSE) is certainly there.

Occupational health and safety

Tony Connell and Clive Stallwood, BSI

The business case

> Society as a whole pays when things go wrong. We estimate that the total cost to society of health and safety failures could be as high as £18 billion every year. We can and should do something about this.
>
> (John Prescott, UK Deputy Prime Minister, 2000)

At a macroeconomic level there is substantial evidence that poor health and safety practices represent a significant cost to the economy and that improving health and safety has a positive impact on economic performance. However, the costs to companies are hidden by the fact that the National Health Service (NHS) provides free treatment at the point of delivery. Costs only become visible in the form of insatiable demands for NHS funding through the taxpayer.

Much progress has been made in this field, but the UK Department of Work and Pensions (DWP), in its report on employee liability insurance, noted, 'Our safety performance in the UK is good – that is one reason why the costs of employers' liability are still much lower than our international competitors'. But there is more to be done, particularly on occupational health...'

Accidents and injuries grab the headlines, and inevitably companies focus on prevention in the form of various high-profile safety initiatives. The United Kingdom's Health and Safety Executive (HSE) is now keen to shift the focus to health. While less spectacular, the social and economic damage caused by work-related ill health is in many ways more significant than accidents. Stress, bad backs, repetitive strain injury (RSI) and other largely work-related conditions are estimated to affect some 2 million workers in the United Kingdom.

Securing Health Together, a report by the HSE launched in 2000, states:

Despite good progress in reducing the number of accidents at work, Great Britain still needs to strive to achieve similar success in tackling the current high levels of work-related ill health. We need a long-term occupational health strategy for several reasons: to stop people being made ill by work; to help people who are ill go back to work; and to improve work opportunities for those not able to work because of ill health or disability.

Defined within the Occupational Health and Safety Assessment series of standards as 'the conditions and factors that affect the well-being of employees, temporary workers, contractor personnel, visitors and any other person in the workplace', occupational health and safety affects every workplace, employee and employer.

Manley considers the United Kingdom's NHS and provides the following example of the significant benefits of conducting sound occupational health practices:

In the NHS bad backs are common causes of absenteeism and nurses scarce and difficult to replace – with temporary nurses a significant drain on resources. One NHS trust, Wigan and Leigh, with 5000 staff, decided to address the problem. In 1993 they commissioned a report into sickness among staff and found 44,000 hrs/yr were lost at an estimated cost £3.9 million. Losses due to industrial injuries were 11,635 hrs/yr, with nurses most commonly affected, and heavy lifting a key reason. They then developed a comprehensive package to address the problem, involving risk assessment, training risk assessors, purchasing equipment, and educating staff. The non-staff costs were £80,000 in the first year, £50,000 in the second. The results were that time lost due to lifting injuries fell from 6720 hours to 1082 in the first year, with further reductions in subsequent years until only 192 hours were lost. The cost of this lost time fell from £800,000 to £24,000. (M Manley, *Health and Safety Indicators for Institutional Investors*, HSE, London, 2002)

Statistics published in the *Occupational Health Statistics Bulletin* 2002/03 show that an estimated 33 million working days were lost from the UK economy. The two main causes are, first, stress, depression and anxiety, and second, musculoskeletal disorders, resulting in 13.4 million and 12.3 million days lost respectively (Figure 10.3.1).

Further review of the statistics shows the relationship between illness levels and occupations. Police officers and nurses have the highest levels, followed by builders, teachers and agricultural workers (Figure 10.3.2).

Occupations appear to have very distinct risk profiles that cause specific types of illnesses. The fight against crime exposes police officers to violent individuals, resulting in

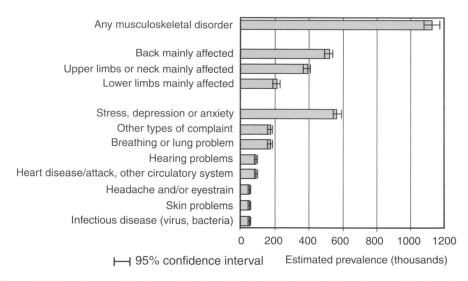

Figure 10.3.1 Causes of lost working days in the United Kingdom (Source: National Statistics, Occupational Health Statistics Bulletin, 2002/03)

injuries in the line of duty. Lifting heavy and awkward patients means that back pain is commonplace among nurses. Unruly pupils, constant change and high workload mean that teachers suffer from stress.

Occupational health and safety can no longer be viewed as the exclusive domain of a small team of 'OHS' experts. All employees and organizations are affected, and risk profiles

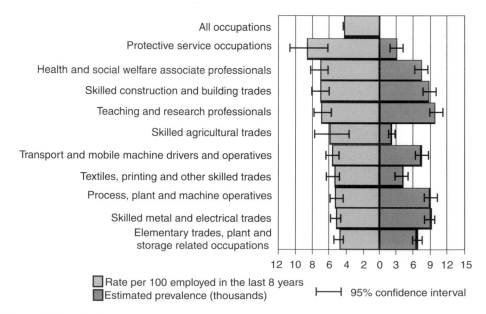

Figure 10.3.2 Relationship between illness levels and occupation (Source: as Figure 10.3.1)

can have a significant impact on the bottom line. A poor safety record means that today's insurance premiums will be high. Tomorrow, the business may no longer be viable, and a brand that has taken many years to create might be destroyed overnight by hostile publicity. All other factors being equal, who would choose to travel with an airline known to have a poor safety record or buy a new car with low crash test ratings?

Legislators and regulators

The World Health Organization (WHO) recognizes occupational health as one of its fundamental priorities, and has set out a global strategy with eight major priority areas:

■ strengthening of international and national policies for health at work;
■ promotion of a healthy work environment, healthy work practices and health at work;
■ strengthening of occupational health services;
■ establishment of appropriate support services for occupational health;
■ development of occupational health standards based on scientific risk assessment;
■ development of human resources;
■ establishment of registration and data systems and information support;
■ strengthening of research.

Occupational health is a fundamental part of the European Union's strategy on safety and health at work. This is made apparent in communications from the European Commission. A Community strategy on health and safety at work in the period 2002–06 advocates that we adopt a global approach to well-being at work, taking account of changes in the world of work and the emergence of new risks, especially of a psycho-social nature. With proposals for a directive on bullying and violence at the workplace, and consultation with social partners on the issue of stress-related conditions, the Commission is establishing stress as a key issue in the management of occupational health and safety.

Following a series of high-profile accidents on Britain's rail network, there is growing public concern at the lack of success of UK criminal law in convicting companies of manslaughter where a death has occurred as a result of gross negligence by the organization as a whole. The debate on accountability rages, with the Government and many business leaders preferring to hold organizations to account, while critics argue the case for a 'corporate killing' Bill to focus on individual directors.

The investors' perspective

Historically, most pension funds have had little focus on health, safety and environmental issues. However, recent pension fund regulation on the topic of disclosure has meant that both the pension fund and the investment management communities are more interested in socially responsible investments.

Mainstream pension funds now expect the boards of companies in which they invest to work to the spirit of Turnbull guidelines – that is, they expect the boards to have considered and be actively managing risks associated with these issues. (The Turnbull Report, *Internal Control: Guidance for Directors on the Combined Code*, was issued by the Institute of

Chartered Accountants in England and Wales (ICAEW) in 1999.) Occasionally, fund managers may raise social and environmental issues with companies, checking that the board is properly managing such issues.

A smaller but growing number of funds take social and environmental issues into account when they are selecting companies for their investment portfolios. Their concern can be driven from one of two perspectives: ethical funds require exemplary management of social and environmental issues as a prerequisite, while other investors see them as indicators of well-managed businesses. This is of particular interest where health and safety data can be linked to financial performance.

From a negative perspective, investors consider that poor health and safety risk management suggests a generally weak approach to risk management and therefore an increased financial risk of unexpected liabilities. It can also be seen as an indicator of employee morale and the respect shown by the company to staff, potentially linking to the concept of measuring human capital and the state of corporate culture.

A clear message from investors is that they do not see themselves as 'policemen' in this area. A growing number of investors are concerned that they are being pressurized by government to 'enforce' health and safety within companies.

The skills gap

The WHO paper *The Way to Health at Work* (1994) acknowledges that occupational health means far more than providing conventional primary healthcare to workers (and at the workplace). Occupational health is a preventive activity aiming at identification, assessment and control of hazardous factors at the workplace, and the generation of competent and effective actions to ensure a healthy work environment and healthy workers. Such activity cannot be carried out with primary healthcare competence alone; specialized occupational health competence and knowledge of the real needs (eg knowledge on industrial and other chemicals, physical factors at work, ergonomics, safety, work psychology, occupational medicine) of the working life are needed.

It is apparent that the scope of occupational health embraces a wide variety of issues, skills and competencies, much more so than what are traditionally labelled safety issues. The health and safety professional needs to be fully aware of these issues; they cannot be ignored, as statistics show that ill health is now a much larger problem to tackle than in the past. The old guard of health and safety professionals generally come from backgrounds in industries with high safety risks, such as building and construction, and petrochemicals, not necessarily the industries carrying high health risks (transport, food, waste). With the rise of the service sector, bringing issues such as the increase of peripatetic working and emergence of issues such as stress, awareness and knowledge need to be increased. The majority of professional bodies and stakeholders have recognized this.

The Confederation for British Industry advocated in December 2001 that business management of occupational health and rehabilitation should be improved, remarking that 30 per cent of employers do not give occupational health provision. Unfortunately, a subsequent report on preventive services, prepared by Laurent Vogel and published in the *TUTB Newsletter* of June 2003, paints a rather damning picture. Although the report embodies a trade union slant, it suggests that the number of UK workers with access to preventive services has fallen 'dramatically'. Specialized health and safety staffs exist in about half the firms with organized prevention activities, and it claims that companies 'do not have the development of preventative services as a priority'.

Management attitudes

Given that business schools can be considered as the source of the next generation of business leaders, it is perhaps surprising that so little time is devoted to the topic of health and safety. Coverage of occupational health and safety on full-time MBA courses in business schools in Great Britain was commissioned by the HSE, which found that 'the explicit occupational health and safety content of the eight MBAs was either non-existent or very limited' and that 'MBA staff tended to think that occupational health and safety was vitally important in major hazard industries but a bureaucratic, legalistic imposition for most other organisations'. Even where they recognized that occupational health and safety was an important corporate goal, business educators had not fully made the link between safety management and the management skills taught on MBA programmes. They questioned the academic rigour of the subject, and did not perceive occupational health and safety as a topic worthy of inclusion in a postgraduate course.

Fortunately, employers are generally beginning to take a more enlightened attitude towards the subject. For example, the Engineering Employers Federation (EEF) recognizes that occupational health is a serious issue for UK manufacturing and engineering companies; it appointed a Chief Medical Adviser in 2002 and has in place an occupational health strategy:

> The EEF's Occupational Health Strategy carries the broad aim of improving the health of companies and their employees, presenting and championing the business case for occupational health. Our campaigning in this area will engage the EEF more in policy development and profile on many issues including workplace stress, absence management, rehabilitation, management development.

Tools, techniques and standards

Research by Manley mentioned earlier in the book suggests that companies should report against the following set of indicators to demonstrate best-practice levels of health and safety management. These indicators have been chosen because they satisfy the data needs of investors while offering comparability across various economic sectors. They provide a broad overview of health and safety performance at a company level, and should allow investors to work out whether the issues are being managed appropriately:

1. appointment of a director with the responsibility of being the health and safety champion;
2. the levels at which health and safety management systems are reported;
3. number of fatalities;
4. lost time injury rate;
5. absenteeism rate;
6. cost of health and safety losses.

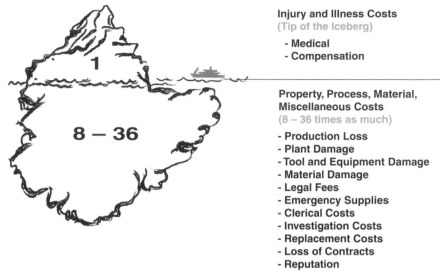

Injury and Illness Costs
(Tip of the Iceberg)

- Medical
- Compensation

Property, Process, Material, Miscellaneous Costs
(8 – 36 times as much)

- Production Loss
- Plant Damage
- Tool and Equipment Damage
- Material Damage
- Legal Fees
- Emergency Supplies
- Clerical Costs
- Investigation Costs
- Replacement Costs
- Loss of Contracts
- Reputation

Figure 10.3.3   The cost of loss iceberg

A standard methodology needs to be agreed to calculate and report indicators 4, 5 and 6, with significant input from qualified accountants on indicator 6.

Organizations are generally able to identify and calculate the direct costs associated with injury and illness, but they find it far more difficult to relate specific incidents to indirect costs borne by separate departments. These include lost production caused by an accident, lost revenue where a client cancels a delayed order, and damage to tangible assets, including product and plant. Indirect costs can be between 8 and 36 times as large as the direct costs. A company that has lost £20,000 in one year due to injury and illness costs will typically incur additional losses of £120,000–£1,060,000. The scale of the costs will depend on the type of industry in which the organization operates.

The Health and Safety Executive has established a website to promote the message that 'Good Health and Safety is Good Business' and has provided 'ready reckoner' interactive tools to assist business in identifying the costs of poor management of health and safety.

Meanwhile, the environmental standard ISO 14001 and the occupational health and safety system OHSAS 18001 have introduced the concept of a risk-based approach to management systems standards. The standards are designed to enable organizations to identify, evaluate and manage the risks they face, through reduction and elimination of those risks.

As a result of adopting these process and risk-based approaches, organizations improve their focus on the requirements and expectations of their stakeholders, including customers, regulators and employees. They are also in a better position to manage the way in which they interact with their physical environment as well as looking after the health and safety of people at work. Thanks to the use of performance measures, organizations can measure progress against objectives, a process that in turn can be used to help drive continual improvement, competitiveness and therefore success in an increasingly demanding environment (Figure 10.3.4.).

Organizations that have successfully applied ISO 14001, the environmental management system standard, have undertaken an environmental review of which an integral part is to consider significant environmental aspects relating to emissions to air, releases to

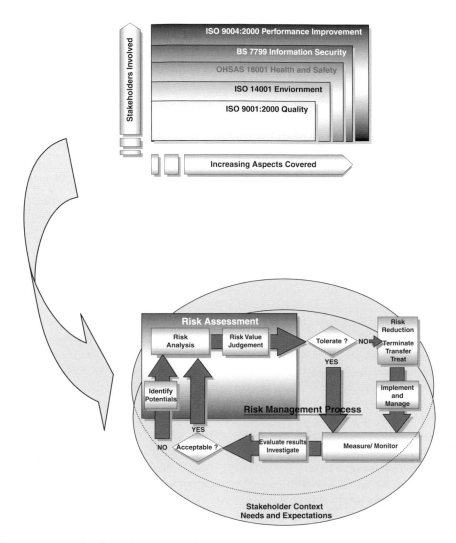

Figure 10.3.4 The drive for continual improvement

water, waste management, contamination of land, use of raw materials and natural resources as well as local environmental and community issues. The mindset in such an organization is repositioned to manage its environmental risks in a systematic manner and to deal with what is often a key stakeholder expectation: managing risk and preventing loss with respect to the environment.

The use by organizations of OHSAS 18001, the occupational health and safety management system specification, demonstrates that they have identified hazards and performed a risk assessment relating to personnel and facilities in the workplace, as well as having put in place programmes to manage these risks. Organizations working in this way address another key group of stakeholders – the people within the organization – helping to establish a culture of risk management.

Conclusion

Harming employees is socially unacceptable and increasingly expensive. Legislation has meant that safety in the workplace has received a considerable amount of attention and accident rates are being driven down. Potential legislation regarding corporate killing will reinforce the need to take safety seriously at board level. Similarly, tough safety requirements are being built into products to ensure that they won't harm the user. Building on this success, the focus of policy-makers now is switching to risk management in the context of occupational health and safety. Long-term chronic injuries caused by repeated exposure to apparently minor irritants, including dust, noise and stress, are now coming under the microscope. Insurers, investors, Turnbull and the Combined Code require companies to have clear systems for managing risks, reporting to stakeholders and shouldering responsibility.

Case 1: the food industry

Hardly a month goes by without another 'food scare' in the media. Is beef safe to eat? Will prawns give you cancer? Are miscarriages caused by coffee?

A food safety scare can start as an unexpected, isolated incident that can rapidly escalate as a result of the complex interrelationships between different parts of the vast food industry, which employs a quarter of the world's population. Food supply chains increasingly transcend national boundaries. Thanks to air travel and refrigeration, fresh meat, fruit and vegetables are shipped thousands of kilometres from producer to consumer. Britain imports 50,000 tonnes per year of chicken from Thailand, and within days of a recent outbreak of avian flu, caterers, manufacturers and supermarkets were cancelling their orders.

Consumer expectations are becoming ever more demanding. Not only should the food industry provide safe and wholesome food without nasty surprises, but it is coming under increasing ethical and emotional pressure for 'foods' that meet specific consumer values and preferences, whether it be food that is organic, health-enhancing, not genetically modified, low carbohydrate, low-salt or whatever else meets current concerns. So-called junk foods, with their relatively high levels of fat and sugar, are being blamed for making children obese.

The United Kingdom is one of very few countries that have a statutory 'due diligence' defence requirement within their legislative framework. The Food Safety Act 1990 puts emphasis on 'due diligence', requiring all companies in the food chain to take reasonable precautions and exercise due diligence.

In response to UK food safety legislation, organizations such as the British Retail Consortium (BRC) have played a central role in developing standards on food safety within their supply chains to help retailers assure themselves that the food they sell is safe. Examples of this are the BRC technical standard for food and the BRC/Institute of Packaging standard for packaging. Fundamental to BRC standards are the premises that top management is responsible for food safety and that all food safety programmes should be built on a foundation of prerequisite programmes (PRPs) or good manufacturing practice (GMP), and the use of risk management approaches to managing food production. These standards are attempts to reduce the proliferation of standards applied by the different food retailers and are designed to allow an assessment, by a competent third party, of the supplier's premises, operational systems and procedures.

In May 2000 the Food Business Forum (CIES), an international trade association, established the Global Food Safety Initiative (GFSI), whose aims include enhancing food safety, ensuring consumer protection and strengthening consumer confidence. The GFSI task force's first priority has been to develop benchmark requirements for food safety schemes used in the retailer supply chains. These requirements are set out in the GFSI guidance document and establish key principles against which food safety schemes will be measured.

The GFSI Task Force brings together over 50 food retailers, which represent 65 per cent of the world's food retail revenue and include household names from the food retail and manufacturing and processing sector. Recently, the first tranche of food safety schemes has been determined as complying with the GFSI benchmark standard for 'food safety' requirements. Key elements of the benchmark standard are a food safety management system, good practices, and hazard analysis and critical control points (HACCP). The schemes that comply are the BRC Technical Standard, the Dutch HACCP code, the EFSIS standard, the International Standard for Auditing Food Suppliers (International Food Standard) and the SQF 2000 code.

The year 2001 saw the start of work by the International Organization for Standardization (ISO) to develop a standard on food safety, 'ISO 22000:200X: Food Safety Management Systems – Requirements'. This standard is due for publication in 2005, is compatible with ISO 9001:2000 and specifies requirements for a food safety management system in the food chain. The key requirements are on communication within the food chain, system management, process controls, HACCP principles and good practice (or prerequisite programmes). ISO 22000 is based on codex, national standards and retailer food safety schemes. The harmonization of food safety schemes is set to continue.

Case 2: noise

Noise is an inevitable by-product from operating almost any piece of machinery. It can be continuous or percussive. Percussive sounds are usually unexpected, significantly louder than background noise, particularly noticeable and very difficult to absorb.

Percussive noise from equipment such as hydraulic jackhammers has an immediate effect on the hearing of the machinery operators. They suffer from temporary hearing loss and often suffer from a ringing sensation (tinnitus) for hours after exposure to the noise. Since the effects are so obvious, most operators are keen to wear earplugs or ear defenders to protect themselves. Usually people eventually recover most of their hearing. Explosions cause the most extreme form of this type of noise; the shock waves cause such brief but very high levels of noise that they can rupture the eardrums of unprotected listeners.

Continuous noise is more insidious and can cause long-term damage to hearing. The ear has the ability to adjust to the ambient level of any noise. This allows people to enter a noisy environment such as an engine room or discotheque, filter out most of the background noise and still be able to hear conversations. Unfortunately, repeated exposure leads a gradual loss of hearing sensitivity, potentially culminating in complete deafness.

In the United States the National Institute of Occupational Health and Safety (NIOSH) claims that 30 million workers are exposed to hazardous levels of noise on the job and that noise-induced hearing loss is one of the most common occupational diseases. In the United Kingdom a recent survey estimated that over 500,000 people suffer from hearing difficulties as a result of exposure to noise at work. Industries with particularly high levels of noise include agriculture, mining, construction, manufacturing, utilities, transport and the military.

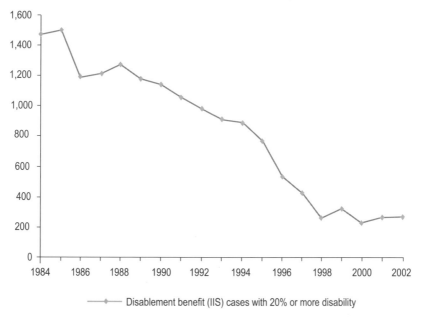

Figure 10.3.5 Cases of occupational deafness in the United Kingdom
(Source: www.hse.gov.uk/statistics/causdis/noise.htm)

Hearing loss is a significant handicap as it reduces the ability to communicate with people or enjoy sounds such as music or birdsong. The costs in terms of disability settlements and medical treatment can be very high.

The good news is that hearing loss is 100 per cent preventable, and noise barriers can be relatively cheap. They range from earplugs and defenders for individual users to absorbent materials and acoustic barriers. A combination of legal enforcement and enlightened management has resulted in a sixfold decrease in cases of impaired hearing as a result of exposure to occupational noise (Figure 10.3.5).

The business case for hearing conservation can be very attractive: between 1987 and 1997 the US military saved over $350 million as a result of a comprehensive conservation programme.

Case 3: stress

In today's 24/7 culture, with mobile telecommunications wherever you are in the world, workplace stress is a seen as a relatively new phenomenon. In reality, it has probably existed ever since prehistoric times, when early humans cooperated to hunt large animals.

Stress is different from a challenge. Challenge is a positive ingredient for healthy and productive work: it motivates staff to learn new skills, and when the challenge is met, everyone involved is able to relax and celebrate. Stress, however, is a harmful physical and emotional response when the challenge simply cannot be met, given the available resources. Symptoms of stress vary from relatively minor complaints including restless sleep and loss of appetite to severe anxiety and a complete breakdown of mental and physical health.

With the relentless drive for efficiency in today's commercial world, stress due to reorganization or the introduction of new technology is commonplace. Shareholder expectations in terms of improving revenue and profitability mean that directors have to 'squeeze the assets'. Within the services economy, staff account for the bulk of costs, so financial performance is linked directly to staff productivity.

Once seen as a boring and secure employer, the UK public sector is attracting bad publicity because of an apparent increase in workplace bullying. With the focus on effectiveness and reporting key performance indicators, public-sector managers face challenging targets and are driving their staff hard. While most use a coaching approach, weaker managers resort to intimidation. The short-term consequences may be a small increase in productivity but at the expense in the medium term of staff losing their self-esteem and creativity. In the worst cases, litigation ensues – a traumatic process for the bully, the victim and the organization. The bully's reputation is usually destroyed, while a shadow of doubt is cast over the whole organization.

Various pieces of research have identified the following primary causes of occupational stress:

- *task design*: heavy workload, infrequent rest breaks, long work hours and shift work; hectic and routine tasks that have little inherent meaning, do not utilize workers' skills, and provide little sense of control;
- *management style*: lack of worker participation in decision-making, poor communication in the organization, lack of family-friendly policies;
- *interpersonal relationships*: poor social environment and lack of support or help from colleagues and supervisors;
- *work roles*: conflicting or uncertain job expectations, too much responsibility, too many 'hats' to wear;
- *career concerns*: job insecurity and lack of opportunity for growth, advancement, or promotion; rapid changes for which workers are unprepared;
- *environmental conditions*: unpleasant or dangerous physical conditions such as crowding, noise, air pollution or ergonomic problems.

High stress levels have been shown to reduce productivity and creativity, and to increase costs in terms of absenteeism, litigation and staff turnover. There is no simple model for measuring the level of stress in an organization and changing it to achieve an optimum level.

As a general rule, organizations should start by performing analysis to establish whether there is a problem and, if there is, how big it is. Group discussions among managers and staff can provide invaluable information, to be followed by wider staff surveys. The main outcome should be a clear picture showing the high stress points within the organization and their root causes.

The next stage is clearly to address the root causes. Some may be quick and easy to deal with (better communication), while others may take many months (redesign of a core process).

Finally, an appraisal should be carried out to establish whether the change has been effective in terms of reducing stress levels, but also in improving the effectiveness of that part of the organization.

Control of major accident hazards

David Wood, Bevan Brittan

Scope of regulations

The Control of Major Accident Hazards Regulations 1999 apply to approximately 1,100 establishments in England, Wales and Scotland that have the potential to cause major accidents because they use or store significant quantities of dangerous substances such as chemicals, explosives, oil or oil products, natural gas, etc.

The Regulations place a duty on every operator at the establishment covered by them to take all measures necessary to prevent major accidents and limit their consequences to persons and the environment. A 'major accident' is defined by the Regulations as being an occurrence (including in particular a fire, explosion or major emission) resulting from uncontrolled developments in the course of the operation of any establishment and leading to serious danger to human health or the environment, immediate or delayed, inside or outside the establishment, and involving one or more dangerous substances listed in Schedule 1 of the Regulations.

Background

The UK Regulations implement the 'Seveso II' European Council Directive (96/82/EC). The first regulatory attempt to prevent or limit the consequences of major incidents was adopted in 1982 following the catastrophic explosion at the Seveso chemical plant in Italy, which killed many local residents and contaminated the local environment with dioxins. The directive was known as the Seveso Directive and was superseded in 1996 by the Seveso II Directive (96/82/EC). It is this directive that has been incorporated into UK law through the Control of Major Accident Hazards Regulations 1999 (COMAH), which superseded the Control of Industrial Major Hazards Regulations of 1984 (CIMAH).

Of the 1,100 establishments in England, Wales and Scotland to which the COMAH Regulations apply, approximately 730 are 'lower-tier' sites where operators must prepare a 'Major Accident Prevention Policy'. The remaining 370 stores or processes, involving larger stocks of dangerous substances, are classified as 'top tier' and are subject to additional requirements, which include submitting a safety report to the 'competent authority': the Health and Safety Executive (HSE), working jointly with the Environment Agency (EA) and, in Scotland, the Scottish Environmental Protection Agency (SEPA). The competent authority is also known as the Hazardous Installations Directorate.

It is mainly the chemical, oil and explosives industries that are affected by the Regulations, but so too are those who store explosives, chemicals or other hazardous materials where the quantities of substances identified in Schedule 1 of the Regulations that are kept or used are above certain threshold levels set out in the Schedule.

Schedule 1 of the Regulations sets two thresholds ('qualifying quantities') for the application of the Regulations. As already mentioned, operators of sites that maintain large quantities of hazardous substances, which are known as 'top-tier' sites, are subject to more onerous requirements than those of 'lower-tier' sites.

Regulation 3 and Schedule 1 set out in columnar form the quantities of dangerous substances that determine whether an operator is a lower-tier or a top-tier site. Thus, in the case of the chemical chlorine, the operator may have on-site at any one time up to 10 tonnes without being affected by the Regulations. Having between 10 and 25 tonnes will classify it as a lower-tier site and having above 25 tonnes will classify it as a 'top-tier' site. Perhaps the most common process that will be affected is the processing or storage of automotive petrol or other petroleum spirits, where the qualifying quantities are 5,000 tonnes and 50,000 tonnes respectively.

Part 3 of Schedule 1 sets out various categories of substances and preparations not specifically mentioned in Part 2 but which are classified by Regulation 5 of the CHIP Regulations 1994 or the Food and Environmental Protection Act 1985 as, for example, 'explosive', 'very toxic', 'highly flammable', 'dangerous for the environment', etc.

Operators of lower-tier sites must notify basic details of their operations to the competent authority. Full details of the information required are set out in Schedule 3 but will include the name and address of the operator, the address of the establishment, the name or position of the person in charge, details of the dangerous substances on-site, the activities carried on at the site, and environmental details.

These details must be given to the authority before operations begin. Commencement of operations is defined by the Regulations as meaning when the quantity of dangerous substances exceeds one of the thresholds.

General duty

Regulation 4 sets out the general duty on every operator affected by COMAH to take all measures necessary to prevent major accidents and limit their consequences to persons and the environment. It is a high standard, and requires measures both for prevention of major accidents and to limit the consequences of such for persons and the environment.

Because all risk cannot be eliminated completely, the competent authority has adopted a proportional response in its enforcement policy. Thus, when the Regulations talk about 'all measures necessary', the proportionality principle will be implied. For example, if hazards are high, then high standards will be necessary to ensure that risks are kept as low as acceptably tolerable.

The ideal objective should be wherever possible to avoid a hazard altogether, but if this is not possible, prevention should be based on the principle of reducing risk to a level as low as is reasonably practicable (ALARP) for human risks and using best available technology not entailing excessive cost (BATNEEC) for environmental risks.

Major accident prevention policy

Regulation 5 requires lower-tier operators to prepare a major accident prevention policy (MAPP), which will usually be a short, simple document setting down what is to be achieved but containing a summary and further reference to the safety management system that will implement the policy. A more detailed explanation will probably be contained in other documentation to which the MAPP will refer, such as risk assessments, job descriptions, training requirements, plant operating procedures, etc.

The preparation of the MAPP will undoubtedly require either a review of existing risk assessments or new risk assessments to identify what can go wrong, how often, the potential for escape of dangerous substances, who will be affected on and off the site, and what might be the consequences of such a major accident. All these taken together will determine the level of risk posed by the substances or processes and enable a risk management action to be developed through the MAPP and its reference documents.

The MAPP also has to address issues relating to the safety management system. These details are set out in Schedule 2 and relate to organization of personnel, the identification and evaluation of major hazards, operational control, planning for emergencies, and monitoring audit and review. The MAPP must be prepared before operations begin at the site.

Safety report

Top-tier operators not only must comply with the above, but also must prepare a safety report that provides information to demonstrate to the competent authority that all measures necessary for the prevention and mitigation of major accidents have been taken. The contents required to be included in the safety report are set out in Schedule 4 and must include a policy on how major accidents are to be prevented and mitigated; a management system for implementing that policy; an effective method for identifying any major accidents that might occur; measures to prevent and mitigate major accidents; information on the safety precautions built into the plant and equipment when it was designed and constructed; details of measures such as fire-fighting to limit the consequences of any major accident that might occur; and information about the emergency plan for the site, which is also used by the local authority in drawing up an off-site emergency plan.

The safety reports will be made available to the public through a register maintained by the competent authority. Safety reports must be submitted to the competent authority before top-tier operation begins, although in the case of completely new establishments some information must be provided before construction of the site starts.

The safety report must be updated every five years or after significant changes or technological advances. For example, if new, more effective systems of controlling fires or explosions become available, the safety report would need to reflect this, together with lessons learnt from accidents or near misses in the past. Even if there have not been any changes, it must be reviewed every five years; unless circumstances so dictate, it should not be necessary to rewrite it completely or to a significant degree. It is sufficient to demonstrate to the competent authority that the operator is treating the safety policy as a responsive, flexible and living document.

Emergency plans

Top-tier operators must also prepare on-site and off-site emergency plans to deal with the consequences of a major accident. Such details as are required in the emergency plan are set out in Schedule 5. They will include the objectives of containing and controlling incidents so as to minimize the effects of a major accident and limit damage to persons, the environment and property; implementing the measures necessary to achieve the foregoing; communicating information about emergency action to the public, emergency services and authorities; and providing for restoration and clean-up. The on-site emergency plan must be prepared before operations at top-tier begin.

Provision of information

Top-tier sites will also need to give information to their local authority. Details of the information required to be given to local authorities are contained in Schedule 5. The reason for the requirement to inform local authorities is that, by statute, local authorities have a key role in the preparation and testing of off-site emergency plans for dealing with the consequences of major accidents at top-tier sites.

Because persons living near to a COMAH establishment could be affected if an accident occurred, they must be given information about the hazards and the consequences and their actions in the event of an accident without their having to request it. This information will be available to the public via public registers.

Safety reports will be put on the register in full unless the operator requests that certain information be withheld – for example, for reasons of national security, or of commercial or personal confidentiality. Schedule 8 of the Regulations outlines the procedure that must be followed in respect of a request that information be withheld from the public register, and such an application must include justification for the request.

Enforcement of the Regulations will be by the competent authority as though the Regulations were health and safety regulations and enforceable by virtue of Section 33 of the Health and Safety at Work etc Act 1974. Prosecutions can be tried either in the magistrates' court, where there is a maximum fine of £20,000, or in the crown court, where unlimited fines are provided for. Fines in such cases are likely to be high, following the Court of Appeal's guidance to courts in the case of *R v F Howe & Sons (Engineers) Ltd.*

Fees are payable by operators to the competent authority. In addition, local authorities may charge by virtue of Regulation 13 for their work in the preparation and testing of off-site emergency plans and for their work in testing and reviewing the consequences of an accident at a COMAH site.

Regulation 21 requires the competent authority to notify the European Community of any major accident meeting certain criteria, which are given in Schedule 7 to the Regulations. These criteria include where an accident, fire or explosion or accidental discharge of a dangerous substance involving a quantity of at least 5 per cent of the qualifying quantity laid down in Schedule 1: an accident directly involving a dangerous substance and causing death or injury to at least six persons who are thereby kept in hospital for at least 24 hours; the evacuation or confinement of persons for more than two hours where the number of persons multiplied by the hours of evacuation or confinement totals at least 500; permanent or long-term damage to terrestrial, freshwater and marine habitats, or significant or long-term damage to an aquifer or underground water; or finally, damage to property and the establishment of at least 2 million euros or outside the establishment of at least 0.5 million euros.

Between April 2001 and March 2002, four COMAH major accidents were notified to the European Community under Regulation 21. They included a fire at the Conoco oil refinery at South Killingholm, Immingham, on 16 April 2001, when, following the release of approximately 179 tonnes of extremely flammable hydrocarbon gases, a fire broke out in the saturate gas plant. Further explosions of vapour clouds occurred, with ruptures of oil lines and subsequent fireballs. Police set up roadblocks in the surrounding area. There were three minor injuries reported, one on-site and two off-site. There was no damage to the environment. It was, however, reportable, as it resulted in a fire and the loss of more than 5 per cent of the qualifying quantity of dangerous substances.

A further reportable incident occurred at the Corus steelworks at Port Talbot in south Wales, where there was a major fire and explosion within a blast furnace. The incident resulted in 13 fatalities and 17 other injuries to employees. Although there was minimal disruption to the surrounding area and no damage was caused to the environment, the incident was reportable as it resulted in serious danger to human health, involved one or more dangerous substances and damage to property exceeding 2 million euros.

David Wood is a Partner at Bevan Brittan.

E-mail: david.wood@bevanbrittan.co.uk

Employment

Employment: introduction

Advisory Conciliation and Arbitration Service

The Institute of Directors (IOD) and the Advisory Conciliation and Arbitration Service (Acas) have something in common: their longevity. The IOD was founded by royal charter in 1903, and Acas' origins go back to 1896, when the Government set up a voluntary conciliation and arbitration service.

Both organizations also support one core value that might be more associated with the Victorian era: social responsibility. Although many of the ideas expressed in this book would be alien to past generations – such as diversity and work–life balance – others would be very familiar. In Victorian times, social responsibility took the form of a rather paternalistic conscience in the workplace, but today it has much deeper connotations. Today, under the umbrella of corporate social responsibility, it takes in everything from environmental reporting to brand integrity, energy efficiency to health and safety.

Wherever you look in business, new ways of working are evolving – and new theories to help us keep up with the changes. For example, the idea of a 'quality of working life' – once a very specific theory – now has much wider associations embracing equal opportunities as well as pay and holidays.

Many directors readily accept their new responsibilities. The old corporate ethos of problem-solving based on confrontation is disappearing fast. Today, businesses solve problems jointly, through communication and consultation.

The subjects covered Part 11 of the book are not just ideas, or even 'issues'; they are the accepted bedrock of good employment relations. They are critically important because they help us to interpret 'responsibility' in a more responsible way.

But is responsibility practical? Do accountability and responsibility make business sense? The quick answer is 'yes'. Prevention is always better, and cheaper, than cure. If Acas has learnt one lesson since its creation, it is that talking first is always best.

Employment: legal overview

Kathryn Mylrea, Simmons & Simmons

There is a large body of employment legislation, some of which (specifically, some the discrimination acts) has been in existence for many years and covers a broad range of issues that can be considered to be part of the sustainability debate. Employment law is a specialist area in its own right, but a few issues that touch on the sustainability of an enterprise are mentioned here.

The Public Interest Disclosure Act 1998 came into force in July 1999. Under this Act, in provisions often referred to as 'whistleblower' protection provisions, a worker can disclose certain information about a company and obtain protection in relation to that disclosure. Qualifying disclosures include any information that, in the reasonable belief of the worker, tends to show that the environment has been, is being or is likely to be damaged or that the health or safety of any individual has been, is being or is likely to be endangered.

Another developing area of employment law is workplace stress. This overlaps with health and safety legislation, but includes measures – such as the Working Time Regulations 1998, which limit the number of hours that an employee can work in a week – that can also be considered to be relevant to the stress issue. Although workers can contract out of these regulations, employers should consider the possible effect on stress levels in their workforce of routinely requiring employees to work hours in excess of those provided for.

There have been a number of cases that provide further guidance on the principles underlying an employer's liability for stress suffered by employees. The EU Equal Treatment

Directive (2000/78/EC) came into force in 2003, although member states have an additional three years to implement the provisions on age and disability discrimination.

The Working Time Directive (93/104/EC) is an ongoing legal issue for the United Kingdom, in part because the United Kingdom currently opts out of the 48-hour maximum working week. The opt-out is the subject of a consultation by the Department of Trade and Industry (DTI) coinciding with the European Commission's review of aspects of the directive, one of which is the working-time opt-out. In January 2004 the Commission concluded that the way the opt-out was used in the United Kingdom showed the difficulties in ensuring that the spirit and terms of the directive were respected and that real guarantees were provided for the workers.

The United Kingdom has also had the Sex Discrimination Act and Race Relations Act since 1975 and 1976 respectively. More recently, the Disability Discrimination Act 1995 has been passed, and an age discrimination Act is in the pipeline.

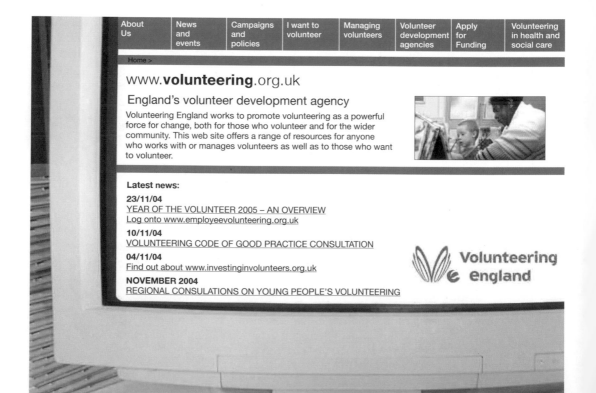

Volunteering England

22 million people volunteer each year, in a wide variety of roles. Yet the protections we take for granted as paid workers – from unfair dismissal, or discrimination – do not apply to them, making good practice a must for volunteer involving organisations.

So where can you find advice and support on the legal and good practice issues affecting volunteer involving organisations?

Volunteering England is the integrated national body for volunteering in England. It works strategically across the private, voluntary and public sectors to raise the profile of volunteering.

Volunteering England is:
- *Relevant* – we develop, disseminate and promote good practice in volunteer management.
- *Diverse* – we work to engage more people, from a wider variety of groups, in higher quality volunteering activity through increasing the quantity, quality and accessibility of volunteering opportunities.
- *Proactive* – we influence the policy agenda, reflecting the needs and views of the local, regional and national volunteering sector and act as campaigning force for change.
- *Visionary* – we lead the strategic development of volunteering in England through the development of a dynamic local and regional infrastructure.

What services do we offer to business?

Consultancy
As an organisation that is passionate about the highest standards in volunteer management, we provide consultancy services that achieve real results.

We can help you ensure that:
- All parts of your organisation understand and value volunteering.
- You have appropriate structures and processes in place to support volunteering.
- You understand the impact of your volunteering programmes through our internationally recognised research arm, the Institute for Volunteering Research.
- Your volunteers are appropriately recognised through our experience of managing internal awards schemes.

We also run the annual national campaign to promote volunteering, Volunteers' Week, 1-7 June.

Who can join Volunteering England?
Membership is open to organisations and individuals operating in England with an interest in volunteering. There are a range of membership packages for different types and sizes of organisations. Full details can be found at **www.volunteering.org.uk** or telephone **0845 305 6979**.

Equal opportunities, diversity and the work–life balance

Ruth Hounslow, Manpower

Equal opportunities

Employment is a social as much as an economic issue. It can play a transformational role in improving health and housing and reducing crime rates and benefit dependency throughout the United Kingdom. Access to employment is key to the social and economic welfare of the United Kingdom, and *improving* access to employment should be a priority for all of us – not just policy-makers, but communities and employers too.

Establishing equality of opportunity goes far beyond the narrow definitions of workplace discrimination: race, gender and disability. It is about responsible strategic business leadership – understanding the role of workforce diversity in labour market dynamics and its value in establishing competitive advantage.

There are economic imperatives accelerating the rate at which companies need to promote equal opportunities. Although we are in a tough economic climate, we are actually close to full employment in the United Kingdom: there is no huge surplus of skilled people looking for work. Similarly, in the emergence from an economic slowdown we cannot expect a resurgence of skills and talent back to the labour market, as was the case in the

1990s. The war for talent continues and is as tough as ever. And UK employers – especially small and medium-sized enterprises (SMEs) – want to recruit more people.

For the fourth quarter of 2004 the Manpower Employment Outlook Survey found that the balance of UK employers expecting to take on more staff was +18 per cent. Employers in small and medium-sized businesses forecast a net outlook of +33 per cent and +28 per cent respectively. If employers are to continue to find sufficient numbers of staff with the right skills, they have to create the widest possible pool of talent from which to choose. Their recruitment methods must be innovative and their pools of labour varied: younger and older workers, newcomers to the labour market as well as those embarking on second and third careers – which means creating a culture of equality of opportunity.

Diversity

Equal opportunities is about judging people only on the basis of their ability to perform a specific job. Diversity is about valuing the differences between people and committing to equality of opportunity and fairness. It therefore encompasses valuing differences of culture, ethnicity, race, gender, nationality, age, religion, disability, sexual orientation, education, life experiences, opinions and beliefs. Diversity is about changing attitudes and eliminating barriers so that everyone who has the ability to do so is able to progress as far as they would like within an organization.

Discrimination often occurs as a result of a lack of awareness or understanding rather than through malicious intent. There is a distinct and very important added value role for intermediaries in addressing these issues effectively. Employment agencies are key in bridging the gap to break down barriers to employment for groups that may otherwise experience discrimination. Businesses like Manpower are trusted to select people to meet clients' requirements to do the job. When we introduce people disadvantaged by age, race, gender or disability into a client's workplace – from which direct selection might have inadvertently excluded them – their good performance encourages the employer to rethink its own recruitment strategy.

Manpower can remove the risk employers may feel they face in sourcing non-traditional pools of labour by providing temporary staff who are our employees. These people demonstrate the value of skills, rather than the limitations of perceived barriers when recruiting people for the job. The employment business also understands the needs of both employees and employers, and can provide practical support to both to overcome the teething problems in adapting to a new workplace or new employment practices.

Employers want good employees; the job of the employment business is to help jobseekers compete and progress in the labour market by developing new skills and career mobility. Providing wider opportunities for people to access the labour market is not just an act of charity or corporate social responsibility, but a chance for employers to recruit and retain the best candidate – who will show greater loyalty, has better skills and potential, and will prove more reliable.

Promoting equal opportunities and diversity goes far beyond the basic legislative requirements. A diverse workforce can offer a wide range of perspectives, ideas, solutions and a wealth of different experiences from which to draw.

The practical promotion of diversity means different things in different areas.

Disability

Employers need to make reasonable adjustments to the working environment, where practicable, to accommodate the needs of a disabled employee, and to retain wherever possible existing staff who develop disabilities during the course of their employment. Unintentional or passive discrimination can be avoided by communicating relevant facts about employment and disability internally and by continually questioning assumptions relating to disability.

Businesses can demonstrate their good practice – and make it easier to attract and retain staff with disabilities – by using the 'positive about disabled people' two ticks on their literature. Doing so commits the company to meet criteria set down by the Department for Work and Pensions (DWP) regarding the employment of disabled people, including:

- to interview all applicants with a disability who meet the minimum criteria for a job vacancy and to consider their application on the basis of their abilities;
- to make every effort when employees become disabled to make sure they stay in employment.

There is also a wealth of organizations that employers can work with to support their recruitment of employees with disabilities. One is St Loye's College in Exeter, which is working to retrain those affected by disability or long-term illness so that they can get back into work with their former employers, or find alternative sustainable employment. Manpower has worked with St Loye's to tackle an area of skills shortage with innovative solutions, and have specifically adapted an assessment tool to support the recruitment of call-centre staff to work in the South West.

Age

Relatively simple measures can promote diversity of age in a company, which is of critical importance to businesses in the United Kingdom, where our ageing population means that by 2020, 40 per cent of the population will be aged over 50.

Not operating a mandatory retirement age for employees, or placing no upper age limit on graduate recruitment programmes, can promote a more age-diverse workforce. Organizations like the Employers' Forum on Age can provide information and guidance on deriving benefits from a mixed-age workforce.

The business case for recruiting on the basis of skills and not age speaks for itself. An age-balanced workforce provides huge benefits to business: higher retention rates; increased flexibility; a broader skills base; and improved reliability, commitment and loyalty. Again, in shortage areas such as contact centres there are some great examples of success. Manpower staffs a Scottish contact centre that breaks all the stereotypes on age. The average age in the contact centre industry is 24, yet at the Scottish centre it's 36. It has a high proportion of older workers – one in seven are over 50, one-third over 40 – and in an industry that is dominated by part-time female workers, more than 50 per cent of the staff are male. The business case is better retention: the average staff turnover in the contact centre industry is between 40 and 50 per cent per annum, but here it is a healthy 10 per cent.

Legal requirements may overtake some businesses in relation to age. Recent Manpower research showed that proposed changes to employment regulations that could prevent employers setting retirement ages for staff and remove the upper age limit for statutory redundancy pay were likely to come as a big surprise to British businesses.

Sixty-one per cent of employers were either unaware of or doing nothing to prepare for the impact of the legislation, the European 'Equal Treatment Framework Directive', on which the UK Government is currently consulting with a view to bringing new rules on age discrimination into force in 2006. Being ready and ahead of the event can mean that employers are first past the post in attracting, recruiting and retaining the best employees, regardless of background.

Race, gender and sexual orientation

Good practice on racial equality in employment includes identifying and removing the barriers that prevent people from ethnic minority groups gaining access to employment, promotion and training opportunities. Likewise, employers have to communicate clearly that they will not tolerate discrimination, victimization or harassment on the basis of someone's sex or sexual orientation.

Work–life balance

Although many companies talk about the importance of work–life balance for their employees, the private sector still lags behind the public sector in this respect. Benefits such as time off in lieu, flexitime and working from home – which all promote a good work–life balance – are far more predominant in the public sector, according to Manpower research. Our experience of working with both public- and private-sector organizations allows us to see this at first hand.

But it's not just employees who benefit from a more balanced approach to the demands of work and home life. Employers with a more open, flexible approach succeed in attracting quality employees and retain a happy and motivated workforce, ultimately resulting in increased productivity. Flexible working attracts many people such as working mothers (many of whom need to fulfil childcare commitments) back into employment.

Again, employment businesses are often in the ideal position to help employees find a good work–life balance. Manpower, for example, will make every effort to accommodate requests for more flexible working arrangements. Our family-friendly policies have been designed to be inclusive and apply to both men and women alike. The very nature of an employment business means people can choose flexible employment opportunities to suit their individual preferences and circumstances, whether working full-time, part-time, in one role or moving across different client companies.

This quotation from one of our recruitment consultants is typical:

> I am now employed as a part-time consultant, which has given me the opportunity to get the right balance of work and home life. Although being a mum is a fantastic experience, it can be isolating. I very much enjoy the social contact that a working environment offers while making progress with my career.

Summary

Respect for the work–life balance of employees helps employers meet the same need as enlightened equal opportunity and diversity policies. In an age of high employment and shifting demographics, which are changing the make-up of the United Kingdom's population and workforce, employers cannot afford to restrict the type of employees they attract.

Diversity is not about altruism. All businesses can promote equal opportunities and diversity through initiatives specific to their own area of operation. And the businesses that succeed in promoting equality of opportunity, in embracing diversity and in encouraging flexibility will not only exceed the requirements of the developing regulatory framework, but become more productive, more proficient and more prosperous. For them, 'People are our business' has become more than just a clichéd mantra: it is a competitive strength in a changing business environment.

Ruth Hounslow is Manpower's Public Affairs and Corporate Communications Manager. Manpower is the United Kingdom's leading recruitment and workforce management company, specializing in permanent and temporary recruitment, HR services, managed services, outsourcing and HR consultancy.

Manpower has been established in the United Kingdom since 1956 and today works with all sizes of business in most industry sectors. Manpower's United Kingdom-wide network of 300 branches allows the company to meet the needs of local and national customers from thousands of SMEs across the country, together with blue-chips including IBM, Xerox, Royal Mail and BT in the private sector, and public-sector organizations such as Hertfordshire County Council, the National Blood Service and the Government's New Deal programme in south Wales.

Right people. Right job.

Jobcentre Plus understands that getting the right people working for you is crucial to the success of your business, whatever its size.

That's why we offer a range of tailored solutions to match your recruitment needs, ranging from sending applicants' CVs directly, to assessing applicants against your criteria for you.

It couldn't be easier.

Just one call and your vacancy will appear on our website which attracts over 1 million visits per week. Access to our large pool of candidates will help you find the right person for your job.

To find out more about all the services we could offer your business, log onto our website, or if you would like to place a vacancy immediately, please call Employer Direct on **0845 601 2001***.

A textphone service is available for those with hearing or speech impairments on **0845 601 2002***.

*Opening hours 8am – 8pm Monday to Friday, 10am – 4pm Saturday. Calls charged at local rates.

What could we add to your business?

www.jobcentreplus.gov.uk/employers

POSITIVE ABOUT DISABLED PEOPLE

jobcentreplus

Part of the Department for Work and Pensions

Right people. Right job

"The concept of corporate trust has assumed greater importance and a one
At Jobcentre Plus we understand that recruiting the right staff for your
business can often be a time consuming and expensive process – whether
it's a permanent vacancy, or just to expand your team to deliver a specific
project. That is why we have developed a wide range of recruitment services
to support employers of all sizes to ease the burden of getting the right
people for the job, quickly and effectively.

Our services have been designed in close consultation with employers to
ensure they meet the needs of individual companies and the economy.
We offer a wide range of recruitment services that can be tailored locally to
meet your specific business needs. Jobcentre Plus staff have an intimate
knowledge of the local labour market that your business operates in, whilst
our national network of account managers are experts in regional and
national labour market issues and work with larger employers to support
their particular recruitment needs. Our Sector Marketing Managers
understand the complexities faced in recruiting across different industry
sectors and they also appreciate how your business methods influence the
way you recruit. They continually analyse business trends to identify growth
industries and sectors to enable Jobcentre Plus to understand the skills and
knowledge required to meet the economies' recruitment needs.

We have also introduced a network of regionally based SME Channel
Managers who provide the focus for our SME services, who will work with
SME representative bodies to continually evolve our services to meet the
changing recruitment needs of these key businesses.

Jobcentre Plus Deliver Successful Recruitment Drive for Dixon's xL Expansion

One of the UK's leading electrical retailers, Dixons, opened its first "xL" store
in Swansea in June 2003. Having previously delivered a successful
recruitment drive for Dixons in Cardiff, Jobcentre Plus was appointed by the
retailer to fill approximately 40 jobs for the new store. Based at Fforestfach
Retail Park, Dixons xL needed to fill most of the vacancies, weeks before the

store opened. This included a range of part-time and full-time jobs in general sales, security and merchandising. In March Jobcentre Plus created a tailored package for Dixons xL, creating a recruitment team to handle telephone enquiries. The team also assessed applications and arranged interviews between Dixons xL and prospective candidates, which took place in a Jobcentre Plus employer suite in its Swansea office.

Jobcentre Plus also worked in partnership with Swansea College during the recruitment drive to deliver a work preparation course for New Deal jobseekers that were suitable for the vacancies. Malcolm Mumford, Dixons HR Manager said: "Once again we have been highly impressed with the efforts of the professional team at Jobcentre Plus. We have worked hand in hand with the team throughout the Swansea recruitment campaign. It's a rewarding partnership that has already helped us recruit a first-rate team for our first Dixons xL store." As a result of the successful recruitment drive in Swansea and Cardiff, Jobcentre Plus will work with the retailer again when the next Dixons xL store opens at the Bullring Shopping Centre in Birmingham later this year.

Got vacancies to Fill?

Informing us of your vacancy couldn't be easier. Employer Direct is a dedicated telephone service available 8am-8pm weekdays, 10am-4pm Saturdays (with an answering service available at other times). Advisers will guide you through our vacancy-taking process. Alternatively you can fax us on **0845 601 2004**, or e-mail us via our website **www.jobcentreplus.gov.uk**

For our English-speaking service, contact Employer Direct on **0845 601 2001**. Our textphone service for people with impaired speech or hearing is **0845 601 2002**.

A Welsh-speaking service is available on **0845 601 4441**, and textphone on **0845 601 4442**.
All calls are charged at local rates.

Our website has further information on the range of Jobcentre Plus services for employers. **www.jobcentreplus.gov.uk/employers**

External relationships

External relationships: introduction

Mallen Baker, Business in the Community

The management of a company's environmental impact is pretty much down to science. For instance, the quantity of greenhouse gas emitted by a production process can be measured, analysed and minimized on a reliable and predictable basis. Every other aspect of the 'corporate social responsibility' agenda, however, is about relationships.

Relationships are rather less predictable. Stakeholders may seem irrational. They may punish the company today for doing what they themselves demanded yesterday. They may expect responsibility but then purchase only on price. Managing stakeholder relationships is not science, but art.

Companies have both direct and indirect stakeholders. Direct stakeholders are those that suffer most if the company is negligent in its duties, or if it should cease trading altogether. The customers, the employees, the shareholders, the suppliers – these are the direct stakeholders of every business. It is hardly a novel idea that a successful business is one that pays attention to such audiences. Companies that are careless of their own people or the needs of their customers have suffered the consequences long before the buzz phrases of sustainable development and corporate social responsibility (CSR) were coined.

Indirect stakeholders include a range that may claim, with varying degrees of legitimacy, an interest in the activities of the company. These include government and regulators, non-governmental organizations (NGOs) and local communities. Over the past decade, increasing numbers of companies have sought to come to terms with growing expectations upon them to engage these stakeholders and to respond to concerns. For many, this is uncharted territory. They have to find ways to achieve due accountability for the power they have, enabling them to create wealth and thereby generate a profit.

There is no certainty that such a process will achieve sustainable development – only that the absence of such a process is guaranteed to fail.

Mallen Baker is Development Director of Business in the Community.

External relationships: legal overview

Kathryn Mylrea, Simmons & Simmons

External relationships are not primarily a legal issue, although there is a legal obligation to consult or inform external stakeholders in a number of situations relevant to sustainability – for example, as part of an application for planning permission, when information must be made available to the public. Also, companies whose processes are regulated under integrated pollution control are required by law to report emissions to air and water of certain pollutants above a specific threshold to the Environment Agency.

The opportunity for shareholder views on matters such as investments to be made known at annual general meetings (which are a legal requirement) is increasingly being utilized by shareholders. The United Kingdom's proposals for an operating and financial review (OFR) are specifically for providing information to shareholders, but the draft guidance notes include the suggestion that the views of customers and other stakeholders may be relevant to the company's prospects and should therefore be included in the OFR in those circumstances. Voluntary engagement on sustainability issues is often adopted by organizations in any event, in particular where there is a clearly identifiable issue associated with an industry.

The United Nations Economic Commission for Europe (UNECE) Aarhus Convention is a new kind of international environmental agreement. The convention is premised on the concept that sustainable development can be achieved only through the involvement of all stakeholders. The Convention has three strands or 'pillars': access to information, public participation and access to justice. Around 40 countries, including the European Union as a whole and the United Kingdom, have signed up to it. Proposals to bring existing EC legislation into line with the Convention are soon to be transposed into UK law.

Increasingly, individuals and companies are requiring their suppliers to have adopted a formal environmental management system – for example, ISO 14001 or EMAS (the European Eco-Management and Audit Scheme) – as one of their formal contractual requirements. Imposing sustainability requirements on suppliers is an important issue, and environmental improvements can be delivered in this way, often in advance of formal legal requirements. A good example of such imposition of requirements is the EC Directive on Waste Electrical and Electronic Waste: automotive manufacturers required supplier compliance with its requirements well in advance of its formal implementation dates.

CSV
make a difference

make a difference
to your working day
employee volunteering

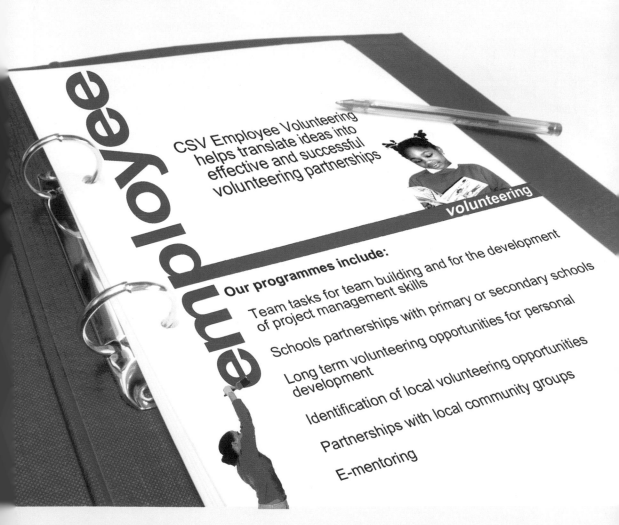

CSV Employee Volunteering helps translate ideas into effective and successful volunteering partnerships

volunteering

Our programmes include:

Team tasks for team building and for the development of project management skills

Schools partnerships with primary or secondary schools

Long term volunteering opportunities for personal development

Identification of local volunteering opportunities

Partnerships with local community groups

E-mentoring

For more information, please contact:
✓ Employee Volunteering ■ 237 Pentonville Road, London N1 9NJ
020 7643 1431 ■ lnicholls@csv.org.uk ■ www.csv.org.uk

CSV Employee Volunteering

As part of the UK's largest volunteering body, with over 10 years of employee volunteering experience, CSV Employee Volunteering is uniquely placed to help employers develop programmes which suit their requirements.

Each year hundreds of volunteers trained and placed by CSV Employee Volunteering assist children in schools with literacy, numeracy and IT, or mentor older children who need one-to-one support to reach the educational and behavioural levels required for employment. Others, whose jobs do not allow them to make the regular commitment required of face to face mentors, are involved in e-mentoring through our specialist website. Every year, over 100 teams of 3 to 150 paint, hammer, garden, make paths, and struggle with brambles. Volunteers report a great sense of satisfaction from watching a child develop or seeing the results of their labours in schools, country parks and community centres from Scotland to Bristol, and express their thanks to their employer for providing the opportunity. The employers reap the benefits in terms of more cohesive teams, improved employee motivation and local and national PR.

CSV specialises in working in partnership to help employers translate their ideas into effective volunteering programmes, placing volunteers in a range of settings with a variety of time commitments. We tailor-make each programme we develop so that it meets the employer's aims in the areas of Community Investment and/or Human Resources whilst meeting a community need.

For those with no experience in this area, we offer consultancy to explore the concept of employee volunteering, devise pilot programmes, and to offer advice on training, research and delivery.

We are totally flexible in the way we work, and can deliver projects on your behalf or provide the support for you to undertake this yourself.

For further information contact:
Lesley Nicholls
Employee Volunteering Development Manager
020 7643 1427
lnicholls@csv.org.uk
www.csv.org.uk/employeevolunteering

Social enterprise

Jeremy Nicholls, The Cat's Pyjamas

There is already a special class of business, recognized by the Department of Trade and Industry (DTI) and the Small Business Service, called social enterprise. The DTI's definition of social enterprises is as follows:

> Social enterprises are businesses with primarily social objectives whose surpluses are principally reinvested for that purpose in the business or in the community, rather than being driven by the need to maximize profit for shareholders and owners. They tackle a wide range of social and environmental issues and operate in all parts of the economy. The Government believes that social enterprises, by using business solutions to achieve public good, have a distinct and valuable role to play in helping create a strong, sustainable and socially inclusive economy.

The Cat's Pyjamas has a different take on this type of business, one that is much less concerned with the use of profits *per se*. For The Cat's Pyjamas, social enterprises are businesses that produce goods and services that reduce inequality. Simply, they are businesses that focus on a particular market – a difficult market, certainly, but a market nonetheless. The founders and managers of these businesses are often driven by a belief that sustainability and an equality of opportunity are interlinked, and by the challenges of running profitable businesses in this market.

So far so good.

The other determining criterion is that these businesses should report on their impact and that the report should be verified. In part, The Cat's Pyjamas believes that engaging with stakeholders, reporting on that engagement and getting someone else to check that the important issues are in the report, that the report is complete and that a response has been made that is accessible to people, is a driver for innovation and improves the business. In part it's because this is one way of taking out risk, but most importantly it's because any-one claming the name 'social enterprise' should be willing to prove it and justify the claim.

But these are businesses that put the social aspects of sustainability at the heart of their operations and then embed these issues in their culture. At their best, they cannot lose this focus simply in order to exploit a sudden new financial opportunity. For any small or medium-sized enterprise (SME) serious about becoming a sustainable business, The Cat's Pyjamas would suggest seeking out examples of these social businesses in order to find out how to make sustainability work.

Jeremy Nicholls, The Cat's Pyjamas, c/o Furniture Resource Centre, Brunswick Business Park, Atlantic Way, Liverpool L3 4BE

Tel: 0151 702 0564
Fax: 0151 702 0551
E-mail: events@the-cats-pyjamas.com

Volunteering England

The definition of volunteering used in the *1997 National Survey of Volunteering* is *"any activity which involves spending time, unpaid, doing something which aims to benefit someone (individuals or groups) other than or in addition to close relatives, or to benefit the environment"*.

When someone volunteers, they are building a relationship. And managing volunteers well requires careful planning. Volunteering England, the national body for volunteering in England, provides comprehensive advice and information on all areas of volunteer management to companies, the public and voluntary sectors.

Employee volunteering can be a particularly useful and fruitful way for companies to build external relationships with public institutions and community organisations.

One key forum for employee volunteering managers, run by Volunteering England, is the Employees in the Community Network. This thriving membership network of employee volunteer managers from the voluntary, private and public sector has been running for 10 years and has grown to over 100 members.

"The Employees in the Community Network is an excellent forum, enabling corporates and the voluntary sector to work together in a non-competitive environment to the mutual benefit of both", The Royal Bank of Scotland Group.

Membership services
The well attended events, on topics as diverse as skills development, virtual volunteering, work-life balance, CSR and employee volunteering in Europe, provide an essential forum for employee volunteering managers to share ideas, concerns and best practice. Members also receive a regular e-bulletin on up-to-the minute news and views on employee volunteering. Members also enjoy all the benefits of being a Volunteering England member, including a free copy of the monthly magazine, Volunteering.

"The Employees in the Community Network is an essential network for practitioners from all sectors, providing a solid and friendly platform for discussion and debate", Business in the Community.

Who can join Volunteering England and the Employees in the Community Network?
Membership is open to organisations and individuals operating in England with an interest in volunteering. There are a range of membership packages for different types and sizes of organisations. Full details can be found at **www.volunteering.org.uk** or **telephone 0845 305 6979**.

The community

David Grayson, Business in the Community

The most valuable contribution that a business makes to the community is to be a sustainably successful business: providing goods and services at a fair price, being a good employer, and treating suppliers as you would like to be treated. Somehow, though, many businesses – large and small – do find time, on top of all that, to provide other help in the community too.

Motives vary: for some owner-managers, helping in the community reflects their personal values – sharing some of the fruits of their success with wider society. For others, it is about enlightened self-interest. There is increasing evidence that supporting the community improves staff morale, raises profile and reputation – and in some cases generates new business. If employees get involved, community work can also enhance staff skills. For many businesses, it is a case of 'all of the above'.

- Forty per cent of business leaders get new business ideas through community activities, according to Roffey Park in 1999.
- Employees involved with a company's community investment activities are significantly more likely to feel pride about their workplace, and this is shown to have an impact on motivation, skills development, team working and likelihood of staying with the company, according to MORI in 2001.
- Ninety per cent of the British public want companies to communicate concerning their community or social activities, according to MORI in 2000.
- Over half (55 per cent) of community organizations and schools say that business support is crucial, according to Impact Assessment, Business in the Community/MORI, 2002.

The most effective business contributions to the community do not try to replace what is properly the role of government or local councils or charities. Rather, they seek to complement these other players and provide the things that only business can provide, or for which business has a comparative advantage. Local schools are a good example of this principle. We pay taxes to fund schools, but a businessman or woman can share his or her time and experience, perhaps by serving as a school governor or as a mentor to a headteacher. Business in the Community (BITC) has been running a very successful programme for more than a decade to twin businesspeople and headteachers, called 'Partners in Leadership'. Most report mutual benefits. Twinning gives a headteacher the much-needed opportunity to test ideas and issues out on a sympathetic outsider. Businesspeople acquire insights, say from helping to run an ethnically diverse organization. Typically, the mentoring lasts a year (although many people choose to continue beyond that) and usually involves a one- to two-hour conversation once or twice a term.

Similarly, a lot of small-business owners and their staff volunteer to help out for (say) an hour a week in a local school to listen to a child read. Again, BITC has a programme for this, called 'Time to Read'. One of the many benefits of this particular scheme is that for many of the children in deprived areas, the business volunteer may be the first non-family adult who has taken a positive interest in them. Most schools are also constantly on the lookout for local businesses that can offer good-quality work experience placements tailored to students' career aspirations – and not just 'shelf-stacking', as the inner-city headteacher of the school where I have been a governor for the past five years describes the poor-quality work placements we used to receive.

HMG Paint

HMG Paints Ltd is a family-owned paint production business based in Manchester. It focuses on education and environmental programmes such as helping many local initiatives with materials and facilities, the provision of outdoor classrooms, work experience opportunities, mock interviewing, industry challenges, career fairs, regenerating the Irk Valley, creating urban community forests and making the surrounding woodland accessible to schools and the community.

Sharing skills and expertise can extend to many other areas of community involvement. BITC's Pro-Help brokers the *pro-bono* assistance of more than 1,000 professional firms – lawyers, accountants, quantity surveyors, architects, advertising agencies and PR companies – often in cross-disciplinary teams to support a wide range of community and charitable groups. This support may involve helping a group of local residents assess the feasibility of converting a disused building into a community centre or incubator space in which people can start up their own businesses.

One of the most valuable contributions that businessmen and women can make is to share their experience of business with people starting out in business: this might involve acting as a volunteer adviser to a Young Enterprise company set up and run by schoolchildren for a school year; or mentoring a young person setting up his or her own business –

perhaps through the Prince's Trust or Shell Livewire, both of which rely on volunteer mentors for the high survival rates of the businesses they support.

Many of the most enduring business–community partnerships involve synergies between the objectives of the business and the community activities that they support – as in the case of Langdale Leisure and Lime Marketing Ltd.

Langdale Leisure

Langdale Leisure is a timeshare and hotel business employing 200 staff with a turnover of approximately £5.5 million a year, based in Langdale, Cumbria. It has three main community initiatives:

- The Lake District Tourism and Conservation Partnership: the first opt-in scheme to raise funds to pay for a full-time footpath repairman working for the National Trust. Langdale has raised over £72,000 so far.
- The Langdale Valleys Initiative Network: formed during the foot-and-mouth crisis to unite all local businesses. It developed a valleys website and promotional leaflet, raised funds for playgrounds, an interpretation centre and obtaining broadband for the area.
- Its commitment to staff participation with other community groups: the Langdale estate – its staff, families and visitors – has always been involved with the local community, where many of its families live and with the landscape that supports it. The estate and its business provide not only jobs directly for local people, but customers for other businesses in the valley as well.

The results

The marketing initiatives undertaken during foot-and-mouth and their close customer relationships were so successful that business trebled. Langdale recognized that true PR value lies in the relationships built between the business and its customers and now its shareholders. When market research was carried out on the value of the Langdale brand, it was identified that the business is unique in its two-way loyalty between its staff and its customers, loyalty that is largely due to its community programmes. Langdale achieved the BITC Community Mark standard in 2003.

Lime Marketing Ltd

Lime Marketing is a marketing, PR and design agency with eight employees based in Brighton. Lime embraces the principles of community involvement by forming lasting relationships with local arts and educational organizations, which it draws upon to develop the agency's creative edge through a combination of sponsorship and training. Staff volunteering and other activities include mentoring and work experience. Lime's designers lecture at schools and colleges; the agency holds team-building days, offers in-kind support and discounted design rates, sponsors the arts, engages in fundraising, brokers support from like-minded businesses and suppliers, draws media attention to community partners, and donates materials.

The results

Lime Marketing won a contract with the Barbican directly as a result of its community programme, excellent press opportunities, positive media coverage, increased networking opportunities, good reputation and customer recognition. It was short-listed for a Sussex business award. Sponsorship has helped to procure training and has improved staff morale through team activities. Mentoring helps staff training and development, and their arts partners speak well of Lime Marketing and recommend the agency, thereby generating new business.

Both these examples illustrate win–win: benefits to the community as well as to the business. Some of the companies at the leading edge when it comes to corporate social responsibility are now going one stage further: they are working with community partners to achieve corporate social *opportunities*.

Businesses are under constant pressure to find new sources of innovation and market insight. Local communities and community groups can be one such source of ideas for new products and services; or for new ways of doing business, such as new marketing and distribution channels; or new ways of finding and training staff. Giant banks such as Citibank and Bank of America are selling mortgages to low-income households in the United States through community development groups in poor neighbourhoods. Tesco is partnering with community organizations to find trainees for pre-recruitment training programmes, who can then go on to work in new Tesco stores in regeneration areas. In such cases the business project becomes viable because of the credibility and connections of the community partners. And that has to be the big prize: taking community learning and experience back into the business.

Corporate community investments are thus most effective for both the company and the community when they:

■ are long-term;
■ involve a range of corporate resources – especially the passion and energy and skills of employees;
■ use the company's 'influence chains' to leverage other support and to lend credibility to the organization or cause;
■ address a business need that is understandable to employees, investors and society at large;
■ if relevant, have the capacity to be taken to scale by others – for example, in the public sector;
■ are not isolated, but complementary to and consistent with wider provision;
■ are based on sound research and assessment of need;

- have been evaluated and modified as necessary to maximize positive impact;
- have been created with opportunities built in to identify and disseminate learning;
- play to the core competences of the business.

And, at their best, they should lead to learning that the company applies to its own core activities, which, as a result, are modified – for example, hiring policies might be changed after a company has participated in a community programme on employability of disabled or homeless people – or lead to other forms of corporate social opportunities.

How to get started in a small way

- Find out more about issues in your local community from newspapers, your employees, customers, suppliers, the internet, the local authority and the local chamber of commerce.
- Make contact with relevant local community groups to understand their activities, consider possible involvement and thereby build a mutually beneficial relationship.
- Find out the opinions of your employees and get them involved in your community programme.
- Look at your existing business resources and how you can use them to benefit the community and your business at the same time.

Who can help?

- Business in the Community (www.bitc.org.uk) provides guidance, information and step-by-step models on business involvement in the community – for example, Community Mark, a national standard recognizing smaller business's involvement in their local communities.
- Arts and Business (www.aandb.org.uk) helps to build communities by developing creative partnerships between business and the arts.
- The Giving Campaign (www.givingcampaign.org.uk) has a simple toolkit available for SMEs on payroll giving.

This chapter is based in part on research for the Small Business Journey, a free online resource for small firms and their advisers who want to build a business that people value. It is from one of 20 individual plus points that make up the Journey – visit www.smallbusinessjourney.com.

David Grayson CBE (www.davidgrayson.net) is a director of Business in the Community and Chairman of the UK Small Business Consortium, which has produced www.smallbusinessjourney.com. He is the author – with Adrian Hodges – of *Corporate Social Opportunity: Seven steps to making corporate social responsibility work for your business* (Greenleaf Publishing, July 2004).

Companies and employees: working together to invest in communities

Graham Leigh, CAF (Charities Aid Foundation)

Introduction

Companies and communities are inextricably linked. Companies pay taxes and employ staff. These employees are, in turn, engaged in communities to a greater or lesser extent. But there is much talk at present about corporate community investment or involvement (CCI) as an answer to some of the responsibilities that companies face. So, what activities tend to be listed under the heading of CCI, why do companies promote these activities and how can employees be included? And while we're on the topic, how much is considered enough?

Sometimes we just don't know what the outcomes of our business choices will be. It would be foolish to rush into decisions without gathering the correct degree of information, but there are some activities that can involve minimum risk and moderate cost while delivering impressive benefits. CCI is one such activity, but it requires adequate planning, focused implementation and willingness to learn on the hoof.

Recent figures from the National Council for Voluntary Organisations (NCVO) suggest that corporate contributions to the UK voluntary sector account for just over £1 billion, equating to 4.3 per cent of the sector's total income, compared to 36.6 per cent from the general public and 37 per cent from the public sector (www.ncvo-vol.org.uk). Furthermore, the 2001 annual corporate social responsibility study produced by MORI reports that 74 per cent of the public believe that 'industry and commerce do not pay enough attention to the local communities in which they operate'.

According to HM Treasury's spending review, 'The Government is determined to do more to build, strengthen and extend the links between the public, private and voluntary sectors.' To this end, the Corporate Challenge was set up 'to increase involvement in community activity in three main areas: corporate support for employee volunteering; corporate support for and promotion of payroll giving schemes; and corporate charitable activity'.

This chapter concentrates on the way in which companies can share or encourage the sharing of resources with communities through either cash, gifts in kind or employee and management time.

Corporate contributions

A company's overall charitable contributions might relate to traditional corporate philanthropy: gifts of cash to charities and community groups. However, companies are increasingly including the measurement of gifts of resources, such as gifts in kind, management time and employee time, in the figures that they report.

Reporting and measuring contributions

All these contributions can be accounted for as a charge against income, which reduces profits and corporation tax in turn. In order to measure these gifts for internal accounting purposes and to measure them against those of other companies, a standard benchmarking model such as that of the London Benchmarking Group may be helpful. (For more information, contact the Corporate Citizenship Company on 020 7945 6130.)

Managing budgets for donations

Gifts may be given gross of tax direct to wholly charitable organizations. They do not have to be registered with the Charity Commission to be considered charitable for tax purposes. Many organizations, such as schools and churches, can automatically benefit from such gifts, and other, smaller groups or projects might not have received a tax-efficient gift before. Where there's a need for charitable donations to be validated, a company charity account could be the answer. This account also allows budgets to be kept separate from other business spend and rolled over from one financial year to the next (contact CAF (Charities Aid Foundation) Corporate Services on 020 7400 2309).

Where a large capital sum is intended to remain untouched and the interest given away to charity, a corporate charitable trust might better fit the bill (for 'off-the-shelf' charitable trusts, contact CAF Trusts on 01732 520000, and for further information on registering your company's own charitable trust, see the Charity Commission website at www.charity-commission.gov.uk).

Support your staff's generosity!

CAF (Charities Aid Foundation) is a registered charity with a mission to increase the resources available to the voluntary sector.

CAF Corporate Services provides solutions that encourage closer engagement between companies and their community. Our services are focused on activities that result in effective and sustainable methods of giving.

- Give As You Earn – the UK's market leading payroll giving scheme
- Matched Giving – allowing your company to support employee donations
- Volunteer Awards Programme- to recognise and reward employees that have contributed their time to the community
- Fundraising Account – designed to hold charitable funds raised by your customers and employees.

If you would like to discuss how CAF can support the design or delivery of your community investment programme, please contact the Corporate Services team on 207 400 2300 or corporate@cafonline.org

sit our website at www.cafonline.org

New developments

There are also new options for community investment that are starting to break the mould of traditional giving. They use other financial tools and tax-free incentives to create broader social benefit.

One option is to bank your money for onward lending while being guaranteed to be able to withdraw it, after a notice period, at some time in the future. If you wanted to commit it for a five-year period, like a bond, you could even get a 5 per cent year-on-year return through a tax credit. (For further information on both of these options, see www.charitybank.org.)

If you wanted an organization to work on your behalf to loan your money in areas of higher financial risk but with strong potential for social return, you could fix your total gift to Venturesome, which will carry out a risk assessment then lend it onwards. Anything that cannot be returned can be treated as a grant. (For further information, visit www.venturesome.org.)

Sponsorship and cause-related marketing

There are some other activities that may fall between charitable contributions and a traditional business exchange, but may also fit within a CCI programme. Examples include corporate sponsorship of charitable organizations and cause-related marketing (CRM).

The distinction between a charitable contribution and sponsorship depends on whether or not a tangible benefit is supplied to the company as a condition of the company's payment. Typically, the benefit comes in the form of exposure of a company logo; it can be displayed either on a charity's promotional information, during the course of its activities or on its material assets. Other supplies of benefit may include a table at a charity banquet or sponsoring a corporate box at the theatre.

Unlike in the case of sponsorship, CRM can use a charity's logo to help market a corporate product. Companies are beginning to see enormous potential in this activity, as it represents a clear business case for corporate investment in communities. According to the Business in the Community (BITC) website (www.bitc.org.uk), BITC's Giving Now survey has discovered that 82 per cent of the population have been involved in a specific CRM programme.

In a sponsorship or CRM agreement it is important for the charity and the company to guard against reputational risk, and for this reason it is prudent to use a commercial participation agreement with clearly stated objectives and expectations.

CCI – how much is enough?

Public opinion

CCI, from charitable activity through sponsorship, CRM and employee involvement, can be seen as a balance of give and take. Is the company seen to give back to the community as much as it takes out?

How does the company compare?

As a broad indicator of 'how much is enough', BITC has set up the Per Cent Standard, whereby 122 companies present their figures for total contributions in terms of cash, gifts in kind, management time and employee time as a proportion of pre-tax profits. Verified holders of the Per Cent Standard give in excess of 1 per cent. Of course, this is easier for some companies than others, and it may depend on the way in which a company is associated. For example, concern for shareholder reactions to unusually high levels of charitable contributions might make PLCs more hesitant to do so than privately owned companies.

At what point can the programme be seen to meet strategic objectives?

The ultimate measure of how much is enough is whether or not the company believes that it has met the strategic objectives that it set out to achieve, and whether or not its opinion can be corroborated by the programme's stakeholders.

Programmes and budgets can be scaled, and it's not always the most costly programmes that return the greatest benefits or make the greatest difference to society. This is a great argument for getting a programme started, but there are plenty of charities out there that will tell you that cash hasn't gone out of fashion after all. Money, in the right quantity and in the right place, can be the backbone of a credible, strategic and sustainable CCI programme. (For further information on the strategic argument for corporate philanthropy, see *The Competitive Advantage of Corporate Philanthropy* by Michael E Porter (http://www.isc. hbs.edu/soci-corporate-philanthropy.htm).)

Involving employees

Involving employees in a company's community investment programme (appropriately referred to as employee community involvement) may also require a little company time and resource, but it can also reap great rewards in terms of staff motivation and morale, employee retention and skills sharing.

Employee volunteering

Employee volunteering schemes allow and encourage employees to give their skills and either their personal time or a portion of the working day for the benefit of charitable organizations. The Home Office produced a citizenship survey in 2001 as part of the Government's Active Community Agenda, which aims to create substantial progress towards actively involving a target of 1 million additional people in their communities by 2004. The findings of the survey are reported in a document called 'Active Communities', available at http://www.homeoffice.gov.uk/docs/infindin.pdf. The report indicated that 67 per cent of respondents were involved in informal volunteering, 39 per cent were involved in formal volunteering and only 4 per cent were involved in employer-supported volunteering. This would suggest that volunteering is already happening and that it might not take too much effort to find employee support for organized workplace programmes.

Volunteer England is one organization that can help to develop these programmes in line with strategic corporate and human resources objectives, as well as providing practical advice on matching companies to appropriate community groups. The Employees in the Community Network (EitCN) provides companies with a regular forum for the exchange of knowledge and experience in this field. (For more information, visit http://www.volunteering.org.uk/missions.php?id=33.)

Payroll giving

Payroll giving allows employees to give monthly donations to any UK charity direct from their pay. It's tax effective and therefore costs employees less to give. For example, a 22 per cent taxpayer would forfeit only £7.80 for the charity to receive £10, and less for those on the higher rate.

There are currently more than 600,000 payroll donors in the United Kingdom, and the latest figures from Charities Aid Foundation (CAF) show that £86 million was given through payroll giving in 2002/03 even though only one in five employees are offered the opportunity by their employer, so there is enormous potential for growth in this area. The administration is minimal for the payroll department, and payroll-giving agency charities provide the administration for collecting and splitting payments among hundreds of thousands of potential UK charity recipients.

The facilitation and promotion of employee giving schemes can also attract benefits similar to those of employee volunteering, eg improved staff morale, team-building and satisfaction, as long as a scheme is introduced and promoted sensitively and with the involvement of staff.

The first thing to do in setting up a payroll giving scheme is to ensure that the company has a contract with an Inland Revenue-approved agency charity. This contract is a legal requirement, and it ensures that funds are deducted from payroll and distributed within a reasonable time-frame. CAF is the largest of these organizations (contact details for all approved agencies are available at www.inlandrevenue.gov.uk/payrollgiving/employers).

There are professional organizations that can help to promote payroll giving. In most cases they will work on a commission basis, payable by the charity on a per donor basis. This arrangement is effectively an outsourcing operation for fundraising, and many charities support this since it offers them reliable income for predictable costs. There are also examples of successful promotions where companies have promoted payroll giving using their own staff and resources.

Key principles for promoting involvement of employees in a community

Community involvement programmes are most successful when tailor-made to the needs of the individual company and its specific stakeholders. There are no generic rules or dos and don'ts for promoting the engagement of employees in these programmes, but there are some things that tend to help.

Laying the foundations

The type of response from employees can depend on the history and culture of community investment within the company, the benefits on offer and the appeal of the promotion; but often the success of a programme is dependent on planning. A conceptually sound and well-planned programme will have greater appeal to employees than a gesture of charity and benevolence from out of the blue.

One way to clear passage for successful engagement of employees in a CCI programme is to get their support ahead of a promotion. When offered the opportunity to give up their own time or money for the sake of the community, employees don't automatically accept that there is a link between their private interests and those of the business. They tend to like a little background information first, such as what the company is hoping to achieve – and why now?

Gathering information about what employees already do in the community and what support they would like can also help lay strong foundations for a promotion. Of course, the first thing that springs to mind is about managing expectations and setting boundaries on budget, timing, scope and policy, and openly stating these limitations at the beginning. At the same time, the survey needs to offer genuine choice. There's little point in lobbying opinion if all the decisions have already been made.

A workforce that has been engaged in the design of a programme is more likely to take ownership of it and maintain sustained enthusiasm for it. This can result in genuine pride in its success, and create a positive impact on employee relations, morale and perceptions of the working environment.

Example benefits

Rockport UK is part of the Reebok corporation, and corporate social responsibility is at the top of its management agenda from labour standards right through to community involvement, but Rockport wanted to match corporate values to practice and so they chose a project in partnership with the Wildlife Trust called Boots and Butterflies. Managing Director Andy Loeber worked with colleagues to help clear Warton Crag, in Lancashire, of invading plant species. The work helped to increase the native food source of two endangered butterfly species, so it delivered great environmental benefits. The Wildlife Trust benefited from an extremely valuable volunteer resource, and there were plenty of business benefits besides.

Rockport already had a culture of 'work hard, play hard', and once the management team had set the scene for the programme, employees quickly took ownership. Andy commented:

> This initiative was great for cross-functional relations. We didn't stick to our regular groups: people from Accounts worked with people from Marketing and so on. Boots and Butterflies really helped to build team spirit... When we're all juggling different projects at different times, the biggest challenge is making time for it, but it has really been great fun and we now have lots of ideas for future events. It helped us understand the full potential for a great working environment, better productivity and a really strong team culture. The senior management team is behind it now more than ever.

Promotion tips

1. Companies often use matched giving programmes to bridge the gap between the company's direct contribution to the community and the contribution of its employees. Such programmes may have various constituent parts, eg matching proportions of

employee donations to charity through their payroll; matching one-off charitable gifts; matching employees' fund-raised money; matching employees' personal time with company time; or awarding gifts of cash for volunteering effort. These can be good options for making granting decisions in an inclusive, democratic and transparent way. They can also aid communication and measurement of the company's criteria for determining the success of a programme. (For assistance in planning, setting up and administering these programmes, call the CAF Corporate Services team on 0207 400 2309.)

2. Human interaction is important. Programmes in which there is a good level of interaction between colleagues are not only more likely to gain high levels of take-up, but are also more likely to provide business benefits such as interdepartmental communication (throughout a company's hierarchy), skills sharing and team-building. This is as true for payroll giving as for volunteering, where there needs to be a definite 'ask' from one colleague to another. Employees need to be given a clear and concise explanation of what they are being offered without being coerced into joining a scheme.

3. Pre-promotion information on the scheme can help build awareness ahead of time, which can encourage a warmer reception.

4. Partnering with charitable organizations can help to provide a deeper insight into popular issues, and sometimes there is no substitute for their enthusiasm.

5. Standard literature can be provided by the agency charity or charity partner, or the company can produce its own information with their help.

6. Electronic promotion systems can help to provide a convenient and immediate sign-up mechanism and therefore help build and maintain campaign momentum.

7. Whatever it is that the company decides to do, it should be fun. Employees remember a good time, even if it involves hard work.

8. Post-promotion information is a great way to maintain awareness of and enthusiasm for the programme for future years.

Corporate community investment is unlikely to be the answer for all of a company's responsibilities to society, but it can be seen to help redress the balance of give and take in the community. A well-organized, inclusive and considered programme that is promoted effectively can have a generally positive impact on the operating environment and the working environment, so while many companies continue to struggle with the question of 'Why run a programme?', the resounding question for the enlightened might be 'Why not?'

13

Process efficiency

Process efficiency: introduction

John Sabapathy, AccountAbility

Responsible competitiveness: from private profit to public good

Corporate responsibility is constantly in the news. Picking up almost any issue of the *Financial Times* throws up a myriad of corporate responsibility issues with implications for the competitiveness of the companies involved. How will Shell move on from its reserves crisis? What will be the effect of The Gap's new sustainability reporting initiative in reducing the risk of labour violations in its supply chain? What is the role of Pret-à Manger's organic and ethical sourcing policies in its seemingly incessant growth? The answers to any of these individual cases are complex and nuanced. The broader trend is clear: more and more companies are trying to increase their competitiveness through greater sensitivity to their stakeholders' concerns about corporate social, environmental and economic impact – that is, through corporate responsibility.

There are by now many instances of how the pattern spreads across sectors: Vietnamese clothing manufacturers' approach to labour standards strengthening their sector's competitiveness in Northern markets; or British financial services' opening up of new markets by developing innovative approaches to financial exclusion.

The bigger question for policy-makers is whether corporate responsibility is or can be a key component in driving national productivity and competitiveness. Recent work by an international responsible competitiveness consortium and using work by the World Economic Forum has shown that when such measures of corporate responsibility are incorporated into existing national competitiveness rankings we get a different picture of countries' likely growth trajectories. The Responsible Competitiveness Index shows countries such as the United States, China, Japan and Korea set to have lower than expected levels of growth, once key aspects of corporate responsibility are factored in. On the other side, countries as far apart as Denmark and Costa Rica are set to achieve higher levels of competitiveness that those suggested by traditional rankings.

We live in a deteriorating environment, working in economies where the renegotiation of responsibilities between the public and private sectors is played out at increasingly globalized levels. If targeted corporate responsibility can improve national competitiveness, then both business and governments need to understand how to deliver this – both improving our environment and strengthening both the public and private goods we have access to.

This introduction draws on work conducted through AccountAbility's Responsible Competitiveness Programme. For more, see www.accountability.org.uk.

John Sabapathy is a Senior Associate at AccountAbility.

Process efficiency: legal introduction

Kathryn Mylrea, Simmons & Simmons

Process efficiency is not primarily a legal issue, although there are numerous examples of legislation containing requirements that may necessarily involve changes to processes. For example, health and safety law requires that safe systems of work be in place. The concept of Best Available Techniques underpinning the pollution prevention control (PPC) legislation includes processes, and PPC specifically requires that the process be operated in a way that delivers improvements in energy efficiency. Changes in legislative requirements regarding the disposal of waste – in particular, landfilling – have meant that many waste streams can no longer be disposed of in landfill, and much more costly options are required. Changes in process to ensure that waste streams are minimized will be a practical necessity.

Office efficiency

Anna Francis, Waste Watch

Making your office as sustainable and efficient as possible has commercial benefits and can entail significant cost savings. It also helps to improve an organization's profile and hence competitive advantage, and can increase staff morale. Taking control of the way your office uses resources improves management control as well as ensuring that your organization complies with legislation. Responsible environmental practice makes good business sense and is synonymous with a well-managed organization.

This chapter will examine four main areas of office efficiency: waste and recycling, equipment, energy use, and management systems that empower the workforce.

Waste and recycling

The way an organization uses and disposes of resources has an impact on both costs and the environment. Waste reduction at source – that is, careful purchasing to prevent waste – is environmentally and commercially the best option and is a growing area of business interest for many organizations. Waste is a commercial issue: the less waste you create, the less you pay to have it removed. Maximizing the efficiency of resources, such as printing double-sided, also means that less money is spent on procurement. Savings in waste disposal costs through reduction, reuse or recycling (see the hierarchy shown in Figure 13.3.1) can be particularly significant, and costs of waste disposal often tend to be underestimated, despite their recent substantial increase with the introduction of the landfill tax. Many companies do not know what they spend on waste, and few companies are aware that the real cost of waste (including the value of raw materials, energy and wasted labour) can be up

Wastebusters Ltd, June 1996

Figure 13.3.1 Savings in waste disposal costs: the waste hierarchy

to 20 times the cost of disposal alone.[1] On average, 70 per cent of office waste is recyclable, so there is significant potential for savings on disposal costs, although there will generally also be a fee for a recycling service.

In the United Kingdom each year the average office worker produces more than two and a half times his or her own body weight in rubbish. That's over 2 million tonnes across the United Kingdom.[2] To take paper as an example, the average UK office employee uses nearly 15,000 sheets of A4 paper,[3] the equivalent of one tree's worth of paper every year. It costs around £30 a tonne and rising to dispose of 'waste paper', yet the paper can be worth far more if it is sorted and recycled. Offices are potentially a major source of high-quality sorted waste papers. More than half of all office waste is made up of paper, most of which is high-grade white paper, the most sought-after type for recycling.[4]

There are also significant environmental savings to be made by recycling. On average, the production of recycled paper involves between 28 per cent and 70 per cent less energy compared to producing virgin paper,[5] producing recycled paper saves 17 trees, 7,000 gallons of water and 4,200 kilowatt-hours of electricity (enough for an average house for six months) per tonne, and also reduces emissions of carbon dioxide and nitrogen.[6]

What can be recycled?

The following common office wastes can be recycled:

- paper;
- cardboard;
- computers and related components;
- toner and ink cartridges;
- office equipment, eg photocopiers;
- mobile phones;
- fluorescent light tubes;
- batteries.

Brother – Committed to Sustainable Development

The technological revolution has radically changed today's office – enabling us to work faster, smarter and more efficiently from anywhere across the globe…but at what price?

One of the UK's leading business technology manufacturers, Brother, has long taken the principles of sustainable development and corporate social responsibility to the heart of its business strategy and throughout its products' entire lifecycle.

Why should businesses place social responsibility top of their agenda? This year new legislation will be passed that will directly affect all businesses – the EU Directive on Waste Electrical and Electronic Equipment (WEEE), with companies having to comply fully by August 2005. The directive promotes eco-friendly product design to reduce the mountains of electronic waste currently going straight to landfill.

The choice of products on the market claiming to be 'green' can be bewildering. To ensure that the legislative requirements are met, the easiest route is to choose a product that has gained TCO accreditation – the definitive catch-all for green credentials.

Brother has pledged to launch all new relevant products under the TCO banner and recently gained the TCO accreditation for a total of eleven business products, including the world's first multifunction laser printer. All Brother products manufactured from August 2004 will meet WEEE product marking requirements – one year ahead of the legislative deadline.

Mr Kayaba, acting managing director of Brother UK, explains why businesses need to act now, "Investing in environmentally friendly, sustainable products is not idealistic – it makes sound economic sense.

"By purchasing products that are endorsed with a TCO badge, businesses know they meet the terms of the EU WEEE Directive.

"More than this, it enables them to become socially responsible businesses with all the benefits this brings."

At Brother UK we're making our mark on protecting and preserving the environment. Our approach to sustainable development is underpinned by the environmental philosophy supported by the Brother Group in Japan. Here, the theory is translated into practice, using five simple but effective operating principles: Reduce waste material by recycling. Re-use products and waste material again. Reform materials and use again. Recycle rather than scrap. Refuse to buy environmentally unfriendly products.

Following these simple rules, efforts are now being co-ordinated on a global scale to reduce our environmental impact by 30% over the next 3 years.

For a full copy of our environmental policy, please contact the Brother Green helpline on **0870 830 4015**

Brother UK Ltd., Audenshaw, Manchester. Brother Industries Ltd., Nagoya, Japan.

At your side.

Business machines that won't cost the earth.

Table 13.3.1 Impact of different recycling collection options

Potential Scenario	Encourages Environmental Culture	Quality of Recyclables		Space Requirement		Admin Requirement	
		Low	High	Low	High	Low	High
Separation							
Waste company reclaims recyclables from waste stream	No	✓		✓		✓	
Separation at source (ie segregation in the office)	Yes		✓		✓		✓
Multiple collection companies	Yes		✓		✓		✓
Contractor							
Single collection company	No	✓		✓		✓	

Office items that can be easily reused include:

■ furniture;
■ IT equipment.

Waste generated by catering services can also be recycled:

■ aluminium cans and foil;
■ cooking oils;
■ glass;
■ plastic bottles;
■ plastic cups from vending machines.

Fruit, vegetable peelings, tea bags and coffee grounds can also potentially be composted.

Options for an office recycling service

There are a number of collection options when selecting a recycling contractor to service an office, each of which requires different levels of staff involvement, space and frequency of collection. As a result of these factors, the quality of the material collected for recycling will also vary. Staff engagement is important, as the more staff an organization has, the more waste it will produce, which therefore increases the amount of material available for recycling.

Moving office

Moving to a new office can create a significant amount of waste as well as offering opportunities for more efficient waste management in the future. However, unwanted office furniture can now be reused (see www.frn.org.uk/code/find/map.asp for details), and, when setting up a new office, recycling facilities can be installed at suitably convenient points to encourage staff to recycle and maximize the effectiveness of the scheme.

How do I start recycling?

The following are suggestions for how to start:

■ Know what waste you are producing and identify what materials you think could be recycled.
■ Identify recycling collection contractors in your area.
■ Gain senior management commitment.
■ Engage the support of other contractors, such as cleaners and interested staff, in implementing a system.
■ Agree a recycling plan, highlighting when schemes will be introduced, reviewed and expanded.
■ Once the infrastructure is in place, run an internal awareness-raising campaign to encourage staff to recycle, and use this as a way of developing 'green teams' or 'recycling champions'.
■ Ask your recycling contractor to record and provide you with information on the quantity of material that you have recycled. Use these data to highlight the positive impact of staff actions and to improve capture rates (ie the percentage of a potentially recyclable material that is actually collected for recycling).
■ Include information on recycling in staff induction programmes and the 'staff handbook', and encourage staff feedback.
■ Buy recycled products.

Barriers to recycling and how to overcome them

The main barriers to recycling are:

■ space restrictions;
■ lack of available recycling services in your area;
■ minimum quantities of material required for collection;
■ cost of collection of material(s) for recycling/implementation of scheme;
■ lack of staff engagement/understanding.

However, good planning, endorsed schemes, reviewed action and good communication with contractors and staff will help to overcome these barriers and will help you keep up to date with legislative changes and changes in service provision.

What is considered to be best practice in office recycling and reduction? The answer is a recycling rate of 70 per cent and a figure of 200 kilograms of waste production per full-time-equivalent member of staff.

If you recycle your waste, it is also important that you buy recycled products ('closing the loop'); unless there are viable markets, recycling is not always cost-effective. For more information about recycled products, see www.recycledproducts.org.uk.

Legislation and regulation

It is essential to comply with legislation and regulations that govern waste disposal, including:

- the Environmental Protection Act 1990, including the Duty of Care Regulations;
- the Environment Act 1995;
- the Landfill Directive;
- the Packaging and Packaging Waste Directive;
- the Waste Electrical and Electronic Equipment (WEEE) Directive.

For further information, contact:

- the Environment Agency for England and Wales, www.environment-agency.gov.uk;
- the Scottish Environmental Protection Agency, www.sepa.org.uk;
- the Northern Ireland Environment and Heritage Service, www.ehsni.gov.uk/default.asp.

Equipment

The choice and management of office equipment can have a huge impact on both the environmental and the organizational costs of an office. How long a piece of equipment lasts, the energy and resources it uses and the way it is disposed of are all significant. While energy use for the heating and lighting of offices is decreasing and becoming more efficient, the energy used by office equipment continues to rise. In fact, office equipment is the fastest-growing user of energy in the business world, and electricity consumption by office equipment now represents 25 per cent of total electrical energy use in offices.[7] Its impact on the environment (and an organization's costs) is therefore considerable. For example, carbon dioxide (CO_2) emissions arising from such consumption are a major contributor to climate change. Furthermore, because of the limited life of most office equipment, substantial waste is produced when equipment is finally disposed of.

Fortunately, there is now an extensive range of environmentally preferable products that can reduce your costs and environmental impact. These products are often no more expensive to purchase and are usually cheaper to operate. Preference should be given to energy-efficient equipment and equipment that reduces resource use (and hence costs), such as printers that can print double-sided and photocopiers that have easy-to-use duplex settings.

Staff awareness and understanding of their impacts in relation to office equipment use is also key to successfully reducing the environmental and cost implications of equipment use – for example, making employees aware of the benefits of turning off their computer monitor if they are away from their desk.

Energy

Office energy bills can often be reduced by 10–20 per cent by introducing a range of measures, many of which involve little or no expenditure. For example:

- Energy-efficient light bulbs last six times as long as conventional types and cost one-tenth as much to run.
- Reducing the temperature of your office by 1°C will reduce your fuel bill by 10%.
- If you do not service your boiler for one year, its efficiency can drop by 10%.
- A photocopier left switched on overnight uses enough energy to make 5,300 A4 copies.
- A PC monitor uses 80 per cent of a PC's energy. If you are away from your desk for more than 30 minutes, it is more cost-effective to switch your PC monitor off. A monitor left switched on overnight uses enough energy to laser-print 800 A4 pages.
- Lighting an empty office overnight uses enough energy to heat water for 1,000 cups of coffee. Even if you are only leaving your office for 5 or 10 minutes, it is still more cost-effective to switch off your lights.

When purchasing office equipment, it is important to consider whole-life energy cost savings; it may save you money in the longer term to pay more initially. For example, over its lifespan a fluorescent tube will save 640 kilowatt-hours of electricity compared with the equivalent 100-watt standard bulb. This reduces the production of carbon dioxide, a greenhouse gas, by half a tonne and that of sulphur dioxide, which causes acid rain, by 3 kilograms. Preference should be given to equipment that has the Energy Efficiency Recommended logo, or a similar standard. When purchasing new equipment, ask your suppliers for information on the average power consumed under normal operating conditions. You could then develop that information into a more formal green procurement policy, establishing a policy of purchasing energy-saving equipment and making it a requirement that the lifetime cost of new equipment is included in the purchasing decision. Once the equipment is purchased, it is important to make sure that the 'power save' feature is activated, as equipment is often set up with it disabled.

How to start greening your office

The most effective approach to setting up a green office is to involve senior management from the beginning, as it is much easier to get things done when an effort has the backing of management. A signed commitment from senior management towards improving the environmental performance of your organization is a good start. This commitment could then potentially be developed into an environmental policy: a written statement outlining an organization's main environmental impacts and aims in relation to managing these impacts. In the absence of senior management commitment, individuals and groups of employees can still achieve significant environmental improvements.

Assign responsibilities

Nominating individuals to take responsibility for a particular environmental improvement is very important, as they can ensure that the changes needed are followed through. Setting up an informal committee to coordinate efforts and share information is also very beneficial. Encouraging in-house suggestions and rewarding initiatives or innovation in the context of recycling can also help to create a successful green office.

Review current performance and collect data

Reviewing existing practice means that opportunities for environmental improvements can easily be identified. It involves examining resource use, energy and water use, transport, procurement, and current waste disposal methods. By collecting baseline data on energy and water consumption and on waste production, future improvements can be compared. This can be done internally or with the help of external consultants.

Set priorities

Improving the environmental performance of your organization is a long-term project. Some changes will take longer and require more resources to implement than others. However, there are lots of things that can be done straight away, such as setting up a paper recycling scheme, so this could be prioritized while more complicated changes could be undertaken later.

Eventually you may feel that the organization needs a more formal approach to improving its environmental performance. Longer-term changes can be incorporated into an environmental management system (EMS), which can be independently audited if required.

Communicate and promote

Communication is central to improving efficiency and environmental performance. Ensuring that everyone understands what you want to do, why and how, and that they receive regular feedback on targets and achievements, can help to ensure continued interest and involvement. Formulating and then communicating an environmental policy is also useful and is key to developing and implementing an EMS. An environmental policy allows an organization to communicate its environmental aims and objectives to employees, shareholders, customers, suppliers and any other interested parties.

Review and improve

In a green office, concern for the environment should be an integral part of everyday operations. Environmental improvement is an ongoing process, and new products and processes are constantly being developed. The best way of maintaining and improving a green office is to establish a more formal EMS, which will put in place a continual process of review and improvement.

Environmental management systems

Adopting a more formal approach through implementing an EMS has a number of advantages: integrating responsibility for environmental issues into day-to-day work ensures that initiatives last beyond initial enthusiasm. An EMS also helps organizations to identify all their environmental effects and potential risks in a structured and systematic way rather than responding to outside pressures on an ad hoc basis. In addition, as more organizations adopt EMSs, they are starting to look at the effect their supply chain has on the environment. By implementing environmental measures, you can comply with your customers' requirements and be in a better position to win EMS-registered clients.

Environmental management system standards

The main EMS standard is ISO 14001. There is also a European regulation, the Eco-Management and Audit Scheme (EMAS). These management standards have created an international blueprint for integrating environmental issues into the management structure of an organization. They are not the only possible designs for an environmental management system, but they do provide an opportunity for independent certification of an organization's commitment to responsible environmental practice. For more information, see http://emea.bsi-global.com/Environment/.

Waste Watch Environmental Consultancy

Waste Watch Environmental Consultancy (WWEC, formerly Wastebusters) provides practical support to businesses wishing to implement efficient and cost-effective sound environmental practice. Our client list features high-profile organizations from both the public and the private sectors, and we can help you with:

- resource management;
- waste audits;
- green procurement policies;
- waste minimization plans;
- environmental reporting;
- education and awareness-raising programmes;
- advice on sustainable transport;
- feasibility studies;
- composting research.

WWEC/Wastebusters also compiled the *Green Office Manual*, which provides businesses of all sizes with clear, jargon-free, concise information about environmental issues and the practical steps that can be taken to create a green office environment. It highlights the opportunities for achieving cost savings through environmental improvements and sets out effective, simple mechanisms to encourage participation and commitment from staff and suppliers.

Waste Watch Environmental Consultancy is managed by Waste Watch Services, the trading arm of Waste Watch (www.wastewatch.org.uk), the national charity promoting waste reduction, reuse and recycling. For more information about WWEC, see www.wastewatch.org.uk/business or call 020 7549 0305.

Notes

1   www.gloucestershire.gov.uk/index.cfm?articleID=5318
2   www.ecoaction.richmond.gov.uk/business_directory.htm
3   www.sweeter-islington.fsnet.co.uk/Officewaste.htm
4   www.green-office.org.uk/audit.php?goingto=factsheet4
5   www.sweeter-islington.fsnet.co.uk/Officewaste.htm
6   www.sustainable.doe.gov/success/sanjose.shtml
7   www.greenconsumerguide.com/domesticll.php?CLASSIFICATION=98&PARENT=92

Capitalising the rewards of energy efficiency

Seeking expert advice at the right time can help companies maximise cost and energy savings. Andrew Thorne, Principal Consultant with BRE Environment, looks at recent initiatives by The University of Glasgow.

As part of the University of Glasgow's continuing programme of enhancing energy efficiency throughout its building stock, it recently formed a partnership with the Carbon Trust in Scotland. The Carbon Trust agreed to fund packages of specialist advice and consultancy as an incentive for the University to further its own activities. Along with several other focus areas, three new building projects presented opportunities to put this policy into practice. The Carbon Trust appointed BRE as advisors for all three projects, each of which had different needs and thus required individual treatment.

The CRUK Beatson New Cancer Research Centre

This flagship laboratory will cost over £15 million and house around 240 researchers. As a first step the Carbon Trust commissioned BRE to carry out a comprehensive energy review of the design. Energy performance was reviewed at RIBA design stage C. This identified opportunities for improvement that could be incorporated as the detailed design developed. The key areas for reducing energy use were through the control of ventilation in areas of high or intermittent demand, a control strategy that increased opportunities for boilers to operate in their most efficient condensing mode, and the construction of an airtight building envelope.

Encouraged by the results of the Energy Review the University took matters forward and commissioned a BREEAM* assessment for the building. BRE is overseeing sustainability issues but in particular is advising how to minimise environmental impacts, whilst maintaining the high levels of performance required by a leading-edge laboratory. A set of environmental criteria has been built into the design brief, aiming for the building to achieve an Excellent BREEAM rating once it is completed.

The Rowardennan Marine Biology Centre

The brief for this project is to exceed environmental Good Practice and create a green building with low running costs and low carbon emissions. BRE's design review confirmed that good environmental practice is being followed with regard to building orientation, landscaping, energy conservation, daylighting, heating, ventilation, solar gain control, use of thermal mass and materials selection. However, the feature that will most improve its environmental credentials is the incorporation of a hydro scheme generating renewable electricity at the site. In energy terms, the building is set to exceed good practice by 19% and be 45% more efficient than a comparable academic building.

The Department of Computing Science

A design review was carried out to see whether it would be possible to improve the overall energy efficiency of this new building and, at the same time, calculate the cost and energy savings that would accrue. The result showed that although energy efficiency had been a key consideration during the development of the design, several of the concepts would require further consideration if they were to be effective.

The most significant opportunity for energy savings was in the area of ventilation and involved the use of variable speed fans that respond to occupancy levels. Further opportunities for savings included: the selection of cooling equipment using a database of operating performance; heat recovery; and refinements to automatic control strategies and user interfaces.

All in all, annual energy savings are expected to be worth more than £2000 a year at current energy prices and equal to 12.5% of site demand. This figure is further increased when the social cost of carbon emissions (which the Government estimates at £70 per tonne) is included.

*BREEAM is a labelling scheme that has become the mark of environmental sustainability for commercial and public buildings in the UK. It assesses the design, construction, management and operation of buildings.

Sustainable businesses operate in sustainable buildings

Buildings have a huge impact on the environment. The energy used within them accounts for nearly half of the UK's CO_2 emissions, and the production of construction materials accounts for a further 10%. Six tonnes of building materials per person are used each year, and the waste from their production and use accounts for 35% of the UK's total waste.

Making your business operate sustainably is not just about the way you work – it is about ensuring your premises are sustainable too.

BRE Environment can add value to your business by helping you to reduce any adverse impacts that your premises may have on the environment. We help our clients create sustainable buildings that meet today's needs and anticipate future demands.

- Energy advice
- Design reviews
- Whole life costing
- Waste minimisation
- Materials selection
- Energy and environmental performance
- Pollution and noise control
- Recycling

BRE Environment
Telephone: 01923 664500
E-mail: environment@bre.co.uk
www.bre.co.uk

The construction industry: responding to the rise of sustainability and corporate social responsibility

Peter Bonfield, BRE Construction

With an annual output of some £75 billion, the construction industry plays a major role in the UK economy, accounting for around 8 per cent of GDP and directly employing 1.5 million people (1 in 14 of the total working population). There are an estimated 164,000 construction companies in the United Kingdom, the vast majority of these being small and medium-sized enterprises (SMEs) with fewer than 24 workers.

The sector has profound and extensive environmental, economic and social impacts, and is therefore a key player in delivering Government policy objectives on climate change, energy, resource use, waste minimization, housing, transport, urban regeneration and sustainable communities. Waste from construction and demolition materials, including soil, equals 70 million tonnes annually (29 per cent of UK controlled waste), with an estimated

13 million tonnes of this made up of materials delivered to building sites but never used. Annually, the industry produces three times the waste generated by all UK households combined, and the amount of construction materials used each year is equivalent to 6 tonnes per head of the UK population. About 17 per cent of waste going to landfill sites is directly related to construction, with indirect arisings such as quarrying and other waste doubling this figure. Around 50 per cent of UK CO_2 emissions are from energy used for heating, cooling, ventilation and lighting in buildings. The sector accounts for 60 per cent of all timber used in the United Kingdom, the majority of it imported.

Clearly, moves to minimize waste, reduce pollution and improve resource use within the sector would make a significant contribution to national sustainable development objectives as well as boosting the sector's profitability and improving its reputation as a socially and environmentally responsible employer. This chapter looks at some of the initiatives that are driving forward improvements across the industry.

Rethinking construction

In July 1998 the influential report *Rethinking Construction* was published by the Construction Task Force, chaired by Sir John Egan. The report aimed to provide a blueprint for the future long-term competitiveness and performance of the construction industry in the United Kingdom by improving efficiency, minimizing waste and focusing on quality. The improvement targets identified in the report were to:

■ reduce capital cost by 10 per cent per year;
■ reduce construction time by 10 per cent per year;
■ reduce defects by 20 per cent per year;
■ reduce accidents by 20 per cent per year;
■ increase predictability by 20 per cent per year;
■ increase productivity by 10 per cent per year;
■ increase turnover and profits by 10 per cent per year.

Following this, the Construction Best Practice Programme (CBPP) and the Movement for Innovation (M4I) were set up to take forward the report's recommendations. CBPP set up a comprehensive website and a network of Best Practice Clubs, and developed other innovative resources and tools. It worked with industry groups to develop key performance indicators (KPIs). M4I concentrated on promoting demonstration projects that demonstrated the 'Rethinking Construction' principles. The programme comprised 374 demonstration projects with a combined value of almost £7 billion covering the whole industry, including housing and local government clients and all types of construction work: new build, refurbishment, repairs and maintenance. KPIs were used to monitor progress. These revealed that the 'Rethinking Construction' projects outperformed the industry average in all areas, with the highest scores being for safety and reduced environmental impact. The demonstration projects achieved astonishing savings: client construction costs 6 per cent below the industry average, accident rates 61 per cent lower and profitability 2 per cent higher. If these figures are extrapolated to apply to a third of the UK construction industry, the cost of accidents could be reduced by £1.2 billion annually, client construction costs could decrease by £1.4 billion and industry profits could increase by £446 million.

Operating in a complex environment

The construction industry is used to operating in a heavily regulated business environment. It is subject to a large number of governmental and legislative requirements that in themselves drive forward sustainability: the planning system, environmental impact assessment, the contaminated land regime, the Climate Change Levy, landfill tax, aggregates tax, the Building Regulations, etc. There will be further legislation on water, energy and planning, and from January 2006 the industry will need to meet the requirements of the EU Energy Performance of Buildings Directive (EPBB), which requires that all buildings have an energy label whenever they change ownership or tenancy.

Following the Better Buildings Summit held in October 2003, John Prescott, Margaret Beckett and Patricia Hewitt established the Sustainable Building Task Group (SBTG) to identify how government and industry could improve the quality and sustainability of new and refurbished buildings. One of the key recommendations coming out of the group's report, published in May 2004, was the establishment of a Code for Sustainable Buildings, based on the Building Research Establishment's Environmental Assessment Method (BREEAM) and EcoHomes. The Code would be used by planning authorities to set standards higher than the Building Regulations for energy, water and waste. 'When you get local authorities, the Government and planning authorities making a label or code higher than the Building Regulations, then the industry will respond,' says David Strong, Managing Director of BRE Environment.

There are numerous non-statutory pressures too, notably on corporate social responsibility (CSR) reporting: the rise of the socially responsible investor, greater community activism, shifting client expectations and growing pressure to comply with corporate good governance rules.

Attracting and retaining high-calibre staff is a well-documented and perennial problem. The construction industry's relatively poor reputation and the perceived lack of job security contribute to its difficulty in employing well-qualified staff. The Construction Industry Training Board estimates an annual shortfall of 6,500 tradespeople in the building trades by 2005. These and other issues are fuelling interest in innovative construction techniques and new construction technologies, including prefabrication and off-site manufacturing.

Lean construction

Borrowing from the concept of lean manufacturing, lean construction is about the management of construction processes to deliver more value to the customer, with the elimination of waste being a core feature. Lean construction focuses on maximizing customer value by seeking to remove all non-value-adding components and processes while improving those that add value.

The Construction Lean Improvement Programme (CLIP), managed by the Building Research Establishment (BRE) in partnership with Constructing Excellence and supported by the Department of Trade and Industry (DTI), has adapted lean tools and techniques to remove waste from all levels of the construction process, including materials and energy use. CLIP engineers provide practical intervention, coaching and team development services for UK construction firms that are seeking to improve their business, management, construction and supplier management processes. Productivity is increased by diagnosing current practices and processes, challenging them, and implementing improvements with the customer's team.

Following a successful pilot scheme in 2002 in which certain projects saw a 40 per cent improvement in productivity and profitability, a five-year programme was launched in 2003, with more than 60 companies initially expressing interest. Project Director Martin Watson believes that CLIP could be of great benefit to many construction companies by encouraging them to look at what they do in a fresh way:

> CLIP is set to have a significant impact on the long-term sustainability of the industry. If the results from the pilot are replicated across the rest of the industry, then widespread performance improvement is imminent. Companies can expect to make improvements of at least 20 per cent to quality, cost and/or delivery.

BRE offers services for both manufacturers and contractors on modern methods of construction, such as off-site manufacture, timber and light-gauge steel frame, prefabrication, and tunnelform concrete casting. For manufacturers, it provides advice on product design and development, and can test and certify the performance of new products and construction methods to ensure conformity to Building Regulations and other relevant standards. For main contractors, design management and supply chain management advice is available to help them fulfil a sustainable brief. To help companies manage their waste more efficiently, BRE has developed a benchmarking tool, SMARTWaste, which enables construction firms to measure the source, type, quantity, cause and cost of their waste.

Client demand

Increasing client demand for more sustainable buildings is a key issue for the construction sector. Companies such as Sainsbury's, Shell, BP and BT have adopted high-profile CSR policies that require their premises to be 'clean and green', with high energy efficiencies and recycled material content, access to public transport, natural ventilation, and low emissions. The design and construction process needs to be to the highest standard, generating low amounts of waste, noise and nuisance, using water and energy efficiently, and specifying recycled or sustainable materials, such as Forest Stewardship Council-certified timber, where appropriate.

Increasingly, clients are turning to tools such as BREEAM for assessing and improving the environmental performance of offices, schools, supermarkets and industrial units. A parallel scheme for housing, called EcoHomes, is also available. The Government, which is responsible for 40 per cent of total UK construction industry output, has set itself the target of achieving a BREEAM 'Excellent' rating for all new public buildings; this is acting as a key driver to shift the sector towards more sustainable outcomes and ways of working. English Partnerships now requires BREEAM 'Excellent' for its developments, while the Housing Corporation makes EcoHomes 'Excellent' a provision of funding for housing associations.

Designing environmentally friendly buildings is extremely complex, so BRE has developed a software program, ENVEST, to help designers identify those aspects that have the greatest influence on a building's environmental impact. And in order to ensure the credibility of 'green' building materials and products, BRE's Certified Environmental Profiling scheme offers a universal measuring system to help designers and specifiers identify suitable materials while enabling manufacturers to demonstrate the environmental credentials of their products.

A collaborative approach reaps dividends

The construction sector is characterized, perhaps more than any other, by its fragmentation into hundreds of thousands of small companies, many of them sole traders. Getting the CSR message across in these circumstances is exceptionally difficult. A report by the Sustainable Construction Task Group, published in December 2003, concluded that most construction industry companies remain ignorant of the benefits that sustainable practices can bring.

Consequently, leading construction companies and industry bodies have focused on partnerships and integration to ensure that everyone in the construction process and supply chain can engage with the CSR agenda, from the smallest operator to the biggest. The Strategic Forum for Construction has set a target for 20 per cent of construction projects to be undertaken by integrated teams and supply chains by the end of 2004, and for 50 per cent to be by the end of 2007. To this end, it is piloting an Integration Toolkit, which is now being used on demonstration projects. The toolkit promises faster delivery times, improved profitability, reduced accidents and greater customer satisfaction.

In order to improve competitiveness, rise to environmental and social challenges and provide better value for its customers, the construction sector has developed an impressive range of demonstration projects, best-practice initiatives, management toolkits, supply-chain networks and innovative working practices, and these are starting to reap tangible benefits. The sector's collaborative approach offers valuable lessons to other manufacturing industries.

Peter Bonfield is Managing Director of BRE Construction.

Using environmental technology efficiently

Martin Gibson, Envirowise

Introduction

The perception of what environmental technology entails has changed markedly over the past few years. Until fairly recently, the words 'environmental technology' conjured up images of expensive investments in treatment systems. These would take a potentially polluting waste and render it less harmful. Such technologies would often have high purchase and revenue costs and would do nothing to help improve the function or quality of a product or service. They would, of course, help improve the environment, but might have their own environmental impact.

Over the past decade or so, the definition of environmental technology has widened considerably. It is now recognized that the best way to deal with pollution is not to generate it in the first place. This means that technologies that improve production process efficiency are some of the most effective environmental technologies. Improving efficiency will give both cost savings and environmental gains. End-of-pipe treatment technologies may still play an important role, but capital and revenue costs can be reduced if the volume of waste requiring treatment is reduced.

Environmental technology is not simply limited to processing. Many businesses use monitoring and control equipment that greatly improves their environmental performance. Such equipment will rarely be sold primarily on its environmental criteria, but it is effectively environmental technology and it can be used in a wide range of businesses. In manufacturing, for example, it can help to improve process control. However, it has a much wider application, as it is also valuable to a large proportion of businesses in the service sector. For example, sensors that control lights can greatly reduce energy use and costs. Sophisticated heating-control systems can often greatly improve comfort while improving energy efficiency. Simple water-saving devices can be used in almost every building, so have a vast potential to reduce water use.

An important approach to environmental improvement is to design products and services that have inherently low environmental impacts. Thus, a television that uses almost no energy when in use may be a very important use of environmental technology. Again this type of application is very widely applicable across business. With computers being almost ubiquitous in the commercial sector, any technology that reduces energy consumption will have a great environmental benefit. Similarly, any technology that reduces the amount of fuel needed to travel greatly reduces pollution and the depletion of natural resources. Even better are technologies that eliminate the need to travel entirely.

Drivers for environmental technology

So, what drives the uptake of environmental technology? For traditional end-of-pipe technology, the primary, and perhaps only, driver is legislation. As it does not add value to a company's products, the only real reason for installing this type of technology is if it is essential for a licence to operate. Not surprisingly, producers of end-of-pipe abatement technologies are keen that regulations are fully enforced. This type of technology has been key to many of the improvements to the environment over the past few decades and is likely to remain vital for many years to come.

An increasingly important driver for many companies is the requirements of customers. Although few UK domestic consumers take environmental issues seriously at the point of purchase, business customers often do. Corporate social responsibility (CSR) and environmental standards are certainly being felt throughout the supply chain. Evidence of environmental compliance is becoming increasingly important for suppliers to many corporations. Certain industries, such as the automotive sector, have seen vehicle manufacturers working with first- and second-tier suppliers for some time.

The most important driver for improving environmental technology for many companies is competitiveness. This is particularly true for process technologies that improve efficiency.

Of course, sometimes more than one factor drive an improvement. For example, Ford Motor Company introduced a computerized solvent management system at its Halewood site to ensure compliance with legislation. It also helped Ford to be far more efficient with solvent use, saving £60,000 per year and reducing solvent emissions by almost 40 per cent.

There is effectively a hierarchy of approach to using environmental technology. When you are faced with the need to upgrade a process or improve environmental performance, the first question needs to be: is there a different business model that might be more efficient in producing the desired customer outcome? A new model could mean redesign of your product and processes, using very different technology. This approach is rarely likely to be the answer, so the next question is: can we improve the process technology to meet any environmental needs? This is likely to mean improved efficiency and better margins. Finally, if neither of those options is open, the question has to be: which treatment technology is best in terms of whole-life cost and environmental performance? It is important to take running costs into account, as these may be substantially different for different technologies.

Environmental technology in action

One of the most common examples of 'end-of-pipe' treatment systems is a water treatment works. Most companies dispose of their wastewater to the sewer. It eventually ends up at a wastewater treatment works, where a combination of filtering and biological action renders the effluent harmless. The companies that dispose of wastewater in this way usually pay under a formula that takes account of both the amount and the strength of the effluent.

Some companies produce strong effluent that gives rise to high charges from their water-service companies. At times, it can pay to treat the effluent on-site to reduce its strength. This was true for British Sugar plc at its site in York. It decided to investigate whether it could have an on-site treatment system that would allow it to discharge its treated effluent into a river, rather than via a wastewater treatment works belonging to the water company. The company found that a modern system that incorporated 'anaerobic digestion' was the best solution. This uses bacteria that grow when there is no oxygen, and converts sugars into a gas that can be used as fuel. The plant cost about £1.5 million but paid for itself in 21 months through avoided discharge costs and a reduction in the need for natural gas.

A simple example of an environmental technology that can improve efficiency is cleaning-in-place. Nelsons of Aintree produces jam for bulk sale. The jam is loaded into tankers for transport. Historically, some product was lost every time the batch of jam changed. Jam remained in part of the feeder pipes to the tankers, and these had to be cleaned. The cleaning meant that jam was wasted, and a lot of water and chemicals were used, producing effluent for disposal. The company realized that it might be able to recover the residual jam by using a 'pigging' system. In this system a one-piece rubber 'pig' is forced through the pipe between batches, pushing any jam in the pipes into the tanker. The system allowed the company to increase yield, effectively eliminate jam waste and dramatically reduce the water and chemicals needed for pipe cleaning.

More radical changes to processes can also lead to environmental benefits even if they are not driven by the need to improve environmental performance. The impact of some processes seems to be inherently environmentally problematical. An example of such a process is the tanning of leather. Traditionally this uses a chemical process to remove hair from hide. The main chemicals involved are sodium sulphide and lime. Much of the hair is degraded into solution, with the remainder remaining as insoluble fibre. As you might expect, this produces a solution that is potentially very polluting and that needs a lot of treatment before release into the environment. However, there are other ways to get rid of the hair, and executives at W J & W Lang Ltd decided to investigate how they might benefit from changes to their processes.

The answer was to try to increase their use of natural approaches. They found a number of suppliers of systems that used enzymes to effectively remove the hair shaft intact. This means the pieces of hair can be removed by simple filtration, reducing the strength of effluent produced. W J & W Lang invited three suppliers to test the enzyme technology at its site. The preferred supplier was selected for the best combination of quality of the hide and reduced effluent strength. The final result was lower overall costs and less treatment.

Another trend in environmental technology is the move towards addressing more stages in the life cycle of a product. At present, most environmental technology targets a single area of the life cycle of a product. For example, a water treatment plant might be used to clean the effluent from one step in the manufacturing stage. Some recycling technologies can link together different stages of life cycle. Recycling waste packaging, for example, can produce raw material for manufacturing. Some companies are recognizing that there are advantages in taking control of more of their products' life cycles. This approach may involve utilizing technology that will allow rapid characterization of components or segregation.

Tax incentives for environmental technology

In general, there is little, if any, funding available for implementing new environmental technologies. If you have to do something to comply with legislation, then the government cannot help you pay for it. However, there are some tax incentives for using more efficient technologies to reduce energy and water use. These are given in the form of enhanced capital allowances for certain energy-efficient or water-saving technologies. If your company buys an approved product, it can claim back 100 per cent of the capital allowance in the first year. This means the purchase is effectively cheaper. Details of the scheme and the products it applies to can be found at www.eca.gov.uk.

Help with environmental issues

While there may not be grants for using environmental technology, there are many free sources of advice. The Government funds Envirowise to provide free advice on environmental issues to companies in the United Kingdom. The programme has a number of guides and case studies available, and also offers free telephone advice through the Environment and Energy Helpline (phone 0800 585 794). The website for the programme is www.envirowise.gov.uk.

Advice on reducing energy use is also available through the helpline, which gives access to the Action Energy programme. Like Envirowise, this programme offers a range of free advice. Its website is www.actionenergy.org.uk.

More specific advice on biotechnology-related treatment is available through Bio-Wise on www.biowise.org.uk. Like the other programmes, this has a range of advice on how to use biotechnology. Most of the case-study projects use technologies that are environmentally superior to traditional technologies.

Use environmental technology wisely

The right environmental technologies will help your business to run efficiently and within the law. The best will give you competitive advantage and, possibly, a new way of meeting your customers' needs. Don't be afraid to think radically about how technology can help you. Remember that environmental technology is not just about improved treatment; it is really about how to use resources more efficiently in a wide range of applications.

Corporate responsibility and innovation

John Sabapathy, AccountAbility

Innovating through corporate responsibility: what Milton Friedman meant to say

We all know the Milton Friedman quotation: 'The business of business is society.' At least, that's what he should have said. Any business not attuned to its customers, the people around whom it operates, the governments that regulate it, the employees that power it and the environmental resources that sustain it will in the end fail to do business. Any business that does these things does business, at least in democratic markets. And if a business does these things, it understands what it means to operate responsively to the needs and preferences of its stakeholders – understands, that is to say, corporate responsibility.

The trick, as always, is to align what the company does with the most important of its social, environmental and economic impacts on society. But much of the controversy surrounding the supposed 'uncompetitiveness' of corporate responsibility has arisen as a downside from understandable and valuable initiatives to define that black box labelled 'corporate responsibility'. Problems only emerge if broadband approaches to corporate responsibility are applied without consideration for the specific sustainability challenges and opportunities any given company faces. Clearly, just as all businesses have their own business model, so too do they need their own model to make corporate responsibility beneficial rather than irrelevant.

A recent Europe-wide survey of business leaders found that 76 per cent of them believe that 'responsible business practice can promote innovation and creativity within the organization'. Specifically, 79 per cent agreed that 'responsible business practice offers us an opportunity to learn from outside the organization', while a further 83 per cent agreed that it also 'allows us to learn more about our marketplace'.

This is, as it were, the bad news. The good news is that increasing numbers of companies are making success stories from corporate responsibility strategies that balance the broadband with bespoke. We know that innovation drives business success. The more that companies are able to derive value from unique products and processes, the stronger their basis of competitive advantage. Corporate innovation at its best is individual. Corporate responsibility can help drive innovation.

This breaks down in a number of ways. Companies' experience shows that corporate responsibility – when it is aligned to companies' core drivers, impacts and business – can:

- help companies understand the needs and concerns of their stakeholders;
- provide insights into customer concerns and new market opportunities;
- give forewarnings of emerging consumer trends and expectations;
- make direct links through to significant communities with whom a company sites, supplies, sells and employs.

The building blocks to this sort of community-enabled innovation can be set out and illustrated quite simply by four practical propositions.

Community-enabled innovation: practical propositions

1. *Community engagement can enable business innovation.*

Corporate experience shows that community engagement can enable business innovation when it is geared towards generating new insights into companies' interaction with society. To benefit in this way requires recognition that applying business skills to important social and environmental issues can result in new insights and innovations. Management strategies are only built around new insights and returns, which is a significant factor in successfully creating community-enabled innovation.

Dow Chemicals has been able to identify a wide range of product and process innovations through its Responsible Care Awards scheme, which encourages staff to develop and pilot sustainability schemes with a range of civil society partners. More broadly, a range of knowledge management systems within Dow encourage local business units to feed insights and views of local environmental and community groups into its decision-making processes.

2. *Community-enabled innovation adds most value when it is part and parcel of a company's product and management processes.*

Often, the limited business benefit and social impact from corporate responsibility programmes arises from a disconnection between core business and the corporate responsibility activity itself. This is one of the drawbacks of many classic forms of corporate philanthropy, which indirectly benefit the business by creating associations in the minds of customers or others between 'good works' and the company. To gain real benefits, the company must engage material social or environmental issues with its core competencies and products.

Travelers Property Casualty has worked with the National Insurance Task Force coalition and community-based non-governmental organizations (NGOs) to both increase the affordability and quality of insurance available in inner-city areas and raise low-income homeowners' awareness of home hazards and their ability to make their homes safer. Drawing on its own core competency – a knowledge of hazards in the home and how to protect against them – Travelers has been able to help make neighbourhoods safer and to improve the market for home ownership insurances.

3. *Responsiveness to relevant community needs is a prerequisite of community-enabled innovation.*

Where a community's own needs are not addressed through corporate engagement, the opportunities for community-enabled innovation will be wasted. The problem has been in putting this theory into practice. Responsiveness to signals in the market is a skill that business managers identify as one of the keys to innovation. In the same way, the art of community-enabled innovation lies in the quality of a company's response to stakeholders' needs. It is only by being responsive that companies are testing the boundaries of learning, and creating new solutions within dynamic market environments. Without a willingness to handle the challenges that communities face, companies *cannot create the reciprocity that will encourage the community to constructively engage with it.*

Tesco's strategic innovation of store development in low- to moderate-income inner-city areas has been highly successful United Kingdom-wide. Enabled by responsive engagement with the transport, childcare and training needs of potential employees, the 'Regeneration Partnerships' have led to the creation of 12 stores in urban areas previously deemed too difficult to serve and invest in. Altering existing processes to accommodate community needs and partnering with local community groups and employment services was critical in getting to the heart of the conditions that would determine the stores' success.

4. *Community-enabled innovation can increase the accountability of the company to key stakeholders... but not always.*

Accountability has become an important driver in defining responsible business strategies. In this regard, part of the attractiveness of community-enabled innovation is that it is manageable and focused. It is therefore relatively easy for a company to be accountable to a community for the duration of a project or partnership. However, it is quite a different proposition to extend and embed a partnership-specific approach to accountability within production and management processes. For example, institutional initiatives within the field of supply chain labour standards that have developed as corporate, NGO (and sometimes) union partnerships have all had to demonstrate who they are ultimately accountable to, and therefore whether they ultimately justify the civil society legitimacy they seek. What is clear is that the longer the partnership, the more critical it is to establish accountability mechanisms that structure the terms of a company's relationship with a particular community. Ultimately, accountability to communities helps companies build the credibility and licence to operate, irrespective of what they sell or how they sell it.

Suez, for example, has developed new forms of collaboration with low-income groups in Central America in order to deliver water projects effectively in newly privatized areas. The result of an acknowledgement that long-term approaches to partnerships are required for such infrastructure investment, these partnerships embody new strategies for engaging with grassroots communities whose needs have not always been incorporated into such development projects. In addition, Suez has developed the *Observatoire Sociale Mondiale* (OSI), a bespoke internal advisory group convening key civil society groups in order to increase the company's learning about emerging issues and concerns.

Reasons why there is not more community-enabled innovation

Besides the fact that companies may not have thought about the potential opportunities of community-enabled innovation, our research suggests two fundamental reasons.

The first is that community-enabled innovation is unlikely to occur unless the expectations, implications and required resources are factored in from the start. If companies don't expect to gain innovation from their engagement with communities, they won't spend much time looking for it and they are unlikely to find it. Why don't businesses expect to find community-enabled innovation? Leadership within a company may be insufficiently convinced about its potential business value. Business executives may have watched the varying financial fortunes of highly branded 'responsible' companies such as The Body Shop, Iceland or Ben & Jerry's and concluded that such approaches could not function as a long-term business strategy. They may have looked at the uptake of 'sustainability reporting' among many of the world's leading companies and not seen the findings of such reports filtering back into the decision-making processes at the very top.

One of the core barriers has in fact been created by a one-size-fits-all approach to 'selling' the business case for corporate responsibility. As the cases show, however, a fundamental characteristic of all the community-enabled innovation approaches is an individually designed response to idiosyncratic market conditions – social and environmental, as well as economic. In no area of business would companies expect to gain performance improvements by simply applying generic principles, and corporate responsibility is no different. Some of the most interesting recent legislation (such as the United Kingdom's draft Operating and Financial Review) acknowledges precisely this through its emphasis on companies' own identification of what are the relevant and material sustainable issues facing them.

The second reason has less to do with problems of perception and expectation than with the fact that not all companies are necessarily in a position to produce community-enabled innovation. There are reasons why BP and Novo A/S have generated innovation through community engagement, while many of their sector peers have not. The question then becomes 'How does a company identify the basis on which it can individually innovate in this area?'

Analysing companies' experience in this regard throws up four key strategic factors that determine the extent to which a company is likely to be able to develop community-enabled innovation successfully.

Community-enabled innovation: strategic factors

1. *The company responds to challenges from community groups as an opportunity for engagement and dialogue with stakeholders.*

Many of the companies we engaged with as leaders in this field have been at the centre of critical debates about their social, environmental and economic impact. In the case of Tesco and other UK supermarkets, the debate has been about the impact of supermarkets on town centres and smaller high street retailers. Dow and other chemical companies have been drawn into discussions concerning the chemical industry's responsibility for accidental emissions.

The existence (often in the media) of such debates is a highly effective means of linking core activities with corporate responsibility strategies and encouraging those at the top to adopt strategies of engagement with such issues. Similarly, it is often harder for companies that have not experienced crises, and the impetus for change they can create, to find effective triggers for engagement within the company.

While a crisis can help focus management's attention on communities, it is not the presence or absence of a crisis that determines whether or not a company can innovate through community engagement. Rather, it is whether the company responds by engagement and dialogue or by defensiveness and distancing. Companies that respond to challenges with vigorous legal and public relations counter-attacks, rather than dialogue, are unlikely to generate innovation in the process.

Action implication

Advocates within companies should identify whether the willingness to embrace dialogue in response to challenges is likely to tip corporate reaction to challenges towards community-enabled innovation or whether the barriers are likely to prove too high.

2. *The company's core skills in innovating are in areas that enable interaction with key stakeholder groups.*

The nature of a company's basic business model and the relationships it encourages between itself and its stakeholders will also influence how it can improve performance through corporate responsibility. It is important in this context to note that 'community-enabled innovation' need not pertain solely to relationships with communities classically defined as those living around a manufacturing or retail site; community-enabled innovation pertains to what we call 'significant communities'. While business-to-business (B2B) models may have fewer points of interaction with retail consumers and the communities associated with retail outlets, they still have significant points of interaction with a wide range of other communities of interest, be they employees, business customers or suppliers. Thus, in footwear manufacture, improvements in factory labour conditions are dependent on the quality of relationships between factory suppliers and high street brand retailers. This is by no means a matter of 'B2B = No basis for community-enabled innovation' while 'B2C = Basis for community-enabled innovation'. There are strong examples (see the Dow case) of B2Bs providing private goods that do generate community-enabled innovation. What is critical in these cases is that the product and production process do not reduce points of interaction with communities, but rather provide the basis for engagement.

Action implication

Advocates within companies should identify where the key points of interaction are with communities of interest who could provide insights into product, process, service or delivery. Where individual companies lack leverage, advocates may explore the basis of collective action as a way of reducing entry costs and increasing learning. Key areas such as ethical trade in supply chains have demonstrated that community-enabled innovation is not necessarily a zero-sum game and that innovation can be the result of collaborative action.

3. *The company can gain competitive advantage in its industry by differentiating itself through corporate responsibility.*

Peer-to-peer competition within a single sector is another under-examined factor in determining how companies are likely to use engagement with communities to innovate and differentiate themselves from competitors. Thus, those campaigning in the United Kingdom for a fair return for agricultural producers in the South have engaged many high street food retailers, leading to the emergence of Sainsbury's and the Co-operative Wholesale Society as first movers and key players within the Ethical Trading Initiative (ETI), a cross-sector partnership established to take forward this agenda in the United Kingdom. While most of the other leading UK food retailers are also now involved, the leadership position of competitors does affect whether 'follower' companies engage with an issue in order themselves to innovate or engage in order to learn from other companies' innovation.

Action implication

Advocates within companies need to carefully identify the trade-offs involved in differentiating themselves from competitors through community-enabled innovation. Key considerations include the relative lead competitors have, the entry costs and the relative corporate importance of the impact area (labour rights, energy use, etc).

4. *Strong cultures of learning or innovation within a company will significantly affect advocates' ability to generate community-enabled innovation.*

Internal cultures of knowledge sharing and cross-unit functioning are indispensable if companies are to generate community-enabled innovation. A corporate responsibility team, or equivalent, housed in a silo separate from and deemed irrelevant to 'core' business functions is unlikely to credibly communicate any insights or patterns derived from engagement with civil society, suppliers, customers, regulators or other stakeholders.

Poor group-wide tendencies to innovate will also make it harder for companies to make significant use of this team since the barriers to change will typically be deemed too high. As a positive counter-example, IBM's research labs have a good reputation for innovation and have reached across business units to draw on the networks of their Community Relations team to develop new software and hardware products for use by visually impaired groups.

Action implication

Advocates within companies should identify formal and interpersonal ways of tapping into key knowledge management systems, whether these be through engaging with intranets or engaging with key board members. Understanding the needs of key players in relation to group strategies is the key to channelling useful information derived from community-enabled innovations and leveraging up isolated cases into group-wide practices.

In summary, companies' own experience shows that community-enabled innovation can be an important approach for developing strategically important innovation. Such an approach to innovation isn't right for every company: a company's culture, competitive position and core skills help determine whether or not the company will be a supportive environment for this approach. Also, community-enabled innovation is not a guaranteed result from community engagement. But as the cases summarized here show, properly managed community engagement can enable companies to capture and create strategically important benefits through community-enabled innovation.

John Sabapathy is a Senior Associate at AccountAbility.

www.accountability.org.uk.

The sustainable supply chain

Darren Ford, Senior Procurement Specialist, Chartered Institute of Purchasing and Supply

Over the past 10 years we have seen a growing awareness in organizations of the critical importance that their bought-in goods and services can have for the environment. It could be said that purchasing and supply management used to be the weak link in the environmental activity chain.

As the purchasing function has gradually moved forward and become an integral part of an organization, businesses have realized the importance and impact that the supply side of the organization can have and how, over the long term, it has a responsibility in helping create a more sustainable world.

Purchasing has a certain responsibility to play in helping to reduce corporate exposure to environmental risk, improving the security of key suppliers, and driving continuous improvement in the supply side. Specifically, it can:

- provide the business case for implementing sustainable procurement, communicating this to senior managers, colleagues and suppliers;
- have a good understanding of how sustainable procurement relates to management systems such as ISO 14001;

■   acknowledge the possibilities for sustainable procurement within the public and private sectors, including how sustainable procurement can be achieved within the EU procurement rules, and learn how some organizations have capitalized on these opportunities.

The case for sustainable procurement

Most large organizations in today's global economy have adopted some aspects of good sustainable procurement practices and are working towards being seen as more corporately responsible, as pressures from both legislation and consumers grows.

Organizational spend on external goods and services can be as little as 30 per cent of total expenditure, but in contrast can be as high as a staggering 80 per cent. Therefore, early adopters of sustainable procurement have already accepted the need to measure both themselves and their supply chains to gain a better understanding of the effect that their bought-in products and services can have on the environment.

Companies such as Nortel Networks and Carillion plc have demonstrated the importance they place on sustainable procurement.

Nortel Networks

'Nortel Networks has implemented its corporate policy and procedures on sustainable procurement, which provides operational control of environmental considerations relative to the purchase of goods and services from suppliers. Wherever Nortel Networks does business it will take the initiative to develop innovative solutions to environmental issues that may arise because of its products, operations and business activities.' Source: http://www.nortelnetworks.com/corporate/community/environment/.

Carillion plc

'Identifying and managing the environmental impacts associated with our subcontractors and bought in products is fundamental to the success of our environmental programme. Engaging Carillion's supply chain in the sustainability programme [will] improve sustainable development performance and assist us in achieving our targets.' Source: http://www.carillionplc.com.

If sustainable procurement is relatively new to an organization, purchasing and supply management professionals and other disciplines such as human resources need to understand the potential benefits it can bring, especially where they are required to make a business case to senior management to help it become a mainstream agenda item. These benefits can include:

- minimizing business risk;
- providing cost savings;
- enhancing corporate image;
- creating markets for new products and services;
- securing the supply of goods and services;
- reducing waste and improving resource efficiency;
- providing added value.

Minimizing business risk

Clearly, as we have seen in the media, an organization can be exposed to business risk through the activities of its supply side – for example, where suppliers themselves may breach environmental regulations. The fact that organizations are now operating on a global scale compounds the issue·of sustainability and adds increasing pressure for them to deal with such environmental matters within their supply chains.

Purchasing and supply management professionals need to understand the nature and characteristics of the products and services provided to them and appreciate the risks they may cause to the environment. Doing so will help them when it comes to finalizing or drafting a contract with their preferred provider, as it will focus on the risks that they can then deal with jointly and effectively.

Providing cost savings

In the United Kingdom's current economic climate, cost remains very close to the top of the boardroom agenda, and the fact that some of the early examples of sustainable products were seen to be of inferior quality led some to believe that value for money was not achievable through sustainable procurement. However, quality has improved considerably, and purchasing and supply management has made a huge contribution to organizations' sustainability programmes by using the whole-life costing approach when buying such goods and services.

There is a continual growing body of evidence among organizations to suggest that an active sustainability programme can bring savings in operating costs. Examples of this have notably been through reducing waste. Therefore, it can be argued that suppliers with a good sustainability programme and good process management could expect to be lower-cost suppliers in the long term.

Enhancing corporate image

Purchasing and supply management professionals (along with marketing colleagues) can justifiably argue that corporate image is enhanced through good sustainable sourcing practices. These demonstrate to a very wide audience that the organization is engaged with the risks and consequences of its operations. Purchasing and supply management looks well beyond the organization's boundary to investigate and analyse the impacts of its products and services on the wider community. It is an integral function of an organization, taking ownership of its products and services from 'cradle to grave' rather than only to consumption.

Creating markets

The collaboration of significant buying power and purchasing and supply management professionals can encourage suppliers to invest in new technologies with the objective of designing and developing new products with higher sustainable specifications. Taking into account the whole life-cycle approach, the collaboration between organizations and their purchasing and supply management function can stimulate markets for: 1) recycled products or products that contain a high degree of recyclable material content; and 2) new services delivering a function equivalent to that of the products they replace, but at a lower environmental cost.

We are now seeing organizations increasingly offering a service based on the function provided by the product. This can help the case for sustainable procurement to make an impact, which in turn may stimulate innovation among suppliers, since they are rewarded for developing services that are more sustainable and less damaging to the environment. Clearly, purchasing and supply management professionals will need to reflect this greater sustainability within their negotiations and contracts with suppliers.

Securing the supply of goods and services

There are some regulations within the sustainability arena that can have an impact on the security of supply of strategic goods and services. Purchasing and supply management professionals need to have a full understanding of potential implications for supply in time to source alternative materials or to ensure that existing suppliers can continue to meet their needs.

Failure to make the necessary improvements can result in the loss of a particular contract or, at worst, the failure of the business. Business failure has consequences for all of that business's customers. Thus, environmental pressure in one element of an organization's supply side can affect suppliers and customers elsewhere.

Products that are more sustainable and have a reduced environmental impact can present their own problems in terms of security of supply. We are seeing markets for products containing recyclable material continue to develop; prices tend to fluctuate, and availability may not be guaranteed at all times. We should see this trend diminish as markets for more sustainable products and services mature.

Reducing waste and improving resource efficiency

Efficient and well-managed purchasing processes can deliver a significant contribution to reducing waste in an organization. This is part of what the Government is calling 'modernizing procurement'. This translates as meaning that organizations should first ensure that they have the right purchasing structures and processes in place before embarking on sustainable procurement.

The aim of improving the efficiency of an organization's procurement and the use of materials, energy and other inputs is key to modern purchasing and supply management activity. This 'resource efficiency', or doing more with less, is also a central component of good sustainable practice.

Building collaborative relationships inside and outside an organization to drive resource efficiency forward is a critical requirement, and one that, when realized, opens up opportunities for joint purchasing and sustainable improvements.

Providing added value

Purchasing and supply management has a significant role to play in delivering an organization's sustainable development objectives. It can add value by stimulating markets for sustainable products and services, particularly through joint working with suppliers to aim for continuous improvement across a range of issues such as environmental ones. The result should be better-quality products from better-performing suppliers.

Getting started

A sustainable procurement policy is a sensible starting point. However, no sustainable procurement policy can be developed in isolation; it needs to be formulated in collaboration with other key disciplines within the organization, and it must be aligned with the sustainability policy of the organization as a whole. For this to be possible, the policy must be robust and meaningful; it must stand up to scrutiny from a wide range of interested parties and must take account of their particular needs, viewpoints and contributions. In this way, another vital criterion for success can be met: ownership.

Just as the sustainable procurement policy needs to fit into the overall policy of the organization, it must also be integrated with the existing sourcing governance and policy structure. A sustainable procurement policy that sits outside the main sourcing governance structure will inevitably create unwanted contradictions and tensions. Joined-up thinking is very important here. The policy needs to convey a strong, clear message to suppliers and contractors about what the organization seeks and expects from them.

Purchasing and supply management professionals who are members of the Chartered Institute of Purchasing and Supply (CIPS) have been provided with an environmental policy document (see www.cips.org) that encourages them to take the lead role in the process of implementing sustainable procurement. The CIPS policy document states that purchasing and supply management professionals should:

■ have a significant specialist influence and role in improving the environmental performance of their organizations and that of their suppliers and contractors;
■ seek to reduce the environmental impact of their own day-to-day activities;
■ seek to develop the environmental purchasing policy and practices of their employers and carry out their professional duties in an environmentally responsible manner, compliant with all relevant legislation and cognizant of the objectives of their organization;
■ aim to reduce the adverse impact on the environment of their own activities and that of their suppliers;
■ work with colleagues and suppliers, as appropriate, to ensure that goods and services purchased can be manufactured, delivered, used and disposed of in a safe, and socially and environmentally responsible, manner.

Those who develop the sustainable procurement policy need to bear in mind such factors as:

- organizational arrangements for purchasing, eg centralized or decentralized;
- the size and buying power of the organization;
- the extent of influence of the organization in its major markets;
- public-sector constraints on purchasing – where these are relevant.

Common failings of sustainable procurement initiatives include the following:

- The initiative has been led by environment managers and not integrated with the purchasing process and wider corporate objectives and targets.
- Inconsistent messages have been sent to suppliers by different parts of the customer's organization.
- Budget holders are able to ignore or reject environmentally preferred alternatives.
- Internal customers have not appreciated their role in delivering sustainable improvement.

The easy option is often to ignore what goes on outside of the four walls of your organization, but in today's global economy, with companies operating across continents, doing so is no longer possible. The remit of the purchasing and supply management function has widened considerably in recent years, and with it has come much greater responsibility. It needs to position itself firmly at the core of managing and dealing with sustainability issues, becoming an internal consultant while monitoring the external obligations placed on every organization to ensure that its suppliers also remain compliant.

Darren Ford is Purchasing and Supply Management Development Officer at the Chartered Institute of Purchasing and Supply.

Weather: how does it affect your business?

Wayne Elliott, Met Office

Planning a weekend break? Alongside the travel arrangements, another key issue for most travellers is the weather. Why then do so few of us give little thought to the weather and climate in our everyday business life?

The weather affects everything from our health and the way we use health services through to what we buy as consumers, and it should affect our business planning. There are very few parts of the economy that are not affected by weather in some way.

Ask people what the Met Office does and the majority will mention weather forecasts on television. Those forecasts are an important part of the Met Office's work, as they allow general weather forecasts to reach significant numbers of people. But businesses are slowly turning to more detailed weather information to help them manage their operations and contribute to their profitability.

To use weather information effectively, a business first needs to know how it is exposed to the weather. If that sounds simple, think of the insurance industry as an example. Across the world, claims arising from severe weather events such as hurricanes, typhoons and floods can total billions of pounds a year. Insurers need to assess risk to set competitive premiums.

As climate change begins to be something that is happening and not just something that is going to happen, the re-insurance industry needs to factor these trends into its longer-term business. At the other end of the scale, most domestic insurers use a call centre for customer service. The volume of calls to those centres is often affected by the weather, and not just because severe weather means more claims. A normal wet winter weekend may not lead to many claims, but more consumers will be indoors browsing the internet and shopping around.

Big players in the insurance industry can find themselves exposed to all these weather-related risks and more. So, how can the Met Office help in these examples? To set premiums in the near future, a client can call on a huge database of historical weather information, allowing weather risk to be assessed with postcode accuracy. Gazing much further into the future, an insurer can tap into climate change experts based at the Hadley Centre. These experts are independently acknowledged as world leaders in climate prediction. Using some of the world's biggest supercomputers, this team predicts with growing confidence how the world's climate will change over the rest of the century. The UK will become warmer, with wetter winters and drier summers leading to a possible rise in flood and subsidence claims. More dramatic changes are likely in other parts of the world.

Call-centre operations will also use more traditional weather advice. Severe weather warnings can give advance notice that telephone claims will soar. Trend forecasts up to a month ahead will show whether the weather is turning warmer or colder, wetter or drier, and give advanced warning that an unsettled spell is just around the corner. Week-ahead forecasts will allow managers to staff call centres efficiently to cope with the weather-related peaks and troughs in call volumes.

Weather experts are best placed to help clients discover their exposure to weather risk. A good example of this is in the retail industry. For many years the Met Office has helped retail companies assess the effect of weather on sales volume. Using historical weather information alongside sales data allows a scientific, objective assessment of the link between product lines and the weather.

A motorway service chain discovered that for every degree the temperature rose in summer, it was selling £75,000 worth less of hot food across its sites. On 10 August 2003 the temperature in south-east England reached a record 38°C, so too much hot food on the counters that day would have been a disaster. However, weather forecasters predicted that hot spell a week in advance. Thus, weather forecasts can enable managers of such outlets to be in a position to make real gains by stocking correctly.

Similar examples can be seen across industry. Power generators need to consider climate change when considering the next generation of power stations. Their distribution colleagues, on the other hand, need to consider the possibility of a storm bringing down power lines in the next week or so, and, like the insurance industry, the domestic power suppliers have call centres that are affected by the weather.

Although weather forecasts are becoming ever more accurate and look further into the future, not every forecast is right, of course. However, nowadays new techniques are used so that businesses that take regular forecasts will see bigger benefits. Traditionally, a single computer prediction has been used to produce a definitive forecast, known as a deterministic forecast. Now weather forecasters increasingly use a technique that uses multiple computer predictions for the same time-frame and looks for a consensus between those forecast. This allows a forecaster to express the probability of a particular event occurring, alongside alternative scenarios. The real value of these forecasts is apparent to a customer over the medium to long term. Ensembles help smooth out the effects of a few wrong forecasts and help decide on the level of response needed on each occasion. For example, a local emergency planning department might have teams on call at home given a 40 per cent probability of a storm but would have them standing by at work if that probability became 70 per cent.

In the longer term there are other ways that businesses can hedge their exposure to weather risk. Weather derivatives are widely used in the United States. Liquidity in that market allows power generators, for instance, to hedge against a series of warm winters, or an ice cream manufacturer to hedge against a cold summer. Across Europe the weather derivatives market is slowly picking up and is yet another weather-related tool that business should consider.

For many years, companies have all too often used the weather as a convenient excuse for poor results. Increasingly, though, shareholders and analysts are beginning to realize that more can be done by most businesses to mitigate weather risks.

So, next time you are planning that short break or watching the TV weather forecast, let your mind wander briefly back to work and ask yourself if your business is using the weather to its advantage.

Wayne Elliott, Senior Press Officer, Met Office, FitzRoy Road, Exeter, Devon EX1 3PB, UK

Tel: 01392 884629
Fax: 01392 885681
Mobile: 07753 880687
E-mail: wayne.elliott@metoffice.gov.uk http://www.metoffice.gov.uk

The Chemical Company

Sustainable Enterprise in Action

BASF is the world's leading chemical company. In its five business segments, BASF posted sales of ₤33.4 billion in 2003. Our strategic goal is to continue to grow profitably. Around 87000 employees on five continents are the key to our success.

It is our mission as one of the world's most successful chemical companies to benefit mankind. We want to create assets that benefit all: our customers, our shareholders, our company, our employees, and the countries in which we operate.

For us, sustainable enterprise means combining economic success with environmental protection and social responsibility, thus contributing to a high quality of life for coming generations. With our management systems and tools for sustainability, we create value for BASF and our partners in business and society. In BASF, sustainability is a Board-level responsibility. The BASF Sustainability Council includes a Board Member and 8 divisional presidents. In 1999, we incorporated sustainable economic success – in other words, sustainable development – into our Values and Principles, and it forms part of the target agreements that we set with all senior executives. At the same time, our measures help ensure that we better fulfil the needs of customers and consumers. We see this as long-term competitive advantage. For example, our eco-efficiency analysis can show our customers which products and processes are superior for their specific applications from both economic and environmental viewpoints. This is increasingly valued by our customers as a feature of our system solutions.

The financial markets have identified BASF as an attractive company for those who want to make investments in accordance with sustainability. BASF shares were included in the Dow Jones Sustainability Index for the fourth year in succession in 2004 and are also represented in other leading sustainability indices.

AccountAbility
institute of social and ethical accountability

Promoting accountability for sustainable development

Established in 1995, AccountAbility is the leading international non-profit institute that brings together members and partners from business, civil society and the public sector from across the world. AccountAbility provides effective assurance and accountability management tools and standards through its AA1000 Series, offers professional development and certification, and undertakes leading-edge research and related public policy advocacy.

Core to the AccountAbility Community are our members, who govern us, support us and participate in our programmes as well as play a vital role in shaping our direction and work.

AccountAbility has always valued and relied upon input from members, and now more than ever is looking towards working with, servicing and developing strong relationships with our members.

Membership

Our membership scheme is based on what our members, partners and collaborators tell us is needed, directly, and indirectly, through our international, representative Council. The comprehensive packages provide you with a range of benefits that can be tailored to meet your specific needs, however developed your corporate responsibility approach is.

Membership of AccountAbility is an invaluable asset for those committed to advancing and promoting greater accountability in business, civil society or public institutions across the world. Joining the AccountAbility Community delivers members access to; our unrivalled international networks, our unique blend of strategic research, professional development, and our prominent position in standards and public policy development.

AccountAbility has developed a series of membership levels that have been designed to meet the requirements of different types of members. Packages are accessible to both large and small businesses, service providers, academic institutions, NGO's and individuals.

To find out more about AccountAbility membership packages, and how you can benefit by joining, please visit **www.accountability.org.uk/membership** or email **membership@accountability.org.uk**

The business of weather

The Met Office is the national weather service for the UK. Founded in 1854 as a small department of the Board of Trade serving the Royal Navy, its modern day status is a world leader in the provision of weather products and environment-based services to business and industry everywhere.

In achieving such high standards, the organisation has teamed the expertise of its people with the awesome power of the latest supercomputers. The result of this union is a proactive 'can do' approach leading to unique products tailored to customers' specific requirements.

A Trading Fund since1996, the Met Office's service portfolio reflects the increasing range of business sectors using weather and the environment in their own fields. Dedicated Marketing and Business units within the Met Office ensure that current and potential customers are aware of the 'edge' offered by the weather to businesses in a competitive world. For instance, accurate and timely weather or environmental data allow:

- retailers and manufacturers to match their stock to consumer demand;
- construction companies to plan for 'down time';
- the maritime industry to build suitably designed structures and ships;
- managers of medical facilities to plan for the impacts of seasonal weather on hospital admissions;
- the transport industry to judge the direct and indirect effects of the weather on its infrastructures;
- resource management in the water industry, according to short-term weather forecasts or longer-term climate change;
- agricultural operations to take place during optimum times and conditions.

Risk management in respect of weather conditions is a growing requirement in many business sectors, and the Met Office also helps event organisers, local government, insurance companies and utility services.

Details of Met Office services to business are available from its Customer Centre on **0870 900 0100**, or at **www.metoffice.com**

Funding and investment

Funding and investment: introduction

Andy Hughes, Business in the Community

For businesses of any size, access to capital and cost of capital are fundamental to growth and survival. Corporate strategy acts in a mutual feedback loop with each: a strategy that delivers sustainable competitive advantage is likely to give greater access to capital at cheaper cost than one that does not. Sustainable competitive advantage comes from getting the right balance between entrepreneurial flair on the one hand and minimizing risks of value destruction on the other. The key to understanding how environmental, social and ethical issues fit into the funding arena begins with understanding their function in such a value creation/value protection formula.

For retail and institutional investors, a combination of ethical rating indices and studies revealing variations in risk premium provides valuable insights to inform their investment decisions. There is a growing body of evidence that sound environmental, social and ethical management practices lead to a less volatile share price, which in turn can lead to a lower cost of capital.

More specifically, these rating indices and studies enable further growth in the specialized socially responsible investment (SRI) market. From their original policy of excluding whole industry sectors, funds are now able to apply more sophistication to their analyses and portfolio design, increasing investment opportunities as a result.

Environmental, social and ethical issues also feature in lending appraisals in a mature way. The key issue is risk, in two forms: risk to loan repayments and risk to the value of assets taken as security. Environmental problems that might reduce the value of land taken as security could result in higher borrowing charges. Security of supply and meeting customer expectations are key to maintaining revenue streams to fund repayments. Where environmental, social and ethical issues could threaten supply sources or influence customer choice, wise lenders will factor them into their decisions.

Andy Hughes is Development Manager, Business in the Environment, Business in the Community.

Funding and investment: legal overview

Kathryn Mylrea, Simmons & Simmons

The impact of sustainability issues on funding and investment decisions has been the subject of considerable research and comment. There are quite a large number of ethical or social investment funds that specialize in this area, but there are legal issues governing the structure within which they operate. For example, from July 2000, pension funds have been required to state the extent to which they take social, environmental and ethical considerations into account under the Pensions Act 1995.

The collection and provision of information relevant to investment decisions based on sustainability issues are critical. Although there is no legal requirement for companies to prepare environmental or sustainability reports, however, or even for them to include environmental information within their annual reports in all cases, there are guidelines for voluntary reporting. In practice, many companies do include such information. For example, as of July 2004, 89 per cent of the FTSE All Share companies discuss some aspects of their interaction with the environment in their annual reports, although fewer than a quarter of them make any quantitative environmental disclosures, and fewer still relate them to possible financial consequences or future changes in shareholder value. However, the position is expected to change with the proposed regulations on the new Operating and Financial Review (OFR), which were published for consultation in May 2004.

The proposed new regulations will make it mandatory for directors of quoted companies to prepare an annual OFR, which must contain, 'to the extent necessary to comply with the review objective', key performance indicators relating to environmental matters. The regulations will also require an OFR to include a description of the principal risks and uncertainties facing the company. Reporting standards are expected to be considered by the Accounting Standards Board, but are unlikely to be available until 2005. The OFR proposals have not made mandatory the Association of British Insurers disclosure guidelines on socially responsible investment, although it was considered as an option at one point.

Other initiatives to incorporate environmental issues into company reporting include the FTSE4Good Index Series, launched in July 2001 in response to the increasing focus on corporate social responsibility (CSR) by investors who wanted to measure the social, environmental and ethical performance of companies they invested in. In order to qualify for inclusion, companies must disclose how they identify, manage and report their business, social and environmental material risks to their stakeholders. Increased environmental information is also being required of companies that are seeking a stock exchange listing.

Other non-legal initiatives aimed at encouraging organizations to take an environmentally responsible stance include Business in the Community, which has 700 member companies, with a further 1,600 companies participating in programmes and campaigns. It is the longest-established organization of its kind, and its purpose is to 'inspire, challenge, engage and support business in continually improving its positive impact on society'. Membership of Business in the Community requires a commitment to action, and continual improvement of a company's impact on society.

International leadership is provided by bodies such as the International Finance Corporation (IFC). The IFC is a member of the World Bank Group and invests in private-sector projects. It has had a policy in place for some time that all its operations must be carried out in an environmentally and socially responsible manner. IFC's Environment and Social Development Department is responsible for the environmental and social review, clearance, and supervision of projects in a manner consistent with the requirements contained in the IFC's review procedure. In addition, to achieve better integration of environmental and social considerations within IFC operations and to ensure high performance standards, an IFC Vice President has corporate oversight for environmental and social issues and disclosure matters.

How to be ethical and profitable

Paul Monaghan, The Co-operative Bank

Trust in business is at a low

It is often remarked that the public's trust in organizations and institutions of all types has deteriorated. However, if one looks at the research a little more closely, it becomes clear that there is only one occupation for which there has been a persistent deterioration in trust over the past decade: business. Since the early 1980s the opinion pollster MORI has researched levels of trust among a variety of the United Kingdom's different occupations. Over the period 1993–2002 it found that trust in 'doctors' and 'teachers' increased, and that these professions were trusted by more than 80 per cent of those polled. In contrast, 'business leaders' were trusted by barely 20 per cent, marginally better than 'journalists' and 'politicians', and they were the only profession to show a persistent deterioration in trust over the period. Other research has found that 70 per cent of the UK public believe that industry and commerce do not pay enough attention to their social responsibilities, and that the proportion of people able or willing to name any company that is particularly environmentally or ethically responsible is less than a third.

Bucking the trend

A number of businesses have managed to buck this trend and have succeeded in establishing trust among a wide range of stakeholders. Invariably they have achieved trust via a well-managed programme of corporate social responsibility (CSR). The Co-operative Bank is one of these.

UK MPs cite the bank more often than any other business when asked to 'name companies that best demonstrate the principles of CSR'. Similarly, when members of the UK general public are asked to name 'a financial provider that takes ethical and environmental issues into account', they cite The Co-operative Bank more often than any other. Analysis of media coverage, together with opinion research, finds that the bank receives more positive CSR coverage than any other business in the United Kingdom; in particular, the bank was singled out for 'communicating clearly [its] differentiated values' and for the fact that 'CSR was deeply embedded in [its] strategy'. Research described in the bank's latest Sustainability Report shows high levels of satisfaction with ethical and sustainability performance among personal customers (91 per cent) and corporate and business banking customers (86 per cent). In fact, the bank's customers cite ethics and sustainability more than any other reason when asked why they joined and/or continue to remain with the bank, and the profitability contribution of these CSR-motivated customers was worth almost £40 million to the bank in 2003.

The bank has achieved these results by ensuring that CSR is a core component of its business strategy and communications activities. As with other major components of the bank's customer proposition – innovation and customer service – it has approached CSR with both passion and professionalism, as now described.

Making CSR central to the customer offering

In his foreword to the bank's 2002 Sustainability Report, the Chief Executive, Mervyn Pedelty, discussed how CSR is one of the major pillars of the bank's brand offering:

> Our commitment to sustainability is affirmed in the bank's strategic plan, which sets out our clear market position: 'The Co-operative Bank is a modern bank that goes about its business in an ethical manner', as well as our customer proposition: 'Customer led, ethically guided', which is communicated throughout our advertising and promotional activities.

The bank entered the 'CSR arena' in a serious way in May 1992, with the launch of an Ethical Policy. At the time, the integration of ethical and social issues into business strategy was rare, not least because of an ongoing recession in the United Kingdom during the early 1990s. Moreover, the Ethical Policy was not some side offering or optional extra: it stipulated right across the board the types of business the bank would and would not offer services to. For example, the bank committed itself not to finance or in any way facilitate the manufacture or sale of weapons to any country that has an oppressive regime, and it pledged that it would not invest in any business involved in animal experimentation for cosmetic purposes.

The application of screening to all assets and liabilities (not to mention suppliers) was a significant development at the time, and still is. Many financial institutions have subsequently applied screening to a small proportion of funds under their management (in total, some £20 billion worth of UK managed funds are now subject to some form of ethical screening), but none with a major high street presence has followed The Co-operative Bank and applied screening to all assets and liabilities (and for this reason, arguably, none has tapped into the ethical consumerism market with the same degree of success as The Co-operative Bank). The problem with applying ethics to just a proportion of products and services is that creates an impression of there being no genuine commitment to 'the issues': if something is wrong in one context, how can it be OK in another? Such differentiation also hinders the ability of business to speak and communicate on matters of ethics – which impacts on the ability to generate customer interest and sales.

Of course, the development of tailored ethical and sustainability products is desirable. For example, in addition to its standard range of Visa credit cards, the bank offers branded credit cards with a number of charities. Partners receive a donation from the bank for each new card issued and a margin on the use of the card. During 2003 the RSPB credit cards alone (about 100,000) raised in excess of £500,000, which facilitated the rehabilitation of 550 hectares of UK reed bed and wetland habitat. However, it is important that such products be underpinned by a business-wide programme of ethics and sustainability if charges of profiteering and hypocrisy are to be minimized.

The Ethical Policy, together with its accompanying advertising campaign, created quite a stir when it was launched. The bank came in for criticism from its competitors, with letters and personal approaches to the chairman from people representing various business interests. Fears were even expressed by some magazine editors that in carrying the bank's forthright adverts they might be boycotted by other advertisers. There were complaints to the Advertising Standards Authority from the chemical industry (against an advert on toxic waste) and the cosmetics industry (against the animal testing argument), and editorials from the blood sports lobby asking people to boycott the bank. However, as time has progressed, policies that once seemed controversial are now almost mainstream public opinion.

The Ethical Policy of 1992 responded to the fact that a large proportion of the bank's customers were opposed to animal testing for cosmetics (82 per cent). In 1998 a ban on animal testing for cosmetic purposes was introduced, with the UK Government refusing to issue further licences for such activities.

Since 1992 at least 75 per cent of customers have urged the bank to refuse investment in fur farming: in 2000, the UK Government introduced the Fur Farming (Prohibition) Act, which renders the trade illegal in the United Kingdom as of January 2003.

In 1998 the bank's Ethical Policy committed it to support renewable energies, with over 90 per cent customer support. The bank progressively switched virtually every watt of its electricity supply to renewable energies between 1998 and 2001, and quickly became the largest green energy purchaser of all UK businesses. Today there is hardly a major high street bank that does not source at least some of its electricity from such sources.

The bank's Ethical Policy is subject to regular review. Crucially, this takes place on the back of a programme of extensive customer consultation: almost 1 million corporate and personal customers were polled in 2001, of whom 70,000 responded. The current Policy covers both assets (eg retail and syndicated loans, and corporate leasing) and liabilities (eg retail deposits and savings, and Treasury dealings), together with the investment of all retained balances. Over time, the Policy has broadened and deepened. For example, following the 1998 Ethical Policy review, the position on animal testing was expanded to include a statement precluding investment in businesses that test household products on animals; and following the 2001 review, positions were developed on Fair Trade and genetic modification.

The bank suffered financial losses in 1990 and 1991. Since 1992, the year the Ethical Policy was launched, retail deposits have increased from £1,098 million to £6,158 million (461 per cent), and profitability has grown from £9.8 million (1992) to £130.1 million (2003) – a thirteen-fold increase. Customer research conducted in 2003 found that the bank's ethical and sustainability policies were the most important reason for opening and maintaining a current account. The research also indicated that ethically motivated customers are more likely to hold more than one product and are more likely to 'recommend' than the bank's average customers. Of course, few consumers will pursue ethical preferences in the absence of competitive pricing and good service; however, where these are in place, ethics can act as a crucial differentiator in what is a crowded market. Significantly, The Co-operative Bank is no longer alone in taking such matters seriously: the majority of UK retail banks now claim to factor in environmental considerations, if not ethical matters, when considering the provision of financial services to business.

Report on ethical and sustainability performance – but be honest, or don't bother

There has been a surge in ethical and sustainability reporting by business in recent years. In 2003, 132 of FTSE 250 companies reported on at least one area of social responsibility, up from 105 in 2002. However, there remain some real problems with reporting quality, with just 45 submitting their reports to independent verification and 56 being rated as 'producing no information of substance'.

It has to be said that much of what passes for ethical and sustainability is a bit of a joke – a compilation of all the best bits of a business's performance, with a few exaggerations thrown in to boot. But is it sensible to think that producing a few glossy leaflets and generating a bit of media spin will be sufficient for trust to be built with customers and other stakeholders? Almost nobody considers themself, or others to be entirely perfect: therefore, when a business implies perfection in its communications – which many do – it produces disbelief and ultimately cynicism.

It is The Co-operative Bank's experience that communicating poor performance makes any good performance all the more believable. Furthermore, by and large, media coverage tends to be fair, if not slightly sympathetic. In total, during April 1998 the bank's first Partnership Report was featured in more than 15 million newspapers and reached more than 9 million television viewers and almost 3 million radio listeners. This exposure was subsequently calculated to be worth more than £900,000 in equivalent advertising value.

Reporting not only helps build trust with a wide variety of stakeholders, but also creates a management climate in which improvements in ethical and sustainability performance are more easily prioritized. It is amazing how easily time and resource are found when the prospect of disclosing poor performance looms over the horizon. One of the first lessons of business management is: 'If you don't measure it, you can't manage it.' And as a result, we see a massive uptake in environmental management standards such as ISO 14001, with their emphasis on measurement. However, a project sponsored by the European Union has found that in general those companies with an environmental management system did not perform significantly better than those without. Indeed, in some cases they appeared to perform worse! The mere presence of management systems is not sufficient to drive the desired improvements in environmental performance (or business performance, for that matter). You might say that 'If you don't disclose it, you won't act on it.'

Investment indexes

Alexander Barkawi, Dow Jones
Sustainability Index

Indexes play an important role in investing. Significant amounts of money are managed against a wide selection of benchmarks offered by providers such as Dow Jones Indexes, FTSE, MSCI, Standard & Poors and STOXX Limited. Asset managers use these indexes to evaluate their performance against the market and as a starting point for building portfolios.

Many asset owners and investment managers would argue that sustainability-driven portfolios eventually need to be compared against mainstream benchmarks – and rightly so. In a world where performance tops the agenda and trustees are increasingly challenged to cover their funds' liabilities, investment decisions need to hold up against total market returns. This is equally true for any focus on a specific subset of financial markets – be it region, sector, size, style or sustainability. Investors will always ask whether they should make a particular allocation to one or more of these boxes and whether – in hindsight – they made a wise decision. Total market indexes help them provide an answer.

Simultaneously, investors need tools to plan, implement and control the individual components of their asset allocation. If they brief an asset manager to invest exclusively into growth stocks, they will want to measure that portfolio against a growth index. Should they invest into emerging market bonds, they will compare their performance against the appropriate benchmark for this segment. And if they decide to allocate a portion of their assets into a sustainability-driven equity mandate, they will be looking for a sustainability index to implement this decision and to assess their manager's skills.

The first benchmark accounting for environmental and social criteria was the Domini 400 Social Index. Launched in 1990, this US index excludes various industries such as alcohol, tobacco and firearms, and applies additional thresholds on environmental impact, product quality and safety, diversity and employee relations to select companies. A different approach is taken by the Dow Jones Sustainability Indexes (DJSIs), launched in 1999. Based on the cooperation of the Dow Jones indexes STOXX and SAM, these products marked an important milestone by providing the first global sustainability benchmarks following the best-in-class approach. Rather than screening out whole industries and applying negative selection criteria, the DJSI family is based on comprehensive sets of general and industry-specific indicators to identify sustainability leaders in each sector. In contrast again to this focus on best practice, the FTSE4Good indexes – set up in 2001 – aim to establish a minimum standard by including every company that meets certain criteria regarding environmental sustainability, human rights and stakeholder relations and that is not involved in a group of exclusion industries.

This diversity among the index providers mirrors the different sustainability approaches taken by investors and asset managers. Notwithstanding their distinct characteristics, all these benchmarks fulfil three important functions. First, they provide an essential tool with which to analyse the risk and performance of specific approaches to sustainability. Second, they allow for efficient implementation of sustainability mandates by applying the indexes as universes as well as through index-tracking portfolios. And finally, they offer a conduit for investors to jointly express their interest in sustainability and thus to collectively move the relevant issues up the corporate agenda.

The function of sustainability indexes as performance indicators is relevant in two areas. On the one hand, there is a growing demand among investors to scrutinize the risk/return characteristics of sustainability investments as a whole. Certainly, researchers can, and do, already use sustainability-driven funds and mandates to target this objective. However, these studies are rarely able to find out whether outperforming or underperforming against the total market can be attributed to the application of sustainability criteria or to good timing and selection skills on the part of the responsible asset managers. Indexes – being based neither on timing nor on stock picking, beyond initial construction – provide the appropriate data with which to separate the impact of sustainability from managers' skills. At the same time, specialized indexes are often needed to control the performance of sustainability-driven asset managers. If a manager is briefed to select exclusively stocks out of a subset of the FTSE Global Index, it would not be fair to compare his or her performance against the entire benchmark. An appropriate evaluation of investment managers matches the performance benchmark with the universe that the manager can choose from. Sustainability indexes provide the platform for that.

Specialized benchmarks also allow for an efficient implementation of sustainability briefs. Obviously, there are many different approaches that asset managers can apply to integrate economic, environmental and social criteria. Diversity will continue to shape the industry and provide an important impetus for constant improvements. Different needs and demands among investors will always be an important feature of the market. And divergent views about the 'right' sustainability criteria will keep the debate lively and the development of proprietary selection methodologies firmly on the agenda. However, at the same time demand is out there – and growing – to use sustainability indexes as objective and cost-efficient universes that active managers can choose from. Rather than building up

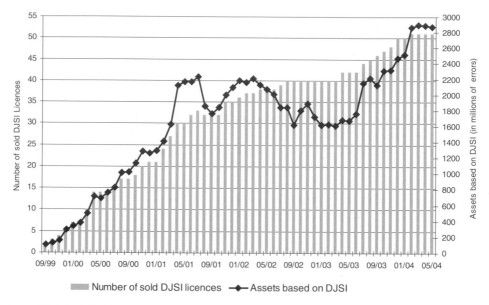

Figure 14.4.1 The Dow Jones Sustainability Index (DJSI): number of licences sold and value of assets

in-house research capabilities, a growing number of sustainability-driven active investors are thus choosing these benchmarks as their starting point for portfolio construction. Similarly, demand is out there – and rising – to apply the concept of sustainability within passive mandates. Again, indexes provide the basis for this option. With the rising amount of passive sustainability investments and the efficiencies of using established benchmarks as universes for active portfolios, the rationale for indexes in this field becomes increasingly obvious. They provide asset owners with the option to profit from the cost-efficiency of passive mandates while at the same time allowing them to apply the concept of sustainability. They allow the market to pool resources efficiently for the assessment of companies. And they eventually also offer active investors a yardstick to find out whether their managers with a proprietary methodology are adding or destroying value – net of fees – compared to the index-based alternatives.

Finally, sustainability indexes also meet the growing interest among investors and the wider public to move long-term economic, environmental and social issues up the corporate agenda. Investors and asset managers have two alternative ways to achieve this goal. They can either directly engage with companies in which they hold shares, or move their money behind an index that puts a spotlight on the issues they care about. Direct engagement is particularly relevant when the focus is on specific concerns. The Pharmaceuticals Shareholder Group's 'Investor statement on pharmaceutical companies and the public health crisis in emerging markets' is a notable example. Developed by ISIS Asset Management and the Universities Superannuation Scheme, this project provides a framework for institutional investors to jointly engage with pharmaceutical companies on access to patented medicines and the response of this sector to the public health crisis in emerging markets.

Carrying the support of several investing heavyweights, the initiative has an influential voice within this focused debate. At the same time, the expanding amount of assets managed against sustainability indexes turns these benchmarks into a growing incentive for companies to improve on a broader front. Today, close to 3 billion euros is managed against the DJSI family, and public recognition of these benchmarks is quickly rising. As a result, firms are placing ever more importance on being a DJSI member and are seeing the indexes as an important driver to improve their sustainability performance.

Against this background, the use of sustainability indexes will continue to expand. The specialized offerings in this field will provide a growing number of investors and asset managers with objective and reliable benchmarks to use when moving into this market. They will continue to support the rising professionalism within this segment by offering tools with which to analyse performance and implement mandates in a cost-efficient way. And they will offer an ever-stronger incentive for companies to integrate economic, environmental and social criteria into corporate strategy and practice.

Socially responsible investment qualifications

Andy Hughes, Business in the Community

The growth in influence of socially responsible investment (SRI) undoubtedly has implications for strategies and practice in the area of corporate social responsibility (CSR), which in turn will increase the importance of the contribution of the CSR Academy to improving responsible business practice.

In their earliest days, SRI funds were primarily concerned with excluding entire industry sectors, such as gambling, arms manufacture or tobacco, from their portfolios. There is still a demand for these types of investment products, but they remain a small niche in the market. The significant growth area for SRI, meanwhile, has been in identifying companies with strong CSR commitments. This movement has not only opened a larger niche in the market, but also begun to influence practices of mainstream retail investors such that the boundary between the SRI niche as a whole and the mainstream is not the cavernous gap it once was.

A major catalyst in this movement has been the growth of rating methodologies, benchmarking tools and indexes that attempt to shed some light on individual firms' approaches to the CSR agenda. They were conceived principally for the benefit of fund managers as a means of simplifying and ranking the CSR performance of many different companies. However, the emergence of common parameters with which to compare CSR performance in this way has had two significant consequences. First, the ratings have led to a spirit of competition between businesses. Second, there is a growing trend for firms to use the components of benchmarking tools, such as Business in the Community's Corporate Responsibility Index, as an internal management tool with which to shape, focus and improve CSR performance.

Increasingly, too, SRI funds actively consult with firms individually on their CSR strategies, which calls for greater knowledge and understanding within companies to be able to engage constructively and meet expectations. Here the CSR Academy has a crucial role to play for firms looking to attract investment from SRI sources, particularly those firms that have no internal CSR function.

Conceived as a web-based resource, the CSR Academy (www.csracademy.org.uk) is primarily aimed at improving knowledge, competency and expertise in CSR issues among non-CSR specialists. Clearly, the advent of the Academy creates a valuable opportunity to integrate CSR principles into mainstream business practices by targeting managers with mainstream business functions. Such a development would in turn serve the interests of SRI funds by strengthening support for their expectations at the very core of the business.

Risk premiums and lending criteria

Paul Monaghan, The Co-operative Bank

This chapter focuses on how banks assess the environmental risks associated with lending to business engaged in environmentally sensitive activities, and extends to the related subjects of leasing and asset finance. It does not seek to cover the related topic of how environmental factors impact on equity and bond investment, as practised by progressive insurers and institutional investors such as the Co-operative Insurance Society (CIS). This is another kettle of fish entirely, one that is covered by R. Sparkes's *Socially Responsible Investment* (Wiley, 2002).

Today, all major banks assess the risks associated with lending to companies engaged in environmentally sensitive activities. For borrowers, this can lead to an increased cost of capital, a requirement for enhanced security or even, in extreme circumstances, the denial of products and services. But on top of such environmental risk evaluations – which are primarily designed to assess creditworthiness and thus protect the lender – a growing number of banks are pledging to restrict finance where projects have a significant negative impact on the environment, regardless of the short-term creditworthiness of a transaction. More and more, it pays for borrowers to understand, and respond to, the banking sector's environmental risk assessment procedures, as described in this chapter.

How banks practise environmental risk assessment

Environmental risk assessment originated in the United States' banking sector in the 1980s and became commonplace among UK banks in the mid-1990s. Curtailment of environmental damage was not the driver for these developments – although a great many banks have subsequently 'spun' this line in correspondence with environmentally conscious personal customers (of which more later). No, the focus of concern was 'lender liability'. Put simply, how could banks ensure that they did not become liable for rectifying environmental damage caused by their customers – a situation that might arise if, for example, they took possession of contaminated land that required clean-up?

Over time, the assessment and management of 'direct' risk have been joined by the assessment and management of 'indirect' and 'reputational' risk, as described in the box at the end of this chapter. However, in all cases when banks assess how environmental factors might impact upon lending decisions, they invariably focus on the potential for negative impacts – for example, the degree to which a client's business could pollute and contaminate buildings or land held as security for a loan, and thus devalue asset values. Rarely are any 'positive' aspects of environmental performance factored in, such as energy efficiency or waste minimization – both of which have the potential to lower costs and thus render a borrower more creditworthy. This is because the environmental risk assessment undertaken by banks is not designed in order to reward good behaviour or punish bad behaviour among borrowers; rather, it exists first and foremost to protect the bank and ensure that any moneys lent have a good chance of being repaid in full. It is also a function of the fact that banks are not half as adept at 'risk-adjusting' the price of a loan as might be imagined. Market pressures are probably a bigger determinant, and it is often remarked that lending is more of an art than a science.

This is not to say that there are now vast swaths of UK business operating in environmentally sensitive sectors that are effectively 'red-lined' by lenders in the United Kingdom (although this has occurred in the United States – see Schmidheiny and Zorraquin's *Financing Change* (MIT Press, 1996, page 104)). Banks will always do their utmost to provide credit to the creditworthy; this is, after all, the primary business of their business, and environmental risk is just one of many risks assessed each time a bank lends to a business.

What to expect as a borrower

In assessing the environmental risk attached to a specific lending proposal, a lender will focus on land issues, the borrower's operations and industrial processes, as well as the quality of environmental management in place to mitigate risks. Of these, a borrower's industrial sector is probably the most important indicator of the potential for environmental risk. For example, a dry-cleaning business or petrol station will present a higher environmental risk than, say, a newsagent.

Typically, the environmental due diligence measures that banks incorporate into their overall credit risk assessment include:

- requiring borrowers to provide information on historical and current property uses, the existence, storage and/or maintenance of hazardous materials and waste, environmental hazards on adjacent properties, and their environmental policies and procedures;
- reviewing borrowers' business plans and/or management systems to ensure compliance with applicable legal and regulatory requirements;
- assessing whether insurance coverage for environmental clean-up and third-party liability might be available and should be obtained by the borrower;

■ if circumstances warrant, requiring a professional audit or assessment to help the bank evaluate its environmental credit risk.

Against this, it should be borne in mind that it is relatively rare for environmental risk assessment to lead to the curtailment of a facility or loan advance. Even when environmental factors emerge as being material, a bank will usually find a way to 'do a deal' (all other things being equal). For example, alternative security might be sought – collateral that is safe from contamination and thus lender liability.

However, if a borrower operates in an environmentally sensitive sector and has a poor credit rating, then the red lights will start flashing within a bank. In such circumstances a lender may seek to reduce, or even eliminate, exposure if it cannot satisfy itself that any land/property offered as collateral is free from contamination. In order to provide itself with peace of mind, the bank may commission an environmental audit or professional site investigation, the cost of which will usually be passed on to the customer.

And in the future...

As stated earlier, through the 1990s the determination and management of environmental risk was the overriding concern of UK banks. However, as a result of pressure from non-governmental organizations and related negative publicity, and also the commercial success of progressive lenders such as The Co-operative Bank (see page 404), a number of major UK banks (including Barclays, HSBC and the Royal Bank of Scotland) are now undertaking to screen the provision of project finance on the basis of ethical and environmental impact, as opposed to merely creditworthiness. Although the guidelines are not yet applied to UK business lending (the majority of which is small-ticket), some regard it as being little more than a matter of time before they are applied.

To this end, the Equator Principles (see www.equator-principles.com) have been developed – a voluntary set of criteria and guidelines based on the social screening criteria and environmental assessment guidelines of the International Finance Corporation and the World Bank. Development began in October 2002, and the Principles were formally launched by 10 financial institutions in June 2003. At September 2004, 27 financial institutions are listed as having adopted the Principles. Between them they account for by far the greater part of project finance worldwide. The Principles apply globally to development projects with a capital cost of US$50 million or over, in all industry sectors. Each project is categorized into one of three groups: high-impact 'Category A' projects, which require a full environmental impact assessment (EIA); 'Category B' projects with lower likely impacts, which require a less extensive EIA; and 'Category C' projects with minimal or no adverse impacts (these do not require an EIA). The Principles also require borrowers in high-impact projects to carry out appropriate local stakeholder consultation. In addition, the borrower or a third-party expert must put an environmental management programme in place to address project compliance, mitigation, action plans and monitoring procedures. For these high-impact projects, compliance with the principles is written into the loan covenants: if a borrower breaches its obligations, the bank can withdraw funding.

Big questions remain as to the consistency of implementation and verification of claims; however, it is still early days, and campaigning groups are sure to be pressing these points further in the future.

Lenders typically categorize environmental risk in three ways:

■ *Direct risk/lender liability risk*. Legislation around the world routinely assigns responsibility for pollution to those who exercise a degree of control over associated premises and land. This principle is often referred to as 'the polluter pays'; however, such legislation may place liability on not just the original polluter, but also subsequent owners, occupiers and operators of a site. A lender may become liable for clean-up costs should it exercise ownership or operational control over a business – that is, as occurs when it takes possession of land or property held as security for a loan. Banks will do their utmost to avoid lender liability risk. It is not something they will entertain – at any price. They will not consider 'risk-adjusting' the price of a loan; and when caught short, they will 'walk away' from security if necessary.

■ *Indirect risk*. Environmental factors (particularly legislation) can add to a business's costs, which in turn may weaken a borrower's ability to service debt. For example, energy-intensive industries may strain under the burden of energy taxes (such as the United Kingdom's Climate Change Levy) if they do not become more energy efficient or source more renewable supplies. Therefore, in environmentally sensitive sectors, banks will routinely ask questions about environmental performance and management as part of the normal credit appraisal process. Environmental management may be as basic as a single employee with responsibility for environmental issues, through to the achievement of external accreditation for environmental management systems, such as ISO 14001 or the European EMAS. Whether or not the company has sought external accreditation, it is important for the borrower to consider that it may need to show evidence of good environmental management.

■ *Reputational risk*. Banks face increasing scrutiny of their lending policies from pressure groups and the media. It is becoming more and more important for them to demonstrate that they act responsibly when providing finance, particularly in respect of major projects in the developing world. It is no longer sufficient to argue that 'if it's creditworthy and legal, it must be OK'. The Co-operative Bank (see page 404) currently has the most advanced ethical and environmental screening of the United Kingdom's retail banks; however, a number of others are now progressing down this track via initiatives such as the Equator Principles referred to earlier in the chapter.

The COOPERATIVE BANK
Customer led, ethically guided

Co-operative Financial Services was formed in April 2002 to bring together The Co-operative Bank, Co-operative Insurance Society (CIS) and smile under the common leadership of Mervyn Pedelty, Chief Executive, CFS. One of thelargest financial services organisations in the UK with more than seven million customers; it has an annual income of £3.5 billion and assets under management of £31 billion.

Both The Co-operative Bank and CIS were first in their respective sectors to introduce corporate social responsibility programmes with fully audited triple bottom line (social, environmental & financial) reports in the UK. The Co-operative Bank's sustainability reporting has been recognised as being the world's best, and it has a well-established Ethical Policy – which reached its 10th Anniversary in 2002. The policy reflects customers' views about how their money should and shouldn't be invested. CIS is a recognised leader in the field of Socially Responsible Investment, and in 2002 was the first UK institutional investor to publish its entire voting record on its website.

In addition to its Ethical Policy, The Co-operative Bank has developed a range of tailored ethical and environmental products for the personal and business sector. Our business banking products are recognised for their high quality service ratings, and we are a major provider of products and services to the public sector and co-operatives, charities and social enterprises. More recently, the bank's ethical positioning has encouraged the development of in-house expertise in renewable energy, sustainable construction and energy efficiency projects – particualrly in relation to leasing and asset finance. For personal customers, there is a range of environmentally-friendly mortgage products that support 'neutralisation' of household carbon dioxide emissions (via projects such as reforestation in Uganda and the provision of fuel efficient cooking stoves in Bangladesh) and a range of Visa credit cards that raise money each time they are used partners such as RSPB, Greenpeace and Amnesty International.

For further details see **co-operativebank.co.uk**

For enquiries, please contact Head of Sustainable Development, Paul Monaghan: **paul.monaghan@cfs.co.uk**

OF banks, lending and environmentally sensitive business

Today, all major banks assess the risks associated with lending to companies engaged in environmentally sensitive activities. For borrowers, this can lead to an increased cost of capital, a requirement for enhanced security or even the denial of products and services in extreme circumstances.

On top of such environmental risk evaluations - which are primarily designed to assess creditworthiness and thus protect the lender – a growing number of banks are pledging to restrict finance where projects have a significant negative impact on the environment, regardless of the short-term creditworthiness of a transaction.

More and more, it pays for borrowers to understand, and respond to, the banking sector's environmental risk assessment procedures, as described below.

How banks practice environmental risk assessment

Environmental risk assessment originated in the United States' banking sector in the 1980s, and became commonplace amongst UK banks in the mid 1990s. Curtailment of environmental damage was not the driver for these developments – although a great many banks have subsequently 'spun' this line in correspondence with environmentally conscious personal customers (of which more later). No, the focus of concern was 'lender liability'. Put simply, how could banks ensure that they did not become liable for rectifying the environmental damage of their customers – a situation that might arise if, for example, they took possession of contaminated land that required clean up.

Over time, the assessment and management of 'direct' risk has been joined by 'indirect' and 'reputational' risk. However, in all cases, when banks assess how environmental factors might impact upon lending decisions, they invariably focus on the potential for negative impacts – for example, the degree to which a client's business could pollute and contaminate buildings or land held as security for a loan, and thus devalue asset values. Rarely are any 'positive' aspects of environmental performance factored in, such as energy efficiency and waste minimisation – both of which have the potential to lower costs and thus render a borrower more creditworthy. This is because the environmental risk assessment undertaken by banks is not designed in order to reward good behavior or punish bad behavior amongst borrowers; rather, it exists first and foremost to protect the bank and ensure that any monies lent have a good chance of being repaid in full. It is also a function of the fact that banks are not half as adept at 'risk adjusting' the price of a loan as might be imagined. Market pressures are probably a bigger determinant, and it is often remarked that lending is more of an art than a science.

Which isn't to say that there are now vast swaths of UK business' operating in environmentally sensitive sectors that are effectively 'red-lined' by lenders in the UK (although this has occurred in the United States). Banks will always do there utmost to provide credit to the creditworthy – this is after all the primary business of their business, and environmental risk is just one of many risks assessed each time a bank lends to a business.

What to expect as a borrower

In assessing the environmental risk attached to a specific lending proposal, a lender will focus on land issues, the borrower's operations and industrial processes, as well as the quality of environmental management in place to mitigate risks. Of these, a borrower's industrial sector is probably the most important indicator of the potential for environmental risk. For example, a dry cleaning business or petrol station will present a higher environmental risk than, say, a newsagent. Typically, the environmental due diligence measures which banks incorporate into their overall credit risk assessment include:

- requiring borrowers to provide information on historical and current property uses, the existence, storage and/or maintenance of hazardous materials and waste, environmental hazards on adjacent properties, and their environmental policies and procedures;

- reviewing borrowers' business plans and/or management systems to ensure compliance with applicable legal and regulatory requirements;

- assessing whether insurance coverage for environmental clean-up and third party liability might be available and should be obtained by the borrower; and

- if circumstances warrant, requiring a professional audit or assessment to help the bank evaluate its environmental credit risk.

Against this, it should be borne in mind that it is relatively rare for environmental risk assessment to lead to the curtailment of a facility or loan advance. Even when environmental factors emerge as being material, a bank will usually find a way 'to do a deal' (all other things being equal). For example, alternative security might be sought – collateral that is safe from contamination and thus lender liability.

However, if a borrower operates in an environmentally sensitive sector and has a poor credit rating, then the 'red lights will start flashing' within a bank. In such circumstances, a lender may seek to reduce, or even eliminate, exposure if it cannot satisfy itself that any land/property offered as collateral is free from contamination. In order to provide itself with peace of mind, the bank may commission an environmental audit or professional site investigation, the cost of which will usually be passed on to the customer.

And in the future…

As stated earlier, through the 90s, the determination and management of environmental risk was the overriding concern of UK banks. However, as a result of NGO pressure and related negative publicity, and also the commercial success of progressive lenders such as The Co-operative Bank (see page x), a number of major UK banks (including Barclays, HSBC and The Royal Bank of Scotland) are now undertaking to screen the provision of project finance on the basis of ethical and environmental impact, as opposed to merely creditworthiness. Although the guidelines are not yet applied to UK business lending (the majority of which is small ticket), some regard this as being little more than a matter of time.

To this end, the Equator Principles have been developed: a voluntary set of criteria and guidelines based on the social screening criteria and environmental assessment guidelines of the International Finance Corporation and World Bank. The Principles apply globally to development projects with a capital cost of US$50 million or over, in all industry sectors. Each project is categorised into one of three groups: high-impact 'Category A' projects, which require a full environmental impact assessment (EIA); 'Category B' projects with lower likely impacts, which require a less-extensive EIA; and 'Category C' projects with minimal or no adverse impacts (these do not require an EIA). The principles also require borrowers in high impact projects to carry out appropriate local stakeholder consultation. In addition, the borrower or a third-party expert must put an environmental management programme in place to address project compliance, mitigation, action plans and monitoring procedures. For these high-impact projects, compliance with the principles is written into the loan covenants: if a borrower breaches its obligations, the bank can withdraw funding.

Big questions remain as to the consistency of implementation and verification of claims; however, it is still early days and campaigning groups are sure to be pressing these points further in the future.

Lenders typically categorise environmental risk in three ways:
Direct Risk/Lender Liability Risk. Legislation around the world routinely assigns responsibility for pollution to those who exercise a degree of control over associated premises and land. This principle is often referred to as 'the polluter pays'; however, such legislation may place liability on not just the original polluter, but also subsequent owners, occupiers and operators of a site. A lender may become liable for clean-up costs should it exercise ownership or operational control over a business – i.e., as occurs when it takes possession of land or property held as security for a loan. Banks will do their utmost to avoid lender liability risk. It is not something they will entertain – at any price. They will not consider 'risk adjusting' the price of a loan; and when caught short, will 'walk away' from security if necessary.

Indirect Risk. Environmental factors (particularly legislation) can add to a business' costs, which in turn may weaken a borrower's ability to service debt. For example, energy intensive industries may strain under the burden of energy taxes (such as the UK's Climate Change Levy) if they do not become more energy efficient or source more renewable supplies. Therefore, in environmentally sensitive sectors banks will routinely ask questions about environmental performance and management as part of the normal credit appraisal process. Environmental management may be as basic as a single employee with responsibility for environmental issues, through to the achievement of external accreditation for environmental management systems, such as ISO 14001 or the European EMAS. Whether or not the company has sought external accreditation, it is important for the borrower to consider they could evidence good environmental management.

Reputational Risk. Banks face increasing scrutiny of their lending policies from pressure groups and the media. It is becoming more and more important for them to demonstrate that they act responsibly when providing finance, particularly in respect of major projects in the developing world. It is no longer sufficient to argue that 'if its creditworthy and legal it must be OK.' The Co-operative Bank currently has the most advanced ethical and environmental screening of the UK's retail banks; however, a number of others are now progressing down this track via initiatives such as the Equator Principles.

Ecology In Action

Established in 1981 Ecology Building Society is an organisation that has prospered directly as a result of its environmental and ethical convictions.

The Ecology promotes the concept of sustainability through its operations and mortgage lending and offers a range of ethical savings accounts to support this. All mortgage applications are judged against its unique lending criteria, assessing the environmental impact of a project, in terms of energy use, pollution and saving resources. This includes looking at properties where new and less conventional ideas are incorporated such as earth sheltering and breathing walls. Features such as the use of recyclable and reclaimed materials, renewable energy and high levels of insulation are encouraged. Typical lending projects include the renovation or conversion of derelict buildings, "low impact" self build, rehabilitating back to back terraced property, community based small businesses with an ecological bias, organic smallholdings, housing co-operatives and loans for small woodlands.

Due to expansion, the Ecology has itself recently moved to new "low impact" headquarters in Silsden, West Yorkshire. Sustainability was again central in the design of the new building, which is powered by a combination of photovoltaic panels generating solar electricity and electricity from other renewable sources. Wherever possible, materials are from renewable sources, recycled or of low toxicity. Paints and finishes are from natural products and solvent free, with the building's insulation being manufactured from recycled paper. Water from a rainwater harvesting system is used to flush the toilets and a nature roof planted with sedum replaces the lost habitat for insects and birds. In 2005 a straw bale meeting room will be added, which will be made available for use by local community groups.

Ecology Building Society now has over £50 million assets and 10,000 accounts.

For further information call 0845 6745566 or visit www.ecology.co.uk

FUNDING CRITERIA

Yorkshire and Humber takes sustainability seriously, so seriously that it has been embedded into the Regional Economic Strategy (RES). Yorkshire Forward, the Regional Development Agency (RDA) also believes in leading by example, and is currently one of only two RDAs to achieve accreditation to EMAS, the European Eco-Management and Audit Scheme – the European environmental management standard. Their CO_2 emissions should reduce significantly over the next 12 months. Following the installation of video conferencing equipment to reduce the need to travel, they have invested in a fleet of environmentally friendly pool cars for use on those occasions when travel by car is essential.

In a recent index of environmental engagement in the region, Yorkshire Forward were ranked 23rd out of 154 entries, scoring 89%.

In addition to demonstrating sustainable practices in its day to day activities, Yorkshire Forward is developing best practice by building them into the funding criteria for the projects which they develop in partnership with both the public and private sectors. This will mean that any organisation applying for funding must demonstrate that reasonable steps have been taken to minimise the environmental impact of the projects they are undertaking.

Mike Smith, Head of Sustainable Development for Yorkshire Forward explains:

"Last year, the RES was independently assessed to ensure that the strategy meets the region's agreed sustainable development objectives. We are now confident that our projects will deliver sustainability as a matter of course. Our project development managers will work closely with our partners to help them to meet all aspects of our funding criteria. We are confident that this approach will encourage other businesses in the region to examine their working practices and adopt sustainability as a way of life."

ART

Social Investment and Loans for Enterprise in the Birmingham Area

THE ART OF SOCIAL FINANCE

It is now widely recognised that a good reputation, born of acting ethically in business and with social responsibly in the locations from which it operates, has a value on a company's balance sheet. There are many ways in which organisations, large or small, can contribute to social purposes and demonstrate Corporate Social Responsibility (CSR), including making social investments in organisations such as Aston Reinvestment Trust (ART).

ART is one of the country's leading area-targeted Community Development Finance Institutions (CDFIs) and a 'social enterprise' itself, being a mutual organisation owned by its members both borrowers and investors. It lends money to businesses and social enterprises in Birmingham and North Solihull which have been unable to secure all or part of the finance they need from conventional sources, but have a viable proposition and will be able to deliver a social benefit as a result.

In the seven years since it started ART has put £3.3m into the local economy in the Birmingham area, lending to over 200 businesses and social enterprises, enabling them to protect or create in excess of 1,000 local jobs. Borrowers, operating in a wide range of markets, have ranged from sole traders starting up to well-established organisations seeking to grow or change direction.

To encourage businesses and individuals to invest in enterprise, the Government has introduced Community Investment Tax Relief (CITR) for investments in DTI accredited CDFIs, of which ART is one. CITR gives 5% per annum of the amount invested off corporation and personal tax liabilities up to a maximum of five years.

Investors since the outset have included well-known companies such as Barclays, IMI, Jaguar, NatWest, Wesleyan and Severn Trent as well as smaller companies and individuals interested in social investment.

Speaking at an IOD event in May 2004, Sir Adrian Cadbury, Chairman of ART, said: "Companies or individuals can invest between £250 and £20,000 in ART and thereby contribute to building a better Birmingham, gaining a measure of tax relief into the bargain. ART's corporate investors are excercising social responsibility by supporting a project which puts their investment to work productively and improves the local economic environment to the advantage of us all. In 2003, ART lend a record £820,000 and is looking to build on that in 2004."

To find out more about investing in ART, call **0121 359 2444** or log on to **www.reinvest.co.uk**.

Making it happen

Sustainability and your organization

Mike Emmott, Chartered Institute of Personnel and Development

What is a sustainable enterprise? Just as there is no single definition of sustainability, there can be no single answer to this question. One answer, however, might be that it is a business with a future. It can look ahead with some confidence because it has considered the needs not only of its shareholders, but also of the wider community. It is managing its business so as to minimize its use of scarce resources and possible damage it does to the environment. It looks after its people and its customers. It behaves strategically by managing risks and identifying opportunities.

Sustainability, or sustainable development (SD), is not something separate from the business: it is a way of thinking about the business and a reminder of some key ingredients underpinning high performance. Sustainability needs to be integrated into business processes; sustainability values need to be embedded into the organization; and policies and processes for which different departments are responsible need to be aligned with one another. Sustainability needs to be built into corporate leadership and strategy. In this sense, sustainability can be seen as essentially a matter of good management, adding business value by ensuring that organizations are able to respond to new or anticipated pressures and opportunities.

The business case for sustainable development

The business case for sustainability policies does not exist at large or in a vacuum; it has to be built in relation to individual companies. Sustainability focuses on a row of changing factors in the environment within which companies have to manage. A basic business case may be grounded in the strategic review process. Most businesses face a rapidly changing environment in which they need to respond to new pressures. The costs of failing to move with the times can be high. SD can focus minds on new factors companies need to take into account.

Research by the International Institute for Management Development (IIMD) suggests that customers are not pushing for more sustainable products and are not willing to pay more for them unless they perceive direct benefits to themselves. A majority of investors say they will react only 'a little more positively' to improved social and environmental performance in the next five years. But surveys also show that people do not want to work for organizations that have a poor reputation for looking after their people or respecting the environment. Companies are having difficulty in recruiting young people who are concerned about financial and other corporate misbehaviour. In tight labour markets, where recruitment and retention are key factors, companies that do not adopt a sustainability agenda could be limiting their own prospects.

The wider argument in support of a sustainability agenda is that it can offer significant help in protecting a company's brand or corporate reputation. The risks of getting it wrong are too big to ignore. By embracing sustainability, organizations can build the trust of their customers and employees. SD can also underpin strategic behaviour, leading companies to anticipate issues they need to handle rather than simply responding tactically. The IIMD survey suggests that the biggest value drivers companies see in sustainability are that it improves their brand value and reputation (23 per cent), is essential to maintaining their 'licence to operate' (18 per cent), and attracts talent and increases employee satisfaction (16 per cent); but the responses vary between one industry and another.

In addition, adopting a sustainability agenda can help employers redefine their corporate purpose or mission; reaffirm their 'licence to operate', particularly where a company's activities give rise to concern about their impact on the environment; help to strengthen their local community; and create a framework for dialogue with a range of interest groups that can extend their strategic awareness.

Managing risk

Risk management is an issue for every business and provides a robust basis for engaging with sustainability. A company's reputation is increasingly on the line as expectations of corporate behaviour increase but trust is withheld. Damage to reputation can seriously undermine a company's share price and the chances of its long-term survival. The range of behaviour that can damage companies' reputation is broad: from condoning child labour to contributing to global warming to lack of respect for women in the workforce. The sustainability agenda can sensitize companies to these risks and support action to deal with them.

The flip side of managing risks is the positive agenda of maintaining trust. Sustainable relationships are essentially built on trust, whether these are with employees or with customers, suppliers or the wider community. A sustainable organization needs to maintain trust-based relationships with all its stakeholders, and that generally means holding dialogue so as to understand their agenda and where they are coming from. A significant benefit of this kind of dialogue is that it extends the strategic information available to the organization and reduces the likelihood of being taken by surprise.

Enlightened employers these days have learnt to pay attention to the psychological contract between them and their employees. Essentially this means respecting the implicit 'deal' between employer and employee, rather than the formal employment contract; it means treating employees fairly and meeting their expectations (or explaining why these cannot be met). A sustainable organization will approach its relations with all its stakeholders on a similar basis so as to establish a reputation for fair treatment and meeting stakeholder expectations. This is the only way in which trust can be built up and maintained.

The big idea

The Chartered Institute of Personnel and Development (CIPD) has undertaken extensive research into the links between human resources (HR) policies and practices and business performance. The link between HR and corporate social responsibility (CSR) emerges clearly from a recent study by John Purcell on 'unlocking the black box'. One of the keys to the link between people management and performance is the existence of a 'big idea' – a clear mission underpinned by values and a culture expressing what the organization stands for and is trying to achieve. Organizations will not energize and empower their people simply by urging them to increase profits. The big idea will generally represent an objective that staff regard as worthwhile and that makes them enthusiastic about coming into work.

Having a big idea means more than just having a formal mission statement: it means that the values are spread throughout the organization so that they are embedded in policies and practices. These values connect the relationships with customers and with employees. They are also enduring and provide a stable basis on which policies can be built and changed. The big idea is a sort of collective glue binding people and processes together in support of a common goal. Finally, the idea can be managed and measured, often through a balanced scorecard approach that provides not just the means of measuring performance, but also a way of integrating different functional areas of the business.

What is HR's job?

Corporate sustainability initiatives are seen to be more or less effective in the majority of organizations that have undertaken them. However, there are problems not only in getting messages across, but also in persuading different functions within companies to work together. Survey evidence suggests that the biggest barriers to sustainability are organizational culture, managers' mindset, lack of knowledge or expertise, and absence of appropriate tools and processes. The issue is fundamentally one of ensuring that systems and processes are properly aligned.

How does the sustainability agenda impact on the role of the HR department? It is HR's job to see that internal processes and practices are aligned with sustainability objectives.

Most organizations are quite good at deciding what they want to do; fewer are good at delivering on their objectives. One problem is that different departments work in their own 'silos' and fail to communicate with each other. HR can be instrumental in communicating a shared vision that is consistent with the organization's values. This can also be a powerful force for building employee commitment.

HR also has a key job to do in building skills and competencies among the management team. It will also need to review its policies on diversity and recruitment. These issues do not represent a technical challenge to HR; no new techniques are required to support sustainability. Rather, HR needs to take on board sustainability objectives and help ensure that the organization is equipped to fulfil them – for example, by seeing that they are reflected in business and people scorecards. Is HR up to the challenge? Increasingly, HR departments are seeking to transform themselves into 'business partners', becoming more knowledgeable about business issues and supporting the line in achieving their targets. By engaging with SD, HR is underpinning its business partner role.

Developing the tools for the job

In July 2004 the Department of Trade and Industry (DTI) published a competency framework listing six core characteristics describing the way all managers need to act in order to integrate responsible business decision-making. These are:

- *understanding society* – understanding the role of each player in society, from government and business to trade unions, non-governmental organizations (NGOs) and civil society;
- *building capacity* – external partnerships and creating strategic networks and alliances;
- *questioning 'business as usual' attitudes* – openness to new ideas and challenging others to adopt new ways of thinking;
- *stakeholder relations* – identifying stakeholders, building relations externally and internally, engaging in consultation and balancing demands;
- *taking a strategic view* of the business environment;
- *harnessing diversity* – respecting diversity and adjusting the approach to different situations.

CIPD is part of a consortium of organizations led by Business in the Community that has contracted with the DTI to promote the competency framework among large and small companies and in business schools. Many organizations may wonder how a competency framework can help in implementing a sustainability agenda. In fact, the competency framework has been designed to be a practical working tool that can perform a range of functions. For example, the six core characteristics define the sustainability (or CSR) agenda by the kind of behaviour needed to sustain it. Second, the standards outline the management training and development needed to support the behaviours. Third, the descriptions of the behaviours can be used as performance indicators and incorporated into the appraisal of individual managers' performance.

The competency framework does not set out to offer a set of professional qualifications to support a functional specialism called 'sustainability' or 'CSR'. The purpose of the framework is to ensure that sustainability is mainstreamed into routine management process, not sidelined as a minority issue. Organizations do not necessarily have to use the language of corporate responsibility or sustainability in order to implement policies and practices grounded in these ideas; the objective is to see that the concepts are applied in practice. Key performance indicators for companies monitoring their progress on sustainability might include a whole list of behaviours and characteristics, none of which includes the words 'sustainability' or 'responsibility' – for example:

- cultural awareness;
- engagement;
- values;
- shared vision;
- understanding stakeholder perspectives;
- dealing with complexity;
- managing change;
- 'futurecasting'.

Accountability

A competency framework can also help towards constructing a 'balanced scorecard' that organizations can use to monitor their performance against social and environmental as well as economic criteria. This is the basis for 'triple bottom line' reporting. In practice, few companies currently publish meaningful information of this kind on a regular basis, but the Operating and Financial Review (OFR), which the Government is expected to incorporate into company law, should give further support to the idea that companies need to be accountable to shareholders and others for their performance on all these dimensions.

It would, however, be a mistake for companies to see sustainability as essentially an issue about compliance. This would be to treat action on social and environmental issues as negative and defensive. Monitoring and measuring performance in these areas should be a means of helping companies manage more effectively to achieve their business goals. HR's role is critical to getting the balance right. The risk of treating sustainability as a compliance issue is that it gets handed to the PR department to manage. HR's job is basically one of seeing that corporate strategy is effectively delivered; that responsible behaviour is embedded in the organization; that the process of leadership development supports sustainability values; and that the activities of different functions within the company are effectively coordinated. It is a major challenge, but one that sits well with the professional values and competencies underpinning good people management and development.

Mike Emmott is Adviser on Corporate Social Responsibility at the Chartered Institute for Personnel and Development.

Employee empowerment

Andy Middleton, Pembroke Associates

Introduction

Academic theory, conferences, presentations and workshops all have their place in the jig-saw puzzle that represents sustainable enterprise. Creation of anything approaching a sustainable enterprise requires managers to balance their management of a new set of requirements in addition to the day-to-day challenges of running a successful business. It is possible to create a culture in which employees are socially, environmentally and ethically aware, playing an active role in keeping the company sustainable, and a few leaders are making significant progress in this area. In making their journey towards a sustainable enterprise, many managers and directors will need to challenge their thinking as well as their behaviour if they are to truly engage their staff as custodians of responsible business and the environment.

Rethinking the challenge

Some organizations' behaviour suggests that they have chosen sustainability as the latest addition to a long line of trends that includes total quality, *kaizen*, just-in-time and business process re-engineering. Of those that follow this route, a few may make progress, yet many will struggle to move any real distance beyond the dreaded territory of initiatives – high-energy, high-resource, expensive, linear approaches that often fail to deliver real value. Initiative-driven change may be wonderful for the people who propose it, yet it often falls short for their clients because of short-term thinking and a lack of feedback, inclusion, relevance and connection.

If linear, short-term thinking is responsible for many of the environmental problems we are experiencing today, then a shift towards systems-based thinking will be fundamental to future success. Acknowledging the connections between people, purpose and place and the interdependencies between different components of the system can do much to drive the change in behaviour that is needed in a sustainable enterprise. Einstein suggested that 'to solve a problem, we need to use a different type of thinking to that which created it in the first place' – a concise summary of the shift in attitude that is needed to start creating a sustainable enterprise.

The challenges caused by use of a traditional, or linear, approach to creation of a sustainable enterprise can be seen in situations where:

■ An organization is concerned only about *elements* of sustainability. Responsibility for sustainability issues is owned and managed exclusively by the CSR team, and hence fails to connect with the wider organization. Yes, a social and environmental report can be produced, and yes, policies help to reduce risk to brand and reputation, but a responsible approach to environmental and social sustainability is still disconnected to operations, processes and people.

■ An enterprise that is seeking more effective ways to motivate and engage staff fails to make the connection between the principles of sustainability (including respect, true value, long-term thinking, goal focus, adaptability and connectivity) and job security, satisfaction and purpose. As we shall see, although levels of staff commitment and inspiration are frighteningly low in many UK companies, few manage to link profit to purpose effectively.

Sustainability through people

There is a lack of understanding of the role that soft skills and people development play in enabling performance in relation and growth of the sustainable enterprise. The increased level of national, European and international legislation and governance requirements is already having an effect on business, requiring many organizations to rethink their policy, reporting and business practice. By themselves, compliance, legislation and governance will do little to ensure the sustained success of an organization without the inclusion of employee motivation and commitment.

The opportunity to connect employee motivation to the challenges and opportunities of sustainable enterprise represents an enormous untapped resource for business owners and managers. Compelling evidence to illustrate this argument has been produced by organizations including the Chartered Institute of Marketing (CIM), the Chartered Institute of Personnel and Development (CIPD) and the Chartered Management Institute (CMI).

CIM quotes a MORI poll that was conducted to investigate understanding and commitment by employees: 'just 27% of respondents strongly agree that they have a clear sense of their organisation's vision and direction for the future, and only 39% of respondents strongly agree that they understand what they need to do as individuals to support business goals'. Levels of commitment and confidence in leaders are even lower, with 'only 9% of those interviewed feeling that their views and participation were valued by their organisation',

Sustainability and young people may not be two images employers often draw together. Gone are the days of 'a job for life' and the expectation that employees, particularly young employees, will stay with one company or one industry for long periods of time. Yet sustainable workforce development – the creation of a workforce, and of workforce practices, which will flex, grow and evolve in line with company needs – is likely to require attention. In either attracting fresh, young talent to the company, or building on the organic promotion of existing talent to achieve the broader aims of a wholly sustainable enterprise.

How, and how well, companies do this will have a big impact on profitability – from protecting their business from the costs of high turnover, to increasing customer business through more knowledgeable, highly trained staff. The Learning and Skills Council (LSC), the organisation responsible for skills development in England, is working with employers to implement Apprenticeships as one key to creating sustainable enterprises. Stephen Gardner, director of work-based learning at the LSC, says: "Apprenticeships offer businesses the means to develop not just the kind of workforce they need today, but to build and protect the workforce they will need in the future."

"By implementing Apprenticeships, employers will support and create a more efficient, motivated and confident workforce with the skills that directly improve bottom lines."

Managed and funded by the LSC, Apprenticeships and Advanced Apprenticeships enable young people aged 16-24, either new or existing employees, to undertake a mixture of on and off-the-job training which culminates in basic skills qualifications, a National Vocational Qualification (NVQ) at level 2 or 3 and the relevant technical certificate. Employers pay their apprentices a wage as an employee, but receive financial assistance, sometimes directly, but often to their training provider, from the LSC for the Apprenticeship training. Local LSC offices provide assessment and advice on the most suitable Apprenticeship for a business's needs, and also on a suitable local training provider for the off-site learning element of the Apprenticeship. Most importantly, it is employers themselves leading the development of Apprenticeships, through Sector Skills Councils, to match the skill and knowledge needs of their industry.

Since opening in 1983, Upper Cut Hair Salons has been driven by Apprenticeship training. Starting over two decades ago with just one small salon in Weston-super-Mare, in Somerset, the company quickly progressed to a network of four small salons across the area. A few years ago, owners John and Carol Burrows made the business decision to consolidate the four salons under one roof. They relocated to their current premises, a spacious ground floor salon with over 25 workstations. The move enhanced Upper Cut's strategic focus on providing quality training to build a highly skilled and motivated workforce. Today, the family-run salon employs 18 full-time and 10 part-time staff. Of the 18 stylists employed, 15 have progressed through the Apprenticeship route. John and Carol believe this strong training culture is integral to the company's success.

John says: "From an employers point of view Apprenticeships make perfect sense. Quality training guarantees growth and the more skills your staff have, the more effective your business will become. From an apprentice's point of view the positives are huge. They get to follow a work-based route with on-the-job, paid training."

Growth continues and future expansion plans are already under way. The company has recently purchased the empty property next to their current salon and they plan to develop one 'super salon', boasting more workstations, a lecture room plus a new beauty salon for their clientele.

John says: "We pride ourselves on making everyone feel valued and this enables us to really get the most out of our learners. On a personal level, the satisfaction from being involved with Apprenticeship training is tremendous and I take great pride in all our apprentices' achievements. It is important to devote this time and energy now. Apprenticeships are an investment in our future success."

and 'a mere 15% strongly agreeing that they have confidence in their organisation's leadership'. Without a clear sense of vision, direction and understanding, opportunities to maximize progress towards sustainability, let alone increased profitability and return on investment, will be severely hampered.

A 2001 CIPD poll showed similar results, suggesting that 83 per cent of the UK workforce were not actively engaged in their work. CMI's leadership research in 2002 reinforced elements of the MCA survey, showing that while inspiration was the most needed trait, only 15 per cent of employees felt inspired by their leaders. These results could alarm anyone with a responsibility to drive the performance of a business; for managers and directors with an interest in creating the sustainable enterprise, they make sober reading indeed. Without confidence and commitment, levels of innovation, creativity and thirst for success will be low at best, and the sustainable enterprise may become little more than a concept.

Using systems thinking

There are strong arguments to support the view that only a system can be sustainable, as components that depend on other elements for their 'lifeblood' cannot be sustainable in isolation. The organs and support systems of the human body need to be in balance for the body to be healthy: the heart depends on strong flows of blood, which depend on clear arteries, and so on. An individual person is most sustainable (and likely to lead a long and healthy life) when he or she has a healthy relationship within a healthy family in a strong community. Following this path of logic would suggest that the sustainable enterprise cannot exist unless the components of the enterprise are geared for sustainability; these components would include employees, shareholders, suppliers and customers as well as the sales, operational and support functions of a business.

Nature has much to teach business, and writers including Janine Benyus in *Biomimicry* and Alan Heeks in *Natural Advantage* give cogent arguments for using natural systems as templates for a range of organizational processes ranging from product design through to change management. Nature *only* works in a systems way, and an organization's profits as well as people are likely to perform at a higher level too when treated in the same way.

Balancing work, life and business

Since the mid-1990s, much rhetoric has been spoken and research conducted into concepts related to work–life balance, a concept that seems flawed in that it suggests a separation between work and life. A truly integrated vision for work–life balance recognizes that work is part of life and that, as such, it needs to meet as many 'life needs' as possible. Recognition, self-esteem, growth, purpose and continual learning need to find a place within an integrated vision.

Understanding the phrase 'work–life balance' is central to progress towards the sustainable enterprise, for as long as work and life are seen as two separate experiences rather than part of the same whole (system), organizations and employees will struggle to maximize levels of involvement and engagement.

A bigger challenge is to create work and business that are in themselves worthwhile, creating value for society and employees as well as for shareholders. This is no easy task, and not one that is suggested lightly. When a business can link an integrated vision with worthwhile purpose, sound operating practices and the performance of an inspired and committed group of employees, an enterprise will be as sustainable as a single enterprise can be.

Goals and timescales

Sustainability is a goal-oriented concept that links current behaviour and outcomes to a clearly defined set of future circumstances. The principles that underpin the connection between goals and sustainability are highly relevant at a personal level, and can have a profound impact on feelings of control, self-esteem and direction. Once personal goals, outcomes and vision start are clear, it is possible to put responsibility, accountability and fear into context, as the yardstick for measurement is something of personal value: personal progress.

One of the greatest challenges in the journey towards environmental, organizational and personal responsibility can be the apparent disconnection between short- and long-term needs. The payback for taking responsibility and courage rarely comes tomorrow, yet the measures of many organizations' success are often based exclusively on short-term outcomes. The compass that directs steps towards sustainability is best created by a clear and detailed vision of a future that is worth fighting for.

Creating an integrated vision

If the levels of inspiration, commitment and motivation suggested by the CIM, CIPD and CMI data are a reasonable reflection of reality, an integrated vision should be the cornerstone of any process that seeks to create a more sustainable enterprise.

An integrated vision will connect people to purpose and place, painting a picture of a future that is worth making an effort for; and will represent a future not only for a business, but for its employees and stakeholders too. Chief executives and business owners who set out a vision to 'be number one in our market' are unlikely to create long-term buy-in.

Linking vision to capital

The concept of 'capital' is useful to bear in mind in relation to the vision that can help make the sustainable enterprise a reality, as the focus is firmly on increasing capacity to give a greater return in future. The environmental charity and consultancy Forum for the Future has developed a model that describes five capitals: environmental, social, human, manufactured and financial. An integrated vision for sustainable enterprise would support strategies for the growth of each capital, to be driven by day-to-day behaviour and underpinned by corporate strategy and goals. The goals for each capital can be interpreted as follows:

- *environmental*: maximizing the likelihood of the environment being able to meet the needs of future generations;
- *human*: matching the performance and capability of employees to the organization's goals and objectives;

- *social*: meeting the needs of the community in which the enterprise operates;
- *manufactured*: minimizing the process and embodied energy associated with operation of the enterprise;
- *financial*: transparency and governance in relation to management and investment of the enterprise's finance and capital.

Leadership for change

Processes relating to sustainability are dynamic rather than static, and enterprises wanting to move down the path of sustainability need to reflect this. Change and dynamic relationships are integral to sustainable systems, and the culture of an organization plays a vital role in driving the behaviours and attitudes that support rather than hinder change.

In their excellent book *The Knowing–Doing Gap*, Pfeffer and Sutton (1999) talk passionately about the need to drive fear out of organizations, as fear creates the 'knowing–doing gap' of their title – the gap between knowledge and action that all too often prevents invention becoming innovation, and creativity becoming change. Pfeffer and Sutton argue effectively that fear is the greatest barrier to change, as it stifles the flexibility of thought and action that are vital to coping with internally chosen or externally driven change.

The role of leaders and leadership cannot be overestimated in creating a culture of change; no amount of words, mission or vision statement can make up for a failure to demonstrate and support the behaviours that are needed. While leadership may too often be the role solely of senior people in an organization, managers hear phrases such as 'we are going through a period of change' – or worse, they displace responsibility and use phrases such as 'they need to change'. It is a manager's job to lead his or her team through change and help them understand that change is an organic, ongoing process that never stops. Putting transformation and change in perspective helps people balance the fears and opportunities associated with change, and to make better choices about the way that they react.

Leadership is everyone's job in an organization, rather than the job of the leader, and it is hard to envision any degree of sustainability without it. Leadership for sustainability is about standing up for beliefs, challenging norms and pushing for what is right; the leader's job in making this happen is in providing the inspiration, the permission and demonstration that principle-based working is worthwhile.

Conclusion

Maintaining progress towards your goal of sustainability is more important than making a start in the first place; starting things is easy in comparison to seeing them through. The points raised earlier about initiative-driven change are key here; if employees sense that something is intended to be short term, then they'll respond accordingly.

Too often, day-to-day business activity can overtake some of the most important aspects of an enterprise's journey towards sustainability, which means that the small steps of feedback, measurement and celebration get left behind. If you are passionate about making your organization more robust, durable and sustainable, be passionate about doing the things that will make it work – make time for fun, focus and friendship, as without them your journey will be both harder and longer than it needs to be.

While directors and managers may have no way of knowing what the ecological, social and technical challenges facing business in 10 years' time will be, there is strong evidence to suggest that by following the paths laid out in the preceding chapters, your organization will be in the strongest possible position to take advantage of future opportunities and cope effectively with the challenges that the future brings.

Inspiring: learning, leadership and change

Annette Rigby, University of Cambridge Programme for Industry

It is encouraging to see how many organizations now take it for granted that they must do more than simply 'operate' in their field; that they must also contribute to the quality of life of people they affect, protect the environment, and perhaps make a broader contribution to society. The reasons for this shift are many and varied: growing uncertainty, high societal expectations, increased accountability and tougher competition all play their part. For many organizations, the business case for sustainable development has become compelling.

The result is that many business leaders are fundamentally questioning and changing the way they manage their organizations:

- What does it mean to hold a position of leadership in an organization today?
- How can we adapt to social and environmental realities while remaining effective and competitive around our core purpose?
- How can we move the issues out of the specialist box into the mainstream?

Leadership development

The modern corporation operates in a society marked by uncertainty, risk and rapid change. The roles and capacities of business, government and civil society are being redefined, resulting in an unprecedented level of expectation that businesses will play a major role as responsible leaders in the shaping of a globalized economy.

Companies must now operate with a high degree of sensitivity to social, cultural and ethical diversity across their markets; they must embrace new forms of collaboration, partnership and local entrepreneurship; they must develop and implement business strategies that are sustainable not just for shareholders, but for stakeholders as well – for government, employees, communities and campaign groups. These demands have prompted a reassessment of the skills and understanding needed by business leaders.

Over the next 5–10 years the skills of sustainable development will become recognized as the skills of leadership. Developing the capabilities to implement sustainable development will be a key source of competitive advantage.

How the Cambridge Programme for Industry can help

New forms of leadership require new forms of leadership development. The University of Cambridge Programme for Industry (CPI) is the university's centre of excellence in work-based, workplace learning. Our goal is to help organizations respond creatively and competitively to the world's changing environmental, social and economic circumstances in ways that contribute to a sustainable society. CPI has become recognized as a global leader in the field of learning, leadership and change within a sustainable development context and runs some of the best-known and most respected learning programmes in sustainable development, worldwide. Some of our programmes are developed for specific companies while others involve a rich cross-section of individuals from various business sectors.

Acquiring board-level commitment to sustainable development is a good start, but the bigger challenge is to bring enough people up to a sufficiently high level of awareness of sustainable development for the issues to be felt more uniformly across the organization. Every employee needs to have at least some understanding of the issues and their practical relevance to his or her work, as well as the skills to make tactical changes in line with business objectives.

Implementing solutions

Many of today's organizations are adept at developing policies and organizational 'vision', but find that getting key, relevant messages through to the employees, in order to effect change, can be challenging. How do you translate an organizational commitment to sustainability into an effective set of practices and procedures resulting in improved performance from individuals in their workplaces?

CPI can help your organization close the gap between vision and reality. Understanding the key stages of change has enabled CPI to develop programmes at each stage of the learning process, all of which are designed to facilitate ongoing learning within both the individual and the organization. Individuals and their organizations must go through three stages of learning in order to embed information permanently into their working practices:

1. *Raising awareness*. Although it will usually begin with senior management, awareness-raising must sooner rather than later include all employees and establish the principles

of sustainable development at all levels within the organization. We offer a range of tools and programmes to help individuals understand the business case for sustainable development and become aware of how the issues affect them, including:

- HRH Prince of Wales's Business & the Environment Programme. This programme, now in its 10th anniversary year, is the largest and longest-running executive education programme on sustainable business. Held annually in four locations (Cambridge, Austria, South Africa and the United States), the Senior Executive Seminars have introduced over 1000 international senior executives and thought leaders to the sustainability debate, and provided insight and support necessary for them to champion sustainable development with profitability in their organizations. With an active alumni network, the programme offers a global forum for debate to identify strategic opportunities of sustainable business practice, a top-level international network, and a unique source of leading-edge contributions and expertise.
- Chronos, our online learning tool. Available via the internet or on CD ROM, this is a highly accessible and easily disseminated tool that makes sustainable development meaningful and relevant to employees at all levels of the organization. Developed in partnership with the World Business Council for Sustainable Development (WBCSD), it is a versatile product that can be blended with other learning initiatives inside the company and used to reinforce the company's principles, policies and practices. Chronos was awarded the 2003 Green Apple National Champion's award for education and training.

2. *Developing a deeper understanding.* This involves translating raised awareness of sustainability into the level of thinking that can form the basis of strategy and implementation. Such practical, work-based learning is a choice readily sought by those who would like to undertake a longer, more in-depth period of training without having to leave their organizations to study theory full-time. Programmes we offer in this phase include:

- Sustainability Learning Networks. This part-time programme, developed and run in partnership with Forum for the Future, focuses on developing middle and senior managers' capability to understand and implement principles of sustainability and corporate social responsibility (CSR) into their jobs and their organizations. The course is accredited by the University of Cambridge as an Advanced Diploma in Sustainable Business, awarded on the basis of continuous assessment and three formal submissions.
- Postgraduate Certificate in International Diversity Management. This programme enables those involved in international teams to manage cultural differences effectively and to profit from diversity in international business relationships. The programme is in itself an intercultural experience, as it is marketed throughout Europe and, in collaboration with international partners, the three three-day workshops are held at different European centres, thus providing a unique atmosphere for exchanging ideas and experiences in an intercultural context.
- The Partnering Initiative, incorporating the Postgraduate Certificate in Cross-sector Partnership. Developed by three established and influential institutions – the

University of Cambridge, the Prince of Wales's International Business Leaders Forum and the Copenhagen Centre – the course has been created in response to a growing recognition that cross-sector partnerships between business, government and civil-society organizations offer an effective means of addressing crucial social, economic and environmental challenges. This nine-month part-time Master's-level programme is designed for senior professionals from any sector whose role requires them to understand, develop or manage cross-sector partnerships.

3. *Embedding good practice.* This is about bringing sustainable development to life within an organization. Embedding good practice and effecting change requires careful planning, the nurturing of champions and, frequently, a willingness to embark upon more fundamental changes than originally expected. To assist client organizations with this phase, we work closely with core teams over extended periods as they develop and put in place learning strategies for their whole organization. An example is the 'learning lab' model. Facilitated by CPI, 'learning labs' are neutral environments in which small groups of leading organizations can meet, discuss their challenges and share positive ideas about successful practices. The organizations involved undertake an informal benchmarking process in which appreciative inquiry is then used to interpret the information generated and unlock successful patterns of practice among the group.

In addition to these programmes, in each of these three phases of learning CPI can offer customized leadership development programmes, training programmes and custom e-learning tools. Underpinning all these initiatives are a number of commissioned research projects that constantly further our knowledge and expertise in learning and sustainability.

A unique approach

CPI's expertise is in both sustainability and learning – a combination whereby we can bring participants to a point of personal understanding from which they can address practical business dilemmas as well as start raising awareness of sustainability within their organization. We help individuals and organizations learn about sustainable development in a way that is personally relevant.

At some stage in their life, most people will have experienced the discomfort of being lectured to by an 'expert' on a topic of little or no relevance to them personally. This experience is typical of a widespread view that learning is a process of transferring knowledge into people's heads, either via an expert or via a computer. In contrast, our approach is not to 'teach' the answers, but to help you develop the insights – the 'thinking tools' and the analytical skills as well as the personal realizations – to take back to your workplace and develop your own solutions. A lot of study time in CPI's accredited programmes addresses the challenges faced by participants in their work settings.

We actively utilize collaborative learning, so that participants on our programmes can benefit from others' experience and best practice, and at the same time share the challenges and dilemmas facing their own organizations. Recognizing that learning is a continuous process, we also support participants after they have attended our programmes via alumni activities. CPI's programmes are based upon the assumption that learning takes place all the time, not just in training courses, and that learning opportunities must connect back to the realities of work in order to succeed. They are underpinned by extensive knowledge of how people and organizations learn, flowing from 15 years of experience of programme design, and a series of high-quality research projects.

As a department of the University of Cambridge, we are able to draw on its full range of intellectual resources and networks, creating challenging interdisciplinary courses and educational services. Our strength lies in our ability to make creative use of this wealth of knowledge that exists in Cambridge and other universities, and combine it with leading-edge insight and experience from business, the public sector and civil-society organizations from around the world. Our philosophy is to work with organizations in as deep a way as possible. This enables us to provide executives with the space, support and intellectual stimulus they need to make a profound shift in the way they perceive the world, their organization and their role in both.

For more information on how CPI can help you introduce sustainable development into your organization, please visit our website (www.cpi.cam.ac.uk) or contact Annette Rigby at CPI, 1 Trumpington Street, Cambridge CB2 1QA, UK (Annette.Rigby@cpi.cam.ac.uk or on 01223 342100).

Schumacher College Business & Sustainability Programme

Schumacher College was founded in 1991 on the conviction that a new vision is needed for society, its values and its relationship to the Earth. Over the last decade, the College, named after E.F. Schumacher, author of *Small is Beautiful*, has established an international reputation for the inspiration, quality and breadth of its teaching. In the beautiful Devon countryside, participants enjoy a mixture of learning, reflection and the exchange of ideas and experiences. The learning at Schumacher College is particularly effective because course-work occurs within a community which is itself striving to live in a more sustainable and responsible way.

In 2000, the College launched a programme aimed specifically at business people. These *Business and Sustainability* courses are shorter than most College courses (four days), have facilitators working with participants to translate what they learn into individual action plans, and are taught by some of the leading thinkers in the sustainability field – Amory Lovins, Tessa Tennant, Fritjof Capra, Karl-Henrik Robert, Jonathon Porritt, and Ray Anderson. Participants from companies such as BP, Ernst & Young, FaberMaunsell, Orange, Tesco and Unilever have attended and gone on to send their colleagues.

The length of the course and the environment in which it takes place (including a field trip to Dartmoor to experience deep ecology and discuss the implications of Gaia theory) enable participants to engage with the issues in a deeper and more fundamental way than other training courses. One early participant commented: "While the College consistently attracts world-class speakers, it retains an informal and participatory atmosphere. Everyone functions as part of the community, sharing the cooking and household chores. Discussions continue and friendships are cemented over potato peelings and freshly mopped floors. At the same time, speakers mingle with delegates, providing the opportunity for in-depth discussion that is seldom replicated on other courses."

Incentives for the sustainable enterprise

Stephanie Draper and Susanna Wilson,
Forum for the Future

The climate that business is operating in has shifted. It's no longer enough to provide employment, to obey the law and pay taxes. These days, business is expected to contribute more broadly to the social good, to exhibit corporate social responsibility (CSR) – the business response to sustainable development, addressing socio-economic and environmental problems and benefiting from a progressive approach. Business is now operating in a low-trust environment and is under pressure from all sides: from non-governmental organizations (NGOs) to shareholders, from employees to governments. NGOs such as Friends of the Earth and Christian Aid publicize the growth in corporate power and criticize those that abuse it; smaller groups scrutinize business at a more local level. Shareholders too are looking to see future risks to assets, reputation and resources managed in a proactive way, as is demonstrated not only through the rise in 'ethical investment' funds, but also through increased shareholder activism more widely. Pressure also comes down the supply chain: big businesses such as Marks & Spencer and Boots are asking questions of their suppliers about their labour standards and use of materials such as pesticides and other chemicals in order to guarantee their own reputation. Governments are asking business to respond positively to social and environmental challenges through legislation, financial incentives and information.

Where there is pressure there is also reward. Employees prefer jobs in responsible businesses; customers and investors reward good practice, and good management of these issues can also result in financial benefits through eco-efficiencies and better access to capital. There has been extensive research into the business case for corporate responsibility and sustainable development. The result has been to highlight that the key question is not 'Will it pay?' but 'When will it pay?'. Responsible business is about doing the right thing today and ensuring longer-term benefits – and this is true for small and large businesses alike.

This chapter takes a look at what these different stakeholders are asking for from businesses, particularly small and medium-sized enterprises (SMEs), and how their expectations are changing the context in which business operates. Also, it looks at how hearing and responding to them contributes to the effective management of a company, enhancing financial sustainability – the incentive for CSR.

Proactively responding to legislation from government

There is a range of environmental legislation in the United Kingdom, much of which can have a significant effect on SMEs as well as large business. The Climate Change Levy, for example, applies to any business that uses electricity, coal, natural gas or liquefied petroleum gas as an energy source. Companies are charged directly to their energy bill, at different rates depending on what energy is being used.

But there are also financial incentives over and above those of compliance: first, the savings made by eco-efficiency and waste minimization; and second, governmental interventions in the market to create financial incentives. For example, in order to encourage energy efficiency in businesses, a variety of legislation has been introduced that will enable businesses to apply for enhanced capital allowances for energy-efficient equipment, to participate in emissions trading and to gain exemption for certain processes and fuels. Landfill tax and aggregates tax have been introduced to encourage efficient use of resources

---

Bovince Ltd

Bovince Ltd is one of Europe's largest users of screen process technology. It has invested in new technology to increase efficiency and reduce pollution. As a result, the company saves around £1,200 (about 20 per cent) on a typical large billboard, and cuts chemical use and waste. Its success stems from a formal, structured approach to assessing its environmental impact, taking steps to reduce it and reporting on the process – traditionally known as eco-efficiency.[1] As a result, in addition to financial savings, Bovince has built a strong reputation as an environmentally responsible company, thereby creating new markets, and is well prepared for possible future legislation.

Sustainable development is not just about the environment; there is a need for businesses to comply with social legislation too in areas of employment, diversity and disability (for customers as well as employees).

Government is also taking a strong interest in the way the business response can move from strategy to implementation. The Department of Trade and Industry-backed CSR academy, launched in July 2004, is likely to push CSR higher up the business agenda and indicates that government is taking seriously the role that business plays in society. The academy will encourage managers to take on the skills and competencies required to respond to wider social and environmental needs.

Getting the most from employees

Treating employees well is a critical element of a sustainable business approach, and there is evidence that doing so can bring benefits in the form of increased productivity and innovation, reduced retention costs and increased customer satisfaction as a result of staff being more motivated. For example, Institute of Employment Studies research into a retailer with 90 outlets across the United Kingdom estimates that a one-point rise (out of five) in employee satisfaction will lead to a sales increase of £200,000 a month per unit for the company.[2]

A recent Institute for Public Policy Research report looked at the main factors that can motivate small businesses to be socially responsible. These range from improved reputation and expanding customer base to better staff development, satisfaction and productivity.[3] A recent report in the *Financial Times* noted that 'Happy staff are more likely to suggest improvements, innovations and new market opportunities. Viewed in that light, the case for treating staff well is so obvious that numbers and data are superfluous.'[4]

The value of a strong team cannot be overestimated. Yet times are changing. Few people now expect to stay in one company for life, but they increasingly expect their employer company to reflect the values that they hold. An Industrial Society (now the Work Foundation) study showed that 82 per cent of UK professionals would not work for an organization whose values they did not believe in and 73 per cent take social and ethical considerations into account when selecting a job.[5]

There is an important link with relationships to the local community too: a shortage of skilled workers can lead employers to focus on improving the quality of education and training in local schools and colleges.

Stable and supportive local communities

Effective relationships with local communities can bring a range of benefits. For example, in the case of small, local enterprises, many customers will be drawn from local communities and will be attracted to a business with a positive reputation. High-quality employees may be attracted from the local area to a company for the same reason, and existing employees can be motivated by the opportunity to volunteer, or by the knowledge that their families are benefiting from corporate community initiatives. Companies can reduce costs associated with complaints of noise and disruption if the needs of local communities are heard and responded to, to prevent this kind of nuisance.

There is an opportunity, particularly for SME owners and managers, to engage with local economic regeneration initiatives as a way of helping to reduce crime and vandalism that have a negative effect on their business. This incentive is recognized by Eddy's Nottingham Ltd, electrical retailers and repairers:

> If you speak to the guys in our shop, they want to have people come in and buy their products – so they want to make sure that people come to their area, and in order for

this to happen, the area needs to be safe, with good parking. The main focus [of CSR] may not be to help the local community, but they do benefit the local community for their own gain.[6]

Business in the Community's Innovation through Partnership programme is exploring how engaging with stakeholders, particularly low- to moderate-income community groups, can enable business innovation and organizational learning – another example in the range of ways in which cooperation between businesses and communities can bring benefits to both parties.

Meeting the demands of business customers

Among the business community, where large businesses have embraced the CSR agenda there is an expectation that they will engage with suppliers to encourage them to adopt similar standards. This affects a large number of smaller companies that make up their supply chain. Sixty per cent of SMEs say that a large corporate customer has asked them to satisfy criteria on health and safety practices, and 43 per cent say they have had this call on environmental practices.[7] This trend is likely to become stronger over the next few years, as more and more large companies start to take CSR seriously, but also because there is a requirement to continuously improve. Even companies that are currently retained as suppliers may need to make changes in order to keep their customers.

Keith MacMillan of Henley Management College has identified this trend, and sees it as an extension of the traditional concept of 'goodwill', familiar to businesses of any size: 'I think the primary value for a business is that it should be there to generate goodwill amongst its stakeholders. I also believe that can be measured; I also believe that in the next 5 to 10 years, investors will demand that it is reported on.'[8]

Consumers

Ethical consumerism is seen by many as a niche market, but evidence suggests that concern for social, environmental and ethical issues is increasingly driving buying patterns among customers. The Co-operative Bank's Ethical Purchasing Index – a tool for measuring growth in ethical consumerism based on sales data – in 2002 reported an increase in sales of £2 billion over two years. In addition, £3.4 billion is currently deposited in ethical banks (an increase of 29 per cent between 2001 and 2002), and £3.8 billion is in ethical investments, bringing the total 'ethical wallet' in 2002 to £13.9 billion.[9]

Ethical brands are becoming increasingly mainstream: Green & Black's chocolate, winner of two Ethical Consumer Awards in 2004, is expected to report sales of £14 million in 2004 and to grow by 40 per cent in 2005. CEO William Kendall sees no conflict between running a competitive business and doing it ethically.[10] Other ethical brands such as Ben & Jerry's and Ecover are rapidly becoming household names.

It is with this in mind that some large businesses are starting to acknowledge that their sustainability programmes cannot stop at the door of the marketing department. However, now that public trust in business is fragile, ethical aberrations affect even the most mainstream brands, so that all companies stand to lose competitive advantage by failing to adopt a risk management approach to brand reputation. Intangible assets such as reputation and brand value, as well as intellectual property and motivation of staff, are now seen to represent 70 per cent of the true total asset value of companies in many sectors.[11]

Reputation, brand and investment

Over 60 per cent of the public say that big business doesn't care about its social and environmental impacts.[12] Yet research by the insurer Aon among leading UK organizations found that loss of reputation was seen as the greatest risk, up from fourth place in 1999.[13] While social and environmental campaigns targeting companies do not always have an immediate effect on the financial bottom line, they can and do affect reputation in general and, in due course, investment.

One key way in which investors and other stakeholders look for evidence of a sustainable business approach is through company reporting – and not only in the case of FTSE listed companies. The Beacon Press, 3re Group, FRC Group, Hammerson plc and Traidcraft have all been shortlisted for environmental or sustainability reporting awards by the Association of Chartered Certified Accountants. Indexes such as the Business in the Community (BitC) Corporate Responsibility Index have a high profile among the peer group of FTSE 250 companies, and, for smaller companies, the Small Business Service's Benchmarking index (www.benchmarkindex.com) includes a section on corporate responsibility.

Awards such as the Queen's Award for Enterprise in Sustainable Development, awarded this year to companies such as KeyMed (Medical & Industrial Equipment) Ltd and Triodos Bank NV, raise a company's profile and enhance its reputation.

Conclusions

All the stakeholders referred to in this chapter are providing incentives for businesses of all sizes to embrace corporate social responsibility. There is growing evidence that companies that take sustainable development seriously are also those that perform well. In-depth research has shown that on share price performance, socially responsible investors will not lose out in the long term. For small businesses, this is a question of longevity in the local community, harnessing the talents of the best employees and responding to the needs to customers and the marketplace. Corporate social responsibility is not a fad; it's the way of the future.

Notes

1   www.societyandbusiness.gov.uk/company/studies/bovince.htm, accessed 6 May 2004

2   Draper, S (2002) CSR Monitor: Workplace Practices, in *Corporate Social Responsibility Monitor*, eds J Rayner and W Raven, Gee Publishing, London

3   Joseph, Ella (2000) *A Welcome Engagement: SMEs and social inclusion*, Institute for Public Policy Research, London

4   Article entitled 'Focus on human resources and leadership development', *FT Management*, 27 October 2003

5   Draper, S (2002) CSR Monitor: Workplace Practices, in *Corporate Social Responsibility Monitor*, eds J Rayner and W Raven, Gee Publishing, London

6   Joseph, Ella (2000) *A Welcome Engagement: SMEs and social inclusion*, Institute for Public Policy Research, London

7   'Engaging SMEs in Community and Social Issues', a consortium research study carried out on behalf of the DTI, led by Business in the Community, with British Chambers of Commerce, the Institute of Directors and AccountAbility (the Institute of Social and Ethical Accountability), published in London, 2002

8   Porritt, J and Tuppen, C (2003) Just Values, BT, London

9   New Economics Foundation and The Co-operative Bank (2002) *Ethical Purchasing Index: 2002*, The Co-operative Bank, Manchester

10 Griffiths, I (2004) Chocolate Soldier, *The Guardian*, 10 April

11 Harpur, O M (2002) CSR Monitor: Protecting and Enhancing Reputation, in *Corporate Social Responsibility Monitor*, eds J Rayner and W Raven, Gee Publishing, London

12 Edelman, R (2003) Edelman Survey on Trust and Credibility, in *Risks, Returns and Responsibility*, Association of British Insurers, www.edelman.com

13 Aon Biennial Risk Management and Risk Financing Survey 2001, www.aon.com

The role of consultants in corporate social responsibility

Entec UK

Simply put, corporate social responsibility (CSR) is the business contribution to sustainability. Not so simply put, it requires companies to take responsibility and be accountable for their relationships and impacts (both positive and negative), now and into the future. Accountable to whom? Stakeholders. Who are stakeholders? Any person or organization that is, or could be, affected by, or could affect, a company and its actions. To make it even more difficult, some stakeholders are impossible to communicate with. When was the last time you hugged a tree or talked to the animals to make sure you understood the impact of your company on them? But don't worry: there are well-meaning non-governmental organizations (NGOs) that speak and lobby on their behalf.

Mind-boggling stuff. It's broad based, and packed full of jargon and non-specific statements. Not the easiest of things to manage, and anyway, isn't it just another fad? Unfortunately not. Continuing tales of corporate woe have shown that CSR continues to be an important issue. Pressure continues to build from several angles. Investors are asking companies difficult questions about their CSR approach and performance. The Government is putting forward further requirements on reporting, which, although they stop short of making reporting mandatory, will support the move to further transparency. The Operating and Financial Review (OFR) will be a statutory requirement for companies to report on their business drivers, strategy and how they identify and manage risk. At present it is anticipated that this will become a requirement for some companies for financial years starting on 1 January 2005. Shareholders and, increasingly, other stakeholders want to know whether companies are being effective about value creation and reputation management and are managing their risks in order to secure their long-term support.

Recent years have seen a plethora of guidelines and standards covering CSR in general and specific issues (labour standards, human rights, etc). They include:

- AA1000 – a stakeholder-led assurance standard;
- the Global Reporting Initiative – a sustainability reporting approach;
- SIGMA – a sustainability management system.

CSR and sustainability require us to take a look into the future and try to plan with this in mind. For instance, what if we lived in a world in, say, 5–10 years' time where we were all financially responsible for the damage due to climate change caused by our emissions? Sounds unlikely? Cast your mind back a decade or so, and a landfill tax, Climate Change Levy and producer responsibility were all new concepts but we've got them now!

Adopting an effective approach to CSR can bring unexpected benefits. For it to be effective, organizations must have positive collaboration across functions. CSR can integrate finance, marketing and communications, operations, human resources, sales, etc. No one knows your business as well as you do, and moving towards CSR involves the progressive opening out of your business to a host of interested parties. This in itself can be risky, as many well-intentioned but ultimately damaging initiatives will testify.

So, before considering a consultant, make sure you can deliver commitment from the very top and resources from all key business functions. A neat way of doing this is to work together to develop an outline business case for CSR, then pool, from existing plans, activities that contribute to individual elements of the CSR spectrum before finally considering opportunities to combine actions to deliver increased value. Take a long, hard look at the result of your deliberations and, if it feels right, move forward carefully, and monitor and review your progress frequently. Build confidence.

It may be that you could bring in a consultant to steer you and facilitate this process. Some consultants have very good mapping tools that can aid the development of the business case.

Consultants can operate at a number of levels within a company on CSR:

- *Strategic* – helping companies to develop an effective approach to CSR. This can include formulating a strategy that identifies key issues and sets objectives to address them, along with ensuring that the strategy identifies the appropriate resources, structures and responsibilities needed to implement the necessary changes.
- *Polices and programmes* – helping companies to develop polices and programmes to support CSR such as appropriate policies and procedures for business conduct, environment, human rights, risk management and non-discrimination.
- *Capacity-building* – helping companies to develop their ability to effectively address CSR issues, eg training and education programmes to ensure that employees understand what's required of them and have the ability to do it.
- *Projects* – helping companies to deliver specific projects such as stakeholder engagement, a CSR report or assurance, and verification of a company's CSR process.

Mapping your company involves setting its purpose, functions, divisions, structures, etc against key CSR issues. This could be done using a simple matrix. CSR issues are typically grouped into broad environmental, social and economic issues, although some companies find it easier to categorize CSR issues into marketplace, workplace, community and environment.

The next step in this mapping process would be to identify the interaction between the two axes. For example, if you are a clothing company and have a manufacturing facility or suppliers in the Far East, is there a risk that they may not be operating to acceptable labour standards? If they weren't, what would the consequences be for your business? Another example would be if you had an authorization for a particular level of discharges or emissions into the air or water from an environmental regulator; what would be the consequences if you exceeded it? There could be a range of consequences in each of these cases, including fines, loss of reputation, loss of production and damage to people's health.

This mapping process is designed to be an opportunity for learning. It could be that you haven't looked at the company from a sustainability perspective before, and it could identify some interesting issues and opportunities. Once you've gone through this stage and identified the priorities – that is, those risks that are most likely to arise and that have the greatest consequences – then you can move on to the business case.

You can see from the text box that consultants can help at different levels across the business process. It may be that a single consultancy or organization can provide effective support, from building the CSR vision to tackling a project designed to identify and manage product level risk. It is, however, unlikely. More likely is that organizations will have already established and trusted external advisers for each business function, and so the role of a CSR consultant will be to bring new thinking and focus to integrate the advice from the existing supply chain.

This is a long game, so the best way to interact with a CSR consultant is to build an effective working relationship over time. Do this by understanding the consultant's capabilities, giving him or her time to understand your business and how it works, being receptive to suggestions and being clear about what you want the consultant to do. The CSR issues will evolve for your company, and having a good working relationship with a CSR consultant will help you make the most of the opportunities he or she presents.

So, a summary of the process towards employing a CSR consultant looks something like this:

- Bone up on what's already been done (standards, best-practice case studies, etc).
- Build commitment from the top and involve all key business functions.
- Review work in progress in the context of CSR and build confidence. Map your business and establish priorities.
- Prepare the business case for CSR and a draft outline action plan.
- Select a CSR consultant and integrate all other relevant external advisers. (This step can be completed earlier, if you prefer.)
- Move forward carefully, secure early success, build.

You can't outsource corporate responsibility. A good CSR consultant will bring specific expertise, general broad-based understanding and an ability to integrate other expert advice, but you make the decisions and, through your passion, belief, creativity and commitment, steer your organization safely into its future.

Corporate social responsibility and small and medium-sized enterprises

Jeremy Nicholls, The Cat's Pyjamas

Under the cosh from the corporate and social responsibility (CSR) community for not doing enough on sustainability while corporates steal the thunder with glossy publications, small and medium-sized enterprises (SMEs) are the new target group. Eurochambres is currently carrying out a programme on behalf of the European Commission to bring CSR to SMEs. So, someone thinks this is important. And yet according to research carried out for the Department of Trade and Industry (DTI) in the United Kingdom, 97 per cent of SMEs' owners or managers thought they were socially responsible. At the same time, though SMEs are much vaunted by government as a source of employment and innovation, they are struggling to access, let alone win, public-sector tender opportunities as e-commerce, financial regulations and consortia bidding squeeze them out.

Not that there aren't voices urging caution. David Grayson, writing on CSR and SMEs for the Copenhagen Centre, urges CSR 'intermediaries' to build alliances with existing organizations that represent SMEs and warns that, 'Any attempt to encourage SMEs to look at their social and environmental impacts using the language of CSR or that relies on the examples of large companies is doomed to failure.' Eurochambres, speaking on behalf of SMEs across Europe, is concerned that, 'It is not possible to trim down or simplify existing approaches to CSR to make them relevant to SMEs. (A bottom-up approach is needed in order to capture SMEs' unique experience.)'

The fact is that many SMEs are already 'social' businesses with an excellent track record on sustainability. Most business owners do not fit the stereotype that results from television programmes on rogue traders and newspapers stories of commercial fraud. People's perceptions of SMEs are often drawn from anecdotes and contacts across a few sectors.

We know the figures, but they get forgotten. Seventy-five per cent of businesses employ fewer than 20 people. Yet providing employment has a social impact, and most small businesses are proud that they are employing people, even with the burdens of employment legislation.

And CSR means a willingness to accept a different viewpoint and to learn to understand a different language. So, it's one thing to say that SMEs can do more on CSR and it's another thing to find out ways of recognizing what they are already doing and finding measures that are not just corporate indicators of CSR transposed across to small business.

So where does a business start? The likelihood is that they are already doing a lot, partly because of legislation, partly because what you think is good business practice has been wrapped up in sustainability and partly because people generally want to be responsible citizens whether or not they own or run organizations.

For the SME, however, it is possible that the material issues are economic as much as they are social and environmental, and yet the economic aspects of sustainability do not get as much coverage as the other areas. It may be that this is because 'economic' and 'profitable' are treated as synonymous, although they aren't. Yet in many aspects of their impact it is SMEs' economic impact that is so important: employing locally, purchasing locally and having been running the business from the same location for many years.

SMEs are already having positive impacts. In giving up time and skills to their local communities they often provide what they know best: informal business advice; active membership of local civic bodies, including Chambers of Commerce; taking on work placements from local schools. They may be involved in 'community' programmes, but their joint involvement in local crime reduction, working with the police, is just as important a part of sustainability.

And the distance between the owner and the stakeholders is a lot smaller in a small organization. In a single day the owner may talk to key suppliers, customers, his or her staff and perhaps the neighbours.

Moreover, SMEs need to respond quickly to any issues that arise. Their cash flows simply won't stand delay. Again, according to AccountAbility, which argues that sustainability comes from accountability and that part of accountability means responding to stakeholders, SMEs may be doing well. The issue may be that as the SME responds to its important issues, other stakeholders feel that their issues are ignored. It is often the role of business networks to act as a clearing house for these issues. Simply, the business cannot take them all on, and where the same issues relate to many SMEs, the 'response' comes from these networks. This all happens already, but the sustainability issue has not included the implication of economies of scale for SMEs and the resulting importance of business networks such as Chambers of Commerce.

Business networks have another role as well: for many small businesses, the potential impact often arises from businesses working together, perhaps for their local economy, recognizing the social benefits that economic growth can bring.

So, in taking on a sustainable agenda SMEs should include, and be proud of, positive impacts that they are having as well as considering the benefits of addressing other elements of sustainability.

Some sources

There are process standards such as those provided by AccountAbility (www.accountability.org.uk) to help organizations develop their accountability, and a wide range of benchmark indices – for example, smekey (www.smekey.org), or the Corporate Responsibility Index offered by Business in the Community (www.bitc.org.uk), which helps organizations compare their performance with that of others.

www.conversations-with-disbelievers.net sets out much of the available quantitative evidence that addressing social challenges can help businesses improve their financial bottom lines in the form of top case studies and special reports, as well as the latest headline news from across the world. There is the Global Reporting Initiative (www.globalreporting.org), described as a collaborating centre for the United Nations Environment Programme, which aims to develop and disseminate globally applicable sustainability reporting guidelines.

There is advice on CSR (eg at www.CSReurope. org as well as all the above sites), competitions on specific areas such as Great Place to Work (www.greatplacetowork.com) or on the sustainability reports produced by organizations (www.acca.co.uk). There is the SIGMA project (www.projectsigma.com), which aims to provide clear, practical advice to organizations to help them make a meaningful contribution to sustainable development and which is supported by the British Standards Institution.

Finally the International Organization for Standardization (www.iso.ch), which brought you ISO 14000, is developing a standard on social responsibility.

Jeremy Nicholls, The Cat's Pyjamas, c/o Furniture Resource Centre, Brunswick Business Park, Atlantic Way, Liverpool L3 4BE

Tel: 0151 702 0564
Fax: 0151 702 0551
E-mail: events@the-cats-pyjamas.com

Sustainable Enterprise at the University of Bath School of Management

The School of Management has a long tradition of excellence in teaching and research and an international reputation for the quality of its programmes. Under the leadership of Professor Andrew Pettigrew, appointed Dean of School in October 2003, the School of Management continues to build its reputation as a top UK business school. One of the oldest established management schools in Britain, the School's faculty has been strengthened with new areas of expertise and Professor Pettigrew has presided over a major step forward in the delivery of tailored executive development programmes for blue-chip organisations including: McKinsey, QinetiQ, PricewaterhouseCoopers and CIMA.

The School has consistently achieved both top research and teaching ratings. In May this year the School was ranked in the 'top 5' UK business schools by *The Times Good University Guide, 2005*. Our highly rated Bath MBA programmes have consistently featured in the *Financial Times* global top 100 MBA programmes and the School's close relationships with a wide range of external organisations ensure that teaching and research remain dynamic and relevant to both the private and public sectors.

The innovative MSc. in Responsibility and Business Practice addresses the issues of sustainable enterprise. It looks at the challenges currently facing society as we seek to integrate successful business practice with a concern for social, environmental and ethical issues. This part-time programme studied over two years, offers participants an opportunity to encounter, debate and evaluate a wide range of alternative perspectives on business. The programme considers the complex relationship between business decisions and their impact on local and world communities and economies, on the environment and on the workplace itself. The course challenges ideas about where "responsibility" begins and ends. Through interaction among peers, academics and guest speakers participants will learn about management techniques and approaches being developed in leading-edge organizations, and will test the relevance of these ideas and practices in their own workplaces.

This is a challenging programme, aimed at managers, consultants and others who are ready to ask searching questions about how modern business is carried out, the consequences and the alternatives.

For more information on the MSc in Responsibility and Business Practice please telephone: **+44 (0)1225 383861** *or email:*
mscrbp@management.bath.ac.uk www.bath.ac.uk/carpp/

Entec

Creating the environment for business

Entec is one of the UK's largest environmental and engineering consultancies, with over 60 years of consulting experience in the public and private sectors in the UK and overseas. Entec's customers are highly diverse, across a range of industry sectors. Examples include: Amec Capital Projects, BAA, Bellway Homes, Bovis Lend Lease, BNFL, BP, Business in the Community, Defence Estates, Defra, EDF Energy, Environment Agency, European Commission, Greater London Authority, Hanson Aggregates, Morgan Est, Northumbrian Water, Scottish Power, Scottish Water, SecondSite Property Holdings, Shanks Waste Solutions, Southern Water, United Utilities and Yorkshire Forward.

Entec offers its clients an integrated approach to environmental and engineering services from policy to projects, capitalising on our experience in environmental, health and safety and engineering consultancy.

The company assists government and regulators develop and implement policy, legislation, and best practice guidance. We help businesses improve their operational effectiveness and comply with legislative requirements, with services ranging from risk assessment, management systems and training through to waste minimisation, process optimisation and pollution prevention and control.

Entec also works with businesses to achieve their development objectives, with services including development planning and site selection, environmental audit (due diligence), environmental impact assessment, project management, feasibility studies and optioneering, design and construction management.

Entec's services
- Contaminated Land
- Development Planning
- Environmental Appraisal
- Environmental Management and Compliance
- Industrial Engineering Services
- Property Engineering Services
- Risk and Safety Management
- Sustainable Development
- Waste Management
- Water Management
- Water Engineering Services

Entec UK Ltd
Northumbria House, Regent Centre, Gosforth, Newcastle upon Tyne, NE3 3PX
Tel: 0800 371733
Fax: +44 (0)191 272 6592
Email: info@entecuk.co.uk
Web site: www.entecuk.com

Also have offices in: London, Crawley, Bristol, Reading, Leamington Spa, Northwich, Shrewsbury, Leeds, Edinburgh, Glasgow and Dounreay.

Lancaster's Environment Centre and Management School developing sustainable businesses

At Lancaster University we know more about the environment and the issues it presents for business leaders. The Lancaster Environment Centre (LEC), just about Europe's largest concentration of environmental scientists, and Lancaster University Management School (LUMS), the top rated business school outside London, provide individual and organisational development, research and training opportunities for policy makers, business leaders and scientists of today and of the future to deliver a sustainable global environment.

Let LEC and LUMS help you raise your productivity, creativity and competitive performance, drawing on our world-class research in the study, remediation and social and financial management of the environment to deliver a sustainable global future.

- ■ **Innovative and flexible professional development programmes for your staff from graduate to Director level.**

- ■ **Exceptional graduates to meet your need for technical and managerial skills required to run a sustainable business.**

- ■ **Understand how enhanced environmental performance can impact on business growth and productivity.**

- ■ **A range of valuable outreach services designed to meet your needs, whether a multinational or a smaller developing business.**

- ■ **Develop your business with Europe's leading leadership, management and technology researchers and teachers.**

For further information visit our websites:
www.lec.lancs.ac.uk or www.lums.lancs.ac.uk
or telephone **+44 (0)1524 510204**

The University of
Nottingham

A New Framework for MBA education

Corporate Social Responsibility (CSR) and sustainability have become prominent in the language and strategies of business. This has been driven by businesses becoming more aware of their responsibilities in the post-Enron era, coupled with growing stakeholder demand for businesses to act in a transparent and responsible manner.

Traditionally CSR was seen to be at conflict with the goal of profit maximisation, however today the emphasis is shifting towards profitability in a responsible manner. CSR has moved from being peripheral philanthropy to being part of the core business. Therefore for CSR to be firmly embedded into the core business, managers need to be equipped with awareness and decision frameworks for making decisions on CSR issues.

The International Centre for Corporate Social Responsibility was founded at the Nottingham University Business School in 2002, in order to contribute to the acquisition of CSR knowledge. The centre takes an international and inter-disciplinary approach to the teaching and research of CSR.

The flagship programme of the ICCSR is the MBA in CSR. This is a unique programme that combines advanced teaching and learning in management with state of the art thinking in corporate social responsibility. This combination allows progressive learning at the leading edge of knowledge in the general discipline of management studies and socially responsible business. Subjects such as Business Ethics, Corporate Social Responsibility, Corporate Governance and Accountability, and Economic Crime are taught alongside mainstream subjects such as Managerial Economics, Accounting and Finance, Organisational Behaviour and Marketing.

The MBA in CSR is designed to enable students
- To study organisations, including private, public, and not-for-profit organisations, their management, and the changing external environment in which they operate.
- To critically evaluate at an advanced level the core business disciplines, while applying business ethics and corporate social responsibility issues across all management disciplines.
- To develop a career in business and management.
- To develop the capacity for lifelong learning in global business and to enhance personal development.

Index

NB: page numbers in *italic* indicate tables

Index of advertisers